RINALDO

TORQUATO TASSO

RINALDO

A NEW ENGLISH VERSE TRANSLATION
WITH FACING ITALIAN TEXT,
CRITICAL INTRODUCTION AND NOTES
BY
MAX WICKERT

ITALICA PRESS
NEW YORK
2017

Copyright © 2017 by Max Wickert

ITALICA PRESS, INC.
595 Main Street, Suite 605
New York, New York 10044

Italica Press Poetry in Translation Series

Library of Congress Cataloging-in-Publication Data
Names: Tasso, Torquato, 1544-1595, author. | Wickert, Max, writer of
introduction, editor translator.
Title: Rinaldo : a new English verse translation with facing Italian text /
Torquato Tasso ; translation, critical introduction and notes by Max
Wickert.
Description: New York : Italica Press, 2017. | Series: Italica Press poetry
in translation series | Includes bibliographical references and index.
Identifiers: LCCN 2017002937 (print) | LCCN 2017021679 (ebook) |
ISBN 9781599103587 (hardcover : alk. paper) | ISBN 9781599103594
(pbk. : alk. paper) | ISBN 9781599103600 (ebook)
Subjects: LCSH: Tasso, Torquato, 1544-1595--Translations into English.
Classification: LCC PQ4639 .R2 2017 (print) | LCC PQ4639 (ebook) |
DDC 851/.4--dc23
LC record available at https://lccn.loc.gov/2017002937

Cover Art: *A Knight of the Rehlinger Family (Bildnis eines Herrn
Rehlinger),* by L.M. (Augsburg, first half of 16th century), 1540.
Gemäldegalerie der Staatlichen Museen zu Berlin.

For a Complete List of
Poetry in Translation
Visit our Web Site at
http://www.italicapress.com/index013.html

About the Editor and Translator

Max Wickert is the author of several volumes of verse and of *The Liberation of Jerusalem*, a rhymed translation of Tasso's *Gerusalemme liberata*, published by Oxford University Press in 2009, as well as the editor and translator of Torquato Tasso, *Love Poems for Lucrezia Bendidio* (Italica Press, 2011). He has taught for many years at the University at Buffalo, NY.

Contents

Contents

PREFACE

Though in the shadow of the spectacular fame of *Gerusalemme liberata* (or perhaps because of that shadow), *Rinaldo* soon attracted notice outside Italy. In England, Edmund Spenser knew the work well enough to comment on it in his preface to *The Fairie Queene*, and to imitate some of its episodes in that masterpiece.[1] Several other Elizabethans, notably Sir Philip Sidney and Abraham Fraunce,[2] almost certainly also knew *Rinaldo*. In the eighteenth century, Samuel Johnson's friend, John Hoole, author of a successful version of *Gerusalemme*, translated it into heroic couplets. After this, the poem, at least in the English-speaking world, sank into obscurity, although later references to it (John Addington Symonds and Thomas Bulfinch come to mind) suggest that it remained familiar to educated readers.

The present volume is, to the best of my knowledge, the first modern translation of the work. It is based on the original 1562 Italian edition printed in Venice. I began it in 2008, shortly after completing my verse translation of *Gerusalemme liberata*,[3] while simultaneously working on my version of Book One of Tasso's *Rime amorose*.[4] In rendering the verse, I was guided by the same principles as in my translation of the *Gerusalemme*. The prose of Tasso's "Letter to the Reader" presents special problems.[5] Its polemical periods and stylistic formulas, if rendered literally, can seem pedantic, over-complicated, archaic or downright fussy. One is tempted to modernize, but this inevitably involves a temptation to improve on the original — not a translator's business. I have sought, allowing myself occasional liberties, to steer a middle course between simplifying Tasso's rhetoric and retaining some of its flavor.

I wish to thank the following for their help, encouragement and courtesy: Gianfranco Bogliari (Università per Stranieri, Perugia), Andrea Guiati and David Lampe (State University College, Buffalo, NY), David Quint (Yale University) and Joseph Tusiani. I have been extraordinarily fortunate in my editors, Eileen Gardiner and Ronald G. Musto, whose common

Preface

sense, sharp eye and tireless attention to detail yielded many a suggestion for improvement and saved me from several blunders. As always, I owe a very special debt to Katka Hammond.

My thanks also to the Just Buffalo Literary Center in Buffalo, NY, for inviting me to present an early section of this book in a public reading (March 10, 2010). Other than that, no part of it has been previously published.

NOTES

1. Spenser's reference to "Rinaldo" in the "Letter to Raleigh" is ambiguous. It may be to either the Carolingian hero of Tasso's first epic or the Crusader Rinaldo in the *Gerusalemme*. Mindele Anne Treip argues persuasively for the former in *Allegorical Poetics and the Epic* (Lexington: University of Kentucky Press, 1994), 269ff. See also 403–4, nn. 50–51 below.

2. Tasso's influence on Sidney seems a promising subject for research. During his continental tour, Sidney arrived in Venice in November 1573. He based himself there for six weeks and then continued for eight more at Padua. It is unthinkable that he should not there have heard about Tasso, though he probably did not meet him, since Tasso was in Rome during most of that time. Abraham Fraunce's *Arcadian Rhetoric* (1588) includes illustrative passages from Tasso.

3. *The Liberation of Jerusalem* (New York: Oxford University Press, 2009).

4. See p. xxv, n. 2.

5. Tasso himself placed his "Letter" in the main text, immediately preceding Canto One, and almost all Italian editions follow his lead. For the modern English reader, this must feel like an invitation to get involved with an obscure theoretical quarrel before getting to the poem itself. While that quarrel, as my Introduction makes clear, is by no means trivial, it has little immediate bearing on the emotional impact of the narrative. The Letter therefore appears in this book as an Appendix. A modernized translation of Tasso's Letter is available; see Rhu (1993) in the Bibliography. The translator there is understandably more interested in clarifying Tasso's critical ideas than in reproducing his style.

—⁓—

INTRODUCTION

…seguii con mal sicure piante,
qual Ascanio o Camilla, il padre errante[1]

AMADIGI AND RINALDO

In late 1559, Torquato Tasso, then a precociously gifted lad of fifteen, moved from Urbino to Venice in the company of his father, the poet Bernardo Tasso, to assist him in preparing his works for publication, a massive project involving five books of lyrics, several volumes of epistolary prose, and —most importantly — *Amadigi (Amadis of Gaul)*, a 100-canto-long chivalric epic that Bernardo considered his masterpiece. Father and son were well received in the palaces of Venice's intellectual elite and, by all accounts, worked together, the younger Tasso serving the older as amanuensis, proofreader and participant in *conversazioni*. For his own part, Torquato now started work on *Gierusalemme*, an epic on the First Crusade, which was destined in due course to grow into his masterpiece, *Gerusalemme liberata (The Liberation of Jerusalem)*, but he put that project aside after 116 stanzas to commence work on *Rinaldo*, a chivalric epic in twelve cantos.

Amadigi saw print in early 1560. In November of that year, Torquato Tasso left Venice to enter the University of Padua. His father was an alumnus, having studied in the faculty of law some forty years earlier, and at his insistence his son enrolled in the same faculty. Law, he seems to have thought, was a more practical preparation for life than literature. In the summer of the following year, during a brief spell at the Este country estate of Bagni di Abano, Torquato met and fell in love with Lucrezia Bendidio, one of Eleanora d'Este's ladies-in-waiting, to whom he addressed his first sequence of love poems.[2] Meanwhile, he continued with *Rinaldo* and, working with astounding speed, completed the entire 7,624-line poem in less than a year. It was published at Venice in 1562 and proved successful enough to be reprinted at least five

Introduction

times during the poet's lifetime, a formidable achievement for a teenager just beginning to write and to measure poetic swords with his elders, to say nothing of the promise it offers of greater things to come. That promise was not hidden from Tasso himself, since he had already in 1561, against paternal advice, changed his university studies from jurisprudence to eloquence and philosophy, with a view to a career as a poet.

For this aim he was both eminently qualified and oddly unsuited — qualified, because he had long shared with his father an intellectual and literary environment of the highest distinction; unsuited, in that both father and son grew entangled in a thicket of rapidly changing literary theory and public taste.

A Ruined Career

Father and son, it should be noted, were initially far apart. Bernardo was over fifty years old when Torquato was born in Sorrento. He was away from home at the time, campaigning with his patron, the Prince of Sanseverino, in faraway Piedmont. He was in fact repeatedly absent during the boy's early childhood. When, in 1552, Sanseverino with his retinue were proclaimed traitors by the Spanish viceroy of Naples, and all their property confiscated, Bernardo Tasso, then Sanseverino's secretary, along with Sanseverino himself, was once again far from home, engaged in intriguing for a military invasion of Naples — Tasso at Henry II's court in Paris and Sanseverino at Suleiman the Great's in Istanbul. These efforts failed, and Bernardo moved to Rome, barred from his family by the decree of exile.

He never again saw his wife — who died, rumored to have been poisoned, two years later — nor his daughter — she was maneuvered, first into a convent and then into a disastrous marriage — but he at last obtained permission for young Torquato to join him. It is probably only then that the ten-year-old boy really began to know his father, who was then in his sixties — an old man by the standards of the time. Except for brief intervals, Tasso's life during the next decade was emphatically life with father.

This entailed some significant advantages. Bernardo, though impoverished and a fugitive, was well connected. Sanseverino had come under papal displeasure and had moved to France and turned Huguenot, but his Italian fiefs had passed into the possession of the Gonzagas of Mantua, relatives by marriage, who were in turn closely allied with the ruling families of Urbino and Ferrara. These three courts, which in the previous generation had rivaled Florence or even Rome in cultural panache, were still glamorous centers of art and learning. Bernardo eventually entered the service of the Gonzagas, but before that (from 1554) enjoyed the protection of the Guidobaldo II della Rovere, duke of Urbino, who granted him lodging and employment, first in Pesaro and then in Urbino itself. So the aging Bernardo came to revisit the haunts of his youth: he had been born in Bergamo, enjoyed his first love affairs and successes as a poet in Ferrara and Venice and had studied law at the University of Padua. And so young Torquato came to pursue his education at Urbino under the choicest humanist masters, with the ducal heir, Francesco Maria, as one of his schoolmates.

Bernardo's career was that of a Renaissance courtier-poet. In the beginning, he perhaps envisioned it on the model of Ludovico Ariosto's, whose skill as a writer secured him a patron and whose services as a diplomat in that patron's employment earned him the governorship of a province. Bernardo's first successes as a writer of love lyrics did indeed bring him to the attention of the cultured prince of Sanseverino, under whose patronage he began *Amadigi* and entered the circle of noted humanists in Salerno. His courtier duties involved repeated travel and the performance of countless secretarial, diplomatic and military tasks. The last of these was his role in the failed negotiations in France. With the collapse of Sanseverino's fortunes, the older Tasso must have felt that his life as a courtier lay in shambles. He now had only one thing left to make his mark: the successful publication of his *magnum opus*.

AN EPIC IN EXILE

The poem he finally published in 1560 was far different from the one that he had begun in the 1540s. At that time, Ariosto's *Orlando furioso*, published some fifteen years earlier, was nearing the peak of its popularity and success. It was attaining the status of something like a classic. Yet many voices were also beginning to question the legitimacy of a poem so manifestly unclassifiable by any known critical standards. The standard of unity of plot was inapplicable in that *Orlando furioso* begins in mid-tale just where Boiardo's *Orlando innamorato* ended. The standard of heroic *gravitas* was undermined by Ariosto's preference of chivalric romance to the epic material of ancient Greece or Rome. Ariosto's bewildering interlacing of narrative threads, his eroticism, his repeated use of sensational sorcery and marvels, his unpredictable intrusions of authorial commentary and above all his pervasive irony made his poem seem at best like an oddball masterpiece difficult to talk about and dangerous to imitate. Even his verse form, the *ottava rima* stanza, though by now standard in popular literature and with a literary pedigree that harkened back to Boccaccio, still carried echoes of improvising, popular entertainers *(cantastorie)*, sounding trivial or excessively "modern" in the ears of humanist readers fed on unrhymed Greek and Latin hexameters. Nevertheless, Ariosto unquestionably ruled the roost. The question remained: Could a good epic be written differently?

One obvious way to buck the Ariosto precedent was to choose a narrative subject differing from the Carolingian — and occasionally Arthurian — chivalric tales, centered on the figure of Roland, which dominate *Orlando furioso*. By the mid-sixteenth century this different subject came ready to hand in the story-cycle centered on Amadis de Gaul and Palmerin. Though these two heroes are in fact English or Welsh and now and then encounter traditional Arthurian characters, their ambiance for *cinquecento* Italians was Spanish rather than French or Breton. This was the material Bernardo Tasso opted for, and the composition of his poem is closely contemporary with the indefatigable Mambrino Roseo's Italian translations and continuations (eighteen installments, 1555–65) of the Spanish source texts by Garcí Rodríguez Montalvo and his successors.[3] Bernardo may also have reached for Spanish sources because Sorrento and Naples were Spanish territory. (In view of future events, this was perhaps an impolitic choice.[4])

A more radical challenge to Ariosto's primacy had been delivered by Trissino's *Italia liberata dai goti (Italy Liberated from the Goths)*, completed in 1527 and printed in 1547, a severely classicizing historical epic in *verso sciolto* (the Italian equivalent of blank verse). This, though a popular failure, was a critical success. It inspired, in form, if not in content, Bernardo's first draft of

Amadigi, composed in *verso sciolto*, with its events presented in a single continuous narrative rather than in the Ariostan profusion of interwoven stories.[5] No copy of this original draft has survived, but both Bernardo and Torquato Tasso later told the tale of its reception: when Bernardo recited it to a courtly audience — presumably at Salerno — the audience walked out one by one until he found himself addressing an empty room. Unwilling to settle for a *succès d'estime* like Trissino's, he rewrote the poem from scratch, in *ottava rima*, greatly increasing its variety of episodes and — one must suppose — its bulk.

The younger Tasso probably had no direct memory of the original unrhymed version (discarded while he was still a toddler), but he grew up watching his father working his way through the complex backdrop of contemporary epic experimentation and literary criticism in the hope of finding and justifying an uneasy compromise. During that period of gestation, ending in the late 1550s, several epics appeared that also presented non-Ariostan subject-matter in a largely Ariostan style (though without the Ariosto's *entrelacement* of plots) and in *ottava rima* versification, among them Giraldo Cinzio's *Ercole Amante* (*Hercules in Love*, 1557) and Luigi Alamanni's *Girone il Cortese* (*Guiron the Courtier*, 1548). Giraldi presents a protagonist unconnected to the world of chivalric romance, the classical Hercules among the Amazons. Alamanni's Guiron is a chivalric figure, but hails from the relatively unknown Arthurian Palamedes cycle rather than Ariosto's familiar Carolingian world.[6] During that same period at least one long poem appeared that frankly emulated Ariosto: Ludovico Dolce's *Sacripante* (1536), with a protagonist who appears in both Boiardo's and Ariosto's poems.

Giraldi, Alamanni and Dolce not merely happened to be contemporaries, but were personally acquainted with the elder Tasso and figure prominently in his correspondence[7] with leading literary critics of the period, including both a growing contingent of Aristotelians hostile to chivalric romance and several rearguard defenders of Ariosto. Among the latter, Giambattista Pigna daringly argued that romance constituted a new and separate genre, to be judged by its own laws rather than those of classical epics. His *I Romanzi* (1554) appeared in the same year as *Modi affigurati* by the already-mentioned Ludovico Dolce, which offers a favorable view of Ariosto in a genial compromise with classicism.

Their Aristotelian opposition includes three other acquaintances of the elder Tasso: Bartolomeo Lombardi, who lectured on the *Poetics* at Padua until 1541;Vincenzo Maggi, who continued his work there; and the great classical scholar, Francesco Robortello, whose edition of the *Poetics* appeared in 1548. Aristotle's *Poetics* is, of course, primarily a discussion of tragedy, but the increasing tendency of these critics was to stretch Aristotle's rules to apply to epic, with special attention to the criterion of "unity," which more and more makes them suspicious of both the multiple plots and the mixing of first-person commentary with third-person narration so characteristic of Ariosto.

The *Amadigi* thatTorquatoTasso saw his father produce under the pressure of these various influences must have seemed like a departure from Ariosto in its subject matter, but a half-hearted return to Ariosto in its mode of story-telling. The Aristotelian push toward "unity," already felt in the epics by Alamanni, Giraldi and Dolce, had certainly dominated the first draft of *Amadigi* but is very feeble in the final version, which contains at least three elaborate and separate plots — though these are, to be sure, presented seriatim, rather than interwoven in Ariosto's manner.

FILIAL AMBIVALENCE

Several of the old friends who welcomed Bernardo toVenice in 1559 now, or a year later in Padua, formed significant, independent relationships with his son. Five of them (Danese Cataneo,[8] Domenico Venièr,[9] Carlo Sigonio,[10] Giambattista Pigna[11] and Sperone Speroni[12]) are singled out by name in Torquato's prefatory letter to *Rinaldo,* and two of them,Venièr and Cataneo, receive handsome verse compliments in the body of the poem.[13] These five are clearly guarantors of the young poet's critical position, midway between Aristotelian and Ariostan, which, he claims, governs *Rinaldo.*They are also presented as witnesses-for-the-defense in his decision to turn poet in defiance of his father's express wishes.That decision, it may well be argued, is the life-blood of the poem.

In consideringTasso's psychological and intellectual coming-of-age, two things seem clear: first, the whole process, transpiring so completely in the paternal shadow, gives the impression that the only poetical career the youngTasso can imagine is one just like his father's; and second, the father is suspected again and again of falling short of his ambitions — not failing, perhaps, but repeatedly needing to revise or buttress a position with which he seems not altogether comfortable. To these, a third consideration, not touched upon so far but crucial, must be added: on the conscious level, Tasso revered and loved his father sincerely, gratefully and intensely. His homage to him at *Rinaldo*'s highly unconventional conclusion ("he gave me breath and speech, yea life and limb: / and all my best gifts are but gifts from him") must be taken at face-value. He not only devotedly attended him during his final illness at Ostiglia but years later at the height of his own creative career worked diligently to secure Bernardo's artistic legacy. Shortly before his death, Bernardo, not content with his hundred-canto *Amadigi*, had elaborated one of its episodes into yet another long epic, *Floridante*. Left unfinished in manuscript, this work was painstakingly corrected, completed and seen into print by Torquato sixteen years later. It was a labor of love, the first task Tasso undertook when finally freed from his long confinement at Santa Anna.[14]

Perhaps the most striking instance of his filial devotion came some months earlier, when, still imprisoned, he learned that his own epic masterpiece was under attack from the powerful Florentine Accademia della Crusca. Disparaging the son by association with the father, one of his detractors had contemptuously ranked *Amadigi* below the work Boiardo and Pulci. Stung to the quick, Tasso began his *Apologia in difesa della "Gerusalemme liberata"* not by defending his own work, but by lashing out furiously and at some length on behalf of his father's, as though a sacred grave had been defiled. By this time, Tasso had himself completed the reform of epic from which his father had retreated. He had emancipated it from Ariosto by choosing a historical subject — the First Crusade — rather than a chivalric subject and treating it in a single, unified action — the Siege of Jerusalem — in a style of far greater *gravitas* than Ariosto could have imagined. It was the audacity of this reform that provoked the Accademia,[15] for whom Ariosto was still god. Ironically Tasso finds himself defending the work of his father who in both *Amadigi* and *Floridante* had compromised the reforming position. However, the son's identification with the father is too strong to let him see that irony. He feels the eminence of the father as an existential need.

Introduction

Tasso's mature lyric poetry includes several plangently fond allusions[16] to his father's passing, but none richer or more mysterious than in "Al Metauro," the poem cited in the epigraph of this introduction. The poem's metaphors involve a series of allusions to Virgil's *Aeneid*: Aeneas driven into exile stands for Tasso's father and Ascanius/Iulus for Tasso himself. Aeneas/ Ascanius's wanderings are figures both of the tribulations of Bernardo/Torquato after their exile from Naples and of their quest for a new poetry. The implicit image of Creusa/Portia vanishing at their rear in the wreckage of Troy/Sorrento seems temptingly appropriate — a lost mother whose absence intensifies alienation from the past — but the absent feminine is curiously smuggled in the form of Ascanius's alter-ego Camilla, Aeneas's future enemy, who is fated to perish. In the final lines, the tribulations of the wandering son seem offered up to Bernardo as to a deified Aeneas/Caesar/Augustus, whose own sufferings, now over, validate the poet's.

THEMATIZING THE FATHER

It is not surprising to find *Rinaldo* marked — even obsessed — from beginning to end by the theme of paternity. The work is framed by two direct references to Tasso's father: the prose preface, in which Bernardo appears chiefly as the inhibitor of Torquato's "genius" whose objections are worn down by a cadre of critical supporters; and the final "Go, little book" stanzas that acknowledge Bernardo as the only begetter of Torquato's "genius"[17] and humbly submit the completed epic to his better judgment.

Between these points, father figures appear in multiple guises. The first is that of the literary patron and dedicatee, in Tasso's case literally a "Holy Father" — Ippolito d'Este, a cardinal and possible future pope. The invocation of a courtly patron is conventional and mandatory in Renaissance literature, but Tasso characteristically makes him the poet's fatherly protector from misery and persecution, and prophesies for him a historical role that the actions of the poem's hero foreshadow.

On the fictional level, the poem features at least four kinds of paternal authority: (1) Merlin, the Daedalian forefather magician, who has long before the poem's beginning determined who falls in love with whom and who fashions or bestows the hero's enchanted steeds and weapons; (2) Charlemagne, Rinaldo's liege lord from whose displeasure Rinaldo must eventually redeem himself; (3) Aymon, patriarch of the Clairmont clan and Rinaldo's actual father, in defense of whose honor Rinaldo proves his manhood; and (4) the godfatherly sorcerer Malagis, a kind of deputy-Merlin who acts as Rinaldo's behind-the-scenes manipulator and corrector. All four of these are also present in Boiardo and Ariosto, but in Tasso's poem, they are far more starkly foregrounded at crucial junctures of the plot.

Two other planes of paternity operate in the poem alongside the fictional plane: the biographical plane, where Bernardo Tasso must either be conciliated or outdone; and on the metapoetical plane where the claims of fathers like Ariosto and Aristotle must be either reconciled or fought out to the end. It is worth pondering that on this metapoetical plane, the biographical father is himself a rival son to Ariosto. When he began *Amadigi*, he tried to give it a classical, Aristotelian pedigree. Failing in this, he rewrote the work in an attempt to regain some of the Ariostan birthright (and limelight) by conceding a greater variety of narrative while sticking to his non-Ariostan subject matter. In *Rinaldo*, Bernardo's son becomes his poetical rival by reversing this process. He claims the mantle of Aristotelian "unity of plot" without altogether abandoning variety of incident.

The modern conception of Aristotelian unity as the inexorable interlinking of causalities toward an inevitable end without disruption by extraneous episodes is obviously irrelevant here. The plot of *Rinaldo* is episodic with a vengeance. Aside from the hero, all but four or five of its 130-odd named characters appear only once or twice, often to be killed off in the same canto. Although Rinaldo's seriatim acquisition of chivalric perquisites — horse, lance, armor, sword, bride — has a primitive logic, his story seems, as in Mark Twain's definition of history, "just one damn thing after another." Tasso requires only that the poem's actions be confined to a single hero engaged in a single quest and narrated in a fairly straight-forward sequence without subjective authorial interruptions.[18] Yet, in his pervasive focus on paternity, Tasso does fuse the heterogeneous episodes in a powerful unity of another sort — a thematic and metapoetical one. Individual episodes succeed each other like variations in a phantasmagorical family romance: the son in quest of the bride, repeatedly challenged by a father, proves his worthiness or identity by outperforming either the father or a potent rival. This pattern oscillates among the poem's planes of paternity with a suggestive repetitiveness that seems to push toward a never-to-be-resolved future.

Returning now to the paternity theme on the fictional plane, it is evident that Tasso has laid his groundwork carefully by "rewriting" a number of source texts. In Pulci's *Morgante Maggiore*, Rinaldo does indeed subdue a monstrous steed ("with teeth and feathers" that has already killed hundreds) but he does so while already mounted on Bayard. In Ariosto, Rinaldo is already in possession of Bayard; the fabulous steed to be overpowered is the winged Hippogriff, first tamed by the sorcerer Atlante, not quite mastered by Ruggiero, and at last ridden by Astolfo. Tasso has fused and modified these hints in an invention of his own, which makes Amadis de Gaul Bayard's original owner, replaces the mediating sorcerer Atlante with Malagis, and (most daringly) destines Rinaldo as the rightful claimant to the horse by making him a linear descendant of Amadis, thus making the hero of Bernardo's poem into a forefather of the hero of his own.

The episode begins with the appearance of the father-figure as an apparently feeble old man (Malagis[19] in disguise = Bernardo as skeptical father-poet), who warns Rinaldo against attempting to master Bayard, but who grows kinder when the lad shows signs of spunk. Encouraged to proceed, Rinaldo is accompanied by an unnamed "English knight" (probably Ariosto's Astolfo) and the "Spanish" Ysolier. Astolfo, who has already failed once, abandons the quest; Ysolier fails and Rinaldo succeeds. In a few neat strokes, Tasso has moved away from Ariosto's paternity and aligned himself with his own father's epic. His hero is, in fact, his father's hero's heir. He has also validated both his and his father's emancipation from Ariosto and his own emancipation from his father. He has, so to speak, acquired Bernardo's Pegasus. The narrative of this early passage is full of verve and assurance. No wonder: Rinaldo rides the paternal steed with the innocent energy of a boy showing off for his dad.

His assurance is short-lived. The paternal hand that bestowed the gift soon takes it away, for when Rinaldo uses the horse to abduct his beloved Clarice, Malagis reappears as a Dragon Knight, causes Bayard to stumble and pin its rider underneath, snatches up the girl and vanishes, pursued by Ysolier, in a storm cloud.

Rinaldo

When the sky clears, the Spanish knight Ysolier, who seemed destined to be Rinaldo's inseparable companion, has vanished along with the magician and the lady. He never reappears, but is almost at once replaced by Florindo, apparently another Spaniard, who does indeed become an inseparable companion, even a kind of alter ego. The two proceed together to the Cavern of Cupid where paternal prophecy (by Merlin/Malagis) predicts the same fate for both: they will attain their lady-loves after they earn fame in warfare.

Rinaldo has Florindo by his side throughout the key events of the next five cantos, but at last loses him also, along with Bayard, the sword Fusberta and the beloved image of Clarice in a shipwreck. He does not find him again until just before the poem's final battle. He then learns that the apparent Spanish shepherd, Florindo, is in fact Laelius, the long-lost son of Scipio, a nobleman descended from the ancient Roman Cornelii. Perhaps Tasso intends a compliment to Scipio Gonzaga,[20] but he more likely means to endow the theme of paternity with the éclat of *Romanitas*. It should be remembered that Tasso's mother's name (Portia) and his sister's (Cornelia), and certainly his own (Torquatus) all have venerable Roman associations. Tasso was self-conscious enough about his to make it the subject of one of his early sonnets,[21] which among other things alludes to Livy's account of the consular severity of the historical Torquatus, who condemned his own son to death for neglecting military discipline. The association of *Romanitas* with heroic fatherhood is eventually thematized in *Gerusalemme liberata* by the heroic joint death on the battlefield of Latinus and his five sons (9.27–39).

A joint father-son death, in fact, also occurs just before Rinaldo discovers Florindo/Laelius's identity. His friend appears as a stranger unfairly beset by a mob. When Rinaldo rushes in and kills them in great numbers, two of his first victims are a father and his son (11.77–79). The scene is a variation on a much earlier one, when Rinaldo kills a crowd of attackers that includes another father–son pair, Aridan and Orin (4.19–22). Both pairs are villains: Maganzans in Canto Four and Saracens in Canto Eleven. Yet their deaths in both cases are related in stanzas of melancholy pathos.

It is tempting to look upon this pair of father-and-son slayings as parenthetically framing a sensational vision of grief-crazed paternity at the poem's center (7.2–11): Hugh's father lamenting over his son, whose head Rinaldo has struck off in Charlemagne's lists. That scene is even more striking because it seems oddly out of place. Hugh had been killed the day before; he has already been mourned in quasi-paternal fashion by Charlemagne, who in his grief and rage has dispatched Orlando to avenge him. Rinaldo's consummate valor in the deadlocked combat with his cousin impresses the Emperor and soothes his rage. He stops the fight, the combatants shake hands and exchange gifts, and finally Rinaldo, refusing both to divulge his identity and to accept an invitation to stay on, rides off into the night with Florindo. It is only now, as the pair are leaving Charlemagne's camp behind, that they somehow come upon Hugh's bereaved father, who acts as if he had just seen his son killed and who at last, in a grisly finale to his lament, picks up and kisses Hugh's still bleeding skull. The scene is really quite dreamlike, especially when Rinaldo is found lingering nearby, lost in a *sunt lacrimae rerum* reverie, wondering somewhat absurdly whether to offer the bereaved old man his sympathy. Its emotions are obviously primal, but their meaning is curiously muddled in a sense of conflicting and overlapping filial/paternal fantasies: any son's natural fantasy of being deeply missed at death; a son's dread that failure to live up to his father will be equivalent to death; the dead son as the father's image of his own failure; the son's terrified projection of time running out.

The effect is uncanny and considerably dampens what would otherwise be a moment of triumph for Rinaldo. He has, after all, just proved himself equal to Orlando, the limit case of his sense of unworthiness since the poem's beginning. In Ariosto, Boiardo and much of the Carolingian tradition before, Rinaldo is often referred to as second-greatest to his cousin among Charlemagne's paladins. Orlando's fame is the fame he cannot match. By fighting Orlando to a draw, hasn't he achieved it now? Or, in another light, since Rinaldo's quest for martial glory always shadows Tasso's quest for poetic fame, has not Tasso, by lifting his Rinaldo material to the level of Ariosto's Orlando material, reached his goal? Evidently not, since we are barely past the middle of the poem, with a hero still resolutely incognito, and many crucial tests still to come.

Rinaldo

ALLEGORIES OF GLORY AND LOVE

For one thing, although Rinaldo has proved himself Orlando's peer, he still does not possess Clarice. After all I have said about paternity and men so far, I have said very little about romantic love and women. But if Tasso's Rinaldo upstages Ariosto's Orlando, Tasso's Clarice upstages Ariosto's Clarice with a vengeance. In *Orlando furioso*, she is never seen acting in her own right and exists only marginally, already married to a husband who spends most of his time in and out of love with Angelica, and who, at a particularly cynical moment, declines to drink a magic potion that will make him know if his wife is faithful to him.[22] Rinaldo's Clarice, on the other hand, is at the core of the poem. In her very first encounter with the hero, her "I never heard of you" touches Rinaldo where he lives. She might as well be Fame personified, and indeed her name etymologically means "glory." Her subsequent appearances in the first half of the poem all suggest allegorical overtones. Her sudden readiness to fall into bed with Rinaldo after his first demonstration of knightly prowess hint at the danger of short-lived "easy fame." Rinaldo's decline of her offer (a charming narrative surprise) does not spring from prudery or adolescent shyness, but from the desire of something more solid — a marriage to glory, not a flirtation with it. On the metapoetical plane, it suggests the poet's need for nurturing a skill that operates on a grander scale than the depiction, however spirited, of an exploit or two.

Clarice next appears, not in her own person, but (in several senses) "by report." The Siren Knight reports her flight, moments earlier, from Ransald's attack; he reports her as the motive of Francard's embassy. Francard himself only knows her by report. His original beloved is "Clarinea" — the wordplay on names cannot be accidental[23] — who seems to embody the "secure local renown" he already enjoys; but he wants more and seeks her image in the Temple of Beauty. Instead he finds the image of Clarice and is enthralled by it. The first result of his infatuation is to have the image replicated in countless copies. This is glory in a kind of mirror stage, and its inevitable consequence is that he is doomed eventually to want the Real Thing. To be sure, the distinction between "fame" and "report" seems a problematic one, as is the question whether "real" glory can be found by means of either.

Introduction

The curious doubling of Clarice as both herself and her image resurfaces in Canto Eight, when Rinaldo finally catches up with Francard, who is still fixated on Clarice's image in the form of a statue. Rinaldo fights him to the death to win it, and from that point on adores and cherishes it like a fetish. It acts as a reminder to save him from betraying his quest in the arms of Floriana. At last he seems to lose it in the Canto Ten shipwreck, along with Florindo and all the other knightly spoils. But once cast ashore in Italy, he recovers it, along with Bayard and Fusberta, from the knight who has ignominiously bought it. And then, no sooner than recaptured, the statue disappears from the narrative. Its place is taken by another image, that of the lady on the shield, which eventually causes his most serious estrangement from Clarice.

Deferring Closure

In the context of the poem's over-arching plot, Rinaldo moves from Fame (Clarice) to the Idea of Fame (the statue) to False Fame (the shield) back to true Fame (Clarice). His battle with Francard for the image of Clarice is a kind of dress rehearsal for his battle with Mambrin for Clarice herself, and to understand the relation between the two goes a long way to understanding the poem. But it also comes as something of a shock to realize that this final battle is not really final. Its ending is deferred to the future and the marriage of Clarice and Rinaldo is not a conclusion, but a prelude to more important business. As in so many earlier instances in a poem, there is a sense of something missing or dropping out or incomplete or not quite realized. [24]

The poem refuses to pause over incidental questions, it always seems in haste to get on to the next thing. Perhaps some of this haste is due to its rapid composition; but more often it seems a sign, not of carelessness or lack of leisure, but of anticipation. Even as he writes, Tasso is rapidly seeing his writer's horizon expand. He knows he is on his way to the "worthier Muse" (12.92) that he promises his patron in the octaves of the postscript, and he is already contemplating a return to the Crusader epic he had begun some two years before. With the hindsight of history, we can see here and there in *Rinaldo* faint anticipations of *Gerusalemme liberata*, such as of Armida in Floriana (with Virgil's Dido as a mediating trope), of Sveno's miraculous tomb in the uncanny sepulcher that unites Clytie's body with her husband's, of powerful pagan villains like Argante and Solimano in Mambrin, and (yes) of Rinaldo the Crusader in Rinaldo of Montalban, or even in incongruous hints now and then of the *Gerusalemme*'s characteristic Christian piety. [25]

It may be relevant to recall that, at least in its author's view, *Gerusalemme* also looked forward to things yet to be realized. Its glory did not satisfy him and he spent the rest of his career rewriting it from scratch, with the well-known disastrous outcome. One of his most striking characteristics was a relentless need for revision, self-correction, even self-censorship. Perhaps this quality was the introversion of the father image that had once tried to turn him from poetry to law. At any rate, Tasso's idea of glory and fame, starting with the *Gerusalemme*, presses toward that of Eternal Glory. The father-figure edges more and more toward that of the Father Inquisitor,[26] the Holy Father and ultimately the Heavenly Father. The energy that carried Tasso to an ever "worthier Muse" reached the aporia of its original intentions. It is in this way perhaps that Tasso's creative self-immolation in *Gerusalemme Conquistata* can be understood.

— Buffalo, June 2016

Notes

1. "I followed with hesitant footsteps, / like Ascanius or Camilla, my wandering father" (from Tasso's incomplete canzone, 'Al Metauro,' S.573). The poem is autobiographical; the "wandering father" is Bernardo Tasso, but neither half of the simile is strictly apt. When Aeneas escapes the sack of Troy, he leads his son Ascanius by the hand, carries his father Anchises on his back and is *followed* by his wife Creusa, who perishes along the way (*Aeneid* 2.720ff) Nor does Camilla, who in due course becomes Aeneas' enemy, "follow" her father Metabus into exile, but is carried by him as a baby (*Aeneid* 11.535ff).

2. See Torquato Tasso, *Love Poems for Lucrezia Bendidio,* ed. and trans. Max A. Wickert (New York: Italica Press, 2011).

3. Montalvo's *Amadis de Gaul,* a chivalric epic in five books, was written in 1499 and published in installments 1508-10. By 1546 seven books of continuations by various other Spanish writers had appeared. Italian translations of these works were published in 1557-58 by Mambrino Roseo di Ferrara, who eventually added six additional books of his own

Introduction

(1559-65). Bernardo Tasso knew Montalvo's poems and perhaps some of Mambrino's but emphatically claimed that his own was an original work, not a translation.

4. Bernardo in fact originally intended to dedicate *Amidigi* to the future Philip II, then Infante of Spain. With Sanseverino's revolt, this became, of course, unthinkable. The next dedicatee to be considered was Philip's enemy, Henry II of France, along with Marguerite de Valois who had patronized the elder Tasso in Paris. With the death of Henry II and France's humiliation at the Treaty of Cateau-Cambrésis in 1559, the wheel had turned back again. The title page of the 1560 Venice printing bears a dedication "a l'invitissimo catolico re Filippo" and the duke of Urbino sent a deluxe copy to Madrid. Philip II ignored it and the real dedicatee of the book remains the duke of Urbino, whose patronage is acknowledged in a dedicatory sonnet on the last page.

5. In his 1585 *Apologia,* Torquato Tasso recalls it as "una perfetta azione di un uomo, non meno che sia quella d'Omero nell'Odissea e di Virgilio nell'Eneida" ("a single complete action of a single man, no less than that of Homer in the *Odyssey* and of Virgil in the *Aeneid*").

6. Alamanni's *Avarchide,* a far more radical work than *Ercole,* appeared posthumously in 1570. Composed in unrhymed verse and imitating Homer's *Iliad,* it treats a historical subject: Julius Caesar's siege of Vercingetorix at Bourges.

7. Dolce also edited the fourth volume of Bernardo's lyrics (1555).

8. *Danese Cattaneo* or Cataneo (?1509-?73): sculptor and poet from Carrara, who, with his master Sansovino, fled to Venice after the Sack of Rome (1527). His friends included Bembo, Titian, Aretino and Vasari, as well as Bernardo Tasso, who, along with Torquato, was his frequent house-guest between 1559 and 1561. As a sculptor Cataneo produced medals, tombs and civic monuments in Verona, Venice and Padua. His best-known surviving large-scale works are a group of four statues for the monument to Leonardo Loredan in SS. Giovanni e Paolo, Venice (1572) and a monumental bust of Bembo in the Basilica del Santo, Padua. As a literary man, Cataneo befriended both Bembo and Aretino and produced works, many of them unfinished, in a variety of forms: *Lucrezia,* a tragedy; *Teseide,* an epic in imitation of Statius; various sonnets, etc. More pertinently, he also began but never completed a narrative poem in quatrains about Rinaldo, *Peregrinaggio di Rinaldo,* and the first thirteen cantos of a chivalric romance, *Dell'amor di Marfisa,* printed in the same year as *Rinaldo.* In the last months of his life, he began an epic on the Battle of Lepanto (1571). Tasso later made him a fictional interlocutor in one of his dialogues (*Il Cataneo ovvero delle conclusioni amorosi,* completed 1591). For more about this interesting personage, see Massimilliano Rossi, *La poesia scolpita: Danese Cataneo nella Venezia del Cinquecento* (Lucca: Paccini Fazzi, 1995).

Rinaldo

Cataneo may in fact have been the first to suggest not only Rinaldo but also the First Crusade as epic subjects to Tasso. For Cataneo, a true Renaissance man, poetry was a sideline to his professional career in sculpture and architecture, but his four narrative poems cover just about all the available options for epic: the *Marfisa* is Ariostan in its choice of heroine, style and versification; the *Teseide* treats a Greco-Roman subject in an appropriately classicizing manner, the *Lepanto* daringly uses recent history as an epic subject, and the *Peregrinaggio* opens the option of evading Ariosto's influence by having his protagonist Orlando displaced by his fellow-paladin and sometime rival, Rinaldo.

9. Domenico Venièr (or Veniero) (1517–82): Venetian politician whom illness forced to retire from public life in 1547. He thereafter devoted himself to extravagantly Petrarchan verse and cultural patronage. Ca' Venièr, across from Santa Maria Formosa, where he entertained a coterie of intellectuals including Tasso's father, still exists. He should not be confused with his contemporary compatriot, Maffei Venièr, a considerably more gifted writer and a spirited debunker of Petrarchism.

10. Carlo Sigonio [also Segonio, Segonia] (1520–84): a student of Castelvetro's, became a leading legal scholar, historian and classicist and first taught at Venice where his poetics, *De dialogo,* appeared in the same year as Bernardo's *Amadigi.* It had a profound influence on the younger Tasso. Sigonio then moved to the university at Padua where he became Tasso's instructor in Roman Law. When Tasso changed faculties in 1561, Sigonio, along with Francesco Piccolomini mentored him in the intense study of Aristotle. A bitter dispute with another famous Aristotelian, Francesco Robortello, soon afterwards led Sigonio to leave Padua for Bologna, where Tasso followed him in 1562. There is a fine portrait of Sigonio by Lavinia Fontana (Galleria Estense, Modena). Tasso's Aristotelianism in the *Rinaldo* preface gives the first inkling of Sigonio's influence.

11. Giovan Battista Nicolucci, "Il Pigna" (1530–75): a Ferrarese apothecary's son. (The sign above the shop showed a pine nut [*pigna*]). He was educated by Giraldi Cinzio and the celebrated Aristotelian, Vincenzo Maggi. He taught Latin and Greek at Ferrara and in 1554 published *I romanzi,* a treatise defending the Ariostan romance as a new modern genre, to be judged by its own laws rather than by Aristotelian strictures, engaging Giraldi Cinzio in a lively polemic. He eventually succeeded Cinzio as ducal secretary and court poet. He also tried his hand at a 'heroic' poem on a modern subject (*Gli eroici,* 1561). Tasso later criticized *I romanzi* in the *Discorsi sull'arte poetica,* but highly praised Pigna as a lyric poet in *Considerazioni sopra tre canzoni di G.B. Pigna intitolate le Tre stelle* (both c. 1572). Interestingly, just as Tasso's father and Speroni had both long before been lovers of Tullia d'Aragona, so the younger Tasso and Pigna eventually both became lovers of the same woman, Lucrezia Bendidio. Most of Pigna's love poems to Lucrezia have only recently been

rediscovered. By the time Tasso himself wrote his *Rime amorose* for her, Pigna, as court poet to Alfonso II d'Este in Ferrara, was also a professional rival. At his death in 1575, Tasso succeeded him in that position.

12. Sperone Speroni (1500–88) and Bernardo Tasso had been friends in their early youth. Both had been lovers of the legendary courtesan-poet, Tullia Aragona. Speroni eventually taught philosophy at Padua, where the became Torquato Tasso's teacher and friend. He was at the time already famous as the author of *Canace,* a classical tragedy, and as a literary critic who had measured swords with no less a rival than Giraldi Cinzio. Along with Pietro Bembo, he was an early defender of the vernacular in literature and the influence of his writings reached abroad to DuBellay, Sir Philip Sidney and others. However, as Matteo Navone points out (ed. 2012, pp. 344–45), Tasso's claim that *Rinaldo* meets Speroni's criteria for narrative unity does not pass muster in view of Speroni's own writings. In 1575, Speroni became a member on the panel of Roman intellectuals invited by Tasso to critique the *Gerusalemme.* A portrait by Titian of Speroni, age 44, hangs in the Museo Civico, Treviso.

13. See 3.58 (Cataneo) and 9.30 (Venièr).

14. In 1587; see Chronology.

15. Galileo Galilei was a member and heartily shared its distaste for Tasso's epic.

16. One of them (S.772) imagines Tasso supplying a belated inscription for his father's tomb; another (S.809) conjures up the memory of an Arabian vase, won by his father at the Siege of Tunis and now a spoil of war preserved in misfortune.

17. The word (Italian *genio* or *ingegno*) is Tasso's own. In addition to the two instances cited here, it occurs thrice more in the poem, once applied to himself as poet (1.3), once to Malagis (1.42) and once to Rinaldo (4.17).

18. See n. 5 above.

19. In the sources, Malagis is Rinaldo's cousin, of an indeterminate age. But in Tasso, after first appearing as a father figure, he seems to get progressively younger in the course of the narrative, from a senescent father in the Bayard episode to a vigorous fellow combatant in the final battle. His very last function, however, is once again that of a surrogate father who licenses Rinaldo's marriage to Clarice.

20. Scipio (or Scipione) Gonzaga (1542–93), educated in the household of Cardinal Ercole Gonzaga, and at Bologna and Padua, where he became a fellow student of Tasso. He founded the Accademia degli Eterei, which Tasso joined in 1564. In Tasso's later years, Scipio oversaw the first corrected printing of *Gerusalemme liberata* (1584), He was named cardinal in 1587 and as a high-ranking ecclesiastic enjoyed the friendship of Carlo Borromeo and Filippo Neri, both future saints.

Rinaldo

21. Here it is the sonnet's octave, in my translation (*Love Poems*, p. 43).

Fetters by which the soul is bound life-long
to its mortal consort are to me less dear
than these you bound me with, which hold me here
in links, once sweet and soft, now hard and strong.
The famous hero with no better cheer
gave death to his son, or made the barbarian die
by throttling him with his own torque, than I,
dragged by my hair, go chained at your chariot's rear.

22. *Orlando Furioso* 43.5-9. Similarly, Ariosto's Rinaldo, who mocks the double standard by which sexually active women are condemned (*Orlando Furioso* 4.63-67), is hard to square with his Tasso namesake, who earns his spurs defending his mother's chastity.

23. If the Clarinea/Clarice name-pairing is suggestive, I leave it to the reader to puzzle out suggestions in Rinaldo/Ransaldo.

24. Some other unanswered questions: Where do the English knight and Ysolier disappear to? If Rinaldo gets Tristan's lance, who gets Lancelot's? What are the back-stories of the scores of named characters who drop out of the poem almost as soon as mentioned — Anachrone and Auristella and Eurybas and Helidonia and Medea and Pandion, to say nothing of about a hundred combatants? Whose portraits hang on the other three-and-a-half walls in the Inn of Courtesy? Rinaldo throws the shield with the fateful image into the river, but what happens to Clarice's statue? What are the names of Clytie's husband, of Floriana's twins? When Rinaldo gets married, why not Florindo also?

25. Incongruous is the operative word here. I am not, of course, referring to the conventional Christian-versus-pagan commonplaces found in all chivalric epic, but to unexpectedly pious intrusions like Rinaldo's scruples at the pagan rites in the Cave of Love (5.63), Florindo's conversion and baptism (11.95), Clarice's dream-warnings to Rinaldo after his seduction by Floriana (9.86), the strangely scrupulous interfaith marriage stipulations proposed by Francard (3.45) and the authorial denunciation of corrupt Christian armies (6.12–13).

26. See Chronology, 1577

—⁂—

Bibliography

(1) Manuscripts and Early Printed Editions

No autograph of *Rinaldo* has survived. Six printed editions appeared during Tasso's lifetime beginning with Francesco Senese's (Venice, 1562), which contains countless errors, a number of which were corrected in a broadsheet inserted in the book some months after its appearance. A second Venetian edition (1570) was printed by Francesco Franceschi. This includes alterations apparently provided by Tasso himself but is marred by misprints and inconsistencies. Subsequent printings are by Osanna (Mantua, 1581 and 1583), Lelio Gavardo (Venice, 1583) and Giulio Cesare Cagnacini (Ferrara, 1589). A curiosity of some interest to Anglophone readers — and opera lovers — is a much later edition, in Italian, prepared in London (1801) by Mozart's librettist Lorenzo da Ponte, nine years after John Hoole's English translation.

(2) Modern Works

(A) Editions

Tasso, Torquato. *Rinaldo.* In *Opere*, edited by Bruno Maier, 2:441–721. Milan: Rizzoli, 1964. The text here reproduced and translated.

—. *Rinaldo: edizione critica basata sulla seconda edizione del 1570 con le varianti della princeps 1562.* Edited by Michael Sherberg. Ravenna: Longo, 1990. A scholarly modern edition based, unlike most previous and subsequent ones, on the second Venetian printing (*see* Manuscripts and Early Printed Editions above).

—. "*Il Gierusalemme.*" Edited by Lanfranco Caretti. In *Studi Italiani* 12 (1993). An edition of the epic fragment dedicated to

Guidobaldo dell Rovere and abandoned in favor of *Rinaldo*. Much of it is recycled in the opening of *Gerusalemme liberata*.

—. *Rinaldo*. Edited by Matteo Navone. Alessandria: Edizioni dell'Orso, 2012. Based on the 1562 text and described by Navone as "«*una nuova trascrizione della* princeps *del Rinaldo, condotta secondo criteri moderatamente conservativi*» (p. 37). Navone adds a fine introduction and useful, up-to-date notes.

(B) SECONDARY WORKS

Battaglia, R. "*Dalla lingua del* Amadigi *a quella della* Gerusalemme Liberata." *Cultura neolatina* 1.2 (1941): 94–115.

Bonadeo, Alfredo. "*L'avventura di Rinaldo*." *PMLA* 81 (1966): 199–206.

Bozzetti, Cesare. "Testo e tradizione del Rinaldo." *Studi Tassiani* 11 (1961): 5–44.

Brand, Carl Peter. *Torquato Tasso: A Study of the Poet and of His Contribution to English Literature*. Cambridge: Cambridge University Press, 1965.

Bulfinch, Thomas. *Bulfinch's Mythology*. New York: The Modern Library, 2004. Bulfinch's third volume, *Legends of Charlemagne*, patches together materials from Pulci, Boiardo, Ariosto and others, many of them more "literary" than "legendary." His account of the taming of Bayard is a near-translation from Tasso's *Rinaldo*.

Capasso, Angelo. *Il "Tassino": L'aurora di Tasso*. Genoa: Albrighi Segati, 1939.

—. *Commento al* Rinaldo *di Torquato Tasso*. Genoa: Società anonima editrice Dante Alighieri, 1940.

—. *Studi sul Tasso minore*. Genoa: Società anonima editrice Dante Alighieri, 1940.

Carducci, Giosue. *I poemi minori di Torquato Tasso*. Bologna: Zanichelli, 1894. A sympathetic, if somewhat dated study by the Nobel-Prize-winning poet.

Caretti, Lanfranco. *Ariosto e Tasso*. Turin: Einaudi, 1961; 2nd. ed., 2001.

Bibliography

—. *Ariosto e Tasso.* Turin: Einaudi, 1977.

Casadei, Alberto. "Il *Rinaldo* e il genere cavalleresco alla metà del Cinquecento." In *La fine degli incanti,* 45–60. Milan: FrancoAngeli, 1997.

Cavallo, Jo Ann. "Torquato Tasso, *Il Rinaldo.*" In *The Romance Epics of Boiardo, Ariosto and Tasso: From Public Duty to Private Pleasure,* 178–85. Toronto: University of Toronto Press, 2004. Also contains a useful discussion of Bernardo Tasso's *Amadigi,* 170–77.

—. *The World beyond Europe in the Romance Epics of Boiardo and Ariosto.* Toronto: University of Toronto Press, 2013. Though limited to the two authors of its title, it contains numerous insights relevant to *Rinaldo.*

Comelli, Michele. *Poetica e allegoria nel* Rinaldo *di Torquato Tasso.* Milan: Edizioni 'La Ragione Critica', 2014. Contains an extremely detailed and useful bibliography.

Corradini, Marco. "Torquato Tasso e il dibattimento di metà Cinquecento sul poema epico." In *La tradizione e l'ingegno: Ariosto, Tasso, Marino e dintorni,* 29–41. Novara: Interlinea, 2004.

Daniele, Antonio. "*Considerazioni sul* Rinaldo" and "*Ancora sul* Rinaldo." In *Nuovi capitoli tassiani,* 56–126. Padua: Antenore, 1998.

Della Terza, Dante. *Dal* Rinaldo *alla* Gerusalemme—Il *testo, la favola: Atti del Convegno Internazionale di Studi Torquato Tasso quattro secoli dopo, 17–19 novembre 1994.* Sorrento: Città di Sorrento, 1997.

—, ed. *Torquato Tasso e la cultura del suo tempo.* Naples: Edizioni Scientifiche Italiane, 2003.

Di Pietro, Antonio. *Il noviziato di Torquato Tasso.* Milan: Malfasi, 1953.

Donadoni, Eugenio. "Il *Rinaldo.*" In *Torquato Tasso: Saggio critico,* 1:41–66. Florence: La Nuova Italia, 1920.

Forti, Fiorenzo. "Aspetti del *Rinaldo.*" In *Torquato Tasso,* Comitato per le celebrazioni di Torquato Tasso, 227–80. Milan:

Marzorato, 1957. Reprinted as "*L'opera prima di Tasso*" in *Fra carte dei poeti*, 78–132. Milan: Ricciardi, 1965, 78-132.

Fortini, Franco. *Dialoghi col Tasso*. Turin: Bollati Boringhieri, 1999. A fascinating meditation by a poet about a poet, with acute and daring psychological and metapoetic speculations.

Fubini, Mario. "*Il* Rinaldo *del Tasso*." In *Studi sulla letteratura del Rinascimento*, 6–15. Florence: La Nuova Italia, 1947.

Getto, Giovanni. "Preludio poetico: il *Rinaldo*." In *Interpretazione del Tasso*, 113–44. Naples: Edizioni scientifiche italiani, 1951.

Gigante, Claudio. *Tasso*. Rome: Salerno editrice, 2007.

Hoole, John. *The* Rinaldo *of Torquato Tasso*. London: Dodsley, 1792. The only previous English translation.

Looney, Dennis. *Compromising the Classics: Romance Epic Narrative in the Italian Renaissance*. Detroit, MI: Wayne State University Press, 1996.

Manso, Giovanni Battista *Vita di Torquato Tasso,* edited by Bruno Basile. Rome: Salerno editrice, 1995. A modern edition of the biography by Tasso's friend, originally published in Naples in 1619. It is of some interest to students of English literature that Milton during his Italian journey met and conferred with Manso.

Mazzoni, Guido. "*Del* Rinaldo." In Angelo Solerti, ed., *Opere minori in versi di Torquato Tasso*. Bologna: Zanicchelli, 1891, i–xlii.

Melli, Elio. "Nella selva dei *Rinaldi*: poemetti su Rinaldo da Mont'Albano in antiche edizioni e stampe." *Studi e problem di critica testuale* 16 (1978), 192–215.

Milesi, Silvana. *Un' idea su Tasso tra poesia e pittura*. Bergamo: Corponove, 2003. A sumptuously illustrated collection of essays, pictures and documents relating to Tasso.

Momigliano, Attilio. "*L'esordio del Tasso*." In *Studi di poesia*, 83–88. Messina: D'Anna, 1960.

Morace, Rosanna. "Il *Rinaldo* tra l'*Amadigi* e il *Floridante*." *Studi Tassiani* 56–58 (2008–10): 11–42.

Bibliography

—. *Dal* Amadigi *al* Rinaldo: *Bernardo e Torquato Tasso tra epico ed eroico.* Alessandria: Edizioni dell' Orso, 2012. A penetrating full-length study that places *Rinaldo* in the context of Renaissance Italian romantic epic.

Navone, Matteo. "Intersezione di generi nel *Rinaldo* di Torquato Tasso." In *La Letteratura degli Italiani: Rotte Confini Passaggi,* edited by Alberto Beniscelli et al; 15–18. Transactions of the 14th National Congress of Associazione degli Italianisti. Genoa: DIRAS, 2012.

Oldcorn, Anthony. "Il Tassino tra 'epos' e romanzo." In *Torquato Tasso e la cultura estense,* edited by Gianni Venturi, 2:155–62. Florence: Olschki, 1999.

Proto, Enrico. *Sul* Rinaldo *di Torquato Tasso: Note letterarie e critiche.* Naples: A. Tocco, 1895.

Quint, David. "The Boat of Romance and the Renaissance Epic." In *Romance: Generic Transformation from Chrétien de Troyes to Cervantes,* edited by Kevin Brownlee and Marina Scordilis Brownlee, 178–202. Hanover, NH: University Press of New England, 1985.

Ragonese, Gaetano. "Sul *Rinaldo.*" In *Dal* Gerusalemme *al* Mondo Creato. Palermo: Manfredi, 1963.

Rajna, Pio. "Rinaldo da Montalbano." *Il Propugnatore* 3.1 (1870): 213–41, 3.2 (1870): 58–127. Reprinted in Guido Lucchini, ed., *Scritti di filologia e linguistica italiana e romanza.* Rome: Salerno editrice, 1998. A survey of romances based on or related to the Rinaldo legend, including the sources and analogues of Tasso's poem.

Ramat, Raffaello. *Lettura del Tasso minore.* Florence: La Nuova Italia, 1953.

Rhu, Lawrence F. *The Genesis of Tasso's Narrative Theory.* Detroit, MI: Wayne State University Press, 1993. Contains a translation (pp. 95–98) of "Torquato Tasso to His Readers," the preface to *Rinaldo.* See Appendix, pp. 438ff.

Sherberg, Michael. *Rinaldo: Character and Intertext in Ariosto and Tasso.* Saratoga, CA: Anma Libri, 1993. Chapters 2 and 3 comprise the most substantial modern critical analysis of the *Rinaldo* in English.

Rinaldo

Solerti, Angelo. *Vita di Torquato Tasso*. Turin: Loescher, 1895. An early pioneering work of biographical scholarship.

Symonds, John Addington. *Renaissance in Italy: The Catholic Reaction*. London: Smith, Elder & Co., 1886. Chapter 8 contains an extended discussion of *Rinaldo* in relation to both Bernardo Tasso's *Amadigi* and Torquato Tasso's *Gerusalemme*.

Tortoreto, A. "*Bernardo e Torquato*." In *Studi Tassiani*, supplement to no. 1, 71–74. Bergamo: Biblioteca A. Maj, 1969.

Venturi, Gianni, ed. *Torquato Tasso e la cultura estense*. Florence: L.S. Olschki, 1999. A three-volume collection of essays, covering the whole range of Tasso's activities. The articles by Marina Beer (1.53–67), Anthony Oldcorn (1.155–62), and Vania De Maldé (1.317–32) are relevant to the present work.

Williamson, Edward. *Bernardo Tasso*. Rome: Storia e Letteratura, 1951. A detailed study of the life and work of Tasso's father.

Zatti, Sergio. *L'ombra di Tasso*. Milan: Mondadori, 1996.

——. *Torquato Tasso*. Milan: Marzorati, 2000. See especially pp. 135–300.

——. *The Quest for Epic: From Ariosto to Tasso*. Toronto: University of Toronto Press, 2006. A selection of essays translated from various works by this superb Italian critic.

—ᴀ—

PLOT SUMMARY OF *RINALDO*

CANTO ONE: Orlando's feats in Charlemagne's wars fill Rinaldo with shame at his own obscurity. One day he chances upon a steed, armor, shield, lance and sword (secret gifts from his sorcerer-protector Malagis). Obedient to an earlier vow, he does not take the sword, but sets out with the rest. Malagis arrives, disguised as an old man, to warn him of the monstrous steed Bayard, and Rinaldo sets out to tame it. On his way, he meets the princess Clarice and identifies himself as Aymon's son, Roland's cousin, and Charlemagne's liegeman. She says that she has heard of all three, but never of him. Humiliated, he proves his prowess by unhorsing all her attendant knights. She is impressed and invites him to her bed, but he refuses, still feeling unworthy.

CANTO TWO: Rinaldo meets Ysolier and an English knight, jousts with Ysolier for the right to face Bayard and defeats him. The three make friends. When Bayard approaches, the English knight backs down and rides away. Ysolier is routed by Bayard, but Rinaldo wrestles the terrible stallion to earth and tames him. He and Ysolier then meet a haughty knight, Ransald, who bears a shield depicting Cupid trampling on Mars. Rinaldo defeats him and takes possession of the shield.

CANTO THREE: The Knight of the Siren, seeing the Cupid shield, mistakes Rinaldo for Ransald and attacks him. He is unhorsed and tells this story: Francard, King of Armenia, cousin of Mambrin, loved Clarinea and was loved in return. He traveled to the Temple of Beauty which displays images of the world's fairest women. He found it but discovered that it contained the image, not of Clarinea, but of Clarice. Infatuated, he abandoned Clarinea. He had Clarice's image duplicated in countless copies, but at last wanted the real thing. He then dispatched the Knight of the Siren to Charlemagne, with an ultimatum: "Either give me Clarice in marriage or I will join the Moorish army, destroy you and seize her." Charlemagne temporized and the Siren Knight crossed the Alps to confer with Clarice herself. Upon arrival in France, he accidentally met her on the way. Moments earlier, while they were resting, Ransald attacked them and Clarice ran away. Rinaldo and Ysolier continue their journey and come upon Merlin's statues of Lancelot and Tristan, depicted as though in combat with lances. An inscription declares that these lances are destined for champions even mightier than their bearers. Ysolier tries to seize Tristan's lance but fails. Rinaldo easily succeeds and the statue of Tristan bows to him.

CANTO FOUR: Rinaldo and Ysolier reach the Seine estuary and see a triumphal barge coming from the sea while a triumphal chariot moves by land to meet it. The chariot carries Charlemagne's queen, Galerana, with Clarice among her attendant damsels. After overthrowing the women's escort with Ysolier's help, Rinaldo, thinking Clarice is destined for Francard, abducts her. He is about to rape her, when Malagis, disguised as a black knight, charges and carries her off in a dragon-borne chariot, vanishing in a cloud with Ysolier in pursuit.

CANTO FIVE: Rinaldo sets out alone in quest of Clarice. He chances upon Florindo, a charming lad, who is in deep despair because he, the apparent son of a lowly shepherd, has been spurned by the high-born Olinda. He and Rinaldo ride off to the Cave of Love built by Merlin. There a magical statue of Cupid prophesies that they will both attain their loves, but must first seek renown in war. It also reveals that Florindo is nobly born and identifies the black knight as Malagis.

CANTO SIX: Rinaldo and Florindo reach Charlemagne's camp in Italy, proclaim themselves champions of love and challenge all comers. Both pagans and Christians are invited to the tournament. Rinaldo, unarmed but for lance and dagger, kills the Saracen giant Atlas, thus winning the fabled sword Fusberta. He then kills Hugh, a favorite young knight of Charlemagne's. The enraged emperor calls on Orlando to avenge Hugh's death. The protracted fight between the two heroes comes to an impasse. Greatly impressed, Charlemagne is mollified and stops the match. Rinaldo refuses to divulge his name and concedes victory to Orlando. Orlando responds in kind, and they become friends. Gryphon, a wicked member of the Maganza clan then attacks with a group of others, but is easily defeated by Florindo. He and Rinaldo, still incognito, leave the camp.

CANTO SEVEN: After passing Hugh's grieving father, Rinaldo and Florindo enter a gloomy forest with a vile-looking lake, where a crystal sepulcher contains the incorruptible body of a beautiful lady, her breast pierced by an arrow. All around, hundreds of grieving men are gathered and their leader challenges Rinaldo. Mortally wounded in the ensuing combat, he discloses that the dead woman is his beloved wife Clytie. He has accidentally killed her when she spied on him, made jealous by a malicious rumor. In despair, he caused a sorcerer to cast a spell over the tomb and lake. As he breathes his last, the spell is broken, the mourners return to normal and the sepulcher miraculously unites Clytie's body with her husband's. Florindo and Rinaldo ride on and arrive at the seaside Inn of Courtesy. They are welcomed by Eurydice, the Inn's governess, who also tells them that the magic Ship Adventurous lies at anchor nearby.

CANTO EIGHT: After a tour of the Inn, with its picture gallery of paragons of courtesy, the two knights embark on the Ship Adventurous. It carries them to a distant shore where they liberate a group of captives enslaved by pirates in the employ of Mambrin. The ship then deposits them on another coast and sails off. There they find that a marvelous image, which Rinaldo recognizes as depicting Clarice, is being worshiped by pagans led by Francard. Rinaldo kills Francard, as well as his brother Clarel and the lion who fights alongside him. Seizing Clarice's image, Rinaldo leaves with Florindo. The two champions gain renown for their exploits in Asia, including the slaying of Mambrin's monstrous brothers, Brunamont and Constantine.

CANTO NINE: In Syria, Rinaldo and Florindo are welcomed by Queen Floriana and rout all her champions in a tournament. During a banquet, Rinaldo relates an episode from his early youth: His mother Beatrice had married his father Aymon in preference to a rival suitor, Ginam of Maganza. Years later, when their sons neared manhood, Ginam, still consumed by secret malice, falsely boasted, producing apparent proof, that the boys were the issue of Beatrice's adultery with himself. Rinaldo fought his virgin battle in defense of his mother's honor and killed Ginam with his first lance thrust. He vowed henceforth never to use a sword until he had seized one in fair fight from a great warrior. Floriana meanwhile has fallen in love with Rinaldo. She seduces him in her garden, but he, admonished by a dream vision of Clarice, leaves secretly with Florindo.

CANTO TEN: The abandoned Floriana tries to kills herself, but is whisked away to the Hesperides by her sorceress aunt, Medea. There, true to an earlier prophecy, she eventually gives birth to Rinaldo's twin children, a boy and a girl, both destined to become great warriors. Meanwhile Rinaldo and Florindo find themselves in a storm at sea. Rinaldo puts Bayard, Fusberta and the image of Clarice into a life boat, whose treacherous pilot casts off before Rinaldo comes on board. The main ship sinks and the two friends are swept out to sea and separated. Rinaldo is washed up in Italy where he regains Bayard, Fusberta and Clarice's image from a knight who has bought them from the boat pilot. Rinaldo takes possession of the knight's shield which bears the image of a beautiful lady. He reaches Paris and, maintaining the superiority of his lady's beauty to that of all others, challenges and defeats Gryphon, now Clarice's champion. Clarice, believing that Rinaldo was fighting for the lady on his shield, is seized by jealousy. Meanwhile Rinaldo is recognized by the Court and joyfully welcomed by his father Aymon.

CANTO ELEVEN: At an imperial ball, Rinaldo, smarting under Clarice's scorn, seeks the intercession of Alda, an innocent childhood friend. When, at his approach to her, Anselm of Maganza steps up and calls him a bastard, Rinaldo stabs him to death on the spot. The assembled Maganzans rush upon Rinaldo, but the Clairmonts rally to his defense and he escapes. Charlemagne is furious and banishes him from France. The miserable Rinaldo rides off, throws the fateful shield into the Seine and reaches a dreary wilderness where he almost succumbs to despondency. A mysterious knight (Malagis in disguise) seizes Bayard to lure Rinaldo up a green hill, where he is welcomed by the hill's guardian ladies who restore him to health and cheer. After a while, he hears the faraway sound of combat. Riding toward it, he finds a lone stranger beset by a rabble of attackers. He routs them and recognizes the stranger as his friend Florindo, who, washed ashore near Ostia, was nursed to health by Scipio who recognized him by a birthmark as his long-lost son Laelius, abducted in infancy by pirates.

CANTO TWELVE: One of Florindo's attackers confesses that the ambush was ordered by Mambrin, who has arrived with a huge host to seize Clarice and to avenge his brothers. He has already captured Clarice in Paris and is returning to his fleet anchored nearby. Rinaldo and Florindo speed off toward the pagan army. They are ferried across a swollen river by Malagis. On the far side, they find Mambrin and his hordes, with Clarice held captive in their midst. After an elaborate muster of pagan champions, the battle begins. Rinaldo and his two friends slay crowds of pagans. At last Mambrin enters single combat with Rinaldo, both wearing magic armaments that make them proofed against blows. In the end, Malagis brings the action to a halt by enchantment and conducts Rinaldo, Clarice and Florindo to his nearby palace. There Clarice is reconciled and the two lovers marry. Malagis prophesies glory for Rinaldo in the terrible wars to come.

—⁂—

1493 Bernardo Tasso, the poet's father, is born to a noble family of Bergamo.

1520 Around this year, Bernardo (age 27) at the court of Ferrara, writes love poems to Ginevra Malatesta under the nom-de-plume "Ginepro." His sonnet about his separation from her at her marriage *(Poichè la parte men perfetta e bella)* becomes widely known.

1531 Bernardo (age 38) publishes the first book of his *Amori.* (Three others follow in 1534, 1537 and 1555). He gains substantial fame as a love poet.

1532 Bernardo (39) enters the service of Ferrante Sanseverino, prince of Salerno.

1535 Bernardo (42) fights under Sanseverino at the Siege of Tunis; then moves to Venice where he has a love affair with the famed Tullia d'Aragona. Returns to Salerno at the end of year.

1536 Bernardo (43) marries Porzia de' Rossi, of a noble family from Pistoia.

1537 Bernardo (44) is granted a villa at Sorrento; his daughter Cornelia is born.

1544 Torquato Tasso is born (March 11) at Sorrento; his father (51) is absent in Piedmont as secretary to Prince Sanseverino during the war between the Emperor Charles V and France.

1545 Bernardo (52), after a brief stay in Flanders during peace negotiations, returns to Sorrento. Granted temporary leave from his secretarial duties, he relocates his family to Salerno and begins work on his epic, *Amadigi.*

1547 The Spanish viceroy in Naples attempts to introduce the Inquisition, provoking a violent uprising. Representing the insurgents, Sanseverino, accompanied by Bernardo (54), travels to Augsburg to confer with the emperor.

1548 Bernardo (55) returns to Salerno.

Rinaldo

1551 In November, the Tasso family moves to Naples.

1552 Prince Sanseverino is proclaimed rebel and exiled from Naples, along with his followers, including Bernardo Tasso (59), whose goods are confiscated and whose family is prohibited from following him. Torquato Tasso (8) begins schooling at a Neapolitan convent under the Jesuit Giovanni d'Angeluzzo. Meanwhile his father is sent to Paris by Sanseverino to agitate for a French invasion of Naples. This intrigue fails.

1554 After further wanderings, Bernardo (61) settles in Rome and vainly petitions that his family be allowed to join him. In October, only Torquato (10) is allowed to do so, who upon arrival in Rome, continues his studies, joined by a cousin from Bergamo, Cristoforo Tasso.

1556 The poet's mother Porzia dies unexpectedly. His father suspects poisoning. In September, fearing an attack on Rome after hostilities between Pope Paul IV and Philip II of Spain, Bernardo (63) sends Torquato (12) to live with relatives in Bergamo. He himself leaves Rome for Pesaro and Urbino, finding patronage under Guidobaldo II della Rovere.

1557 Torquato (13) joins his father in Urbino and there continues his studies. Guidobaldo's heir, Francesco Maria della Rovere, is a fellow student. Their tutors include Girolamo Muzio, Antonio Galli and other noted humanists.

1558 Tasso's sister Cornelia (21) marries Marzio Sersale. The humiliating match is instigated by a relative, Abate della Fosse, and vehemently but unsuccessfully opposed long-distance by Tasso's father (65). In June, during a Turkish raid on Sorrento, Cornelia narrowly escapes death or slavery. A false report of her death reaches Torquato (14) in Urbino.

1559 Bernardo Tasso (66) moves to Venice to oversee publication of his epic, *Amadigi*. He is joined by Torquato (15), who, while assisting his father, begins an epic on the First Crusade, but abandons it after 116 stanzas to compose *Rinaldo*.

1560 Bernardo Tasso's *Amadigi* published. In November, Torquato (16) enters university at Padua to study law and befriends Sperone Speroni, Cesare Pavesi and Vincenzo Pinelli.

1561 Torquato (17) abandons the study of law and inscribes in courses of philosophy and eloquence. Under Speroni,

Francesco Piccolomini and Carlo Sigonio, he embarks on a deep study of Aristotle. In late summer, he is in attendance at the Este summer palace of Bagni di Abano where he meets and falls in love with Lucrezia Bendidio, a lady-in-waiting to Eleanora d'Este, and begins composing lyrics in her honor. His father (age 68) enters the service of Cardinal Luigi d'Este.

1562 *Rinaldo* is published at Venice. Torquato Tasso (18) composes further poems for Lucrezia and continues to do so after she marries Paolo Machiavelli that autumn. Still at Padua, Torquato resumes work on his projected Crusader epic. His father (69) transfers to the service of Guglielmo Gonzaga and moves to Mantua. In November, Torquato Tasso (18) leaves for Bologna to commence his third year of university study.

1563 Torquato (19) visits his father (70) at Mantua, where he meets Laura Peperara, falls in love and begins writing verses for her. He continues his studies at Bologna. His father begins work on *Floridante*, a thirty-four-canto recasting and continuation of *Amadigi*.

1564 In January, Torquato (20), accused of authoring an anti-university satire and forced to flee Bologna, moves back to Padua under the patronage of Scipione Gonzaga. He joins the Accademia degli Eterei under the pen-name "Pentito" and resumes study under Francesco Piccolomini and Federico Pendasio. He composes a funeral oration on his friend Stefano Santini and begins writing *Discorsi dell'arte poetica*.

1565 In October, Torquato (21) enters the service of Cardinal Luigi d'Este and is in frequent attendance at the court of Alfonso II d'Este at Ferrara. He finds favor with Alfonso's sisters, Lucrezia and Leonora, for whom he eventually writes some of his finest lyrics.

1566 In the spring, the poet (22), during a brief visit to Scipione Gonzaga and other friends at Padua, compiles an arrangement of *Rime Amorose* for publication in *Rime de gli Accademici Eterei*.

1567 *Rime de gli Accademici Eterei* published. Torquato (23) is living at Ferrara, where he cultivates close relations with Giovanni Battista Pigna, Ercole Cato, Giambattista Guarini, Antonio Montecatini and Annibale Romei. He composes various inaugural orations for the Ferrarese Academy.

1569   On September 5, tended by his son (age 25), Tasso's father Bernardo (age 76) dies at Ostiglia near Mantua, leaving *Floridante* unfinished. It is eventually completed and published by his son in 1587.

1570   On January 18, Lucrezia d'Este marries Francesco Maria della Rovere, duke of Urbino. Tasso (26) begins composition of the dialogue *Il Cataneo ovvero delle conclusioni amorosi* (completed 1590). In October, he travels to Paris in the suite of Luigi d'Este, befriends Iacopo Corbinelli and meets Ronsard.

1571   Tasso (27) returns to Ferrara and quits the service of Cardinal Luigi d'Este.

1572   On January 1, Tasso (28) is admitted into the service of Duke Alfonso II d'Este. He writes *Considerazioni sopra tre canzoni di G.B. Pigna detto le tre stelle.*

1573   In January, Tasso (29) moves in Alfonso's entourage to Rome. In the late spring, he returns to Ferrara and writes *Aminta*. In the summer, *Aminta* is performed at Belvedere, the Este summer residence. The poet is appointed Ducal Lecturer in Geometry and Astronomy at Ferrara. He begins his tragedy, *Galealto, Re di Norvegia,* later retitled *Torrismondo*.

1574   In July, Tasso (30) moves in Alfonso's retinue to Venice for a state meeting with Henry III of France on his return from Poland. He assists in preparing festive entertainments for Henry in both Venice and Ferrara.

1575   In April, Tasso (31) completes *Goffredo,* the first draft of *Gerusalemme liberata*. That summer he reads his epic to the duke and Lucrezia d'Este. In November, Tasso becomes historiographer to the court. He is troubled by nervous disorders amid increasing discontent with his position in Ferrara and doubts about *Goffredo*. While traveling to Rome for jubilee celebrations, he is presented to Cardinal de' Medici and submits *Goffredo* for revision to a panel of Roman literati chosen by his friend Scipione Gonzaga and including Luca Scalabrino, Flaminio Nobili, Silvio Antoniano and Sperone Speroni. Alfonso d'Este is suspicious of Tasso's overtures to the Medici and displeased by his irresolution over the publication of his epic.

Chronology

1576 In January, Tasso (32) returns to Ferrara and begins extensive revisions of the *Gerusalemme*. His discontent and persecution mania escalate. On September 7, he is attacked and wounded in the head during a dispute with Ercole Fucci over courtly precedence. In disgrace at court, he takes refuge in Modena as a guest of Ferrando Tassoni, and there meets the poet Tarquinia Molza, for whom he writes the *Discorso della Gelosia* (published 1585).

1577 In January, Tasso (33) returns to Ferrara and resumes life as a courtier. During a stay at Comacchio, he composes his comedy, *Gl'intrichi d'Amore* (published 1603). Amid increasing symptoms of neurosis, he suspects himself of heresy. In June, he confesses to the Ferrarese Inquisitor, is absolved, but remains in doubt. On June 17, he attacks a servant with his dagger, suspecting him of spying. Released after a brief imprisonment, he accompanies Alfonso's court to Belriguardo. When his condition deteriorates, he is ordered back to Ferrara under house arrest in a Franciscan convent. Alfonso fears that Tasso's behavior may rouse suspicion from the Inquisition. On July 27, Tasso secretly leaves the convent without authorization, flees Ferrara and travels incognito to Sorrento. Still in disguise, he finds his sister Cornelia and announces his own death. When she faints, he reveals his identity. After a happy but brief stay in Sorrento, he begins to miss Ferrara and sets out for Rome.

1578 In April, Tasso (34) arrives back in Ferrara, but is still restless. In July he begins wandering again, with frequent changes of residence: Mantua, Padua, Venice, Pesaro. In August, he is received as a guest by the della Rovere at Urbino. At nearby Fermignano, he writes *Il Metauro*. In September he leaves Urbino, briefly visits Ferrara and Mantua and then moves to Turin to offer his services to Emanuele Filiberto. At first refused admission by the city guards, he enters and is presented at court by his friend Angelo Ingegneri. He writes many lyric poems and a dialogue, *De la nobiltà*.

1579 In February, Tasso (35) suddenly leaves Turin and reaches Ferrara during the wedding celebrations of Alfonso and Margherita Gonzaga. On March 13, while a guest at the Bentivoglio household, he is seized by sudden fury and rushes to ducal castle to denounce the court. Put under arrest by order of the duke, he is committed to the Ospedale di Sant'Anna as a madman.

Tasso's later life may be briefly summarized as follows: He spent eight years of confinement in Sant'Anna. At first under brutal restraint, he was gradually granted liberty to write, receive visitors and correspond. After a pirated version of *Gerusalemme liberata* appeared in print, he oversaw an authorized version (1581), composed the rearrangement of his *Rime Amorose* (the Chigi autograph, 1584), and wrote *Apologia in difesa della Gierusalemme liberata* (1585) in response to attacks by Leonardo Salviati and other members of the Florentine Accademia della Crusca. During his imprisonment, his former passion, Laura Peperara, married his friend Annibale Turchi. He was finally released in 1587 at the age of 43 into the custody of Vincenzo Gonzaga at Mantua. His first work upon his release was the completion and revised publication of his father's *Floridante*.

His late wanderings included a stay in Naples, where he met his future biographer Giovan Battista Manso and the composer Carlo Gesualdo, before he settled at 47 in Rome. During his last years he rewrote *Gerusalemme liberata* in its entirety (retitled *Gerusalemme conquistata*, published 1593), composed a number of religious poems, published a final revision of his *Discorsi dell'arte poetica e in particolare sopra il poema eroico* (1594) and oversaw the publication of the *Rime* in their final arrangement (1591–93). He died at the age of 52 — the approximate age at which his father began writing *Amadigi* — on April 25, 1595 at the Roman monastery of Sant'Onofrio on the Gianicolo. Just before his death, the pope had made plans to crown him poet laureate. Tasso did not live to receive the honor.

—ɯ—

RINALDO

—⁓—

Canto primo

Canto i felici affanni e i primi ardori   1
    che giovanetto ancor soffrì Rinaldo,
e come il trasse in perigliosi errori
    desir di gloria ed amoroso caldo,
allor che, vinti dal gran Carlo, i Mori
    mostraro il cor più che le forze saldo;
        e Troiano, Agolante e 'l fiero Almonte
        restar pugnando uccisi in Aspramonte.

Musa, che 'n rozo stil meco sovente   2
    umil cantasti le mie fiamme accese,
sì che, stando le selve al suono intente,
    Eco a ridir l'amato nome apprese:
or ch'ad opra maggior movo la mente,
    ed audace m'accingo ad alte imprese,
        ver' me cotanto il tuo favor s'accresca,
        ch'al raddoppiato peso egual riesca.

Forse un giorno ardirai de' chiari fregi   3
    del gran Luigi Estense ornar mie carte,
onde, mercé del suo valor, si pregi
    e viva il nostro nome in ogni parte;
non perch'io stimi ch'a' suoi fatti egregi
    possa dar luce umano ingegno od arte,
        ch'egli e tal ch'altrui dona e gloria e vita,
        e vola al ciel senza terrena aita.

E voi, sacro signor, ch'adorno avete   4
    d'ostro la chioma e di virtude il core,
e sì lucidi raggi omai spargete
    che se n'oscura ogni più chiaro onore,
quando ai gravi pensier la via chiudete,
    prestate al mio cantar grato favore:
        ch'ivi vedrete al men, se non espresso,
        adombrato in altrui forse voi stesso.

CANTO ONE

I sing of the sweet joys and youthful fire   1
    Rinaldo as a lad was made to bear,
and how Love's ardor and his great desire
    for glory drew him into Error's snare,
in times when Charlemagne made the Moors retire,
      whose force proved feeble, much as they might dare,
        and Troyan, Anglant and the fierce Almont
        lay dead on battlefields in Aspromont.

O Muse, whose rustic style in days gone by   2
    aided my humble song and fed my flame,
until the woods attentive to my cry
    heard Echo ring out the beloved name:
now that my mind seeks grander themes,[1] and I
      gird up its powers high exploits to proclaim,
        augment your favor, and with no less great
        success help it to bear the double weight.

Some day perhaps I'll dare to deck my rhyme   3
    with great Luigi d'Este's proud device,[2]
whence, by his valor, in all future time
    our name shall everywhere delight men's eyes.
Not that I deem mere human art can climb
      those heights and his great worth imparadise,
        for his renown in others is displayed,
        and he soars heavenward without earthly aid.

You, reverend lord, your head with purple crowned.[3]   4
    your heart with virtue's palm, whose face
scatters such generous rays that all around
    the brightest lights, eclipsed, leave scarce a trace,
when musing in your cell on thoughts profound,
      bestow upon my song your welcome grace.
        There you may see your high worth and your glory
        dimly foreshadowed in another's story.

Rinaldo

Ma quando, il crin di tre corone cinto,   5
    v'avrem l'empia eresia domar già visto,
e spinger, pria da santo amor sospinto,
    contra l'Egitto i principi di Cristo,
onde il fiero Ottomano oppresso e vinto
    vi ceda a forza il suo mal fatto acquisto,
        cangiar la lira in tromba e 'n maggior carme
        dir tentarò le vostre imprese e l'arme.

Già Carlo Magno in più battaglie avea   6
    domo e represso l'impeto affricano,
e per opra d'Orlando omai giacea
    estinto Almonte e 'l suo fratel Troiano;
pur in sì rio destin si difendea
    ne' forti luoghi ancor lo stuol pagano,
        che molti in riva al mar, molti fra terra
        pria n'occupò nel cominciar la guerra.

Ma Carlo, il pian ridotto in suo potere,   7
    e l'uno e l'altro mare a quel vicino,
stringea più sempre con l'armate schiere
    da varie parti il campo saracino,
ch'avendo gran cagion del suo temere
    paventava il furor d'empio destino;
        pur, con audace e generoso core,
        era a' nemici suoi d'alto terrore.

E ciascun giorno sempre alcun di loro   8
    fuor da le mura e da' ripari usciva,
per provar s'al francese il valor moro
    pari al men ne' duelli riusciva.
Poi, quando il sol celava i bei crin d'oro,
    e sotto l'ali il ciel notte copriva,
        tutti assaliano insieme il nostro campo,
        per tentar con lor gloria alcuno scampo.

Ma sempre il primo onore, il primo vanto,   9
    in generale e in singolar battaglia,
rapporta Orlando il giovanetto, e intanto
    gli antichi eroi d'alte prodezze agguaglia:
guerriero alcun non è feroce tanto,
    né piastra fatta per incanto o maglia,
        ch'al suo valor resista; e Marte istesso
        avria forse la palma a lui concesso.

Canto One

But when your brow shall bear the three-tiered crown,[4]   5
    when impious heresy cowers at your sight,
when, moved by sacred Love, your holy frown
    shall make Christ's princes against Egypt fight,
and the fell Turk, confounded and cast down,
    shall yield his ill-won conquest[5] to your might,
        my trumpet, not my lyre,[6] may proclaim
        in ampler song your deeds and martial fame.

Already Charlemagne in many a fray   6
    had crushed the African and made him yield,
and by brave Roland's exploits Almont lay
    slain with his brother Troyan in the field,
but still the ill-starred pagans barred the way,
    in many a castle or strong fort concealed
        that inland or upon the shore they won
        in times when the great conflict had begun.

But Charles, now once more master of the plain,   7
    supplied by sea from both the east and west,
with his armed bands, time after time again
    from various sides the Saracen forces pressed,
who, finding ample cause for fear, in pain
    and rage saw Fate strike at the pagan crest.
        Indeed, his high, audacious spirit froze
        with shock and awe the hearts of all his foes.

Yet day by day their venturing sallies rolled   8
    down from their ramparts or their walls to try
whether a Moor or Frank would prove more bold,
    at least in private duel, and, by and by,
when the bright sun concealed his locks of gold
    and night's black pinions covered up the sky,
        they in a mass assailed our camp to crown
        by some success their glory and renown.

But ever the first honor, the first boast,   9
    be it in general fray or single fight,
was young Orlando's, who, always foremost,
    rivaled the ancient heroes in his might.
No man there was so fierce in all that host,
    no mail or armor charmed by magic sleight
        safe from his valor. Mars himself might yield
        if he should meet him in the open field.

Rinaldo

Oh quante volte e quante ei fece solo   *10*
   a mille cavalier volger le piante,
e quante ancor rendette il terren suolo
   del mauro sangue caldo e rosseggiante!
Quante volte colmò d'estremo duolo
   i miseri seguaci d'Agolante,
      ch'alzar gli vider sanguinosi monti
      de' duci lor più gloriosi e conti!

Tosto la vaga fama il suo valore   *11*
   e l'opre sue va divolgando intorno:
picciola è prima, e poi divien maggiore,
   ch'acquista forze ognor di giorno in giorno.
Ovunque arriva sparge alto romore,
   e finge quel d'ogni virtute adorno:
      col vero il falso meschia e in varie forme
      si mostra altrui, né mai riposa o dorme.

Fra gli altri molti del figliuol d'Amone   *12*
   ella giunge a l'orecchie, e i fatti egregi
del valoroso suo cugin gli espone
   a parte a parte, e gli acquistati fregi.
Sùbito a quel magnanimo garzone,
   c'ha ne la gloria posto i sommi pregi,
      invidia accende generosa il petto,
      che negli altieri spirti ha sol ricetto.

E tal invidia ha in lui maggior potere,   *13*
   perché gli par che 'l fior de' suoi verdi anni,
quando l'uom deve tra l'armate schiere
   soffrir di Marte i gloriosi affanni,
ei consumi in fugace e van piacere,
   involto in molli e delicati panni,
      quasi vil donna che 'l cor d'ozio ha vago,
      e sol adopri la conocchia e l'ago.

Da queste cure combattuto geme,   *14*
   e sospir tragge dal profondo core;
d'esser guardato vergognoso teme,
   ché desta l'altrui vista in lui rossore;
crede ch'ognun l'additi e scioglia insieme
   in tai voci la lingua a suo disnore,
      come de' suoi maggior le lucid'opre
      con le tenebre sue questi ricopre.

Oh how, time after time, he all alone   10
　　took on a thousand knights and drove them back!
How often, too, the ground below him shone
　　as Moorish blood dyed red its loamy black!
How he made Anglant's wretched followers groan
　　in grief's extremity at his attack,
　　　　who saw him piling up in blood-drenched mounts
　　　　the trunks of their most famous dukes and counts!

Soon eager Fame runs everywhere to extol   11
　　his sovereign valor and his every deed.
Though young at first, she soon grows old
　　and gathers day by day in force and speed.
Wherever she arrives loud rumors roll
　　of his great merits that all hopes exceed.
　　　　She mingles truth with fiction as she leaps
　　　　from ear to ear and never rests or sleeps,

and racing through the world, she comes to find   12
　　good Aymon's son, and one by one makes rise
his cousin's deeds that leave all praise behind,
　　his victories in every enterprise,
and thus in that magnanimous youth, whose mind
　　is set on glory as the highest prize,
　　　　kindles his generous heart with envy's glow,
　　　　for only noble hearts can envy so.

That envy burns the more, since to his mind   13
　　the flower of his green age passed away,
when among weaponed bands a man should find
　　hardship and glory in the martial fray,
while he at ease, on a soft couch reclined,
　　wrapped in soft garments, lingered day by day,
　　　　like some weak girl who in her pleasant bower
　　　　with needle and distaff plies her feeble power.

Racked by such cares he weeps, and deep groans came   14
　　heaving up from his heart. He fears his base
and slothful life has marked him out for shame,
　　so that a crimson blush overspreads his face.
He thinks men point at him, that at his name
　　tongues without number whisper of disgrace,
　　　　and that the blaze of glorious fame that shone
　　　　upon his forebears' deeds blotted his own.

Tra sé tai cose rivolgeva ancora,   15
   quando il tetto real lasciossi a tergo,
e da Parigi uscio, ché quivi allora
   insieme con la madre avea l'albergo;
e caminando in breve spazio d'ora
   giunse d'un prato in sul fiorito tergo,
      che si giacea tra molte piante ascoso,
      ond'era poi formato un bosco ombroso.

Quivi, perché gli pare acconcio il luoco   16
   a lamentarsi, e non teme esser visto,
si ferma e siede, e 'n suon languido e fioco
   così comincia a dir, doglioso e tristo:
— Deh! perché, lasso! un vivo ardente foco
   di dolor, di vergogna e d'ira misto
      non m'arde e volge in polve, onde novella
      di me mai più non s'oda, o buona o fella?

Poi ch'oprar non poss'io che di me s'oda   17
   con mia gloria ed onor novella alcuna,
o cosa ond'io pregio n'acquisti e loda,
   e mia fama rischiari oscura e bruna;
poscia che non son tal che lieto goda
   di mia virtute, o pur di mia fortuna,
      ma il più vil cavaliero, al ciel più in ira,
      che veggia il sol tra quanto scalda e gira;

deh! perché almeno oscura stirpe umile   18
   a me non diede o padre ignoto il Fato,
o femina non son tenera e vile,
   ché non andrei d'infamia tal macchiato;
perciò ch'in sangue illustre e signorile,
   in uom d'alti parenti al mondo nato
      la viltà si raddoppia e più si scorge,
      che 'n coloro il cui grado alto non sorge.

Ah! quanto a me de' miei maggior gradito   19
   poco è il valor e la virtù suprema;
quanto d'Orlando a me di sangue unito
   l'ardir mi noce e la possanza estrema.
Egli or, di fino acciar cinto e vestito,
   l'alte inimiche forze abbatte e scema,
      e con l'invitta sua fulminea spada
      fa ch'Africa superba umil se 'n vada.

Such were the thoughts that racked his bosom while,   15
    turning his back upon the royal rooftops, he
left Paris, where he kept his domicile
    together with his mother. Presently,
having proceeded no more than a mile
    or two, he lifted up his gaze to see
        a spacious, flower-strewn and hidden glade
        ringed with dense trees that cast a pleasant shade.

There, since the place seemed apt for groans and sighs,   16
    not fearing to be seen, he stopped to mourn
and languidly, tears welling in his eyes,
    spoke thus, in accents dolorous and forlorn:
"Ah, why does not a living fire rise
    of endless sorrow, mixed with shame and scorn,
        to burn me into ash so that no word
        of me may ever, for good or ill, be heard?

For I do nothing that could bring me praise,   17
    or gain me glory, or achieve renown;
I win no prize and scale no heights to raise
    me from obscurity that drags me down.
I am not a man who confidently weighs
    his worth, or even his fortune, but a clown
        despised by heaven and by the lowliest knight
        on whom the sun bestows his burning light.

Ah why at least did not my fate allot   18
    some lowly state to me, some unknown sire,
or make me a weak woman, so as not
    to be defiled by infamy so dire!
For in a man illustriously begot
    and born of noble parentage, the mire
        of vileness doubles, made more hideous by
        the gentle blood that raises him on high.

How little of my elder brothers'[7] worth   19
    and dauntless valor my deservings show!
How much Orlando, our next of kin by birth,
    in his high prowess lays my honors low!
He, sheathed in fine steel, even now rides forth
    to batter and strike down the haughty foe
        and with his blade's indomitable might
        puts the proud African to humble flight.

Rinaldo

Io quasi a l'ozio, a la lascivia, agli agi 20
  nato, in vani soggiorni il tempo spendo,
e ne le molli piume e ne' palagi
  sicuri tutto intero il sonno prendo;
e per soffrire i marzial disagi
  tempo miglior, età più ferma attendo,
    ai materni conforti ed a que' preghi
    cui viril petto indegno è che si pieghi. —

Mentre così si lagna, ode un feroce 21
  innito di cavallo al cielo alzarsi;
chiude le labbra allor, frena la voce
  Rinaldo, e non è tardo a rivoltarsi,
e vide al tronco d'una antica noce
  per la briglia un destrier legato starsi,
    superbo in vista, che mordendo il freno
    s'aggira, scuote il crin, pesta il terreno.

Nel medesmo troncone un'armatura 22
  vide di gemme e d'or chiara e lucente,
che par di tempra adamantina e dura,
  ed opra di man dotta e diligente.
Cervo che fonte di dolc'acqua e pura
  trovi allor ch'è di maggior sete ardente,
    od amador cui s'offra a l'improviso
    il caro volto che gli ha il cor conquiso,

non si rallegra come il cavaliero, 23
  che così larga strada aprir vedea
per mandar ad effetto il suo pensiero,
  che tutto intento ad oprar l'arme avea.
Corre dove sbuffando il bel destriero
  con la bocca spumosa il fren mordea,
    e lo discioglie e per la briglia il prende,
    e ne l'arcion, senz'oprar staffa, ascende.

Ma l'arme che facean, quasi trofeo 24
  sacro al gran Marte, l'alboro pomposo,
distaccò prima, e adorno se 'n rendeo,
  di tal ventura stupido e gioioso;
conosce ben che chi quelle arme feo,
    fu di servirlo sol vago e bramoso,
      ch'erano ai membri suoi commode ed atte
      qual se per lui Vulcan l'avesse fatte.

Canto One

I, as if born to luxury and ease,   20
   waste all my hours in a gilded cage,
and in soft featherbeds and palaces
   sleep soundly, all unhurt and safe from rage,
and, shunning martial toil like some disease,
   wait to grow strong and reach a riper age,
      by a mother's care and comforts kept apart
      in sloth unworthy of a manly heart."

While thus he spoke and wept and sighed   21
   he heard a loud neigh nearby suddenly.
Rinaldo checked his tongue then, stupefied,
   and turning quickly was surprised to see
a mighty courser by the bridle tied
   to the gnarled trunk of an old walnut tree.
      Chewing the bit, impatient to be bound,
      tossing his mane, he wheels and stamps the ground.

On the same trunk a suit of arms is hung,   22
   adorned with gems and shining with bright gold,
which seems of adamant temper, tough and strong,
   worked by a master's hand in days of old.
A stag that burns with thirst and finds among
   the rocks a spring of water sweet and cold
      or a lover who chances, with a sudden start,
      upon the face that has enslaved his heart

was not so overjoyed as now the knight   23
   who saw a broad path opening in this wise
to move from thoughts of fighting to the fight
   with the arms he dreamt of right before his eyes.
Toward that steed he hastens in delight,
   who chews the bit with foaming mouth, unties
      his bridle, leads him towards the track,
      and, scorning stirrups, leaps upon his back.

But first the arms, which on the tree's trunk shone   24
   like trophies sacred to great Mars, he took
and decked his body with them one by one,
   amazed with joy and grateful for his luck.
And he grows certain that for him alone
   whoever made them plied his skill — for look! —
      he finds the parts so molded to each limb
      that they seem forged by Vulcan just for him.

Rinaldo

Oltra che de lo scudo il campo aurato   25
    da sbarrata pantera adorno scorge,
che con guardo crudel, con rabbuffato
    pelo terror ai rimiranti porge:
ha la bocca e l'unghion tinto e macchiato
    di sangue, e su duo piedi in aria sorge.
        Già tal insegna acquistò l'avo, e poi
        la portar molti de' nepoti suoi.

Poi che saltando sul destriero ascese,   26
    e tutto fu di lucide arme adorno,
l'usbergo, l'aureo scudo e l'altro arnese
    si vagheggiava con lieto occhio intorno.
Indi con ratta man la lancia prese,
    la lancia ond'ebber molti oltraggio e scorno;
        ma la spada lasciò, ché gli sovenne
        d'un giuramento ch'ei già fe' solenne.

Avea di Carlo al signoril cospetto   27
    vantando fatto un giuramento altero,
quando da lui coi frati insieme eletto
    al degno grado fu di cavaliero,
di spada non oprar, quantunque astretto
    ne fosse da periglio orrendo e fiero,
        s'in guerra pria non lo toglieva a forza
        a guerrier di gran fama e di gran forza.

Ed or come colui ch'audace aspira   28
    a degne imprese, ad opre altere e nove,
ciò por vuole ad effetto, e 'l destrier gira,
    e 'l batte e sprona ed a gran passi il muove;
e sì lo sdegno generoso e l'ira,
    e 'l desio di trovar venture dove
        la lancia adopri, in suo camin l'affretta,
        ch'in breve tempo uscì de la selvetta.

Come al marzo errar suol giumenta mossa   29
    dagli amorosi stimoli ferventi,
onde non è che ritenerla possa
    fren, rupi, scogli o rapidi torrenti;
così il garzon cui l'alma ognor percossa
    è da sproni d'onor caldi e pungenti,
        erra di qua di là, raddoppia i passi,
        per fiumi, boschi e per alpestri sassi;

And next to them a great escutcheon hung   25
 on which a spotted leopard was displayed
whose mottled pelt and cruel gaze and tongue
 made all that saw it faintheart and afraid.
With blood-stained muzzle and sharp claws it sprung,
 paws rampant, as if to an ambuscade.
   And this device, which his grandfather bore,
   those of his line did often use in war`.

Then, having leapt upon that strong destrier,   26
 sheathed head to toe in shining armor, he
a hauberk, golden shield and other gear
 saw brightly shimmering beneath the tree
and swiftly grasped the great lance lying near,
 destined to wound so many grievously,
   but left the sword, because a solemn vow,
   made long before, strikes his remembrance now.

He had, in Charles' princely presence made   27
 by way of vaunt a sacred pledge — when he
with his two brothers was by him arrayed
 in all the signs of noble chivalry
and dubbed a knight — never to wield a blade,
 no matter how extreme the peril be,
   unless he first by main force seized it from
   a famous warrior he had overcome.

Now like a man for bold adventure bound,   28
 bent upon glory, welcoming the chance
to wreak his will, he turns his steed around,
 applies the whip and spur and makes it prance.
His generous scorn and wrath and his profound
 need for some test in which to try his lance
   so haste him on his way and fire his mind,
   that he soon leaves the forest far behind.

As a brood-mare in March is wont to range,   29
 impelled by lusty heat to nature's goal,
bolting unchecked from pasture or from grange,
 overleaping walls and streams without control,
so now the youth, who feels a new and strange
 foretaste of honor well up in his soul,
   roams everywhere and with redoubled speed
   past fields and woods and mountains spurs his steed

tal ch'allor che 'l villan, disciolti i buoi   30
    dal giogo, a riposar lieto s'accinge,
e ritogliendo il sol la luce a noi
    l'altro avverso emispero orna e dipinge,
giunge in Ardenna, ove de' fati suoi
    l'immutabil voler l'indrizza e spinge;
        quivi nuovo desir l'alma gli accense,
        che quel primier in lui però non spense.

Errò tutta la notte intera; e quando   31
    ne riportò l'Aurora il giorno in seno,
uom riscontrò d'aspetto venerando,
    di crespe rughe il volto ingombro e pieno,
che sovra un bastoncel giva appoggiando
    le membra che parean venir già meno;
        ed a tai segni, ed al crin raro e bianco,
        mostrava esser dagli anni oppresso e stanco.

Questi, verso Rinaldo alzando 'l viso,   32
    così gli disse in parlar grave e scorto:
— Dove vai, cavalier, ch'egli m'è aviso
    vederti tutto omai lacero e morto?
Ché già più d'un guerriero è stato ucciso
    ch'errando per lo bosco iva a diporto,
        e, troppo altero del suo gran valore,
        ha voluto provar tanto furore.

Sappi che novamente in questa selva   33
    è comparso un cavallo aspro e feroce,
di cui non è la più gagliarda belva
    o dove aghiaccia o dove il sol più cuoce.
Da lui qual lepre fugge e si rinselva
    il leone, il cinghial e l'orso atroce;
        dovunque passa l'alte piante atterra,
        e intorno tremar fa l'aria e la terra.

Dunque fuggi, meschino, o in cavo e fosco   34
    luogo t'ascondi, ché d'udir già parmi
rimbombar al suo corso intorno il bosco,
    né contra lui varran tue forze e armi:
ch'io quanto a me, s'a segni il ver conosco,
    cagion non ho di quinci allontanarmi,
        per servar questa spoglia inferma e vecchia
        cui Natura disfar già s'apparecchia. —

till, as the hour when the plowman will   30
    unyoke his team and turn to rest draws near,
and the sun averts his face from us to fill
    with his fair beams the other hemisphere,
he reaches Arden, for the changeless will
    of Destiny directs and drives him here.
        Here fresh desire makes his spirit soar
        even beyond the heights it climbed before.

All night he rode, and when Aurora's glow began   31
    to show the new day borne upon her breast,
he met a venerable, ancient man,
    his brow by countless wrinkling lines impressed,
who, leaning on a stick, moved span by span
    his faint limbs, pausing at each step to rest.
        He seems, with his scarce strands of thin, white hairs,
        too feeble for the weight of years he bears.

He, toward Rinaldo raising up his sight,   32
    speaks to him thus in grave and courteous wise:
"Where are you going? Ah, be warned, sir knight,
    you seem a dead man to my prescient eyes!
Already more than one man of great might
    lies slain whose overweening enterprise
        led him into this forest to engage
        in futile fight a monster's brutal rage.

Know this: Of late into this forest there   33
    has come a wild, enormous stallion.
There is no fiercer courser anywhere,
    be it in realms of ice or scorching sun.
The boar, the lion and the savage bear
    from him like rabbits to the thickets run.
        His passage knocks huge trees down to the ground
        and makes the earth and air quake all around.

So flee, you doomed, unhappy wretch, or hide   34
    in some dark cave. It seems even now I hear
the thunder of his fast-approaching stride.
    Your strength is useless, and your warlike gear.
For myself, if by sure tokens I descried
    the truth, I have no cause to flee from here.
        He will not seize this feeble, aging prey
        whom Nature leads already to decay."

Rinaldo

Al parlar di quel vecchio il buon Rinaldo
   non si smarrì, né di timor diè segno,
ma d'ardente desir divenne caldo
   di farsi qui d'eterna fama degno;
e con parlar rispose audace e saldo,
   acceso dentro d'onorato sdegno,
      che co' detti a vil fuga altri l'esorte,
      quasi ei paventi una famosa morte.

— Fugga chi fuggir vuol, ché cavaliero   36
   non dee più che la lancia oprar lo sprone;
e quanto è più il periglio orrendo e fiero,
   più francamente il forte a lui s'oppone;
ed io già stabilito ho nel pensiero
   di far del mio valor qui paragone;
      e se ben fussi ov'è più ardente il polo,
      qui ratto ne verrei per questo solo. —

Allor l'antico vecchio a lui rivolto,   37
   in voci tai l'accorta lingua sciolse:
— Con gran diletto, o cavaliero, ascolto
   il grande ardir ch'in te Natura accolse;
né vidi uom mai più dal timor disciolto,
   da poi che 'l mio parlar non ti distolse
      da l'alta impresa, né tue brame estinse,
      ma loro infiammò più, te più sospinse.

E credo che conforme abbia a l'ardire   38
   infuso in te 'l valor l'alma Natura,
e che per le tue man deggia finire
   tosto sì perigliosa alta ventura.
Segui pur dunque il tuo gentil desire,
   e di gloria e d'onor l'accesa cura:
      ch'a degne imprese il tuo destin ti chiama,
      e vivrai dopo morte ancor per fama.

E perché possi, quando a cruda guerra   39
   ti troverai con quel destrier possente,
la furia sua, che l'altrui forze atterra,
   vincere e superar più agevolmente,
vedi di trarlo mal suo grado in terra,
   ché mansueto ei diverrà repente,
      ed a te sì fedel che non fu tanto
      fedel al magno Ettorre il fiero Xanto.

Rinaldo, by these words nowise dismayed,   35
 showed not the slightest sign of fear, for he,
hot with desire for fame, saw ready-made
 at hand a glorious opportunity.
Thus he in daring words this answer made,
 with generous anger burning inwardly
  to hear a man urge him to coward flight,
  as if a famous death were cause for fright:

"Let him who wishes flee. A knight won't run   36
 or use his spurs when he can use his lance.
The more he seems by danger and pain undone,
 the fiercer will a worthy man advance.
Even now I am determined not to shun,
 in trial of my valor, this fair chance.
  Yea! Were the burning pole to bar my path
  I'd meet this one opponent's utmost wrath."

At this the old man looked up earnestly   37
 and courteously replied: "I'm pleased to learn,
sir, of your mettle and delight to see
 how Nature makes your noble boldness burn.
No man I've ever known more fearlessly
 heard words like mine, which, meant to make you turn
  from danger, did not chill your hot desire
  but stoked and added fuel to the fire.

And I believe that Nature has endowed   38
 your daring heart with needful courage too
and that your hands shall, even as you vowed,
 conclude the perilous venture you pursue.
Go then, follow your high desires, be proud
 to strive for honor and success, and you,
  destined to prosper in your every aim,
  shall live long after death in glorious fame.

And that you may, when you at last are found   39
 at war with that huge steed — who did not spare
others — withstand his fury in his lair
 and break him the more readily, take care
to drag him will he nil he to the ground,
 for then he will grow mild and gladly bear
  your weight and be as easily controlled
  as Xanthus by great Hector was of old.

Di lui quel ti dirò ch'a molti è ignoto,   40
   che ti parrà quasi impossibil cosa.
Amadigi di Francia, a tutti noto,
   che la bella Oriana ebbe in sua sposa,
solcando il mar fu dal piovoso Noto
   spinto a l'isola detta or Perigliosa;
      ch'allor con nome tal non fu chiamata,
      ma tra l'altre perdute annoverata.

Quivi il destrier vins'ei già carco d'anni,   41
   ed in Francia suo regno il menò seco;
ma poi ch'a volo glorioso i vanni,
   di sé lasciando il mondo orbato e cieco,
spiegò felice in ver' gli empirei scanni,
   incantato il destrier entro uno speco
      fu qui vicin dal saggio Alchiso il mago,
      di far qualch'opra memorabil vago.

Sotto tai leggi allor quel buon destriero   42
   fu dal mago gentil quivi incantato,
che non potesse mai da cavaliero
   per ingegno o per forza esser domato,
se dal sangue colui reale altero
   d'Amadigi non fusse al mondo nato,
      e s'in valor ancor no 'l superasse,
      o pari almeno in arme a lui n'andasse.

Dopo che 'l mago la bell'opra fece,   43
   non s'è 'l cavallo se non or veduto,
ma da ch'apparve, diece volte e diece
   ha 'l suo torto camin Cinzia compiuto:
onde da segno tal comprender lece
   che 'l termine prefisso è già venuto,
      ch'esser disfatto dee lo strano incanto,
      e domato il destrier feroce tanto.

Né ti maravigliar se 'l destrier vive   44
   dopo sì lungo girar d'anni ancora,
ch'il fil troncar d'alcun le Parche dive
   non ponno, s'incantato egli dimora;
né fra l'imposte al viver suo gli ascrive
   il fato di quel tempo una sol'ora.
      Grande è il poter de' maghi oltra misura,
      e quasi eguale a quel de la Natura.

Canto One

There is a tale, to many men unknown,   40
    though you may doubt it. I will tell it now:
Great Amadis, whose glory all men own,
    fair Oriana's husband, while he steered his prow
across the sea, was by dry Notus blown
    ashore on the Isle Perilous. (Yet how
        it was named then is lost to memory —
        I use the name men give it currently.)

And there he tamed that horse, though bowed by years,   41
    and took it back to France. But when his lot
was full and his soul mounted toward the spheres,
    leaving the whole earth lightless and distraught,
to join on heavenly thrones his deathless peers,
    his steed was to a cavern near here brought
        by the great sorcerer Alchiso, who
        wished to bring forth some marvel strange and new.

A spell placed on that stallion by this good   42
    and excellent magician's power meant
that no knight in the whole world ever should
    by wit or force make it obedient,
except a man born of the royal blood,
    from Amadis derived by due descent,
        and one whose valor, if it not exceeds
        his forebear's, equals it by warlike deeds.

The sorcerer's task being done, no tidings nor   43
    signs of that steed till lately did appear,
but since they did, ten circuits and ten more
    has Cynthia made round her celestial sphere,
and it is licit to conclude therefore
    that even now the fated term is near
        for that enchantment's spell to be undone,
        and the fierce courser to be tamed and won.

Nor marvel that the stallion is not dead   44
    after the passing of so many years,
for even the Parcae[9] cannot cut the thread
    of a life enchanted with their dreaded shears.
Since he was charmed, just one short hour instead
    of centuries in the Book of Fate appears.
        Great is the power of sorcery. It excels
        or rivals Nature in its potent spells.

Rinaldo

Nel fin di questa selva un antro giace: 45
    indi il cavallo mai non si discosta,
ma misero colui che troppo audace
    a quella parte ov'egli sta s'accosta.
Tu perché partir vuo', rimanti in pace;
    e s'a l'impresa ancor l'alma hai disposta,
        in oblio non porrai, ché s'ei la terra
        col fianco premerà, vinta hai la guerra. —

Non avea detto ancor queste parole,   46
    che ne la selva si cacciò più folta,
veloce sì che più veloce il sole
    dechinando il suo carro al mar non volta.
Restò Rinaldo allor sì come suole
    debile infermo rimaner tal volta,
        cui ne' sonni interrotti appaion cose
        impossibili, strane e monstruose.

Questi, ch'era apparito al giovinetto   47
    in forma d'uom ch'a vecchia etate è giunto,
era il buon Malagigi, a lui di stretto
    nodo di sangue e d'alto amor congiunto:
mago de la sua etade il più perfetto,
    che 'l buon voler mai dal saper disgiunto
        non ebbe, anzi ad ognor suoi giorni spese
        altrui giovando in onorate imprese.

Egli avea ritenuto il suo germano   48
    Rinaldo alquanto in Francia e quasi a forza,
sin ch'un influsso rio gisse lontano,
    e cresciesse con gli anni in lui la forza.
Or, passato il furor troppo inumano
    del ciel, cui spesso uom saggio e piega e sforza,
        gli permise il partirsi e fegli appesi
        tornar al tronco i necessari arnesi.

Rinaldo intanto per la selva caccia   49
    il suo destrier per vie longhe e distorte,
e de l'altro corsier segue la traccia,
    senza saper qual strada a quello il porte;
e per ogni romor che l'aura faccia,
    par che rallegri l'animo e conforte,
        credendo allor trovarlo: e così in vano
        errò fin che 'l sol gio ne l'oceano.

Where this wood ends, a cavern yawns, and there 45
    that stallion dwells. He never leaves that nest
except to trample all who unaware
    too boldly to his hiding place have pressed.
Since I must go, stay if you will and dare,
    and since you are determined on the quest,
        do no forget: when his flanks press upon
        the ground, he'll falter, and you will have won."

This said, he vanished and so quickly sped 46
    into the forest's thick obscurity,
the sun no more abruptly hides his head
    when his bright chariot plunges in the sea.
Rinaldo stayed behind, assailed by dread,
    like a weak man on a sickbed dizzily
        in broken sleep dimly imagining
        some strange, impossible, or monstrous thing.

That seeming old man whom the woods now hide 47
    was Malagis in an old man's disguise —
good Malagis to Rinaldo long allied
    by noble love's and closest kinship's ties:
the best mage of his days, who always tried
    to be as good of will as he was wise,
        wherefore he honorably spent his days
        in aid of others' honorable ways.

He had used his spells to make Rinaldo stay 48
    for a long while in France, since he had fears
some evil force might spirit him away
    before his strength should ripen with his years.
But now, since more propitious stars held sway —
    no wise man will oppose contrary spheres —
        he let him go his way and made him see
        the gear he needed hanging on that tree.

Rinaldo meanwhile through the gloomy wood 49
    spurred on his steed by paths that loop and wind,
tracking that other steed, clueless of what road
    to take toward the goal he sought to find.
At every rustling noise he heard, he slowed
    his speed while wild hope leapt up in his mind,
        imagining he had found him. Thus in vain
        he wandered till the sun plunged in the main.

Rinaldo

Allor su l'erba a piè d'un fonte scese,   50
  ch'era de' quattro l'un che fe' Merlino,
e con frutti selvaggi ed acqua prese
  ristor de la fatica e del camino.
Ma quando Febo in Oriente accese
  di nuovo il vago raggio matutino,
    ritorno fece a la primiera inchiesta,
    e 'l viaggio seguì per la foresta.

Per quello andò gran spazio, avendo intenti   51
  gli occhi e 'l pensiero a l'alta impresa solo;
ed ecco, allor che co' suoi raggi ardenti
  insino a l'imo fende Appollo il suolo,
strepito pargli d'animai correnti
  sentir nel bosco; onde ne corre a volo
    là ond'il suono a le sue orecchie viene,
    e raddoppia nel cor desire e spene.

E in questa apparir da lungi vede   52
  leggiadra cerva e più che latte bianca,
che ratta move a tutto corso il piede,
  ed annelando vien sudata e stanca;
e sì il timor il cor le punge e fiede,
  e la lena e 'l vigor in lei rinfranca,
    ch'ov'è 'l garzone, arriva e inanzi passa,
    e gran parte del bosco a tergo lassa.

Vien dietro a lei sovra un cavallo assisa,   53
  che veloce se 'n va come saetta,
di nuovo abito adorna in strana guisa
  disposta e vaga e snella giovinetta,
dal cui dardo ferita e poscia uccisa
  fu la fugace e timida cervetta,
    dal dardo ch'ella di lanciar maestra
    tutto le fisse entro la spalla destra.

Mira il leggiadro altero portamento   54
  Rinaldo, e 'nsieme il ricco abito eletto,
e vede il crin parte ondeggiar al vento,
  parte in aurati nodi avolto e stretto;
e la vesta cui fregia oro ed argento,
  sotto la qual traspar l'eburneo petto,
    alzata alquanto discoprir a l'occhio
    la gamba e 'l piede fin presso al ginocchio:

Then he dismounted near a grass-grown well —   50
    one of the four that Merlin fashioned there —
and let its waters and some berries quell
    fatigue and hunger with their simple fare.
But as soon as Phoebus' radiance once more fell
    out of the East and brightened all the air,
        he rose and turned back to his quest once more
        and galloped through the forest as before.

He rode a long way, mind and eyes intent   51
    on nothing but his yearned-for enterprise,
till, at the hour when Apollo sent
    rays perpendicular down from the skies,
he heard the air of all the forest rent
    by a noise of running beasts, wherefore he hies
        toward the sound, while with a joyful start
        he feels his hopes redouble in his heart.

At last he sees out of the gloom appear   52
    a graceful doe, whiter than milk in hue,
that borne on nimble hooves is drawing near,
    panting and drenched in sweat, and yet unto
her tired limbs and fainting heart her fear
    seems to lend desperate strength. She drew
        near him and hurtled past and at her back
        left a still growing span of woodland track.

But soon he saw how, mounted on a steed   53
    swift as an arrow, charging at its rear,
dressed in apparel of outlandish brede,
    a lovely, slender maiden aimed her spear,[10]
and overtook it with impetuous speed
    and struck and slew the timid, fleeing deer,
        for she, an expert huntress, plunged her dart
        haft-deep through the right shoulder, in its heart.

Rinaldo sees her sprightly, noble air   54
    and fine attire. He trembles to behold,
abandoned to the breeze, her golden hair,
    with some few locks tied up in knots of gold,
and the heaving of her ivory bosom where
    her gown's brocade is parted, fold on fold,
        and her upgathered hem that lets him see
        her foot and white leg almost to the knee,

la gamba e 'l piede, il cui candor traluce 55
fuor per seta vermiglia a l'altrui vista.
Degli occhi poi la dolce e pura luce,
e la guancia di gigli e rose mista,
e la fronte d'avorio, ond'uom s'induce
ad obliar ciò che più l'alma attrista,
e le perle e i rubin, fiamme d'amore,
rimira, ingombro ancor d'alto stupore.

Non quando vista ne le gelid'acque 56
da l'incauto Atteon fusti, Diana,
tant'egli ne stupì né tanto piacque
a lui la tua beltà rara e soprana,
quant'or nel petto al buon Rinaldo nacque
fiamma amorosa e maraviglia strana,
vedendo in selva solitaria ed adra
sì vago aspetto e forma sì leggiadra.

La vaga e cara imago in cui risplende 57
de la beltà del ciel raggio amoroso,
dolcemente per gli occhi al cor gli scende,
con grata forza ed impeto nascoso;
quivi il suo albergo lusingando prende.
Al fin con modo altero imperioso
rapisce a forza il fren del core e 'l regge,
ad ogn'altro pensier ponendo legge.

Ma come quel che pronto era ed audace, 58
e Fortuna nel crin prender sapea,
e tanto più quant'era più vivace
quel dolce ardor che l'alma gli accendea,
disse: — V'apporti il ciel salute e pace
sempre, qual che vi siate, o donna o dea;
e come vi fe' già leggiadra e bella,
così beata or voi faccia ogni stella.

E s'a la grazia, a la beltà del viso, 59
pari felicità dal ciel v'è data,
ardisco dir che non è in Paradiso
alma di voi più lieta e più beata;
ché tai son quelle in voi, ch'egli m'è aviso
ch'angiola siate di là su mandata:
onde per me felice io mi terrei
di spender, voi servendo, i giorni miei.

her leg and foot that, soft and snowy white,   55
   through silken fringes of vermilion peek,
then of her eyes the pure and kindly light,
   the mingled rose and lily of her cheek,
her alabaster brow that by its sight
   dispels worst woe and leaves the strongest weak,
      the pearls and flaming rubies of her smile —
      he sees them all, astonished all the while.

Not when, Diana, in your limpid bourn   56
   incautious Actaeon your form espied,
was he, seeing your beauty and your scorn
   by awe and wonderment so stupefied,
as now in good Rinaldo's breast was born
   an amorous flame he scarcely could abide,
      seeing in dark and lonely woods appear
      a shape so lovely and a sight so dear.

The dear and lovely image in which glowed   57
   celestial beauty's bright and amorous ray
from his eyes with pleasing might by a swift road
   down to his heart pursued its secret way
and there, a flattering guest, made its abode.
   At last it seized with high, imperial sway
      utter control of all his heart and taught
      new laws to govern every other thought.

But then, like a quick man and bold, who knows   58
   how to seize Fortune by the forelock, and
the quicker since the lively fire that glows
   in him is by desire and longing fanned,
he said: "Heaven give you health and fair repose,
   be you the queen or goddess of this land!
      Even as your stars have made you fair, so may
      their blessings shower you day after day!

Yea, if heaven's blessing lend as much delight   59
   as the glad grace that shines out from your eyes,
I will make bold to say that not a sprite
   happier than you will dwell in paradise;
for as you now appear unto my sight,
   you seem a blessed angel from the skies,
      wherefore I should indeed be most content
      to see my whole life in your service spent.

Ma da poi che mostrarvi il ciel cortese   60
   ha per sì raro dono a me voluto,
facciamisi or per voi chiaro e palese
   quel che sin qui nascosto ei m'ha tenuto;
ch'avendo l'altre qualitati intese,
    come quelle apparenti ho già veduto,
      rimarrà sol che con onor divini
      voi mia dea riverisca, a voi m'inchini. —

Al parlar di Rinaldo la donzella   61
   d'un onesto rossor le guancie sparse;
e qual veggiam del sol l'alma sorella,
   quando vento minaccia, in volto apparse:
il che più la rendette adorna e bella,
   e di fiamma più calda il giovin'arse.
      Indi mosse ver' lui parole tali,
      che gli fur tutte al cor fiammelle e strali:

— Non son qual mi formate, o cavaliero,   62
   né va 'l mio merto al parlar vostro eguale;
ma di Carlo soggiaccio al magno impero,
   come ancor voi da Dio fatta mortale;
ben è 'l fratello mio prode guerriero,
   e di sangue chiarissimo e reale;
      ei che Guascogna, ond'è signor, governa,
      or segue Carlo a fiera guerra esterna.

Ed io ch'al giogo maritale unita   63
   non sono, e seguir Cinzia ancor mi lice,
in un castel vicin tranquilla vita
   vivo, e meco ne sta mia genitrice,
e compagnia, qual bramar so, gradita;
   resta or che 'l nome dica: egli è Clarice.
      Ma chi sète, guerriero, e di qual merto,
      voi che 'l vostro servir m'avete offerto? —

Allor Rinaldo a lei così rispose: 64
   — Traggo l'origin io da Costantino,
che l'imperial sede in Grecia pose,
   lasciando altrui d'Italia il bel domino.
Amone è 'l padre mio, le cui famose
   prove al grado l'alzar di paladino:
      Chiaramonte il cognome, io son Rinaldo,
      solo di servir voi bramoso e caldo. —

But since all-gracious heaven has pleased to make   60
     so rare a gift as your fair sight to me,
do you reveal what I must undertake
     that heaven till now has hid in secrecy.
For surely, if you speak, your words shall shake
     and pierce me like the beauty that I see,
         and it but remains that I with holy zeal
         adore you as my goddess. Here I kneel."

At these words from Rinaldo, a chaste blush rose   61
     on the fair damsel's cheeks. As in her sphere,
when storms impend, the sun's kind sister glows
     with a rosy tinge, so did her face appear,
which made her lovelier still and made the throes
     of burning love the youth felt more severe.
         And then she spoke, her every word a dart
         or torch that kindled or transfixed his heart:

"I am not, sir knight, what you imagine, nor   62
     are such high words to my poor merit due.
Subject to mighty Charles, the emperor.
     I am a mortal, made by God, like you,
though my brother is a mighty warrior,
     of pure descent from the blood royal, who
         is lord of Gascony, but now ventures far,
         serving great Charles in the fierce, foreign war.

And I, not yoked in marriage nor a bride,   63
     still follow Cynthia's path with service true.
In a nearby castle by this forest's side,
     with my dear mother and a chosen few
companions, whom I cherish, I abide.
     My name is Clarice. That is all. But you,
         sir, who are you? What merit should allow
         your seeming eagerness to serve me now?"

After a pause, Rinaldo thus replied: 64
     "From Constantine[11] I trace my origin,
who raised his throne in Greece with joy and pride,
     while viceroys ruled far Italy's demesne.
Aymon's my sire, whose deeds, known far and wide,
     have raised him to the rank of paladin:
         I am Rinaldo, of Clairmont lineage, who
         stand here to serve and would serve none but you."

Rinaldo

— Chi de' vostri avi invitti e del gran padre 65
  non ha sentito l'onorato grido?
S'è testimon de l'opre lor leggiadre
  ogni remota piaggia e ogni lido:
e chi d'Orlando, a le cristiane squadre
  prima difesa contra il Mauro infido?
      Ma di voi null'ancor la fama apporta. —
      Così a lui disse la donzella accorta.

E con que' detti gli traffisse il core, 66
  e 'l colmò di dolore e di vergogna,
onde in se stesso, d'ira e di furore
  acceso, morte e più null'altro agogna.
Tratte dal petto al fin tai voci fuore,
  rispose a quella tacita rampogna:
      — Affermo anch'io che molto Orlando vaglia,
      e che raro è colui che se gli aguaglia.

Ma 'l suo valor però non tanto parmi, 67
  ch'io col vostro favor punto temessi
seco venir al paragon de l'armi,
  senza che biasmo a riportar n'avessi;
e s'occasion tal vorrà mai darmi
  il ciel, voi ne vedrete i segni espressi. —
      Fra tanto ei scorse e la donzella altera
      di donne e di guerrier leggiadra schiera.

Eran costor la nobil compagnia 68
  di Clarice, che lei givan cercando,
non ben sicuri che Fortuna ria
  non venga il lor seren stato turbando,
ché lasciati gli avea ella tra via,
  dietro la cerva il suo destrier spronando,
      sì che, vedendola ora a l'improviso,
      segni mostrar d'alta letizia al viso.

Ella, veduto i suoi, tosto rivolse 69
  sorridendo a Rinaldo il vago aspetto,
e gli disse: — Baron, s'il ciel raccolse
  tanto ardir e valor nel vostro petto,
ch'ad Orlando, in cui porre il tutto volse
  che se richiede a cavalier perfetto,
      ne gite par nel gran mistier di Marte,
      mostrate qui vostra possanza in parte:

"Who of your matchless forebears' excellence   65
     and your great father's has not heard before?
The whole world testifies to their immense
     prowess and wondrous feats from shore to shore.
Who does not know Orlando, first defense
     of Christian bands against the faithless Moor?
        But of you Fame as yet makes no report."
        So went the lady's courteous retort.

It stings him to the heart, and grief and shame   66
     consume him, so that in his inmost soul
he seems to die, while wrath's and envy's flame
     wound him more sorely than all sorrows past.
Wrung from his bosom then, these brief words came,
     with which he met her tacit taunt at last:
        "I too say that Orlando much excels,
        and that his worth is matched by few men else.

And yet to me his valor does not seem   67
     so fearful as to make me shy away
from matching him in arms, however supreme,
     without the least reproach or shame some day.
And if heaven grants, to merit your esteem,
     I'll shortly give you proof of what I say."
        Meanwhile a troop of knights and ladies fair
        had ridden up to join the gentle pair.

These were Clarice's noble followers,   68
     riding in search of her and full of fear
that envious Fortune with some hapless curse
     had come to trouble their peace and mar their cheer,
since they had lost her when she put the spurs
     to her palfrey to pursue the fleeing deer.
        Thus, as they chanced upon her in this place,
        signs of great joy appeared on every face.

She, seeing her own, upon Rinaldo now   69
     turned back her lovely countenance and addressed
him thus: "My lord, since heaven seems to endow
     with such presumptuous confidence your breast,
that with Orlando, whom all men avow
     to be of knighthood's flower the first and best,
        you match yourself in strength and martial skill,
        now show some portion of your power and will.

Rinaldo

ché se d'Orlando voi non men valete, 70
 questo de' miei guerrier ardito stuolo
giostrando superar ancor potrete,
 benché contra lor tutti andiate or solo.
Io dirò poi che tal ne l'arme sète
 che mostrate d'Amone esser figliuolo,
  e che voi con la spada e con la lancia
  alzate al par di lui l'onor di Francia. —

A sì grate parole ingombra l'alma 71
 nova dolcezza al buon figliuol d'Amone,
che spera aver di quei guerrier la palma,
 e far del suo valor qui paragone;
pur a lei disse: — Assai difficil salma
 quella è, che 'l parlar vostro ora m'impone:
  ma quest'alma beltà tai forze aviva
  in me, che spero addur l'impresa a riva. —

Così detto, il destrier veloce gira, 72
 e tosto gionto a quei guerrieri a fronte,
pria le fattezze altere intento mira,
 poi così parla con audace fronte:
— Valorosi signor, non sdegno od ira,
 non da voi ricevute ingiurie ed onte,
  ma più bella cagion ora mi sforza
  provar quanto s'estenda in voi la forza.

Accingetevi dunque a la battaglia, 73
 che si vedrà chi di servir più degno
sia l'alta dama, e più ne l'armi vaglia,
 tosto con chiaro ed apparente segno. —
Il forte Alcasto allor, cui di Tessaglia,
 morto 'l padre, obedir doveva il regno,
  qual uom d'amore acceso e qual superbo,
  così rispose con parlare acerbo:

— Ben come hai detto, folle, or or vedrai 74
 quanto sia questa lancia e soda e dura;
e qual error commette ancor saprai
 quel che le forze sue non ben misura. —
Avea di Grecia in Francia a trager guai
 costui condutto empia sua ventura,
  ch'in Clarice non pria fisò lo sguardo,
  ch'al cor sentio d'amor l'acuto dardo.

For since you boast to be no less in might   70
    than Orlando, here is something to be done.
Joust with this bold band of my warriors, fight
    against them, all at once or one-on-one.
At least go prove yourself a worthy knight
    and show that you are truly Aymon's son
        by wielding your intrepid sword and lance
        to advance, like him, the honor of fair France."

These welcome words made a great sweetness stir   71
    in the heart of Aymon's son, for eagerly
he wished to gain the palm of victory there
    and to make manifest his bravery.
"Hard is the task," he therefore said to her,
    "that your commandments here impose on me,
        but, by your beauty spurred, my best hopes rise
        that I'll achieve this weighty enterprise."

This said, he grasps his courser's bridle tight   72
    and turns the steed where all those warriors stand.
He scans their features first with piercing sight,
    then boldly speaks to the assembled band:
"O valiant lords, not scorn or wrath, no slight
    or shame or injury suffered at your hand,
        but a fairer cause makes me here challenge you
        to a sharp trial of what your powers can do.

So gird yourselves for combat that it may   73
    be seen which of you is most worthy of
serving this noble lady and in the fray
    prevails to show his strength and prove his love."
And strong Alkast, who held in Thessaly¹² sway,
    his father being dead, then forward strove,
        like a man pricked on by burning love and pride,
        and thus in fierce and bitter words replied:

"Madman, you've spoken well, but now you'll see   74
    how well this lance can strike, and you'll soon know
the error of a man who hastily
    mistakes his strength and courts his overthrow."
He had from Greece to France crossed recently
    to sow his mischief, where he came to know
        Clarice and, knowing her, soon felt the dart
        of Love lodged painfully within his heart.

E sendo tra il re Carlo e 'l genitore   75
   molti anni pria grave odio e sdegno nato,
non si volse scoprir, ch'ebbe timore
   di non essere offeso e oltraggiato;
ma spinto, lasso! dal tiranno Amore,
   esser fingendo di più basso stato,
      s'era a' servigii posto ei di Clarice,
      ch'in ciò la sorte alquanto ebbe adiutrice.

E perché amor da gelosia diviso   76
   rado o non mai del tutto esser si vede,
con fiera voce e con turbato viso
   la superba risposta allor ei diede.
Ma Rinaldo, che sente a l'improviso
   che con detti orgogliosi altri lo fiede,
      volge 'l cavallo e pon la lancia in resta:
      né men tardo di lui quegli l'arresta.

L'uno e l'altro la lancia a un tempo impugna,   77
   e l'un si move e l'altro anco in un punto;
ma l'un mira che 'l colpo a l'elmo giugna
   là dove è con la fronte il crin congiunto;
l'altro che via men dotto è di tal pugna,
   cerca che 'l petto sia dal ferro punto;
      nessun l'asta nerbosa indarno corse,
      ma con quella al nemico affanno porse.

A mezo 'l petto il fier garzon fu colto   78
   dal forte Alcasto col nodoso legno,
ch'ogn'uom più saldo avria sozzopra volto,
   ed ei non fece di cader pur segno.
Fu il nemico da lui più offeso molto,
   che la terra calcò senza ritegno,
      ferito in testa d'aspra e mortal piaga,
      sì che 'l terren di sangue intorno allaga.

Rinaldo in sella si rassetta, e poscia   79
   verso gli altri guerrier ratto si scaglia:
un ferisce nel capo, un ne la coscia,
   e pon fin con duo colpi a la battaglia.
Indi agli altri col tronco estrema angoscia
   porge, e con l'urto ancor gli apre e sbaraglia:
      ma in pochi colpi rotti in su la strada
      convien ch'in mille pezzi il tronco vada.

And since his sire and Charles, for many a year,   75
    had lived in hate and dire suspicion,
he wished not to be recognized, for fear
    of outrage or attack, and so, spurred on
by tyrant Love, caused himself to appear
    of mean estate, and let himself be drawn
        in Clarice's service, using this disguise
        to find advantage in his enemies' eyes.

Since love means jealousy par excellence,   76
    and its whole force is oft discovered so,
with savage voice and troubled countenance
    he now in haughty words assailed him so
that good Rinaldo, who perceived at once
    defiance in the proud speech of his foe,
        wheeled round his horse and put his lance in rest.
        Nor was the other slow to face the test.

To charge both in one instant now prepare,   77
    each firm as rock behind his saddle-bow,
but one of them aims at the helmet, where,
    above the brow, the hair begins to show,
the other makes his iron lance-point bear,
    with lesser skill, against the chest below;
        with quivering shafts they gallop to engage,
        each bent to meet his foe with utmost rage.

Straight in the chest the fiery youth received   78
    ferocious Alkast's knotty shaft, whose force
would have the best of champions heaved
    from the saddle, but he remained upon his horse
His foe was less unshaken and more grieved,
    for he, struck in the forehead in mid-course
        by a bitter, deadly thrust, dropped to the ground
        and drenched with blood the black earth all around.

Rinaldo in his saddle reared up high,   79
    and toward the other swiftly made his way.
One more thrust at the head, one at the thigh,
    and with two thrusts he ended thus the fray.
The rest attacked then, but he made them fly
    raking their ranks with his great lance, and they
        scattered in terror, till by evil luck,
        his great shaft fell in splinters as he struck.

Nel cader del troncon, speme e baldanza   80
    negli aversarii suoi poggiando sorse;
non già l'ardir si rompe o la speranza
    nel fier garzon, che rotto esser lo scorse,
ché questa e quello in lui tanto s'avanza,
    quanto 'l suo stato più si trova in forse:
        così ben spesso core invito e forte
        prende vigor da la contraria sorte.

Clarice in questa con immote ciglia   81
    mira 'l valor del nobil giovinetto;
dal valor nasce in lei la maraviglia,
    e da la maraviglia indi il diletto:
poscia il diletto che in mirarlo piglia
    le accende il cor di dolce ardente affetto;
        e mentre ammira e loda 'l cavaliero,
        pian piano a nuovo amore apre 'l sentiero.

Erano corsi più feroci a dosso   82
    al gran guerriero i suoi nemici intanto,
ed altri l'elmo del cimier gli ha scosso,
    altri lo scudo in varie parti infranto,
altr'il viso, altr'il braccio, altri percosso
    gli have l'armato corpo in ogni canto.
        Rinaldo or spinge inanzi, or si ritira,
        e coraggioso a la vittoria aspira.

E 'l cavallo volgendo a la man dritta,   83
    il più feroce a mezzo 'l collo afferra;
e scrollandolo poi ben lungi il gitta
    da sé disteso e tramortito in terra.
Un che la lancia a lui ne l'elmo ha fitta,
    e crede omai finita aver la guerra,
        con l'urto del corsier manda sozzopra,
        poi con un altro il grave pugno adopra.

Di sì terribil pugno un ne percosse,   84
    che, rotto l'elmo, gli stordì la testa,
e d'ogni senso e di vigor lo scosse.
    Né per questo il furor degli altri arresta,
ché Linco, un di color, ver' lui si mosse
    ratto sì che la fiamma è via men presta,
        e venne seco a perigliosa lotta,
        credendo aver la man più forte e dotta.

That lance being gone, his enemies assail 80
    him from all sides with bolder hope once more;
Yet neither hope nor boldness in him fail
    but both grow even stronger than before,
and he, now without weapon, does not quail,
    although from every side they press and pour.
        So will a dauntless heart wrest strength and power
        from adverse Fortune in an evil hour.

Clarice meanwhile stands motionless as she 81
    beholds that young man's valor in the fight.
His valor begets wonder presently,
    and wonder begets pleasure and delight,
and her delight, the more she comes to see,
    makes a sweet fire in her heart burn bright.
        So, as she watches and calls him the best
        of knights, love step by step invades her breast.

His enemies now at the great warrior's back 82
    rushed up more fiercely: one from behind
strikes off his helmet's crest, while others hack
    and batter at his shield, and sharp points find
his face, his thighs, his arms, and crack on crack
    his armor shows from blows of every kind.
        Rinaldo now attacks and now retires
        and unto victory gallantly aspires.

He grips, turning his courser to the right, 83
    the fiercest by the neck, and with one thrust
wrenches him downward from his saddle's height
    and hurls him, crushed and dying, to the dust.
Another, who his helmet seeks to smite
    and in his lance's force has placed his trust,
        he makes sprawl low with the impact of his horse,
        and then employs his fists' tremendous force.

Here one was struck with a buffet so immense, 84
    it smashed all through his helmet, cracked his head,
and robbed him of all vigor and all sense.
    And yet the others' fury is not dead,
for Lyncus, one of them, rides to the offense,
    more speedily than raging flame is sped
        and to oppose his power makes a stand,
        thinking in vain he has the stronger hand.

Rinaldo

Ma da l'arcion Rinaldo il leva a forza,　　　　　　　85
　e rotandol per l'aria entorno il gira;
indi con strano modo e molta forza
　tra l'inimici suoi scagliando il tira,
onde a ritrarsi al fin gli induce e sforza,
　ed a schivare il suo disdegno e l'ira.
　　Clarice allor d'alto stupor ripiena
　　n'andò con fronte a lui lieta e serena,

e disse: — Alto guerriero, a pruova aperta　　　86
　già tutte viste abbiam la virtù vostra,
e qui nulla è di noi che non sia certa
　ch'oggi vinta riman la gente nostra,
e che la palma sol da voi si merta.
　　Cessi omai dunque sì terribil giostra:
　　e poi che cessa la cagione, insieme
　　cessi il furor, ch'ogn'uom vi cede e teme. —

Come, allor che 'l Tiren torbo e sonante　　　87
　leva al ciel l'onde, e i legni al fondo caccia,
se Nettuno in sul carro trionfante
　scorge ir con lieta e venerabil faccia,
la furia affrena e 'n placido sembiante
　par che senz'onda nel suo letto giaccia:
　　così al caro apparir, a l'amorose
　　note, ogni sdegno il cavalier depose.

Ma perché Appollo in ver' gli esperii liti　　　88
　già dechinava l'auree rote ardenti,
sopra più barre por fatto i feriti
　ed inanzi portar quei da' serventi,
donne e guerrieri in vaga schiera uniti
　partir di là con passi tardi e lenti;
　　e con la sua bellissima Clarice
　　gia ragionando il cavalier felice,

che tra via pur tal volta a lei movea　　　89
　d'amor parole e tacite preghiere:
ma sempre o non intenderle fingea,
　o gli dav'ella aspre risposte altere,
con le quai l'alma al giovin traffigea
　e sciemava in gran parte il suo piacere;
　　ché, benché eguale ardore al cor sentisse,
　　non volea ch'in lei quello altri scoprisse.

But Rinaldo heaves him bodily from his horse   85
    and whirls him roundabout high in the air.
Then with miraculous and tremendous force
    flings him among his enemies, who stare,
amazed, and yield at last and take recourse
    in flight to shun the rage that meets them there.
        But Clarice, full of admiration, now
        came toward him with glad and serene brow

and said: "O noble warrior, you have shown   86
    clear proof of your great valor. There is none
here present to deny that, overthrown
    by you, all these brave men have been undone,
and that high victory's palm is yours alone.
    Cease then this dreadful jousting. You have won.
        Therefore forget your quarrel, quit the field,
        since all men here unto your fury yield."

As when Tyrrhenian surges crash and rave   87
    sky-high and swallow ships and still increase,
till Neptune, borne in triumph, with his grave
    and gracious countenance bids their war to cease,
and all the sea grows placid, wave on wave,
    and scarce a ripple stirs to break its peace:
        so at her loving speech and charming sight
        the knight checks all his wrath and calms his spite.

But since Apollo in the Hesperian Sea   88
    already dipped his wheels of golden fire,
the wounded on their stretchers presently
    were sent ahead, each tended by his squire,
as slowly homeward the fair company
    of lords and ladies set out to retire.
        And soon the happy champion, as they walk,
        with his fair Clarice fell in pleasant talk,

and on the way he now and then let fall   89
    some word of love, or looked and heaved a sigh,
but she seemed not to understand at all
    or gave some proud, indifferent reply
that pierced his soul and like a bitter gall
    greatly curtailed his pleasure by and by.
        For though her heart concealed an equal glow,
        she was not yet disposed to let him know.

Lassa! non sa che l'amorosa face,   90
    se vien celata, più ferve e s'avanza,
sì come fuoco suol chiuso in fornace,
    ch'arde più molto ed ha maggior possanza.
Pur il guerrier, che ciò ch'ascoso giace
    sotto sdegnosa e rigida sembianza
        scorger non puote e crede al finto volto,
        si trova in mille acerbe pene involto.

Deh! quante donne son ch'aspro rigore   91
    mostran nel volto ed indurato sdegno,
c'hanno poi molle e delicato il core,
    degli strali d'amor continuo segno;
incauto è quel che ciò ch'appar di fuore
    tien del chiuso voler per certo pegno:
        ch'un'arte è questa per far scempi e prede
        d'uom che drieto a chi fuga affrett'il piede.

Quel che più rende il cavalier doglioso   92
    è, perché non gli sembra esser amato
per lo suo poco merto, a lei d'ascoso
    fuoco il cor non vedendo arso e infiammato;
ma speme ha pur di farsi ancor famoso,
    sì che da lei ne deggia esser pregiato:
        così ad un nobil core amor sovente
        è qual lo sprone ad un destrier corrente.

Giunto intanto al castel, congiedo prese   93
    l'acceso cavalier da la donzella,
ch'a restar seco l'invitò cortese,
    raddolcendo lo sguardo e la favella;
ei, che prima ha disposto illustri imprese
    condur al fin per farsi grato a quella,
        ai dolci umani inviti il cor non piega,
        e ciò che brama a se medesmo niega.

Alas! She knows not that Love's torch will burn   90
    hotter if hidden and with brighter flame
as fires pent up in a forge will turn
    to a heat that blasts their iron vessel's frame.
Yet the young warrior, who does not discern
    what lies concealed beneath her scorn or shame,
        believes her feigned demeanor and is caught
        in pangs of doubt and agonies of thought.

Ah! Many a lady will in her haughty face   91[13]
    show bitter scorn, although her heart is still
a mark for Love to shoot at and a place
    of welcome for that wily archer's skill.
Incautious is the man who thinks to trace
    in outward semblances the hidden will.
        For there is an art to make a foolish prey
        of him who runs toward her who runs away.

What most afflicts the knight with grief and woe,   92
    since she seems not to share his ardent flame,
is that he thinks his merit is too low
    to be considered by so a high a dame.
Yet he still hopes to rise in glory and so
    to make her prize and love him for his fame.
        Thus, as a spur drives a swift steed, Love's fire
        makes noble hearts to noble deeds aspire.

As they draw near her keep, the amorous knight   93
    bids farewell to the lovely maid, and she
invites him to repose with her that night,
    with pleasant looks and courteous words and free,
but he, who earlier fought with all his might
    to do her will and please her fantasy,
        now, when she frankly seeks his love, retires
        and turns his back on what he most desires.

Canto secondo

Parte Rinaldo, e nel partir si sente 1
    dal petto acceso ancor partirsi il core;
null'è ch'allegri la dogliosa mente,
    nulla che l'alma oppressa alzi e ristore;
vorrebbe esser rimaso, e già si pente
    d'aver lasciato il suo gradito amore:
        la bella donna di cui fatto è servo,
        di liber ch'era più ch'in selva cervo.

Sei volte e sette a dietro il corsier volve, 2
    e per tornar verso il suo ben s'invia;
poscia tutto al contrario si risolve,
    ed oltre segue la primiera via;
instabil è vie più ch'al vento polve,
    e ben par che d'amor seguace ei sia;
        fa diversi pensier, e in un non ferma
        pur breve spazio l'egra mente inferma.

Al fin con l'aspre cure e co' sospiri 3
    accompagna il parlar tremante e basso,
e dice: — Ove, o disio d'onor, mi tiri
    per forza, ahi folle! a periglioso passo?
Come vuoi tu ch'ad alte imprese aspiri,
    s'io son privo del cor, s'a dietro il lasso?
        Più che la forza in guerra il cor bisogna;
        senz'esso andrò dunque a mercar vergogna?

Deh, perché, lasso! a quel parlar cortese, 4
    a quelle dolci ed amorose note
non rimas'io con lei, di cui s'accese
    l'alma, e senza cui pace aver non puote?
Chi, se non tu, crudel, ciò mi contese?
    Tu le preghiere sue fêsti gir vuote,
        e me l'invito a ricusar sforzasti,
        misero! e lunge dal mio ben tirasti. —

Canto Two

Rinaldo leaves and, leaving so unkind,   1
  feels that his heart has left his burning breast.
Nothing he meets can cheer his woeful mind,
  nothing can lift the weight his soul oppressed.
He should have stayed, he thinks, not left behind
  that pleasing love or scorned her kind request,
    that lovely maid, whose slave he is now — he
    who, more than woodland deer, was lately free.

Six times or seven he turns back his horse   2
  to seek his true love at her castle door,
then he resolves on the contrary course
  and travels onward as he did before.
As dust is driven by some wind's mad force,
  he wanders, lovelorn, with his soul at war.
    Lost in a thousand thoughts, his mind is caught
    in coils that cannot grasp a single thought.

At last he speaks in bitter care mid sighs   3
  and tears that on his trembling eyelids mass:
"Would you, Desire for Honor, have me rise,
  yet bring me — madman! — to this perilous pass?
How could you bid me seek high enterprise,
  if I have left my heart behind. Alas!
    War calls for hearts, not merely skill and power.
    Without a heart, must shame then be my dower?

Ah why, so courteously by her besought   4
  in such sweet, amorous tones, did I not stay
with her, without whom I must err, distraught,
  burning, bereft of peace, day after day?
Who, if not you, cruel Honor, turned to naught
  her prayers and ordered me to turn away?
    You forced me to refuse; compelled by you,
    I — wretch! — to my own good became untrue."

Rinaldo

Qui tace, e china a terra i lumi e 'l volto;   5
 poi così ancora il suo parlar ripiglia:
— Ahi! quanto è quel desir fallace e stolto
 che tornar a Clarice or mi consiglia,
e 'n quanti errori è 'l mio discorso involto.
 Lasso! poi ch'al peggio ognor s'appiglia,
  anzi donna sì chiara e sì gentile
  apparir non deve uomo oscuro e vile

Né fec'io giamai cosa onde sia degno   6
 del suo cospetto, e ciò negar non vale;
e già n'ho visto più d'un chiaro segno,
 ch'ella prudente ancor mi stima tale:
ch'a le parole mie, colma di sdegno,
 risposta diede al mio vil merto eguale;
  e se poi m'invitò, ve la sospinse
  sua cortesia, che la viltà mia vinse.

Né stato il mio restar le saria caro,   7
 né bramar degg'io quel ch'a lei non piace:
quando sarò ne l'arme illustre e chiaro,
 non mi si disdirà l'essere audace;
e 'l volto ove a sprezzar tutt'altro imparo,
 che m'arde il cor d'inestinguibil face,
  a ciò mi porgerà forza ed ardire,
  e darà piume e vanni al mio desire.

E benché priv'or sia del core il petto,   8
 l'alma imago in sua vece entro rinchiude,
che potrà più che 'l core in ogni effetto
 rendermi ardito, e in me destar vertude. —
Clarice intanto d'amoroso affetto
 non meno aviene ancor ch'agghiaci e sude,
  e non meno di lui si duole e lagna,
  ma 'l bel viso di più piangendo bagna.

Bagna il viso di pianto, allarga il freno   9
 ai sospiri, ai lamenti, e così dice:
— Qual or sì novo e sì mortal veleno
 t'attosca il petto, o misera Clarice?
Qual dolce mal d'alta amarezza pieno
 dilettando ti fa mesta e 'nfelice?
  Donde 'l desire in te, donde l'ardore,
  donde la speme ancor nasce e 'l dolore?

Canto Two

He paused, eyes fixed upon the ground, then thus   5
    resumed his speech with dark and troubled brow:
"Ah! How desire with mad and spurious
    counsel bids me return to Clarice, how
false my whole discourse seems, how fatuous,
    that leans on such poor props to disallow
        that a low, caitiff knight must never appear
        before a maid so noble and so dear.

Never — no use denying it — did I   6
    do deeds to make me worthy of her sight;
her prudent mind can show no reason why
    I should to her least notice claim a right.
To my first words, the scorn in her reply
    was but my due; and if she did invite
        me later on, high courtesy prevailed.
        I knew it well, and so my courage failed.

My stay would not have pleased her, and I should   7
    not dream of actions she considers ill.
Were I renowned and proved in arms, she would
    have less fear of my boldness and my will,
and her dear face, which stirs up all my blood,
    and kindled all its fires and feeds them still,
        would lend me strength and daring to aspire
        and offer wings and sails to my desire.

Yet now my breast, reft of my heart, instead   8
    is by her image utterly controlled,
by which it, more than by my heart, is sped
    toward virtue and enlivened to grow bold."
Clarice meanwhile, by amorous longing fed,
    no less complains, her cheeks now hot, now cold.
        No less than he she suffers and complains —
        nay weeps, beset by even harsher pains.

She bathes her face in tears and, giving rein   9
    to sighs and to laments, thus vents her woes:
"What deadly venom with such ceaseless pain
    poisons, O wretched Clarice, your repose?
What sickness, sweet yet bitter, can contain
    such tender joy in such tormenting throes?
        What lends your burning heart this wild desire
        and with both hope and grief sets it afire?

Rinaldo

Già ben m'accorgo apertamente, ahi lassa! 10
or che l'accorger più nulla mi giova,
ch'Amor, che l'alme più superbe abbassa,
or in me fa così spietata prova;
e ch'egli è quel che sì feroce passa
dentr'al mio cor come in sua stanza nuova;
e ch'egli è quel che in lui desire e speme
ed ardor ed affanno aviva insieme.

Ma s'egli è quel ch'in un lieta e dolente 11
mi fa, quando giamai meco contese?
Quando, meschina ancor, così repente
o per forza o per arte egli mi prese?
Come a schermirmi allor non fui possente,
ed a fuggir l'ascoste insidie tese?
Come, no 'l sapendo, io vinta restai?
Come a lui volontaria io mi donai? —

Segue intanto Rinaldo il suo viaggio, 12
né pur l'alma o le membra alquanto posa;
e giunge u' dal notturno umido raggio
face altrui schermo quercia alta e frondosa.
Ivi scorge nel suol, che 'l vago maggio
copria di veste allor verde ed erbosa,
assisi duo guerrier che 'l corpo stanco
rendean col cibo vigoroso e franco.

L'invitan questi con parlar cortese, 13
ed ei l'invito lor ricusa alquanto;
ma, non giovando il ricusar, discese
al fin di sella e lor si mise a canto.
Poi che ciascuno il nutrimento prese,
il ragionar ch'avean lasciato intanto
ripigliaro di nuovo, e quel tal era
qual conveniasi a sì onorata schiera.

A caso venne al bon Rinaldo detto 14
ch'a la ventura gia di quel destriero.
Uno di lor, che cavalier perfetto
tenuto ed appellato era Isoliero,
allor rispose con turbato aspetto:
— Deh! cangia omai, baron, cangia pensiero,
ché tal ventura solo a me conviensi,
e folle sei se di tentarla pensi.

Too clearly now — alas! — I've come to see —   10
    and find no joy at all in what I've learned —
that Love, who makes the proudest bend the knee,
    makes trial of me, for he is the one I spurned:
that he has entered in my heart, that he
      claims it like a new mansion he has earned,
        who in hope's heaven and desire's hell
        makes heat and tender sense together dwell.

But when did I and he, who now somehow   11
    both gladdens me and grieves me, come to fight?
When did he — wretch that now I am! — allow
    my capture, either by main force or sleight?
Why will he therefore not defend me now
    but by some hidden treachery takes flight?
      How shall I yield, not knowing him, at his pleasure?
      How willingly surrender all my treasure?"

Meanwhile Rinaldo rode upon his way,   12
    restless in soul and body, till he found
a place where from the damp, nocturnal ray
    a high and leafy oak shaded the ground.
Seated upon on a knoll that lovely May
    with verdant garlands of new herbage crowned,
      two warriors were restoring their oppressed
      spirits and weary limbs with food and rest.

They courteously invited him to sit,   13
    and he at first refused, but when
he saw that this displeased them, he alit
    from his high saddle and sat by these two men.
They, when their meal was over, bit by bit
    broke silence and began to talk again,
      their converse being lively, frank and free,
      such as befits a gallant company.

It chanced that good Rinaldo learned they too   14
    were on a quest that savage steed to find,
and one of them, a perfect knight and true —
    his name was Ysolier — slowly inclined
his head and said with troubled face, "And you
    my lord, must change, and quickly change, your mind,
      for such a quest for me alone is fit.
      You are a madman even to think of it."

Rinaldo

Rise Rinaldo e disse: — A l'apparire 15
  del sol serò con quel cavallo a fronte,
né lasciarlo altrui vo', né di soffrire
  uso son io sì gravi ingiurie ed onte. —
Isolier lo spagnuol non può sentire
  ch'altri gli parli in sì orgogliosa fronte;
    onde, tratta la spada: — O qui morrai,
    disse, o l'impresa a me tu lascierai. —

Il lor compagno era un gentil barone 16
  de' più pregiati ne l'inglese regno,
forte ed ardito ad ogni paragone,
  e di molti famosi assai più degno;
egli avea col destrier fatta tenzone,
  e van gli era tornato ogni dissegno,
    benché non gisse a la ventura ei solo,
    ma di guerrier menasse ardito stuolo.

Questi che del corsier la forza ha visto, 17
  la forza c'ha 'l suo stuol morto e conquiso,
sì che soleva dir che fece acquisto
  di vita, allor non sendo anch'egli ucciso;
volto al pagan, che d'elmo è già provisto
  e minaccia al garzon con fiero viso,
    gli disse: — Alto guerrier, ascolta, aspetta:
    non correre a ferir con tanta fretta.

Non ti sdegnar in così strana impresa 18
  compagno aver, perché non poco fia
se tu con belva tal prendi contesa,
  avendo un sol guerriero in compagnia. —
Il pagan che di sdegno ha l'alma accesa,
  e che finir tal lite omai disia,
    qui gli tronca 'l parlar e 'l brando stringe,
    e verso il fier garzon ratto si spinge.

Tutta la sua possanza in un raccoglie, 19
  e poi dechina giù l'orribil spada.
Nel forte scudo l'aversario coglie
  e gliel manda in duo parti in su la strada;
passa oltre il colpo, ed a l'elmetto toglie
  il bel cimiero, e fa ch'a terra cada:
    non rompe quel, ma ne la spalla scende,
    e l'acciar che la copre alquanto fende.

Rinaldo laughed and said, "At sunrise I   15
   confront that horse, and I have no intent
to leave him to another. Your reply
   insults my honor. Is that what you meant?"
The Spaniard Ysolier was wroth to hear such high
   terms uttered in a tone so confident,
      wherefore, "You either die right here," said he
      sword drawn, "or you must yield this quest to me."

The third among the three companions there   16
   was an English baron,[14] one of Britain's best,
bold, stout and strong almost beyond compare,
   more famed than most and rivaling the rest.
He once had tracked the stallion to his lair
   and fought him yet had failed to meet the test
      though he had not unaided faced that horse,
      but with a band of daring warriors.

He had seen the stallion's savage power displayed,   17
   a power that killed or conquered all his crew,
which made him say lucky was he who made
   his escape from that steed without dying too.
He now to the pagan, who, in steel arrayed,
   with threatening face at the young warrior flew,
      said: "Noble warrior, hear me and be still,
      and do not be in such great haste to kill.

In such a strange adventure, do not shun   18
   companions. For if you should choose to fight
so terrible a beast, to have even one
   man at your side will much assist your might."
Impatient for the contest to be done,
   the pagan, whose proud spirit burns with spite,
      cuts off his speech and rushes headlong toward
      the fierce young warrior, brandishing his sword.

He gathers all his power in one blow,   19
   and makes his horrid sword descend to pound
and cleave the upraised buckler of his foe
   and sends it in two pieces to the ground.
The stroke passes beyond and, downward bound,
   knocks off his helmet's crest yet does not go
      further but, glancing sideways, slightly dents
      the steel plate of his shoulder's armaments.

Rinaldo

Posto per segno a' campi ivi giaceva 20
    sasso d'immenso pondo antiquo e grosso;
con man robusta allor Rinaldo il leva,
    là 'v'altri non l'avria di luoco mosso.
Stretto l'affera, e poi s'alza e solleva,
    ed al nimico suo l'avventa adosso,
        col corpo il braccio accompagnando e insieme
        qui congiungendo le sue forze estreme.

Non gian presso a Pozzuol con tal furore 21
    gravi pietre per l'aere intorno errando,
pietre cui natural impeto fuore
    da l'imo centro al ciel spingea tonando,
quando dentro 'l terren, chiuso il calore,
    quel ruppe, strada d'essalar trovando,
        con qual dal paladin tirata è questa,
        che stridendo al pagan fiede la testa.

Stridendo il grave sasso al fier pagano 22
    percote il capo e frange pria lo scudo,
ch'opposto avea perché del tutto in vano
    se 'n gisse il colpo, o men gli fusse crudo.
Si riversa Isolier tremando al piano,
    privo di senso e di vigore ignudo,
        ed a lui gli occhi oscura notte involve,
        ed ogni membro ancor se gli dissolve.

Non morì già, ma come morto in terra 23
    un'ora giacque, e man non mosse o piede.
Rinaldo, che finita aver la guerra
    con aspra morte del pagan si crede,
a lo sdegno, al furor il petto serra,
    ed affetto gentil l'alma gli fiede:
        sì ch'altamente ei se n'affligge e lagna,
        ché pietade a valor sempre è compagna.

Rivenuto Isolier, benché assai grave 24
    si senta, ché 'l fier colpo ancor gli noce,
pur stringe in man la spada e nulla pave,
    e ver' Rinaldo il piè drizza veloce.
Ma il buono Inglese con parlar soave
    tempra lo sdegno che sì il cor gli coce,
        e le non lievi differenze accorda;
        ma pria l'alto periglio a lor ricorda,

Placed as a signpost on the field nearby   20
    lay an old boulder of tremendous weight.
Rinaldo now with strong hand lifts it high —
    that no strength else could even dislocate —
and swiftly hurtling forward makes it fly
    toward his enemy, following the great
        strength of his arm with his whole body's force
        to endow with utmost speed and power its course.[15]

Not with more fury on Pozzuoli's plains[16]   21
    do heavy boulders plummet from the air,
that Nature's force from the abyss unchains
    and spews forth skyward from the craters there,
when pent up heat the Earth's deep bowels strains
    to the bursting point and rips them from her lair,
        as this which by the paladin was sped
        and with a loud crash struck the pagan's head.

With a loud crash the huge stone strikes to split   22
    the savage pagan's skull, first shattering
the shield he vainly holds opposed to it
    to guard himself against the dreadful thing.
Ysolier, trembling, spins around, thus hit,
    reft of all sense and strength and tottering.
        Lost in dark night, he feels his eyes grow dim
        and all his power sapped from every limb.

He does not die, but like a dead man lies,   23
    unable to stir hand or foot, an hour
or more, so that Rinaldo, thinking in this wise
    in death to have made that furious pagan cower,
at once his wrath and fury mollifies
    to yield his heart to gentle pity's power,
        and, touched by noble sadness, sighs and weeps,
        since in true valor pity never sleeps.

Ysolier then, recovering, though he still   24
    feels queasy, for the fierce blow gives him pain,
snatches his sword and with intent to kill
    at once toward Rinaldo speeds again.
But the good Englishman with gentle skill
    and soothing words persuades him to restrain
        his anger, and soon puts their quarrel to rest,
        but first reminds them of their perilous quest,

e gli dice: — Signor, io vi consiglio 25
   di non gire a provar questa ventura,
perciò che sotto 'l ciel maggior periglio
   non è, né cosa ad asseguir più dura;
non val contra 'l destrier forza o consiglio,
   arma non è dal suo furor secura.
      Ma se pur fisse in ciò le voglie avete,
      ambo uniti a l'impresa insieme andrete.

E colui col destrier venga a battaglia 26
   verso 'l quale egli prima i passi muova;
l'altro stiasi a veder quanto che vaglia
   il suo compagno in così orribil pruova.
Vi prego ben, signor, che non vi caglia,
   se pur la morte di tentar vi giova,
      d'usar con belva tal vani rispetti,
      ma che pugniate insieme uniti e stretti. —

Rimasero a que' patti ambo contenti, 27
   e più che 'l buon Rinaldo anco Isoliero.
Ma come il sol co' suoi bei raggi ardenti
   ruppe de l'atra notte il velo nero,
a levarse i guerrier pigri né lenti
   non furo, ed a montar sovra 'l destriero.
      Il britanno guerrier ch'a loro è scorta
      gli guida a l'antro per la via più corta.

A l'antro onde il corsier mai non solea 28
   scostarsi, come ei lor narra per strada,
questi, che senza scudo ir ne vedea
   Rinaldo e senza lancia e senza spada,
gli disse: — Credi tu la belva rea
   domare inerme, o di morir t'aggrada? —
      E quelli a lui: — Nel cor consiston l'armi,
      onde il forte non è chi mai disarmi. —

Al disiato luoco intanto giunge 29
   la bella compagnia. Quivi l'Inglese
da lor toglie combiato e 'l destrier punge,
   ma degli altri ciascun su l'erba scese
e lascia il corridore indi non lunge,
   ch'a piè vogliono far l'aspre contese
      per ferir meglio e meglio ancor ritrarsi,
      e più veloci intorno raggirarsi.

saying: "My lords, I urge you to desist   25
    from this adventure, for (as I believe)
no greater dangers anywhere exist
    nor any purpose harder to achieve.
No mortal force or wisdom can resist
    that savage steed, no sharp blade can aggrieve.
        But if your fixed wills needs must have it so,
        together on that undertaking go.

Then one of you might first ride out to greet   26
    that steed's encounter on the woodland track,
and the other in the saddle keep his seat
    to see his friend's performance, and hold back.
Still, do not tempt your deaths, my lords, but meet
    his furious onset in a joint attack;
        don't stand on courtesy with him, but ride
        to engage him both together, side by side."

At these terms, both were pleased, and Ysolier   27
    still more than good Rinaldo showed delight.
But when the sun's fair rays began to tear
    through the black, cloudy veil of sullen night,
the knights rose eagerly and mounted their
    chargers, both keen for the impending fight,
        and, guided by the Briton warrior, they
        rode toward the cavern by the quickest way.

Nearing the cavern where (he said) the horse,   28
    never long absent thence, was wont to hide,
and seeing Rinaldo toward it make his course,
    swordless and without lance or shield, he cried:
"Do you think to overcome that monster's force
    unarmed, or are you bent on suicide?"
        He answered him: "No brave man can be harmed,
        though he bears no weapons, if his heart is armed."

Meanwhile the fair troop reached the wished-for place.   29
    and there the Englishman bade them farewell
and, giving spur, galloped away apace.
    But the other two dismounted in the dell
and left their steeds behind some little ways,
    for they on foot meant to confront the fell
        encounter, thinking thus with more success
        to strike, to turn, to draw back, or to press.

Rinaldo

Ecco appare il cavallo e calci tira, 30
    e fa saltando in ciel ben mille ruote;
da le narici il fuoco accolto spira,
    move l'orecchie e l'ampie membra scuote;
a sassi, a sterpi, a piante ei non rimira,
    ma fracassando il tutto urta e percote:
        col nitrito i nemici a fiera guerra
        sfida, e co' piè fa rimbombar la terra.

Baio e castagno, onde Baiardo è detto: 31
    d'argentea stella in fronte ei va fregiato,
balzani ha i piè di dietro, e l'ampio petto
    di grasse polpe largamente ornato;
ha picciol ventre, ha picciol capo e stretto,
    si posa il folto crin sul destro lato;
        sono le spalle in lui larghe e carnose,
        dritte le gambe asciutte e poderose.

Tal già Cillaro fu, pria che 'l domasse 32
    con forza e arte l'amicleo Polluce,
e tai, prima che lor Marte frenasse
    quei furo, ond'ei l'alto suo carro adduce.
Ma benché tal, benché al furor sembrasse
    furia da l'imo centro uscita in luce,
        raddoppia al paladin pur l'ardimento,
        e desta in Isolier poco spavento.

Prima verso Isolier s'invia Baiardo, 33
    e quei l'attende con la lancia in resta;
l'asta fracassa l'animal gagliardo,
    e 'l corso suo non però punto arresta.
Non fu l'Ibero a ritirarsi tardo,
    ed a dar luoco a così gran tempesta;
        sì che quel non l'urtò, ma tornò ratto
        contra di lui ch'avea già il brando tratto.

Tratta la spada avea, perché non era 34
    per domar il cavallo ei qui venuto,
sendo da chi ne avea notizia intera
    per impossibil questo allor tenuto,
ma per ferir la poderosa fera
    e dargli morte ancor col ferro acuto.
        Sol Rinaldo s'avea vario consiglio
        preso dagli altri, e con maggior periglio.

Now the great stallion, kicking high, draws nigher 30
    with a thousand skyward leaps, curvets and veers,
and from his nostrils breathes ingathered fire;
    he stirs his massive limbs and flicks his ears;
heedless of rocks, thorns, tree-trunks in his ire,
    crashing through every hindrance, he appears.
        and with loud neighs his enemies defies ,
        while thunder from his hooves shakes earth and skies.

Bayard he is named, for his bay-chestnut hue. 31
    A star of silver marks his forehead and
white fetlocks top his hooves. Massive of thew,
    the sinews on his mighty chest expand.
His belly tight, his face fine, straight and true,
    with a curled mane falling rightward, see him stand,
        his shoulders huge and muscular — a steed
        whose lithe legs promise ample power and speed.

Such was Cyllaros[17] once, until, by force 32
    and skill, Amyclean Pollux made him tame;
and such, before Mars bridled him, was the horse
    that draws the war-god's chariot. All the same,
though in his rage he speeds upon his course
    like a fury bursting from earth's central flame,
        he doubles courage in the paladin
        and causes Ysolier but scant chagrin.

First Bayard turns on Ysolier, who receives 33
    his thunderous attack with lance in rest.
The great shaft strikes the noble beast, but leaves
    no mark nor slows his onslaught. Sorely pressed,
the Spaniard is not slow to yield and gives
    him ground, unable to confront that test.
        But then the steed veers back and gallops toward
        the knight who stands to face him with drawn sword.

With drawn sword did he stand, since he well knew 34
    that all attempts to tame the steed were vain.
(His first encounter taught him this was true.)
    This being impossible, he had come again
merely to fight the mighty beast and drew
    his sharp blade now to give it death or pain.
        Only Rinaldo, counseled otherwise,
        risked greater peril to obtain the prize.

Rinaldo

Ratto contra l'Ispan Baiardo torna   35
   feroce, alzando or l'uno or l'altro piede;
dove la fronte è da la stella adorna
   con la spada il baron veloce 'l fiede;
ma fiede indarno ed ei di ciò si scorna,
   ch'aver percosso debilmente crede:
      né sa che del corsier la pelle è tale
      che presso lei l'acciaro è molle e frale.

Sibilando in giù cala il suo tagliente   36
   ferro di nuovo, e 'l fier con maggior possa,
sì che l'aspro corsier se ne risente,
   e china il capo sotto la percossa.
Ma poi di rabbia e di furore ardente
   gli dà con l'urto così fiera scossa
      che 'l pagan cadde, e seco cadde insieme
      quella d'aver vittoria altera speme.

Rinaldo che cader vede Isoliero,   37
   e che sua vita al fin n'andria ben tosto,
perché giacea disteso in sul sentiero
   privo di forze, il primo ardir deposto,
ratto il passo drizzò verso il destriero;
   e come giunto fu tanto d'accosto
      che 'l potesse ferir, il pugno strinse:
      indi la mano impetuosa spinse.

Con tal forza il campione il destrier tocca   38
   che quel che prima o poi mai non gli avvenne:
di vermiglio color tinse la bocca
   il sangue ch'in gran copia a terra venne.
Fuor l'arco stral sì presto mai non scocca,
   né sì presto falcon batte le penne,
      come presto il corsier ver' lui si volse,
      e co' denti afferrargli il braccio volse.

Si ritira il guerriero, e poi raddoppia   39
   il pugno, e lo colpisce in su la fronte.
Volto Baiardo i calci spinge a coppia,
   ch'avrian gettato a terra ogn'alto monte.
Sta su l'aviso, e forze ed arte accoppia
   insieme il cavalier di Chiaramonte:
      dove volge il destrier la testa o 'l piede,
      ei ragirando il passo il luoco cede.

Now Bayard in precipitous rage attacks   35
    the Spaniard with both fore-hooves. Now,
where his forehead bears the star, Ysolier hacks
    with his swift blade but vainly hacks that brow.
The horse ignores him, though he never slacks,
    thinking he must have wounded him somehow:
       He little knows the courser's hide is such
       as makes hard steel seem soft wax at its touch.

Whistling, the sharp steel once again descends   36
    and strikes with yet more potent force, so that
the savage courser feels the blow and bends
    his head a little. In great rage thereat,
he rushes forward with such power, he sends
    the pagan to the ground and lays him flat.
       He falls, and with him falls all hope that he
       could ever entertain of victory.

Rinaldo saw Ysolier fall and thought   37
    his friend's life near its end, because he lay
stretched by the roadside senseless and distraught,
    sapped of all force, all courage drained away.
He hastens thither and, having reached a spot
    sufficiently near the destrier to assay
       a sally at him, balls his great fist and
       strikes at his muzzle with impetuous hand.

The great steed feels such power in that blow   38
    as he felt never after or before.
His mouth foams all vermilion and below
    his hooves the ground is glistening with gore.
More swiftly never arrow left the bow,
    nor wing-borne falcon ever downward bore
       than now the courser veers round in alarm
       and with his teeth snaps at the champion's arm.

The knight withdraws, but then returns to smite   39
    with force redoubled the great stallion's brow.
Bayard wheels, kicking with both hooves, whose might
    could send high mountains to the depths, but now
the Clairmont youth foresees each thrust, each bite,
    and, joining skill to force, succeeds somehow,
       wherever the stallion turns his feet or face,
       to move aside and prudently give place.

Sempre al fianco gli sta, dove il cavallo   *40*
   non lui con morsi o con gran calci offenda,
ché vuol che la destrezza, e no 'l metallo,
   dal suo furor terribile il difenda;
pur, mettendo una volta il piede in fallo,
   colpito fu d'aspra percossa orrenda:
      un calcio recevè nel destro fianco,
      e quasi sotto il colpo ei venne manco.

Non cadde già, ma si ritenne a pena;   *41*
   e se 'l fier calcio era men scarso alquanto,
con tal vigor fu tratto e con tal lena
   che gli avria l'armi insieme e l'ossa infranto.
Non qui Baiardo il suo furore affrena,
   ma 'l cavalier riprese forze intanto:
      la seconda schivò crudel percossa
      ch'avea ver' lui con maggior forza mossa.

Non perciò i piedi a ferir vanno in vano,   *42*
   ma grossa quercia e tant'entro sotterra
ascosa, quanto sorge alta dal piano,
   è da lor colta, rotta e posta a terra.
Rinaldo quei con l'una e l'altra mano,
   pria che gli tiri a sé, stringe ed afferra.
      Cerca Baiardo uscir di questo impaccio,
      ma troppo è forte del nemico il braccio.

Move indarno le gambe, indarno ancora   *43*
   per morderlo ver' lui la bocca volta;
si crolla indarno e s'alza e sbuffa, e fuora
   sparge anitrendo l'ira dentro accolta.
Durò tal zuffa lungo spazio d'ora:
   con gran vigore al fin, con forza molta,
      ma con arte maggior a terra il pone
      il gran figliuol del valoroso Amone.

Sì come il mar che dianzi alto fremendo   *44*
   orribil si mostrava e minaccioso,
lo suo sdegno e 'l furor poi deponendo
   or tranquillo ed umil giace in riposo:
così il destrier che prima era tremendo,
   ed in vista crudele e spaventoso,
      tòcco il suol poi, si sta placido e cheto;
      ma serba de l'alter nel mansueto.

He ever keeps to one side of the horse   40
    where it can neither kick nor bite, for he
intends that nimbleness, not metal's force,
    should countervail his foe's ferocity.
Yet once a slip of foot led him off-course
    and he was buffeted most bitterly:
        a kick in his right side hurt him so much,
        he nearly swooned to feel that horrid touch.

He did not fall, but with an effort stayed   41
    upright; and had more frequent kicks then flown,
their force and vigor would have quite unmade
    his armor and cracked or crushed his every bone.
Bayard his unchecked fury now displayed,
    but then the knight recovered with a moan
        and dodged the second cruel blow that came
        toward him with yet more power to stun and maim.

Yet do those hooves not fall on nothing: no,   42
    a great oak with its hidden tap root thrust,
deep as it soars above ground, down below
    to nourish it, they shatter into dust.
Those hooves Rinaldo now, before their blow
    can hit him, reaches for and grasps. Now must
        Bayard attempt to shake off this strange thong
        but finds his enemy's vise-like grip too strong.

In vain he shifts his hind-legs, and in vain   43
    he once more turns his mouth on him to bite;
in vain he stoops, leaps, kicks, venting his pain
    and pent-up wrath in loud neighs as they fight.
For one long hour thus they strive and strain:
    At last with utmost force and consummate might,
        but with a skill yet greater and profound,
        brave Aymon's great son pulls him to the ground.

Even as the sea surge, earlier churning high   44
    with horrid menace in its ebb and flow,
at last permits its furious rage to die
    and comes to lie at rest, tranquil and low,
so now that steed, at first so apt to fly
    into a fit of cruel rage, bends low
        and, having touched the ground, is pacified,
        though even in mildness he maintains his pride.

Rinaldo

Gli palpa il collo e gli maneggia il petto 45
    il cavaliero, e gli ordina le chiome;
nitrisce quegli e mostra aver diletto,
    perché 'l lusinga il suo signore, e come.
Rinaldo che se 'l vede esser soggetto,
    e c'ha le furie sue già tutte dome,
        la sella e 'l resto a l'altro corsier toglie,
        e questo adorna de l'aurate spoglie.

Era l'Ispan risorto allor che fèa 46
    col destrier pugna il giovinetto ardito;
e vedendo ch'omai dòmo l'avea,
    stava per lo stupor cheto e smarrito:
ché 'n membra giovenili ei non credea
    che fosse tal valore insieme unito.
        Rinaldo lo saluta, e chiede poi
        s'alcun rio male ancora forse l'annoi.

Ed inteso di no prendono il calle 47
    ove torse il destrier la lor ventura,
che fuor di quella selva in una valle
    gli scorse al fine assai profonda e scura.
Scontrano ivi un guerrier che verdi e gialle
    le sopravesti avea su l'armatura,
        e dimostra a l'aspetto alto e superbo
        esser di gran vigore e di gran nerbo.

Dipinto questi porta in aureo scudo 48
    con l'ali al fianco il faretrato arciero,
le belle membra pargolette ignudo,
    bendato gli occhi e di sembiante altero,
sotto i cui piedi giace avinto il crudo
    Marte. Rinaldo allor da lo scudiero
        del suo compagno una gross'asta tolse,
        e così ver' colui la lingua sciolse:

— Molto a me più ch'a te conviensi questo 49
    scudo, o barone; e se no 'l credi, io sono
accinto e pronto a fartel manifesto.
    Vien dunque a giostra, o pur quel dammi in dono:
a me più si convien, ché provo infesto
    più ch'altro amor, né spero indi perdono,
        e più son ch'altri di sue fiamme caldo,
        e più in seguirlo ancor costante e saldo. —

The champion pats his neck and strokes his chest   45
  and smoothes the tangles of his mane away;
the other by loud, joyful neighs expressed
  his wish to please his master and obey.
Rinaldo, seeing his fury laid to rest
  and overmastered quite, without delay
    takes saddle and trappings from his old destrier
    and decks his new mount with the gilded gear.

The Spaniard in the meantime had regained   46
  his senses while the bold youth struck the steed
and, seeing him tamed already and restrained,
  stood silent and bewildered at the deed,
incredulous that those youthful limbs contained
  such peerless strength and such relentless speed.
    Rinaldo hailed him, and inquired if he
    had suffered some disabling injury.

Told he had not, they once more took the road   47
  by which the steed had drawn them to their quest.
They followed it until they left the wood
  and down into a deep, dark valley pressed
where they encountered a fierce knight who stood
  all armed, in green and yellow surcoat dressed,
    and by his proud and noble bearing gave
    a show of being wondrous fierce and brave.

Painted upon his golden shield was shown   48
  the quiver-bearing archer[18] on the wing,
a naked child scarcely to boyhood grown,
  blindfolded, but in posture threatening,
beneath whose feet ferocious Mars lay prone
  as in defeat. Rinaldo then alone,
    seizing a huge lance from his comrade's squire,
    challenged that strange knight thus with eyes afire:

"To me, far more than you, my lord, this shield   49
  is due. If you deny this, I am fain
to prove it on your body in the field.
  Give it to me or fight, for it is plain
it suits me better, since to Love I yield
  more truly than all men, whatever the pain.
    No man alive more sorely feels his heat
    nor serves him with devotion more complete."

— Ciò vedrassi la pruova, allor l'estrano   *50*
    rispose, e se tu vinci, egli tuo fia:
ma spero tosto riversarti al piano,
    s'ora minor non è la forza mia. —
Detto così, tolse la lancia in mano,
    e prese al corso un gran spazio di via,
        ed in quel tempo ancor volse Baiardo
        l'altro baron, nulla di lui più tardo.

Fu dal guerriero estran nel petto colto   *51*
    il buon Rinaldo, e quasi a terra spinto,
ch'era quel forte e valoroso molto,
    e rade volte avezzo ad esser vinto;
con la lancia egli a lui percosse il volto
    con forza tal che ben l'avrebbe estinto,
        se di tempra men fina era l'elmetto:
        pur di sella lo trasse al suo dispetto.

Sùbito in piedi lo stranier risorse,   *52*
    d'infinito stupor ingombro e pieno:
ché rade volte caso tal gli occorse,
    e gli occorse or quando il credette meno;
e 'l forte scudo a l'aversario porse
    dicendo: — Or, cavalier, uscito a pieno
        son da l'obligo mio; tu con la spada,
        se pur la vòi, guadagnar déi la strada. —

Isolier che mostrarsi al paragone   *53*
    degno compagno di Rinaldo ha spene,
disse a lui volto: — A me questa tenzone
    ed il francarvi il passo or s'appertiene;
in imprese maggior voi mio campione
    sarete. — E così detto a terra viene,
        e s'incomincia il periglioso assalto,
        ed a girare il ferro or basso or alto.

Ambo sanno ferir, sanno pararsi,   *54*
    ambo han possenti membra, ardito core;
ambo spingere inanzi, ambo ritrarsi
    san quando è d'uopo, e dar luogo al furore;
tal ch'or con pieni colpi, ora con scarsi,
    senza vantaggio alcun pugnar due ore.
        Qui si comincia a rivoltar la sorte,
        ed appar Isolier più destro e forte.

"We'll try this out," the stranger said and frowned,   50
    "and if you win, the shield is yours, although
I trust I'll shortly cast you to the ground,
    unless my strength is feebler than I know."
This said, seizing his lance, he wheeled around
    and paced off a long stretch to charge his foe,
        and the other lord, no tardier than he,
        made Bayard turn back simultaneously.

Taking the impact full upon the chest   51
    the good Rinaldo almost plunged to earth,
for that man's power and pluck was of the best
    and rarely met a man of equal worth,
but his own lance struck home beneath the crest
    and would have killed him had the girth
        of steel upon his helm been weak or thin,
        yet it unhorsed him, to his great chagrin.

At once the stranger leapt back on his feet,   52
    bewilderment and stupor on his brow,
for he had rarely chanced to lose his seat
    and scarce believed it could have happened now.
Grasping his strong shield, he advanced to meet
    his foe, shouting: "Sir, do you think somehow
        I've paid my debt in full? Now draw your sword[19]
        and clear the path I'll make you earn. *En garde!*"

Ysolier thereupon, who hopes to shine   53
    as a worthy peer of good Rinaldo, draws
up to his friend and says, "That quarrel is mine.
    I'll clear your path, for in a better cause[20]
you'll as my champion in the future shine."
        This said he leaps to the ground and without pause
        begins the perilous attack. Now high,
        now low, he makes his blade lunge, slash and fly.

Both are expert to strike or parry, and   54
    both have stout limbs and valiant hearts afire.
Both well know when to press ahead or stand
    or when to yield to fury and retire,
so that they fight two long hours hand-to-hand,
    venting in blows now fast, now slow, their ire.
        Then luck begins to turn, and before long
        Ysolier seems more dexterous and strong.

Rinaldo

L'audace Ispan, ch'avere il meglio scorge   55
    di questa pugna, l'animo rinfranca,
e tanto in lui la forza accresce e sorge,
    quanto dechina nel nemico e manca;
tal che sì gravi colpi a l'altro porge,
    e sì lo preme, lo raggira e stanca,
        ch'egli loro la strada a forza cesse,
        come che regger più non si potesse.

The doughty Spaniard, sensing victory,   55
    enfranchises his spirit, and the more
he gains in power, the more his enemy
    declines in strength from what he was before.
Soon the great blows descend so heavily
    and press him, hem him in and tire him sore,
        that he perforce gives way and, thus controlled,
        yields them the road he can no longer hold.

CANTO TERZO

Poi che partir l'Ispano e 'l buon Rinaldo,   *1*
*   onde già vinto avean l'estran guerriero,*
l'estran, cui 'l genitor nomò Ransaldo,
*   e poi cognominar gli effetti il Fiero,*
per molte parti, or al lucente e caldo
*   ciel giro errando, or a l'algente e nero;*
*   né giamai ritrovar ventura alcuna*
*   nel chiaro giorno, o ne la notte bruna.*

Scontrano al fin un dì, la manca sponda   *2*
*   calcando ch'a la Senna il corso affrena,*
un cavalier che l'arme sue circonda
*   con sopravesta d'or trapunta e piena,*
cui ne lo scudo la maritim'onda
*   mostra il mezzo più bel de la Sirena.*
*   Grande è 'l guerriero e di robuste membra,*
*   e tutto nerbo ed osso in vista sembra.*

Questi, scorto Rinaldo: — Ah, pur t'ho giunto,   *3*
*   grida, malvagio cavalier villano! —*
Fu ciò dire e ferir tutto in un punto:
*   grave il ferir con l'una e l'altra mano.*
Raddoppia il colpo, e ne la tempia a punto
*   il garzon coglie, e già no 'l coglie in vano:*
*   ché lui, ch'allor di ciò non si guardava,*
*   da l'arcion quasi tramortito cava.*

Rinaldo, ch'al colpir doppio e possente   *4*
*   s'era a Baiardo su la groppa steso,*
risorto su dopoi, come si sente
*   in cotal modo ingiustamente offeso,*
raggirando il destrier sprona repente
*   tutto di rabbia e di furore acceso;*
*   sprona il destriero al suo nemico addosso,*
*   come verso il cinghial suole il molosso.*

CANTO THREE

When good Rinaldo and the Spaniard came 1
    away from where they had left to his defeat
that stranger knight (Ransaldo was his name,
    later surnamed "the Fierce" for some great feat),
they wandered far and wide without fixed aim
    in chilling dark and bright sun's scalding heat,
        nor did a new adventure meet their sight
        either by day or in the gloom of night.

One day at last they found, skirting the shore 2
    by which the river Seine's course is controlled,
a knight who over his plated armor wore
    a tasseled surcoat damasked all in gold,
upon whose shield the fair siren of yore
    was shown amid great waves that round her rolled.
        He was a warrior huge and stout of limb,
        all bone and sinew by the look of him.

He, seeing Rinaldo, cried: "Ha! Do you now 3
    come back again, you foul, dishonored knight?"
and even as he cried thus, struck a blow,
    grasping his sword in both hands, of such might,
and struck again, so that upon the brow
    he smote the youngster, nor did vainly smite,
        for, caught off guard, he reeled and bowed his head
        and slumped in his saddle like a man struck dead.

Rinaldo, who at that strong, double blow, 4
    had bent down over Bayard's croup, at once
recovering and feeling himself so
    unjustly set upon, at this mischance
gave spur and turned his steed upon his foe,
    mad fury flashing in his every glance.
        Toward his enemy he spurs his steed,
        like mastiff at a boar, but with more speed.

Rinaldo

Ma quel con un fendente al capo mira,   5
    e poi la spada in giù fischiando abbassa;
l'altro il suo bon corsier da parte tira,
    sì che senza toccarlo il colpo passa;
indi ver' lui velocemente il gira,
    e sotto gli si caccia e l'urta e squassa;
        poi, fuor tratto il pugnale, il destro fianco
        percotendo gli piaga e 'l braccio manco.

Lo stran col pomo de la spada il tocca   6
    ne le tempie, nel viso e ne la testa,
con forza tal ch'a terra ogni altra rocca
    avria gittata, e lui conquassa e pesta;
e gli trae fuor per l'elmo e da la bocca
    sangue e dal naso. Intanto non s'arresta
        Rinaldo, ma col ferro il destro ciglio
        di piaga doppia a quel rende vermiglio.

Mentre fan pugna i due guerrieri atroce,   7
    atroce pugna ancor fanno i destrieri:
e questo a quello, e quello a questo noce
    con urti, calci e morsi orrendi e feri.
Ma Baiardo a la fin, il più feroce
    tra gli animai, non solo intra' corsieri,
        manda con l'urto sol l'altro sossopra,
        e sotto va 'l signor, resta egli sopra.

Sopra resta il destrier, sotto 'l signore,   8
    con la diritta gamba e 'l dritto braccio;
opra egli per levarsi arte e vigore,
    né puote uscir però da quello impaccio.
Intanto il sangue, da le vene fuore
    fuggendo, reso omai l'avria di giaccio,
        ma Rinaldo gentil non men che forte
        non soffrì che 'n tal modo ei gisse a morte.

Smonta il barone e lo disgrava, e ancora   9
    con mano il leva ond'egli steso giace;
poi si ritira indietro e gli dice: — Ora
    finiam la guerra, se così ti piace. —
Quegli che 'n stato tal si trova allora,
    che bramar dee più ch'il pugnar la pace,
        con atto umile il capo a lui chinando,
        gli porse per lo pomo il forte brando,

Canto Three

The other, parrying, over his head took aim   5
    and his blade, whistling, fell with force immense,
but he by a side-ways pivot of his charger came
    safely away. At once, back on the offense,
he wheels back, ducking, hurtling toward the frame
    of his opponent, grapples him and sends
        his dagger's point into his right flank. Then,
        slashing his arm, he stabs and stabs again.

The stranger to his temples, brow and head   6
    addressed his pummel with such monstrous power
that a great cliff would have groundward plummeted
    thus beat upon, and at those buffets' shower
Rinaldo through his helmet's openings bled
    from mouth and nose, and still he did not cower,
        but with his point twice made vermilion trace
        a gory trail across his foeman's face.

While the two knights pursue that horrid fight   7
    their coursers also wage atrocious war
They leap and push, they kick and thrust and bite,
    both causing painful wounds that drip with gore.
Bayard at last, that creature of most might
    among, not merely steeds, but all beasts, bore
        in a leap the other down and made him drop,
        tumbling his master with his horse on top.

His horse on top, his master lies below,   8
    right foot and right arm quite pinned down. He tries
by strength and skill to raise himself, but no
    efforts to wrench free of that weight suffice.
By then the blood's uninterrupted flow
    from out his veins had left him cold as ice,
        but Rinaldo, no less courteous than strong,
        thought that to let him die like this was wrong.

The knight dismounts, and as he groans, confined,   9
    puts out his hand to raise him whence he lay.
Then he steps back and says, in accents kind,
    "Now let us, if it please you, stop this fray."
He, who by then was truly of a mind
    to prefer peace to warfare, straight away,
        bowing with a most humble gesture, tendered
        his sword to him hilt first, and so surrendered.

e gli dice: — *Guerrier, mi chiamo vinto*   10
      non men che di valor, di cortesia,
ché già sarei miseramente estinto
      se non m'aitava tua bontà natia;
e credo che l'altr'ier tu fussi spinto
      d'altra cagione, e non da villania,
            a farmi quanto allor tu mi facesti,
            quando i nostri cavalli ambo uccidesti. —

A tai voci le ciglia il giovinetto   11
      per meraviglia inarca, e dice poi:
— Non fu 'l mio onor mai sì da me negletto,
      che 'l ferro oprassi contra i destrier tuoi,
perché d'ogni guerriero è 'ndegno effetto
      piagar cavalli de' nemici suoi:
            né mai t'offesi ancor, s'io non vaneggio,
            né mai visto altra volta aver ti creggio. —

Questo sentendo lo stranier barone,   12
      per maraviglia anch'egli immoto resta,
e intentamente il buon figliol d'Amone
      prende a mirar dal piè sino a la testa.
Tutto con gli occhi il cerca, e la cagione
      de l'error chiara scorge e manifesta:
            scorge lo scudo, ov'è dipinto Amore,
            esser stato cagion di questo errore.

Onde dice: — Signore, un cavaliero   13
      tanto villan quanto tu sei cortese,
ch'anco ei ne va di quell'insegna altero
      ch'adorna te, fu quel che già m'offese;
ed io cui l'ira e 'l giusto sdegno e fero,
      il distinguer da l'un l'altro contese,
            da lo scudo ingannato al primo sguardo
            a ferirti non fui pigro né tardo. —

Voleva oltre seguire e 'l tutto dirgli   14
      di quel villan guerriero a parte a parte;
ma Rinaldo che vede il sangue uscirgli
      in molta copia da più d'una parte,
vol, pria che segua il resto a discoprirgli,
      ch'Isolier, che sapea la medica arte,
            la qual già tra guerrieri in pregio fue,
            la cura prenda de le piaghe sue.

"I confess myself defeated, Sir," he said,   10
    "no less by your great courtesy than by
your bravery, for I would now be dead
    had not your native goodness aided me.
And surely you the other day were led
    by different motives than mere villainy
        to attack us so unfairly as to pounce
        upon us and to slaughter both our mounts."

The youth, astonished, opens wide his eyes   11
    hearing these words, then says: "Indeed,
never could I my honor so much disprize
    as to use my weapon's edge against your steed,
since it is foul disgrace for any knight who tries
    to make the horses of his foemen bleed.
        I don't know when I slighted you or how.
        I swear I never saw you until now."

The stranger warrior, hearing this, stood quite   12
    motionless also, addled and distressed.
Then with more careful scrutiny that knight
    eyed Aymon's gallant son from heel to crest.
He looked and soon discovered in plain sight
    the cause of his mistake made manifest:
        the painted shield where Cupid stood displayed
        had led him to the error he had made.

Wherefore he says "There was a knight who came,   13
    as full of vice as you of courtesy,
bearing a shield embellished with the same
    device as yours. He struck and wounded me,
and I, in whom fierce anger and hot shame
    burned and contended for the mastery,
        deceived at first glance by the shield you carry,
        in my assault upon you did not tarry."

He was going to say more and in detail   14
    relate that miscreant's actions from the start,
but now Rinaldo, seeing his spirits fail
    since blood gushes in streams from many a part,
desired, before attending all his tale,
    that Ysolier, skilled in medicinal art —
        in those days prized in warriors — should attend
        the hurts he had received and make them mend.

Poi che d'ogni sua piaga ei fu curato,   15
    così ragiona il cavaliero estrano:
— Io me 'n venia là donde assediato
    si tien da Carlo il popolo africano.
Ne l'orride alpi a pena avea passato,
    che donzella trovai d'aspetto umano,
        da cui pregato fui ch'io la menassi
        al suo castel, ch'in riva a Senna stassi.

Io gliel promisi, e di più ancor m'offersi   16
    d'assicurarli in ogni parte il calle;
così insieme n'andiam, luoghi diversi
    lasciandoci ad ognor dopo le spalle,
ove per lei fatiche aspre soffersi.
    Giunghiamo al fine un giorno in una valle:
        quivi scontriamo un cavalier feroce,
        il qual mi disse con superba voce:

"Dammi tosto, guerrier, questa donzella,   17
    né punto replicare a quel ch'io chieggio:
perché poscia non sol perderai quella,
    ma t'avverrà, se son qual fui, via peggio.
Dama sì vaga, sì leggiadra e bella,
    a te non si convien, per quel ch'io veggio,
        quanto essa è bella, ed io gagliardo sono:
        tu per lei sembri inutile e non buono."

All'altero parlar di quel superbo   18
    diedi io risposta qual si convenia,
dicendo con la lancia: "Or mi riserbo
    a provar quale in te la forza sia;
ben crederò che la possanza e 'l nerbo
    risponder deggia a la tua cortesia."
        Che più parole? Al fine si viene a giostra,
        e ognun di noi la sua virtù qui mostra.

Il primo incontro, ancorché fero e greve,   19
    nullo trasse di noi fuor del cavallo;
ben nel petto colui piaga riceve,
    che 'l rosso aggiunge al color verde e giallo.
Egli, ch'a ciò conosce che non leve
    il vincer fora, accorto del suo fallo,
        ver' me tornando con l'intera lancia
        passò scortese al mio destrier la pancia.

Canto Three

After his wounds were seen to and his pain   15
    had eased, the stranger warrior spoke anew:
"I was returning from where Charlemagne
    besieged the African's unnumbered crew
and had just crossed the Alps' harsh passes, when
    I met a maid[21] of pleasant aspect who
        begged me to be her escort on the way
        to her castle on the Seine. Without delay

I promised — yea, I deeply vowed— that I   16
    would see her safely anywhere she went.
Together, hour by hour, we rode, through high
    and low, onward till she was nearly spent
by sheer exhaustion and began to sigh.
    At last we met, while making our descent
        into a vale, a knight by the roadside
        who me in haughty words like these defied:

'Resign this maid to me at once, good Sir,   17
    nor hesitate an instant, for — I fear —
to hesitate will cost you not just her,
    but, if I'm what I was, something more dear.
So fine a girl, so noble and so fair,
    befits you not as she whom I see here.
        For she's as beautiful as I am brave,
        and you seem worthless even to be her slave.'

The arrogant words thus uttered out of spite   18
    by that proud man I answered fittingly,
saying with lance uplifted high, 'The right
    to test your strength now falls to me.
Though I would rather that your sinews' might
    were matched by courteous grace and chivalry.'
        What need for more words? We without delay,
        mustering our courage, charged into the fray.

At the first onset, though we fiercely pressed,   19
    neither of us threw the other from his steed,
yet he received a wound square in the chest
    that stained his green and yellow jerkin red.
He, knowing by this that triumph in that test
    would be no easy matter, now instead
        lowered his lance and with discourteous force
        thrust it into the bowels of my horse.

Poi sotto la donzella il palafreno 20
    uccide ancora in un medesmo punto;
e veloce se 'n va sì che 'l baleno
    e 'l vento a pena ancor l'avrebbe giunto.
A piedi io resto di stupor ripieno,
    e d'ira insieme e di dolor compunto;
        e come accompagnata ebbi colei,
        in cercar lui rivolsi i passi miei.

Cinque volte ha la notte il suo stellato 21
    manto disteso per lo cielo intorno,
ed altretante Febo a noi recato
    ha nel candido seno il lieto giorno,
da ch'io cotale inchiesta ho cominciato
    per vendicarmi de l'avuto scorno;
        né ritrovar di lui vestigi od orme
        ho mai potuto, o pur chi me n'informe.

Ciò sentendo Rinaldo, allor s'avisa 22
    che questi il cavalier vada cercando
che di verde e di giallo ha la divisa,
    cui lo scudo d'amor tolse ei giostrando;
onde per lui gradir, narra in qual guisa
    ebbe lo scudo, ed in che luogo e quando.
        Del campo chiede poi novella alcuna,
        e come affliga i Saracin Fortuna;

e come ei, che guerrier d'alto valore 23
    gli sembra in vista ed a le fatte prove,
dal campo si diparta, ove 'l suo onore
    molto più chiaro far potria ch'altrove.
E quegli a lui: — Di questo dubbio fuore
    trarrotti, e la cagion ch'a ciò mi move
        pienamente dirò: ma pria ti piaccia
        ch'a la prima dimanda io sodisfaccia.

Tien Carlo la campagna in suo domino, 24
    e le strade del mar liquide, e 'l lito;
ne' forti luochi il campo saracino
    si sta dentro rinchiuso e mal munito;
né soccorso si trova alcun vicino
    che far lo possa in tal periglio ardito;
        e scorge, omai giunto a l'estrema sorte,
        in faccia orrenda la futura morte.

Canto Three

In that same instant, with a sudden slash   20
    of his lance, he killed the lady's palfrey too
and fled so quickly that a lightning flash
    or raging whirlwind scarcely could pursue.
I was left on foot, struck speechless by his rash
    depravity and racked with wrath and rue,
        then turned my steps to seek him by the same
        path upon which I and the lady came.

Five time since then across the sky the night   21
    has come to spread her starry cloak, and five
times Phoebus has brought back the glad daylight
    in his warm bosom, nor could I contrive,
since I began my quest for that vile knight,
    to right my wrong. I found no man alive
        who knew of him or put me on his scent
        or told me who he was or where he went."

Hearing these words, Rinaldo knows straightway   22
    that the man this knight was searching for was he,
decked out in yellow and in green array,
    whose shield of Love he conquered recently.
Therefore, to please him, he proceeds to say
    how, where and when he won it, then feels free
        to ask him about Charles' camp again
        and Fortune's dealings with the Saracen

and how it was that he, who seemed like so   23
    valiant a knight, so apt to do and dare,
had left that camp, in which his honor's glow
    could shine with brighter luster than elsewhere.
Then he to him: "That doubt, I'll have you know,
    racked me as well, and why I came from there
        you presently shall plainly hear rehearsed,
        but let me answer your first question first.

Charles now controls the high sea's watery ways   24
    and all the coast and the adjacent plain.
The Saracen force in scattered strongholds stays
    pent up with scant supplies of arms or grain,
with no help from allies nearby to raise
    its spirits in that peril. Hope seems vain,
        and in the extremes of danger and of fear,
        horror on every face shows death is near.

Di Garba intanto il re, ch'è Sobrin detto,   25
    e d'Arzila il signore, il crudo Atlante,
de' Mori scudo son: quegli perfetto
    cavalier, questi orribile gigante;
fra' paladin d'Orlando il giovanetto
    null'è che più in valor si pregi e vante,
        sì ch'al suo nome il campo avverso trema;
        né meno Atlante e 'l buon Sobrin n'han tema.

Or se tu di sapere hai pur desio   26
    dal campo qual cagion lunge mi mova,
ove assai più ch'in Francia il valor mio
    potrei mostrar con apparente prova,
convien che d'alto ora cominci, e ch'io
    cosa d'un re ti narri estrana e nova;
        d'un re che m'ha mandato al magno Carlo:
        e questi è 'l mio signor, di ch'io ti parlo.

Francardo, che nell'Asia il regno altero   27
    tien dell'Armenia ed altri a quel vicini,
di cui non vede il sol miglior guerriero
    tra quanto chiudon d'Asia i gran confini,
fuor che Mambrino il suo cugin, cui diero
    sovr'umano valor numi divini,
        garzone essendo, de l'amor s'accese
        d'una nobil princessa alta e cortese.

S'accese de l'amor di Clarinea,   28
    del gran re degli Assiri unica figlia;
costei ch'alta prudenza e senno avea,
    oltre ch'era poi bella a maraviglia,
e di Francardo il merto a pien scorgea,
    gli mostrava ad ognor tranquille ciglia,
        e co' casti favori a poco a poco
        in lui maggior rendea d'amore il foco.

Il giovin, che si vede esser sì caro   29
    a la sua donna, al suo sommo diletto,
e ch'essa l'ama di sua vita a paro,
    come si scorge agli occhi ed a l'aspetto,
tanto mostrarle più brama alcun raro
    e de l'alto amor suo condegno effetto,
        e pensa pur con qual più chiaro segno
        le dia del suo voler sicuro pegno.

Only the king of Garba,²² Sobrin hight,   25
   and Atlas, lord of Algiers, in some wise
safeguard the Moors: the one a perfect knight
   the other a giant of appalling size.
But among the Christian paladins in that fight
   no fame higher than young Orlando's flies.
      Hearing his name all foes feel courage fail,
      and even Atlas and Sobrin grow pale.

Now if you still wish me to tell you why   26
   I parted from that martial gathering —
where I indeed more than in France might try
   to give of my true worth a reckoning —
I'll start afresh, so hear me now, while I
   bring strange, unheard-of news about a king —
      a king who sent me to great Charles, for he
      of whom I speak is lord and liege to me.

Francard, who in the Orient holds the proud   27
   rule of Armenia and the lands nearby —
no finer warrior lives where sun or cloud
   dazzle or shade vast Asia's bounds than he,
except perhaps his cousin Mambrin, endowed
   by heaven with more than human bravery —
      was as a boy inflamed with amorous heat
      for a princess high-born, gracious, fair and sweet.

He burned with love for Clarinea who —   28
   sole daughter of Assyria's king, possessed
of wondrous wisdom and discernment too,
   besides her beauty, which was of the best —
at once saw Francard's merit and in due
   course, with calm brow receiving him, expressed,
      little by little, by chaste signs her pleasure,
      thus fueling his love's fire beyond measure.

The young man, finding himself grown so dear   29
   in her eyes, to his infinite delight,
since all her acts and looks have made it clear
   she loves him better than her life or sight,
is all the keener to display some rare
   effect of his own high love and its might
      and ever thinks how he might satisfy her
      with some more absolute pledge of his desire.

Rinaldo

Al fin, per lei gradire, un dì le giura　　　　　30
　　d'andar per l'Asia con proposta tale,
che giamai donna non formò Natura
　　a lei di grazia e di bellezza eguale;
né 'l corpo pria sgravar de l'armatura,
　　che in ogni terra, ogni città reale,
　　　　ed in ogni altro luogo ov'egli vada,
　　　　abbia ciò mantenuto a lancia e spada.

Con tal proposta il mio signor Francardo　　　31
　　si mise a gir per l'Asia intorno errando,
e vinse Dulicon, Tisbo ed Algardo,
　　feri giganti, e 'l re di Tiro Olbrando,
e qual altro più forte era e gagliardo,
　　e sapea meglio oprar la lancia e 'l brando.
　　　　Vinse anco in Babilonia anzi il Soldano
　　　　un mezzo pardo e mezzo corpo umano.

Già vincitor altier se 'n ritornava　　　　32
　　d'ostili spoglie adorno e glorioso,
quand'egli a caso udì che si trovava
　　un tempio in India allor meraviglioso.
Tempio della Beltà quel si nomava,
　　perché di bei ritratti era pomposo:
　　　　quivi eran pinte le più vaghe e belle
　　　　che fêa o sono o fian donne e donzelle.

Vi sono cinque o sei le più pregiate　　　　33
　　d'ogni secol dipinte, e propio quali
le formarà Natura o l'ha formate,
　　perciò che non son quelle opre mortali,
ma già mago, il miglior de la su' etate,
　　che fêa gli effetti al gran sapere eguali,
　　　　v'adoprò gli rei spirti, e mostruose
　　　　orrende fere in guardia poi vi pose.

E nissun può veder quel ch'entro serra　　　34
　　il ricco tempio in sé di vago e bello,
se con due belve pria non viene a guerra,
　　e non le vince in singolar duello.
Ma non produsse mostro unqua la terra
　　o 'l mar, né l'aria ha sì feroce augello,
　　　　che movere a terror Francardo possa:
　　　　ed a l'ardire in lui pari è la possa.

At last, to please her mind, he vowed to ride   30
    the length and breadth of Asia and to face
in mortal battle any who defied
    his challenge that her loveliness and grace
exceeded all, and do so unsupplied
      with armor, till he had in every place
        and in whatever royal seat or land
        maintained this claim with lance and sword in hand.

Armed with that challenge then my Lord Francard   31
    throughout great Asia's lands went sojourning,
felled Dulicon, slew Thisbos and Algard,
    fierce giants both, crushed Olbrand, Tyre's[23] king,
most expert in the use of lance and sword,
      as strong as brave, and in the dust did fling
        the sultan who, half leopard and half man
        ruled Babylon and savage Kurdistan.[24]

The noble victor was now homeward bound,   32
    loaded with glorious enemy spoils, when he
by chance discovered that there might be found
    a temple in India, wonderful to see.
The Temple of Beauty it was called, renowned
    for its array of painted imagery,
        where the loveliest women that had ever been
        alive, or would be living, could be seen.

Culled from the fairest whom each age did prize   33
    some five or six are there portrayed. Each stands,
in the shape that Nature did — or will — devise,
    her effigy not formed by mortal hands
but by a peerless sorcerer and wise
      who could effect all his deep mind's commands
        with demon aid, and he all entry barred
        by a pair of monsters conjured for their guard.

None could behold the riches hid among   34
    that temple's treasures, marvelous and fair,
unless he first engaged two beasts that sprung
    at him in single fight and slew them there.
But never a monster spawned by earth or flung
      from ocean depths or pouncing from the air
        could cause dismay in Francard's heart, for he
        had strength that equaled his audacity.

Questi, di tempio tal la fama udendo,   35
    girne a vederlo si dispose al tutto;
né temeva il ferino impeto orrendo,
    ch'altrui spesso recò di morte lutto;
ma tra sé nel pensier gia disponendo
    d'eguare al basso suol quel tempio tutto,
        s'ivi non era, e nel più degno loco,
        lei che è cagion del suo vivace foco.

Al tempio giunto, i guardiani uccise,   36
    e l'entrata per forza egli s'aprio;
indi a mirar il bel lavor si mise,
    il già fatto pensier posto in oblio,
ché quella vista allor da lui divise
    il primiero amoroso suo desio,
        tanta quivi s'unia grazia e bellezza,
        che poco Clarinea più cura e prezza.

Ancor ch'in Clarinea Natura accolti   37
    aggia bei doni e doti illustri e rare,
tanti ivi son sì ben formati volti,
    che non più vaga o bella essa gli pare;
quel di colei non v'è tra' varii e molti
    che si veggiono il tempio intorno ornare,
        e più d'un altro ancor leggiadro e vago
        non stimò degno di tal luogo il mago.

Sotto i vaghi ritratti in lettere d'oro   38
    la patria, il nome e 'l sangue è dichiarato,
e quando dee de le bellezze loro
    la terra adorna far cortese fato;
ma fra quante seran, sono o pur foro
    donne giamai di vago aspetto e grato,
        una che sotto avea Clarice scritto
        ha 'l cor del mio signore arso e trafitto.

O fosse suo destino, o perciò ch'ella   39
    vive ed è di su' età nel primo fiore,
sì che puote sperar di possedella,
    ché da la speme in noi nasce l'amore,
o che vincesse l'altre in esser bella,
    per lei solo arse d'amoroso ardore.
        L'altre ben pregia sì molto ed ammira,
        ma per lei solamente arde e sospira.

Canto Three

Soon as he learned that temple's fame, to find   35
     it out was his first thought, to force access
his next, despite those beasts of hellish kind
     that unnerved all else with extreme distress.
But he determined in his inmost mind
     to level the temple to the ground, unless
        he found her there, and high above the rest,
        who lit the flame that burned within his breast.

He finds the temple, dares the guards to fight,   36
     kills them and smashes down the gate, then lets
himself begin the labors of sweet sight —
     and all he first resolved upon, forgets.
For what he now sees separates him quite
     from what first tangled him in amorous nets —
        a vision of such loveliness and grace,
        it makes a blank of Clarinea's face.

Though Nature in Clarinea made appear   37
     the rarest gifts fame blazoned in her day,
he sees so many such well-formed faces here,
     she seems to him no lovelier than they,
nor does her picture hang where, far and near,
     the temple of its beauties makes display,
        for many as fair as she, or fairer, were
        found wanting by the cunning sorcerer.

Name, land and lineage of each maid on view   38
     were stamped below in characters of gold,
and when her godlike form moved known unto
     mortals on earth in courtly wise was told.
But of all future beauties, or those who
     were now alive or lived in days of old,
        one, beneath whom the name of 'Clarice' shone,
        burned and transfixed my master's heart alone.

Whether by fate, or else because he knows   39
     she lives, and in the flower of youth, whence came
hope he might have her — for love ever grows
     from hope and hope gives it an aim —
or since her beauty all others' overthrows,
     for her alone his heart is set aflame.
        The others he might prize and much admire,
        but sighs for her, for her burns in love's fire.

Tôrre ei l'imagin volse che sospesa   40
    era presso l'altar gemmato e sacro,
ove in chiaro cristal lampade accesa
    fêa lume di Ciprigna al simulacro;
ma fu sua cura in ciò fallace resa
    dal mirabil saper del morto Anacro,
        che così nome avea quel negromante,
        Zoroastro novel, novello Atlante.

Sì che vedendo vana ogni fatica   41
    pur riuscirsi, e vano ogni disegno,
indi ritrar fe' la sua cara amica
    in carta, in tela, in bronzo, in marmo e 'n legno.
Gli artefici fur tai ch'oggi a fatica
    altri si troveria di lor più degno;
        ed opra fe' ciascun che viva sembra
        a l'aria, agli atti, al garbo de le membra.

Con quei cari ritratti egli a se stesso   42
    fece più giorni dilettosa froda.
Al fine il crudo Amor non gli ha concesso
    che di sì dolci inganni omai più goda;
ma gli ha fero desio nel petto impresso,
    nel petto che più sempre arde ed annoda,
        desio di non fruire il falso e l'ombra,
        ma 'l vivo e 'l vero che gl'inganni sgombra.

Sì che omai non potendo il suo desire   43
    sofferir più, ch'ognor cresce e s'avanza,
ha mandato al gran Carlo ad offerire
    domar de' Mori ei sol l'alta possanza,
e fargli tosto dall'Europa uscire,
    togliendo lor del ritornar baldanza,
        s'egli per moglie li darà la bella
        Clarice, ch'è del re guascon sorella.

Egli sa ben che sia Clarice suora   44
    d'Ivon, ch'a la Guascogna il freno impone,
e che di quello il magno Carlo ancora
    come di re vassallo suo dispone;
parte di ciò lesse nel tempio allora
    che di novello amor restò prigione,
        e parte ancor d'un suo baron n'intese,
        cui ben è noto ogni signor francese.

He thought to seize the image, which hung near   40
   a jeweled, consecrated altar-stone
whence, burning in a crystal chandelier
   held by the Cyprian, a fierce radiance shone,
but found his every care frustrated here
   by wizard spells of long-dead Anachrone —
      such was the name of that rich temple's master,
      that new Atlante, that new Zoroaster.[25]

Thus seeing that all effort was in vain,   41
   vain all designs to carry it away,
he had it copied over and over again
   on canvas, bronze, in marble, wood and clay.
His artists were so skilled and took such pain,
   none worthier of that task exists today.
      Each wrought a work that seemed alive, exact
      in every garment, gesture, air and act.

In these beloved likenesses he now   42
   for many days took solitary pleasure.
But cruel Love at last will not allow
   the sweet deceit of that imagined treasure
and makes his heart to fierce desire bow —
   his heart that burns and aches beyond all measure —
      desire that, weary of shadows, ever vies
      for life and truth to melt the mist of lies.

So that, impatient with this hot desire   43
   that grows and plagues him so incessantly,
he now has sent to Charlemagne to inquire
   whether, if his great power set him free
of the Moorish hordes and forced them to retire
   at once with no hope of returning, he
      might deign to let him wed and eastward bring
      fair Clarice, sister to the Gascon king.

That Clarice had a brother, and that his name   44
   was Ives, the ruler of the Gascons, who
was a vassal from whom Charlemagne could claim
   allegiance — all of these were things he knew.
He had partly read them in the temple when he came
   to leave his old love's service for his new,
      and partly heard one of his barons tell,
      who knew the French nobility full well.

Rinaldo

Se Carlo gliela dà, come si crede,   45
    e come in campo chiaro grido suona,
ei le concederà che la sua fede
    ritegni, se le par verace e buona:
e nascendo di loro alcuno erede
    a la real d'Armenia alta corona,
        vol che di Cristo ancora sia quel seguace,
        com'è ciascun ch'al franco re soggiace.

Io tai condizioni ho già proposto   46
    in nome di Francardo al magno Carlo,
né gli ho tenuto il rimanente ascosto:
    che s'ei ricusarà di sodisfarlo,
ha l'invitto mio sir tra sé disposto
    di congiungersi a' Mori, e di spogliarlo
        di quanto tiene, e poi Clarice tôrsi,
        mal grado di ciascun che voglia opporsi.

Ma benigna risposta il re m'ha dato,   47
    piena di cortesia, piena di spene.
Al fin nulla ha concluso e s'è scusato,
    ché 'l risolvermi a lui non si conviene;
onde ad Ivone io ne son poscia andato,
    a cui dispor di ciò più s'appertiene:
        rispost'ha quel che, pria ch'affermi o nieghi,
        vol saper se Clarice il cor vi pieghi.

Vol pria che si risolva, esso mi dice,   48
    saper qual la sorella aggia pensiero,
e qual la lor antiqua genitrice,
    c'ha sovra lei via più d'ogn'altro impero.
Mi mossi io stesso a ritrovar Clarice
    per far quanto conviensi a messaggiero,
        e quei che 'l re mi diede in compagnia,
        nel passar l'alpi mi smarrir tra via.

Or questa, o cavalier, è la cagione   49
    che mi trasse dal campo in queste parti,
e diedi alto principio al mio sermone,
    perciò ch'in tutto a pien bramo appagarti;
e perch'ancor venendo occasione,
    se vali in ciò, possi con quella oprarti,
        sì che non sdegni in Asia esser reina,
        né tiri Francia a l'ultima ruina. —

If Charles gives her to him — as many say   45
    he will, and so the whole camp's rumor flies —
she may keep her religion, if that way
    seems true and good in her eyes, he agrees.
And if an heir is born to wield the sway
    of great Armenia's royal seignories,
        he too may follow Christ, he fully grants,
        since all kings must who are subject to France.

In Francard's name, empowered to produce   46
    these terms, I brought them to great Charles' court
nor hid the rest: that if he should refuse
    or say they are ungenerous or fall short,
Francard will join the Moorish cause and use
    his matchless power to work his ruin: in short,
        strip him of all he has and by main force
        seize Clarice, and no man shall stop his course.

But the king makes kind reply and thus contrives   47
    politely to keep hope alive, without
concluding matters, and I see he strives
    to keep his council and keep me in doubt.
Wherefore I later went to seek out Ives
    and told him what the parley was about,
        who answered that he first would have to know
        Clarice's mind ere he said yes or no.

He had to know, said he, before he made   48
    any decision, where his sister stood,
and his old mother, whose opinions weighed
    in the family's mind more than all others could.
I then set out for France, bent to persuade
    Clarice myself, as a trusty envoy should.
        I had escorts from the king, but as we crossed
        over the Alps, they, to a man, were lost.

So now, sir knight, you know the reason why   49
    I left the camp and why you find me here.
That is the gist of all I say, and I
    to you above all want it to be clear,
since you might have occasion by and by
    to tell her if you chance to gain her ear
        that her refusal to be Asia's queen
        would doom all France to endless grief and teen."

Mentre parlava il cavalier pagano,   50
 d'ira Rinaldo ardeva e di dispetto,
e du'o tre volte a farli un fero e strano
 gioco fu quasi da lo sdegno astretto.
Poi che si tacque, disse: — Ahi! quanto insano
 e cieco il tuo signore ha l'intelletto,
  se pur si crede con sua spada e lancia
  porre spavento ai cavalier di Francia.

Venga oltre pur con le sue genti indotte,   51
 vili e poco atte al bel mistier di Marte,
che fian le corna a sua superbia rotte
 e l'alto orgoglio suo dęmo in gran parte.
Ma se dormir non brama eterna notte,
 ed ha di sana mente alcuna parte,
  tra noi moglie giamai più non ricerchi,
  né la sua morte con minaccie or merchi. —

Così detto, da quel commiato prende   52
 col cavaliero ispan in compagnia,
il qual di gir con lui tanto contende
 ch'ei gli concede quel che men desia;
tacito vanne, e l'aria intorno accende
 di cheto foco che del petto uscia,
  di cheto foco ne' sospiri accolto,
  che muti uscian dal cor tra pene involto.

Volve e rivolve quanto dianzi gli have   53
 de la Sirena il cavalier narrato,
e gli apre in questa Amor con dura chiave
 a pensier varii il core arso e piagato;
desira e spera e 'n un dubbioso pave,
 da varii affetti afflitto e conturbato:
  ed ora quello a questo, or questo a quello
  cede, e fan nel suo petto aspro duello.

Non quando avien che ne l'aereo regno   54
 aspro furore i venti a pugna tiri,
e 'n dubbio stato a l'inimico sdegno
 or l'uno ceda, or l'altro, e si ritiri,
gira intorno sì spesso il mobil segno,
 che d'alto mostra a noi qual aura spiri;
  come a diversi affetti egli sovente
  raggira e piega l'aggitata mente.

Rinaldo, while the pagan warrior spoke,   50
    felt indignation well up in his breast
and twice or thrice felt tempted by some stroke
    to vent a wrath too strong to be repressed,
then broke his silence, crying: "Is this some joke?
    Your master must be mad, or blind at best,
        if he indeed thinks that his sword or lance
        could ever terrify a knight of France.

Let him come on then, this way let him ride   51
    with his unwarlike, faint-heart regiments,
he'll see how we can break the horns of pride
    and tame his arrogance and drive him hence.
But if he is loath that endless night should hide
    his name and keeps some scrap of common sense,
        let him not seek for wives from us and by
        threats purchase nothing but defeat and die."

This said, he took his leave, and again set out,   52
    accompanied by the Spanish knight, who pressed
to go with him with ardor so devout
    that he agreed, though solitude seemed best.
He rides in silent thought, but round about
    the air feels the still fire from his breast,
        the silent flame that speaks in sighs he heaves
        from the depths of a mute heart that aches and grieves.

Over and over he revolves each thing   53
    the Siren Knight had said that made him smart.
Love's iron key unlocks the gates to bring
    fierce foes into his burnt and wounded heart.
Desire fights Fear, Fear fights Desire, the sting
    of Doubt poisons all fancies from the start.
        Now this, now that seems better or worse to do,
        and both in bitter war his breast imbrue.

No more inconstantly with furious din   54
    do whirlwinds rush to battle to and fro
in the black sky and turn, now out, now in,
    each bent upon the other's overthrow,
no faster flags on summits flap and spin,
    to show which way the fitful tempests blow,
        than he now reels in thoughts of every kind
        and twists and racks his agitated mind.

Rinaldo

Con occhi chini e ciglia immote e basse 55
gran pezzo andò 'l garzon poco giocondo,
sin che trovò per via cosa che 'l trasse
e lo destò da quel pensier profondo;
e fe' che gli occhi a rimirar alzasse
spettacol vago, a pochi altri secondo:
due feroci guerrier d'arme guarniti,
che dotta mano in bronzo avea scolpiti.

Sta l'uno contra l'altro a dirimpetto 56
in vista altera, audace e minacciosa;
tengon con l'una man lo scudo stretto,
e l'altra in resta pon lancia nerbosa;
di ferro ella non è, ma del perfetto
mastro è pur opra, come ogni altra cosa;
lor per mezzo attraversa un breve motto,
l'un "Tristan" dice, e l'altro "Lancillotto".

Spiran vive dal lucido metallo 57
le faccie ove il valor scolpito siede;
annitrir sotto loro ogni cavallo
diresti, e che co' piè la terra fiede.
Indi, discosto poi breve intervallo,
ampio e vago pilastro alzar si vede,
ove ne' bianchi e ben politi marmi
son scritti in note d'oro alquanti carmi.

Mira Rinaldo la bella opra, e 'ntanto 58
novo ed alto stupore il cor gli assale:
l'opra ch'a l'altre toglie il pregio e 'l vanto,
cui Fidia alcuna mai non fece eguale,
o il mio Danese, ch'a lui sovra or tanto
s'erge quanto egli sovra gli altri sale;
indi risguarda il marmo in terra fitto,
e vede che così dicea lo scritto:

"Qui già il gran Lancillotto e 'l gran Tristano 59
fêr parangon de le lor forze estreme;
quest'aere, questo fiume e questo piano
de' lor gran colpi ancor rimbomba e geme.
Questi guerrier che da maestra mano
impressi in bronzo qui veggonsi insieme,
sono i ritratti lor, tali essi furo
quando fêro il duello orrendo e duro.

Eyes on the ground, with frozen countenance   55
    the youth rode a long while in little cheer,
distracted, nor did any circumstance
    to break his deep thought meet his eye or ear.
At last one day, chancing to raise his glance,
    he saw a strange, uncanny sight draw near:
        two powerful knights, in armor cap-a-pie,
        sculpted in bronze with peerless artistry.

In their posture, as they faced each other, true   56
    daring and pride and menace were expressed.
Grasping a shield in one hand sat those two,
    and in the other a strong lance at rest —
a lance not made of bronze, though the master who
    wrought it here too wrought at his best.
        Beneath that pair, inscriptions marked the spot.
        Tristan was one, the other Lancelot.[26]

From glinting bronze a living valor glows   57
    on their bold faces as they gaze around,
and seeing their horses, you'd almost suppose
    you heard their neighs' and hoof-beats' thunderous sound.
Then, after a brief interval, there rose
    a high and shapely column from the ground
        on whose smooth, white marble letters of pure gold
        in verse the legend of these statues told.

Rinaldo gaped in wonder seeing how   58
    that splendid work all marks of beauty bore,
a work so fine that experts would allow
    Phidias[27] could not improve upon it, nor
my own Danese,[28] who outdoes him now
    as much as he outdid all those before.
        Then, looking at the column again, he read
        the inscription on its marble base, which said:

"Great Lancelot and great Tristan here of old   59
    made trial of the utmost of their might.
Through the air of these hills and these valleys rolled
    the thunderous echoes of that furious fight.
Here now their effigies, in bronze and gold
    wrought by a master's hand, gleam in the light.
        These are their likenesses, even such were they
        when they in horrid combat met that day.

Queste le lancie fur, ch'a scontro acerbo   60
   reggendo sì restar salde ed intere,
perciò che tutte son d'osso e di nerbo
   d'alcune strane incognosciute fere.
Io per due cavalier qui le riserbo,
   ch'abbin più di costor forza e potere:
      chi non fia tale, altrui lassi la prova,
      ché nulla in van l'aventurarsi giova."

Il paladin, che già più volte avea   61
   di tal ventura l'alta fama udito,
disse a l'Ispan, che nulla ne sapea
   e stava tutto stupido e smarito,
che 'l gran mago Merlin, che sol potea
   tai cose far, coloro avea scolpito,
      e fatte ancor le strane lancie, e poi
      datele in dono a' due famosi eroi;

ma che le pose qui, morti i guerrieri,   62
   u' da lui posti anco i ritratti foro,
fin ch'altri duo via più ne l'arme feri
   venghino a trarle da le man costoro.
Ciò sentendo l'Ispan, che tra gli altieri
   portava il vanto, disse: — Or forse soro
      ti parerò più che parer non soglio;
      pur sì strana ventura io tentar voglio. —'

Così detto la man bramosa stende,   63
   e di Tristan la grossa lancia afferra;
ma 'l suo desir la statua a lui contende,
   e col calcio di quella il caccia a terra.
Oh quante cose orribili e stupende
   fece in Francia Merlino e in Inghilterra,
      ch'eccedeno del vero ogni credenza,
      e di sogni e di fole hanno apparenza!

Ponvi Rinaldo anch'ei tosto la mano   64
   con somma forza e con dubbiosa mente.
China 'l capo la statua di Tristano,
   e 'l pugno aprendo l'asta a lui consente:
l'asta, da molti già tirata in vano,
   ora concede al cavalier possente.
      Egli s'inchina, ché 'l suo gran valore
      fu di quel di Rinaldo assai minore.

These were the lances wielded by these two,   60
    still sound and whole, for they are made
of bone from a strange creature hitherto
    unknown to men. Here they now stand displayed,
destined by me for two great champions who
    shall be still mightier and more unafraid.
        Let lesser men from the attempt refrain,
        for no man should go venturing in vain."

The paladin, to whom this quest was known   61
    through intermittent rumors formerly,
now told the Spaniard, who knew nothing, thrown
    into mute wonder that such things could be,
that the great magus Merlin, who alone
    could do such work, had carved these, and that he
        had made these wondrous lances too and then
        freely bestowed them on these two great men,

but after their demise had placed them here,   62
    each statue gripping his enchanted lance,
until another brave pair should appear
    in days to come and wrest them from their hands.
The Spaniard — who was known to have no peer
    for courage — then exclaimed: "Now I perchance
        can show you what I'm made of. Perhaps I
        am destined for this venture. Let me try."

This said, he reached out eagerly to take   63
    the mighty shaft of Tristan's lance, but found
the statue made him toil and strain and quake,
    then with a great kick threw him on the ground.
Ah, Merlin, what great portents you would make
    once upon French and English soil abound!
        Beyond belief, each of your wonders seems
        a lying fable or the stuff of dreams!

Then did Rinaldo also place his hand   64
    fiercely upon it, after some delay.
Lo! Tristan's statue bowed before him and
    opened his fist, yielding the shaft straightway.
That shaft that many vainly would command
    he now entrusts to that great warrior's sway.
        He bows, and by that bow makes clearly known
        Rinaldo's worth as greater than his own.

Rinaldo

Simplice infante non sì lieto coglie
    dal suo natio rampollo il frutto caro,
né lieto sì, né con sì ingorde voglie
    prende ricco tesor povero avaro,
come ei con pronte brame allegro toglie
    la grave antenna ch'altri in van bramaro;
        ma perché il più fermarsi a lor non giova,
      se 'n vanno a ritrovar ventura nova.

65

Canto Three

A simple child will from its native bough
    pluck the desired fruit with no more pleasure,
nor greedy pauper with more joyous brow
    gather a lavish, long-desired treasure,
as he what many sought before him now
    seizes. He pulls the heavy shaft at leisure,
        then, with no wish to linger longer, they
        in search of new adventure rode away.

Canto quarto

Mentre di Senna la superba sponda
   premendo van Rinaldo ed Isoliero,
veggion, là donde al mar la rapida onda
   porta dal natio fonte il fiume altero,
barca venir con lieta aura seconda
   solcando il molle e liquido sentiero,
     di fiori e frondi e d'aurei panni ornata,
     e la vela d'argento al ciel spiegata.

Quivi vaghe donzelle ai dolci accenti
   con mastra e dotta man rendon concorde
il chiaro suon de' musici stromenti,
   toccando a tempo le sonore corde;
molce l'alta armonia gli irati venti,
   e 'l lor corso raffrena a l'acque sorde,
     e tragge fuor da le stagnanti linfe
     guizzanti pesci e lascivette ninfe.

Se 'n viene a par al bel legno reale,
   per l'onde no, ma per l'erbose rive,
con strana pompa un carro trionfale,
   portando un coro di terrestri dive.
Ha l'asse aurato, e varia orientale
   gemma indi sparge fiamme ardenti e vive;
     ha le rote anco aurate, e 'n varii modi
     distinte poi d'argentee lame e chiodi.

La somma parte del bel carro intorno
   purpura copre a vaghi fior contesta,
cui fregia e parte un bel ricamo adorno
   di perle sparse a guisa di tempesta.
Bianco elefante, che farebbe scorno
   de l'Apennino a la nevosa testa,
     de' seggi è la materia, e poi va l'opra
     a l'eletta materia assai di sopra.

1

2

3

4

CANTO FOUR

While riding swiftly by the Seine's proud shore   1
  Ysolier and the good Rinaldo mark,
reaching a place where rushing currents bore
  the river seaward from his source, a bark[29]
swiftly propelled over the liquid floor
  by a fresh breeze along a gentle arc,
    decked in green boughs and flowers and cloth of gold,
    with sail of silver to the sky unrolled.

Aboard it lovely damsels stand and sing.   2
  playing upon sweet instruments that fill
the air with dulcet music, voice and string
  moving in time and with such peerless skill
that the clear notes tame raging winds and bring
  deaf roaring waves to note them and be still.
    From oozy depths they lure the fish that glisten
    and make lascivious sea-nymphs rise and listen.

To meet that royal carrack presently —   3
  not through the waves, but through the grass —
    draws nigher
a wondrous chariot, rolling solemnly,
  on which terrestrial deities sing in choir.
Its golden axles, etched with filigree
  make orient gems shoot living sparks of fire.
    Its wheels, too, are of gold, chased with details
    of shining silver on their rims and nails.

That lovely chariot's upper deck is bound   4
  with flower-studded crimson tapestries,
which trim and intersect a silken ground
  all strewn with pearls like wave-tips in a breeze.
A ivory white sufficient to confound
  the blaze from brows of snow on Alpine screes
    sets off the stuff whose workmanship transcends
    the rich material in its excellence.

Rinaldo

Diece gran cervi c'han candido il netto   5
   pelo, e dipinte le ramose corna,
cu' il collo cerchio d'or lucido e schietto,
   e freno d'auro ancor la bocca adorna,
scorti da donne avezze al degno effetto,
   tirano il carro dov'Amor soggiorna;
      e vanno intorno a quel cento guerrieri,
      di bei cavalli e di ricche arme alteri.

Sorge in mezzo del carro un'ampia sede   6
   fra molte altre più basse e meno ornate:
ivi dama real posar si vede
   piena di riverenza e maestate,
che nel pensoso e grave aspetto eccede
   le più vezzose in grazia ed in beltate;
      le fan poscia sedendo un cerchio altero
      donzelle vaghe oltre ogni uman pensiero.

Tal, nel seren d'estiva notte, suole   7
   per le strade del cielo aperte e belle
sul carro gir la suora alma del sole,
   intorno cinta di lucenti stelle;
tal Tetide menar dolci carole
   con le sue ninfe leggiadrette e snelle,
      tirata da' delfin per l'ampio mare,
      quando son l'onde più tranquille e chiare.

L'alta beltà che ne' leggiadri aspetti   8
   tra lor diversi era con grazia unita,
piagato avria quai son più duri petti
   di soave d'amore aspra ferita,
e mosso a dolci ed amorosi affetti
   gli orridi monti del gelato Scita.
      Che meraviglia è, poi, s'ad or ad ora
      ogni spirto gentil se n'innamora?

Tu, del vicino fiume umido dio,   9
   ancor sentisti l'amoroso foco
che dagli occhi lucenti ardendo uscio,
   e 'l tuo freddo liquore a quel fu poco:
ché 'l grand'ardor sotto l'ondoso rio
   s'andò sempre avanzando a poco a poco,
      come infocato acciar che più s'accende
      se l'acqua a stille in lui gocciando scende.

Ten noble stags with pelts of purest white   5
   and painted branching antlers, their proud necks
circled by golden ribbons shining bright,
   each with a golden bridle-bit that decks
its muzzle, draw that chariot of delight,
   led on by squires of the lovely sex.
      An escort of a hundred warriors speeds
      alongside, richly armed, on splendid steeds.

At the chariot's center a great royal chair   6
   mid many others takes the highest place.
A queenly lady is seen seated there,
   majestic, reverend, whose attitude and face
excel in their sweet calm and pensive air
   the loveliest in loveliness and grace,
      and all about her in a noble ring,
      sit ladies fair beyond imagining.

So, through the calm sphere of a summer night,   7
   on wondrous, open highways of the sky
the sun's dear sister, while the stars shine bright
   all round her, guides her car on high.
So Thetis, while her nymphs sing with delight
   and nimbly sport before her, will pass by,
      drawn by a dolphin through the boundless sea
      when all its crystal waves roll clear and free.

That face where ever-varying charms agree,   8
   by grace rendered harmonious and made one
would let all breasts however hard they be
   with bitter wounds of sweet love be undone,
and cause harsh Scythia's[30] frozen alps to see
   their peaks grow warm, by amorous feelings won.
      What marvel then that it should hourly move
      each gentle-natured soul to fall in love?

Even you, damp god of the adjoining stream,   9
   received a sense of the quick amorous heat
that issued from those shining eyes, a gleam
   that your wet chill was powerless to defeat,
for under your cool bed a warmth extreme
   rose bit by bit until it grew complete
      like a piece of molten steel that grows the hotter
      as it is touched by rushing drops of water.

Rinaldo

Ma del fervente ed amoroso caldo 10
    provò la forza e 'l sùbito furore
via più che ciascun altro il buon Rinaldo,
    già prima servo del tiranno Amore.
Sta tutto immoto, e sol non puogli saldo
    restar nel petto il palpitante core,
        che de la donna sua volar nel seno
        vorrebbe, o pur nel volto almo e sereno.

Sedeva con l'illustre alta mogliera 11
    del re de' Franchi, Galerana detta,
in quella degna ed onorata schiera
    la donzella da lui tanto diletta,
ch'a diporto se 'n gia per la riviera,
    ch'i risguardanti a sé leggiadra alletta;
        ond'egli, quella a l'improviso scorta,
        nova fiamma sentio ne l'alma sorta.

E mentre il caro e fiammeggiante viso 12
    di dolce ardor ch'al ciel gli animi tira,
con le ciglia e con gli occhi immoto e fiso,
    e co' pronti desir guardando ammira,
e da diversi affetti entro conquiso,
    or quinci or quindi il pensier vago gira,
        quel gli sovvien che di Clarice udito
        pur dianzi avea dal cavalier ferito.

Qui si ferma egli, e 'l non leggier sospetto 13
    da l'amata beltate in lui s'avanza,
e ricercando in ogni parte il petto
    quasi tutto se 'l fa sua preda e stanza.
Né men dal duolo è oppresso ogni diletto
    in lui, che dal timor sia la speranza;
        e come dentro si conturba, fuora
        sospira, duolsi e si lamenta ancora,

e dice: — Lasso! dunque altrui pur fia 14
    questa bellezza in cui mio cuore alberga?
Rimarrà senza lei la vita mia,
    qual privata di fronde arida verga?
Ahi! crude stelle, ahi! sorte iniqua e ria,
    quando serà che fuor del duolo emerga?
        S'altri d'ogni mio ben, d'ogni mia gioia
        godrassi, oh quando almen serà ch'io moia?

Canto Four

But more than this, the force and sudden heat   10
    of amorous fury wrought inside the breast
of good Rinaldo, already a complete
    slave in the ranks by tyrant Love oppressed.
He stood, not moving, and the pounding beat
    of his poor heart would not be put to rest,
        for it seemed to leap from him toward a place
        within her bosom, or at least her face.

Enthroned among those glorious, ravishing   11
    damsels — they formed the noble retinue
of Galerana, spouse to France's king —
    the maid whom he loved best had met his view.
Anon she stepped ashore, seeming to bring
    perfect delight to every gaze she drew,
        and he, as she approached him, gave a start,
        feeling a new blaze kindled in his heart.

And while he turns his still-fixed brow and eyes   12
    toward that face so dazzling and so dear,
which draws souls heavenward, and his yearning flies
    impetuously toward that cause of all his care
and shifting feelings shake him as they rise
    and vague thoughts pull his mind now here, now there,
        he recollects what on the previous day
        he heard the wounded knight of Clarice say.

At this he stops and feels Suspicion start   13
    to sow grave doubt of his love's faith and grace
and to ransack his breast in every part
    as if it were her fated prey and place,
till he feels Grief drive all joy from his heart,
    and Fear no less all hope of joy erase.
        Thus troubled inwardly, in outward action
        he sighs, laments and sobs in wild distraction.

"Alas!" he cries, "shall then another man   14
    possess the beauty that my heart requires?
Without her my whole life is nothing than
    a leafless branch, a sheaf of shriveled briars.
Ah, cruel stars! Ah, spiteful Fortune! Can
    I be condemned always to feel these fires?
        If another takes my one good, my one joy,
        oh when, at least, will my time come to die?

Morir conviemmi, ché la morte è vita   15
  a chi vivendo muor negli aspri affanni;
e se la doglia in ciò non dammi aita,
  la doglia nata da gravosi danni,
quello farà questa mia mano ardita,
  ch'avrian girando ancor poi fatto gli anni.
    Morir conviemmi, e con la vita insieme
    sveller di miei martiri il fertil seme. —

Poi si ripente e dice: — Io dunque deggio   16
  morir, s'altro rimedio ha 'l mio tormento?
Come, come meschino erro e vaneggio,
  come ho de la ragione il lume spento?
Che mi può de la morte avvenir peggio,
  s'ella non sol non mi farà contento,
    ma tutta mi torrà quella speranza
    che di fruire il mio bel sol m'avanza?

Se non m'ha la Fortuna imperio e regno,   17
  o gemme ed or con larga man donato,
onde ad alcun parrò di quella indegno,
  sendo sì diseguale il nostro stato,
tolto non m'ha che con valore e ingegno
  venir non possa al fin tanto bramato.
    Dunque colui ch'è del mio mal radice,
    mora, ma pria divenga mia Clarice.

Come, ucciso il pagan, presa costei   18
  avrò, chi serà mai che mi divieti
che seco i santi e liciti imenei
  non celebri co' modi or consueti,
e nel suo casto seno i desir miei
  felice non appaghi e non acqueti? —
    Tal pensier fatto, ad Isolier l'accenna,
    ed indi arresta l'acquistata antenna.

Giunto ove i cavalier fanno corona   19
  al ricco carro in bella schiera uniti,
con altero sembiante a lor ragiona,
  e gli sfida a giostrar con detti arditi.
Il maganzese Oren, nato in Baiona,
  allor sentendo i perigliosi inviti,
    ad Alda dice, ond'ha piagato il petto:
    — Di darvi costui preso or vi prometto. —

Yes, death befits me, death is life to one   15
   who living dies of sentiments that kill.
And if grief does not give me aid — if none
   of its sharp agonies dispatch me — still
what turning years would in good time have done
   my own audacious hands can do and will.
      To die befits me, yes, and with my life
      to cast away all seeds of inner strife."

Then he repents and says, "Why should I die,   16
   if there is other remedy for woe?
How, as I lose myself in vaunts of misery,
   how have I quenched the light of reason? No,
much worse than death would be my fate if she
   not only should not yield, but at one blow
      cut off all hope I cling to that I may
      obtain fruition of my bliss some day.

Though gold or gems or an imperial reign   17
   are barred to me by bounteous Fortune's will,
wherefore some think me worthless to attain
   her hand, our states being so unequal, still
Fate has not barred me from the chance to gain
   the yearned-for goal by bravery or skill.
      Yes, he who makes me suffer thus and pine
      must die, but Clarice must also be mine.

Who shall gainsay me when the pagan is dead,   18
   and she my captive, if I then omit
the sacred hymeneal rites and wed
   sans ceremony, and so at once get quit
of pain when in her chaste and virgin bed
   I quench desire and gain my peace by it?"
      So thinking, he rides back to Ysolier,
      and snatches up the newly-conquered spear.

Arriving where the knights on splendid steeds   19
   ring the rich chariot in fine array,
he proudly and in fiery words proceeds
   to challenge them unto the deathly fray.
Bayonne-born Oren of Maganza heeds
   the perilous summons and without delay
      tells Alga, who has pierced his breast, "I vow
      I'll thrash and capture him for you right now."

Rinaldo

Già movono a gran corso ambo il cavallo,   20
   da questa l'un, l'altro da quella parte;
nissun pose di lor la lancia in fallo,
   ma differenti fur di forza e d'arte:
ché la lancia d'Oren per lo metallo
   sfuggendo, punto non l'afferra o parte;
     e lasciandolo intier, di novo ancora
     intera torna a ferir l'aria e l'ora.

Ma quella poi che 'l giovinetto impugna,   21
   lo scudo apre per mezzo al Maganzese,
lo scudo che già prima in ogni pugna
   da ciascun colpo ostil colui difese;
né men la tien, ch'al vivo ella non giugna
   il ben temprato adamantino arnese;
     onde con nova e via più cruda piaga
     de la prima amorosa, il cor gli impiaga.

Destò l'atroce colpo alto spavento   22
   negli altri tutti, e 'n te rabbioso sdegno,
o superbo Aridan, vedendo spento
   il tuo figliuolo, il tuo più caro pegno;
onde a chi ferì lui ratto qual vento
   corresti incontro col ferrato legno;
     ma stordito e tremante al pian cadesti,
     e danno a danno, ad onta onta aggiungesti.

Rinaldo l'asta ancor salda ed intera   23
   di novo arresta e nell'arcion si stringe;
ma verso lui da la contraria schiera
   l'orgoglioso Galven presto si spinge,
il qual così gli parla in voce altera,
   mentre vittoria in van s'augura e finge:
     — Al primo colpo avrà di questa giostra
     or certo fine la battaglia nostra. —

Così quel disse, e poi seguì l'effetto,   24
   quanto conforme al dir, tanto al pensiero
contrario: ché, percosso in mezzo 'l petto,
   perdé la guerra al colpeggiar primiero.
Allor Rinaldo in sé raccolto e stretto
   spinse contra degli altri il suo destriero,
     e ne la torma si cacciò più folta,
     l'aspro tronco fatal girando in volta.

Already galloping, their stallions go   20
    charging from one and from the other side.
Neither contestant errs in aim, although
    power and skill are differently supplied,
for Oren's lance-tip with a glancing blow
    can't pierce or stop the rider in his ride,
        in neither shield nor mail makes dent or tear,
        itself left whole to wound the wind and air.

But the shaft the youth wields with huge force right through 21
    the middle of the Maganzan's buckler goes,
that buckler that in earlier fights held true
    against all thrusts from his most potent foes,
and nothing can his adamant harness do
    to keep it from his breast or to oppose
        its final plunge, causing more grievous smart
        than his earlier wound of love, into his heart.

At that atrocious blow all others stood   22
    appalled, and you, O mighty Aridan,
gaped in blind rage to see your flesh and blood,
    your son, your dearest pledge lie slain. You ran,
swift as the wind, with iron-pointed wood,
    to face and fight his killer, man-to-man.
        But thunder-struck and trembling down you came,
        compounding death with death and shame with shame.

Rinaldo puts his shaft, still whole and hale,   23
    at rest once more, strains forward in his seat
and sees proud Galven, eager to assail,
    come hurtling toward him in the utmost heat,
shouting these haughty words, a foolish tale
    feigning to prophesy assured defeat:
        "At first blow of this contest, you'll discover
        our battle, barely started, shall be over."

So said he and his words, put to the test,   24
    were both confirmed and quite contrary to
his thought. For he, pierced midway through his chest,
    at first encounter fell. This done, anew
Rinaldo gathered strength and straight addressed
    on his great stallion the remaining crew,
        charging their herd in a yet more fierce advance,
        holding aloft his fearful, fatal lance.

Rinaldo

Nel furor primo tre n'abbatte e sei 25
    n'impiaga, e quattro d'ogni senso priva:
misero chi veloce i colpi rei,
    lor sottraggendo il corpo, non ischiva;
ché mai non fece il vostro fabro, o dei,
    per la gente troiana o per l'argiva,
        scudo sì forte, elmo sì fin, che saldo
        stesse al lungo colpir del gran Rinaldo.

Isolier che la pugna accesa scorge, 26
    e Marte errar con faccia orrida e mesta,
ne l'usato ardir suo tosto risorge,
    e i bellici furor nel petto desta;
indi la mano a un grosso cerro porge,
    e con sommo vigor lo pone in resta;
        s'addatta in sella e 'l corridore sprona,
        e le redine al collo gli abbandona.

Fra gli altri adocchia il vercellese Arnanco, 27
    ch'allor di due gran colpi avea percossa
a Rinaldo la fronte e 'l braccio manco,
    e 'l fiede tuttavia con maggior possa.
Avea questi il vestir candido e bianco,
    ma v'aggiunse Isolier la sbarra rossa:
        ché 'l sangue uscendo con purpurea riga
        dal petto fuor le lucide arme irriga.

Quinci oltra passa, e mentre il fero Ernando 28
    inalza il braccio contra 'l novo Marte,
gli ficca nell'ascella il crudo brando,
    e tra' nerbi la via dritta si parte;
quel col braccio sospeso in aria stando,
    né lo movendo a questa o a quella parte,
        ché da la spada ciò gli era conteso,
        voto sembrava in sacro tempio appeso.

Ma perché i duo magnanimi compagni 29
    faccian queste e molt'altre eccelse prove,
tal che già 'l sangue in tiepidi rigagni
    da' corpi ostili al suol discende e piove,
pur spesso avvien ch'ognun di lor si lagni
    sotto la spada che 'l nemico move;
        e se la carne ben non han piagata,
        han piste l'ossa, e quella nera e 'nfiata.

Three die at his first onslaught, while six more   25
    fall earthward, stunned, with bleeding wounds agape.
Unhappy he, who does not flee before
    those dreadful blows and with safe limbs escape!
For never did your smith,[31] O gods of yore,
      for Trojan or for Argive heroes shape
        a shield or helmet any man could trust
        to bear the brunt of great Rinaldo's thrust.

Ysolier, who has seen the fight begun   26
    with grim-faced Mars moving with giant strides,
beholding valor now recalls his own
    and rouses warlike fury in his sides.
He seizes a huge trunk, mounts at a run,
      putting that mighty shaft in rest, and rides
        high in the saddle on his great steed's back,
        letting the reins about its neck grow slack.

Among the men he charges in that fight   27
    is Arnanque of Vercelli, man of dread,
who has just, wounding an arm, rushed in to smite
    with two tremendous blows Rinaldo's head,
when, seeing him all dressed in shining white,
      Ysolier adds to it a stripe of red,
        for, running down his chest, a sudden stream
        stains his bright armor with a scarlet gleam.

Then he passed on, where fierce Ernando made   28
    to bar, with raised arm, the new Mars his way.
He in the armpit thrusts his cruel blade
    and right between the sinews makes it stay.
Arrested thus, the stiff arm stands displayed —
      a thing apart, immobile either way.
        Pinned by the sword, it will not move or fall,
        like a votive hung upon a temple wall.

But since these two magnanimous friends achieved   29
    such feats and many like them, and all 'round
a multitude of bodies writhed and heaved,
    raining warm blood in torrents on the ground,
soon countless numbers for good reason grieved
      beneath the sword blows from the pair who pound
        their skins to pierce the flesh, or at least crack
        the bones beneath and leave them bruised and black.

Come, allor che ne l'arsa ed arenosa   30
   Libia, stuol di pastori e di molossi
viene a battaglia orrenda e sanguinosa,
   con due leon da fame a predar mossi,
si duol la greggia timida e dubbiosa
   tra pastoral ripari e brevi fossi,
      né sa fuggir né star, ché la paura
      di fuggir o di star non l'assicura;

così, dipinte di color di morte,   31
   tristi, sospese e sbigottite stanno
le belle donne, e ne le faccie smorte
   gli interni affetti loro espressi elle hanno;
e come varia del pugnar la sorte,
   varia la tema in lor, varia l'affanno,
      e come varia il duol, varia il timore,
      dipinge il volto ancor vario colore.

Mentre dura la pugna in tale stato,   32
   né a questi più ch'a quei Fortuna arride,
un cavalier là sotto l'Orsa nato,
   dove i nevosi campi il Ren divide,
una asta afferra e di gittar sul prato
   con quella il paladin par che si fide;
      né tal pensiero ancor chiuso egli tiene,
      ma con tai detti ad incontrar lo viene:

— Or qui vedrai di tue vittorie il fine,   33
   e di tua vita insieme; ora, infelice,
ti sovrastan quell'ultime ruine,
   a cui sottrarti omai più non ti lice! —
Mentre ignaro di ciò che 'l ciel destine
   così diceva ancor, la lancia ultrice
      Rinaldo per la bocca entro gli mise,
      e la lingua e 'l parlar per mezzo incise.

Quegli al grave colpir sovra 'l sentiero   34
   accennò di cadere, e lo facea,
se no 'l ritenea Fausto in sul destriero,
   ch'infausta pugna con l'Ispano avea;
ma questi ebbe al ben far merito fiero,
   perché 'l pietoso braccio, onde reggea
      l'amico suo, gli fu d'un colpo tronco,
      ed ei ne visse poi stroppiato e monco.

Even as, when in Libya's[32] desert air   30
   a band of shepherds and their mastiffs may
risk horrid, bloody battle with a pair
   of lions whom starvation moves to prey,
a timid flock shifts bleating here and there
   by shallow troughs and scattered bales of hay,
      in doubt whether to run or stand, since fright
      seems safe neither in staying nor in flight,

so, painted with the hues of death, all white,   31
   watching with sad eyes moving to and fro,
the fair maids stand, feeling now grief, now fright
   and what they feel their pallid faces show.
With all the varying fortunes of the fight,
   their feelings vary between fear and woe,
      for as their sorrow varies, or their fear,
      so in their faces varying[33] hues appear.

And so the fight continues, and nowhere   32
   will Fortune smile for either side to win,
when a king born in the sign of the Great Bear,[34]
   where fields of snow are parted by the Rhine,
comes galloping and shakes a giant spear
   as if in challenge of the paladin,
      nor does he hide his thoughts, but in this wise,
      while speeding into battle, loudly cries:

"Here now will all your triumphs have an end   33
   together with your life. Here now mischance
and ruin will overtake your life and send
   your soul whence there is no deliverance!"
He spoke, nor guessed what heaven did intend,
   for even as he spoke, Rinaldo's lance
      entered his mouth and made therein a breach
      that in mid act cut off both tongue and speech.

At that grave blow he slumped as if to fall   34
   down to the road and would have fallen too,
had Faustus not been there to check his sprawl,
   who had engaged the Spanish knight, but who
for his good deed had no reward at all,
   for his pitying arm, where it was clinging to
      his friend, was severed by one huge slash and,
      he found himself a cripple with no hand.

Rinaldo

Non perciò impune il cavaliero ispano   *35*
  se 'n gio d'avergli tronco il braccio manco:
ché quel, come uom che di valor sovrano
  era e di cor più sempre ardito e franco,
feroce gli piagò la destra mano,
  ed ancor poi, ma leggiermente, il fianco;
    indi a Rinaldo fe' non lievi offese,
    che su la sella del corsier lo stese.

Ma mentre il gran figliol del chiaro Amone   *36*
  per la percossa ria disteso giace
mezzo stordito sul ferrato arcione,
  e tutta adosso gli è la turba audace,
alzando il ferro un cavalier guascone
  cerca ferirlo, e 'l suo fratel Corace
    per istrana sciagura in cambio coglie,
    ministro, lasso! de le proprie doglie;

ché quel meschino a la percossa atroce,   *37*
  ch'a chi drizzata fu, non fu molesta:
cadde languendo con tremante voce,
  insanguinato il crin, rotto la testa.
Rinaldo intanto più che mai feroce
  su risalito fulmina e tempesta:
    ben tu, Fernando, il sai, ma più tu, Niso,
    l'un ferito aspramente, e l'altro ucciso.

Come rapido suol pieno torrente,   *38*
  che ruinoso da l'Apennin cada,
tanto più gonfio girne e violente
  quanto impedita più gli vien la strada;
così questo più fero e più possente
  tra gli nimici suoi par che se 'n vada,
    quanto ei contrasti in lor trova più fermi,
    ed intoppi maggior, maggiori schermi.

Ma già del suo colpir grave ed orrendo   *39*
  è l'avverso drappello esterrefatto,
e con la speme di vittoria avendo
  perduto il cor, fugge veloce e ratto;
ed a Rinaldo il gran furor tremendo
  fugge da l'alma in un medesmo tratto,
    c'ha 'l furor dal pugnar sol nutrimento
    in nobile alma; e, quel finito, è spento.

Canto Four

On boasts of severing that left hand, the knight   35
    of Spain did not have leisure long to dwell.
Faustus, a man of supremely skilled in fight,
    endowed with courage ever free and fell,
at once slashed back to wound his foeman's right
    and cut some gashes in his side as well,
        then with no slight hurt made Rinaldo bleed
        and totter in the saddle on his steed.

But while great Aymon's mighty son hangs low,   36
    half-stunned and gasping after that attack,
clinging onto his steel-clad saddle-bow,
    with the whole crowd of bold foes at his back,
a Gascon knight rides up, heaving a blow
    to wound him, but by strange mischance — alack! —
        his brother Corax there receives instead
        the sudden summons to his own death-bed.

For that unlucky youth, caught squarely by   37
    a blow quite harmless to its object, now
falls languishing with a last quavering cry,
    his head smashed in and blood upon his brow.
Rinaldo meanwhile rallies, rising high
    in the saddle, thundering, blazing there — and how
        you, Fernand, know; you, Nisus, even more —
        one of you slain, the other wounded sore.

Even as a mountain torrent's swollen stream   38
    rushing in ruin from its Alpine height
foams with a force more deadly and extreme
    the more impediments oppose its might,
so do the power and speed he musters seem
    to wax still greater in his foemen's sight
        when their resistance grows or when he senses
        their charges strengthening or their defenses.

But now the cohorts of the enemy,   39
    at his horrendous blows, waver and doubt
and, having lost all hope of victory,
    lose heart as well and flee in a great rout.
So in Rinaldo's spirit presently
    the fire of rage grows gentler and goes out.
        For wrath in noble mind finds nourishment
        in war alone, and, when war ends, is spent.

Egli, che già costoro a tutto corso   *40*
    sparsi vede fuggir per la campagna,
così la tema, ond'hanno il petto morso,
    gli sollicita sempre e gli accompagna,
del veloce destrier ritiene il morso,
    ed u' la schiera feminil si lagna,
        palida i volti, i cuor mesta e tremante,
        si volse in lieto e placido sembiante.

Giunto a la bella e nobil compagnia,   *41*
    le fa cortese e riverente inchino;
né men che prima forte apparso ei sia,
    cortese or si dimostra il paladino,
ch'adornato è 'l valor da cortesia,
    come da fregio d'or perla o rubino.
        A Galerana poi, fisso converse
        le luci, a voci tai le labra aperse:

— *Alta reina, a lo cui scettro altero*   *42*
    lieto soggiace il gallico paese,
quanto mi duol che, dov'è 'l mio pensiero
    e le mie voglie ad onorarti intese,
ora mi sforzi Amor con duro impero
    ch'io villan mi ti mostri e discortese,
        di queste dame ch'or se 'n vanno teco,
        una menando in altra parte meco.

Ma quel che sotto sopra ha spesso volto   *43*
    l'alme più saggie e le più ferme menti,
il mio volere e 'l disvoler m'ha tolto,
    né convien già ch'a lui d'oppormi tenti:
questo iscusi appo te l'error mio stolto,
    ch'è lieve error tra l'amorose genti;
        ch'io poscia ognor per discolparmi in parte
        serò pronto a servirti in ogni parte. —

Così disse egli, e poi dal carro tolse   *44*
    Clarice, che sorgiunta a l'improviso
restò stupida e immota, e le s'accolse
    il sangue al cor, lasciando smorto il viso.
Ben la reina a questo oppor si volse,
    ma vano al fin riuscille ogni su' aviso:
        ch'a lasciar la donzella ei non piegosse,
        benché pregato e minacciato fosse.

Canto Four

He — who now sees them flee in full career   40
    and scattering through the wide plain, heap on heap,
even as, gnawing at their entrails, Fear
    drives them forever, Fear that will not sleep —
pulls at his trusty stallion's reins to steer
    his course where the fair maidens stand and weep,
        trembling and pale, exchanging troubled glances,
        and toward them at a gentle pace advances.

Arrived at that fair, noble company,   41
    he with respectful courtesy bowed down,
nor less in courteous breeding seemed to be
    than earlier in valorous renown,
for valor is ever graced by courtesy
    as pearls and rubies grace a victor's crown.
        He then on Galerana fixed his eyes,
        and oped his lips to greet her in this wise:

"High queen, to whose proud scepter Gallia's land   42
    is gladly subject, how I rue my case,
since, although my whole thought and will demand
    that I should honor you and seek your grace,
Love now by his harsh law forces my hand
    to churlishly affront you to your face,
        by carrying off with me a maiden who
        stands here among your lovely retinue.

"But he[45] who has often turned from high to low   43
    the wisest heads and strongest wills, now quite
controls my power to say 'yes' or 'no'
    nor is it fit that I oppose his might:
Thus I excuse my foolish error, though
    the error to true lovers will seem slight.
        If any time I can in part repair
        this wrong to you, I'll serve you anywhere."

So said he, seizing Clarice where she stood,   44
    who had risen to her feet in sudden fright,
all dazed and motionless and felt her blood
    rush to her heart as her whole face grew white.
The queen indeed then turned to him and would
    have stopped him, but all she could do was quite
        in vain, for neither threats nor prayers could make
        him leave the maid he was resolved to take.

Rinaldo

Anzi sovra un destrier tosto la pose, 45
    ch'avea l'andare accomodato e piano,
e di quinci partir poi si dispose
    e girne in luogo incognito e lontano.
Umida i gigli e le vermiglie rose
    del volto, e gli occhi bei volgendo al piano,
        gli occhi onde in perle accolto il pianto uscia,
        la giovinetta il cavalier seguia.

Il guerrier, che nel viso aperti segni 46
    scorge del duol ch'entro la dama accora,
e che di lei paventa i feri sdegni,
    tra sé si duole e si lamenta ancora;
e perché di venir seco non sdegni,
    e sgombri quel martir del petto fuora,
        con dolci modi a lei cortese parla,
        e sol con umiltà tenta placarla.

E gli dice: — Signora, onde vi viene 47
    sì spietato martir, sì grave affanno?
Perché le luci angeliche e serene
    ricopre de la doglia oscuro panno?
Forse fia l'util vostro e 'l vostro bene
    quel ch'or vi sembra insopportabil danno.
        Deh, per Dio! rasciugate il caldo pianto,
        e 'l soverchio dolor temprate alquanto;

ché già non vi meno io per oltraggiarvi, 48
    ahi! più tosto il terren s'apra e m'ingoi,
che picciola cagion deggia mai darvi
    ch'i begli occhi vi turbi e 'l cor v'annoi;
anzi potete ben sicura starvi,
    che 'l mio voler dependerà da voi;
        e che cosa io giamai voler potrei,
        che non piacesse al sol degli occhi miei? —

Indi soggiunse ch'egli lei rapito 49
    non avea già qual folle e qual leggiero,
né guidato da van cieco appetito,
    ma da prudenza e da giudicio intero;
e quanto avea da quel pagano udito
    conto le fe', molto accrescendo il vero;
        ultimamente poi le disse il nome,
        e scoperse il bel volto e l'auree chiome.

Then hastily he lifts her on a horse   45
    that has a soft and comfortable gait
and rides away, planning to set their course
    toward some far-away and nameless place.
She, turning earthward her fair eyes, the source
    from which the rose and lily of her face
        grow moist as tears like pearls well up and drop,
        follows the knight, who does not turn or stop.

He, when he looks on her at last to see   46
    her face clear signs of inward pain express,
and dreading her fierce scorn, is inwardly
    troubled as well and grieved by her distress,
and fearful, too, that, scorning him, she'd flee,
    to soothe the torments that her heart oppress,
        attempts to comfort her and, mild and meek,
        thus in sweet courteous words begins to speak:

"My lady," says he, "why so sad? why so   47
    lost in your anguish do you agonize?
Why let the murky mantle of dark woe
    obscure the angel torches of your eyes?
Perhaps in time a greater good may grow
    out of the acts you fear now and despise.
        Alas, for God's sake, dry your hot tears now
        and to your torment some relief allow.

No outrage, seizing you, did I intend.   48
    Else let earth gape and swallow me! I've done
what I did in honor and never would offend
    your eyes or heart, and I have only one
desire: your happiness, my only end.
    My will depends on yours, my light, my sun!
        What is there I could ever wish to do
        to force a tear or wring a sigh from you?"

He adds that he abducted her that day   49
    not led by vanity or giddy youth
nor by blind appetite's impulsive sway,
    but by sound judgment, chivalry and ruth,
and of what he heard the pagan gallant say
    gives full account, which much confirms his truth.
        At last he lifts his visor and confesses
        his name, baring his face and golden tresses.

Rinaldo

Come, allor che tra nubi i rai lucenti 50
   mostran di Leda i figli, amiche stelle,
si quetan l'onde irate e violenti
   e le dianzi crucciose attre procelle;
così al vago apparir degli occhi ardenti,
   ond'usciro d'amor vive facelle
      il mar del duolo e i venti del timore
      si tranquillar nel tempestoso core.

La giovinetta il su' amador rimira 51
   soavemente e con pudico affetto,
ed egli in lei gli occhi bramosi gira,
   or nel bel volto, or ne l'eburneo petto;
e fatto audace e baldanzoso aspira
   di pervenire a l'ultimo diletto;
      né meraviglia è s'ei, per gli anni caldo,
      nel suo casto pensier non riman saldo.

Ma mentre ei pensa come dare e dove 52
   fine al desio che tanto ha già sofferto,
tutto che 'l calle per ciò far si trove
   da lei preciso ed intricato ed erto,
veggono un che ver' loro i passi move
   egli insieme e 'l cavallo a brun coperto:
      di vista orrenda, ch'un macchiato drago
      tien ne lo scudo entro un sanguigno lago.

Costui da lunge alteramente il volto 53
   verso Rinaldo alzando alto favella:
— Dove ne vai? dove ne porti, o stolto,
   sì nobil preda, sì bramata e bella?
Deh! rendi tosto a me, rendi il mal tolto,
   e lascia in mio poter la damigella:
      lasciala, dico, omai, se non t'aggrada
      provar quanto il mio brando e punga e rada! —

Isolier, che venia dopo l'amante 54
   buon spazio a dietro, a quel parlar superbo
pose la lancia in resta e fessi avante,
   ma cadde a terra al primo incontro acerbo.
Allor lo strano in via più fier sembiante,
   disse al figliol d'Amon: — Per te riserbo
      altro colpo maggior, s'oltra ne vieni,
      e d'affrontarti meco audacia tieni! —

As when two friendly stars through cloudy skies,   50
    great Leda's twins, send their resplendent rays,
the storm that vexed the sea grows still and dies
    and raging breakers change to gentle sprays,
so at the sunrise of his ardent eyes
      that open on her with love's living blaze
        the waves of woe and gusts of terror cease
        in her storm-tossed bosom, and she feels at peace.

The girl soon to her loving swain addressed   51
    sweet, blushing looks that made her cheeks grow bright,
and he, now on her face, now on her breast
    of ivory whiteness, turned his greedy sight,
till, growing bolder, from the unseen rest
      he thinks to snatch the ultimate delight.
        Nor is it strange if a hot youth should not
        always be sound of heart and chaste of thought.

But while he pondered upon how and where   52
    to accomplish his incontinent desire,
and found many a block and hidden snare
    to hinder him or puzzle him or tire,
they saw toward them a mounted knight repair
      swathed, like the steed he rode, in black attire,
        horrid in mien, whose shield for emblem bore
        a mottled dragon in a lake of gore.

With haughty face upraised, from far away   53
    he greets Rinaldo with a furious cry:
"Where are you running, fool? Where think you to convey
    so noble a spoil, so fine in limb and eye?
Give up, surrender now your ill-won prey
    and in my power leave the maid and fly!
      Leave her, I say, at once, or feel, if not,
      how mightily my sword can strike and cut!"

Ysolier who some way behind the pair   54
    had followed all along, at that proud brave
put lance in rest and charged at him four-square
    but fell at the first thrust the other gave.
The stranger then, with a yet fiercer air,
      shouted to Aymon's son: "For you I have
        a thrust still stronger, if you face me here
        and have the audacity to abide my spear!"

Rinaldo

A tai parole il paladin, destando   55
    fero sdegno nel cor, Baiardo mosse,
ma quel, nel mezzo il correre inciampando,
    cadde nel piano, e tardi indi rizzosse.
Ciò non temeva il giovinetto, e quando
    cadde il cavallo, sotto lui trovosse;
        e benché metta e forza ed arte in opra,
        non può levarlo o torselo di sopra.

Cogli spron tenta e con la briglia in vano,   56
    perché 'n piedi si drizzi il suo Baiardo,
né l'alza o move a questa o a quella mano
    con ogni sforzo il paladin gagliardo,
di ch'egli fatto per la rabbia insano
    omai lo batte senz'alcun risguardo;
        ma quelli, quasi grave inutil peso,
        se 'n giace oltre il suo stil per terra steso.

Mentre Rinaldo ancor vaneggia ed erra,   57
    lo stranier con la lancia il terren fiede,
ed ecco che quel s'apre e si disserra,
    sì che fino al suo fondo in giù si vede.
Con spaventoso suon s'apre la terra,
    ch'al forte incanto la natura cede,
        e fuor, novo miracolo tremendo!
        n'esce tosto sbalzando un carro orrendo.

Tirano il carro quattro alti destrieri,   58
    tinti la bocca di sanguigna spuma,
più de la notte istessa oscuri e neri,
    cui da le nari il foco accolto fuma,
cui similmente i torvi occhi severi
    di furor fiamma orribilmente alluma,
        che col rauco annitrir, col fero suono
        de' piedi, imitan la saetta e 'l tuono.

Messa su questa orribile quadriga   59
    fu da quel cavalier la donzelletta
pallida e tramortita, e poscia auriga
    egli medesmo fu de la carretta.
Isolier, vago ancor di nova briga,
    rimonta in sella e gli va dietro in fretta,
        ma sì veloci van l'accese rote
        che con gli occhi seguirlo a pena il puote.

The paladin then, feeling anger grow   55
　　hot his heart, spurs Bayard forward, who
stumbles in mid-career and, falling down, is slow
　　to rise again. The youth, who hitherto
had felt no fear, finds himself pinned below
　　his fallen steed, for he had fallen too,
　　　　and though he exerts his utmost force and skill,
　　　　he cannot rise or move, do what he will.

With spurs and bridle, mustering all his might,   56
　　he tries to force his Bayard to his feet,
but cannot raise or shift to left or right
　　his bulk, all efforts ending in defeat,
till, in frustrated rage, the furious knight
　　begins to curse and pitilessly beat
　　　　his unresponsive horse, who lies prostrate
　　　　above him on the ground, a useless weight.

Even as Rinaldo errs and struggles so,   57
　　the stranger with his huge lance strikes the ground —
and lo! — it splits and opens up to show
　　the depths beneath and with a fearful sound
from that abyss that reaches far below —
　　as Nature yields, by strong enchantments bound —
　　　　there rolls — tremendous wonder, strange to tell! —
　　　　a four-wheeled chariot as if from hell.

Four great steeds draw that car, as black as night,   58
　　their gruesome muzzles flecked with bloody foam,
their nostrils flared as if in rage or spite,
　　spewing dark gusts of smoke into the gloom,
their eyes deep-set and glistening with the light
　　of intermittent flashing hints of doom
　　　　which to their loud neighs and the pounding under
　　　　their huge hooves seem like lightning before thunder.

The knight now on that four-wheeled chariot's rear   59
　　places the maiden, faint and pale of face.
He himself acting as its charioteer
　　jumps up in front to take the driver's place.
Ysolier, battle eager, without fear
　　leaps back into his saddle to give chase,
　　　　but with such speed on fiery wheels it flies
　　　　that he can scarcely follow it with his eyes.

Rinaldo

Rinaldo s'ange e di furor s'infiamma, 60
   dar non potendo a la sua donna aita,
che se ne va qual timidetta damma
   ch'aggia il lupo crudel pur mo rapita;
misero! in lui non è rimasa dramma
   de la gioia ch'avea somma infinita;
      ma fatto omai tutto dolore e rabbia,
      freme co' denti e morde ambe le labbia.

Rinaldo all this while lies prone, quite mad
    with grief, convulsed with wrath that he can do
nothing to help his love, who, pale and sad,
    a fawn seized by a wolf, now fades from view.
Wretch! Not one pence of joy he owns who had
    an infinite sum an hour ago, but who
        now grinds his teeth and bites his lips to be
        hurled from sheer bliss to deepest misery.

Canto quinto

Già sparito era 'l carro, e nube densa   1
    sparso per l'aria avea d'oscura polve,
che più sempre s'ingrossa e si condensa,
    sì ch'il puro seren del cielo involve,
quando alzato il corsier con furia immensa
    calci accopiando in giro si rivolve,
        ed è presto a lo spron, presto a la mano,
        ché non gli noce più l'incanto strano.

Rinaldo alquanto il cor dal duolo oppresso   2
    solleva, poi che 'n piè risorto il vede,
e per lo segno c'han le rote impresso
    altamente nel suol lo sprona e fiede.
Quel cangia i passi sì veloce e spesso
    che non serba il terreno orma del piede,
        e ne l'aria sospeso augel rassembra,
        che con l'ali sostenga alto le membra.

Ma fermezza maggior la nube prende   3
    a poco a poco, e maggior spazio abbraccia,
tal che vista mortal più non s'estende,
    benché di lince fosse, oltra duo braccia.
Intanto pioggia ruinosa scende,
    e si turba del ciel la vaga faccia:
        il paladin non sa dove si vada,
        né però punto neghittoso bada;

ma con giudizio di Baiardo il corso   4
    regge ed indrizza, e sempre inanzi passa,
lo sprone oprando e rallentando il morso,
    sì che 'l cavallo respirar non lassa.
Al fine, allor che a' suoi corsieri il dorso
    Febo disgrava e sotto 'l mar s'abbassa,
        s'aprì la nube e 'n aria si disperse,
        ed ei né 'l carro né l'Ispano scerse.

Canto Five

The chariot vanished, by a cloud concealed 1
    that spread a dusty darkness everywhere,
growing apace till earth and sky and field
    were all enveloped in its murky glare,
when the stallion, rising in great fury, wheeled
    round on its haunches, kicking at the air.
        ready for spurs and for a bridling arm,
        for the enchantment now had lost its charm.

Rinaldo, though with heart oppressed by woe, 2
    rose, seeing him back on his feet and sound,
and mounting, spurred him on where wheel tracks show
    the magic chariot's path along the ground.
Bayard so swiftly shifts his steps and so
    limberly makes his galloping hooves rebound,
        he almost like a bird appears to fly
        whose beating wings suspend his limbs on high.

But now that foul cloud gains in density 3
    and slowly swells in size till by and by
no mortal more than two arms' length can see
    ahead of him, though with a lynx's eye.
Soon thick rain starts to fall so furiously
    and so obscures the clear face of the sky
        that where he goes the paladin does not know,
        yet pauses not one instant even so,

but leaving to the judgment of his horse 4
    the path and the direction of his ride,
loosens the bridle and without remorse
    presses the spur in Bayard's heaving side.
At last, as Phoebus westward guides his course
    down to the sea, the great cloud opens wide
        and melts into the air but brings to sight
        neither the chariot nor the Spanish knight.[36]

Nulla egli vidde se non piante ed ombre,   5
    e la Senna ch'altera il suol diparte.
Or chi fia mai che con la penna adombre,
    e co l'inchiostro pur dissegni in parte
qual varia passion l'animo ingombre
    al cavaliero in sì remota parte?
        Ciò ben eccede ogni poter mortale:
        tu sol sei, Febo, al gran soggetto eguale.

Fu per uscir di sé, fu per passarsi   6
    col proprio ferro il tormentato core;
fu per morir di duol, fu per gittarsi,
    sì che s'immerga nel profondo umore.
Sospiri accesi a stuol per l'aria sparsi,
    gemiti tratti dal più interno fuore,
        stridi e querele in lamentevol suono:
        di quel ch'ei sente i minor segni or sono.

Ma la speranza, che non prima manca   7
    in tutto altrui che manchi ancor la vita,
benché debole sia, benché sia stanca,
    e quasi oppressa omai, non che smarita,
pur quanto può s'inalza e si rinfranca
    e gli è contro al dolor schermo ed aita;
        e tai cose nel core a lui ragiona,
        ch'a fatto in preda al duol non s'abbandona;

ma determina in fin di gir cercando   8
    Clarice bella ovunque Apollo illustri,
e quando il verno imbianca i campi, e quando
    Flora gli orna di rose e di ligustri,
né, perché a lui più volte il sol girando
    rapporti in sen gli anni fugaci e i lustri,
        lasciar l'impresa, se non trova prima
        lei che de' suoi pensier si siede in cima;

ché poi non teme, se trovar la puote,   9
    di non la riaver mal grado altrui,
benché quanti guerrier son tra Boote
    ed Austro fusser giunti ai danni sui;
ché già gli son l'alte sue forze note,
    e da l'amor l'ardir s'avanza in lui.
        Con tal pensier la via prende a traverso
        negli amorosi suoi pensier sommerso.

Canto Five

There's nothing here but trees and shades of night   5
    and the Seine, whose proud waves cleave the yielding shore.
Now where's the pen that could describe his plight,
    or where the ink that flows with colors for
the countless thoughts that now assail the knight
    and touch his soul and shake it to the core?
        The task defies all mortal power: to you
        alone, great Phoebus, that great theme is due.

Beside himself, he almost plunged his blade   6
    in his own heart, he almost came to throw
himself at once into the stream and prayed
    its floods to take his body far below.
Sobs that with echoing sobs the air invade,
    great groans wrenched from some inmost place of woe,
        loud cries and pleas, wails of lament, appeals:
        these are the least signs of what now he feels.

But hope, never quite absent until life   7
    is also absent, once the harm is done
grows back, though faint and wearied out by rife
    doubt, and is never altogether gone
but works to free the mind of inner strife
    with hints how help and comfort may be won,
        now in his heart plants seeds of the belief
        that he need not yield his soul in prey to grief,

but in a search for Clarice should endeavor   8
    to scour all realms Apollo's rays can show,
wherever Flora strews her buds, wherever
    the fields grow white with winter's ice or snow,
to let no thoughts of fleeting lustra[37] sever
    his will from the fair aim that drives him so
        nor ever to leave off his quest to find
        the maid enthroned on high within his mind;

so that, supposing he can find her, he   9
    feels he can keep her too with valiant arm
from hordes of foes he might assembled see
    twixt Auster and Boeotes to his harm.
Already does he sense new potency
    and ardor in his heart augment their charm
        and, while these hopes his doubts and fears allay,
        he, plunged in amorous thoughts, goes on his way.

Rinaldo

Così ne va ne le sue cure involto,   *10*
   e se tallor riscontra alcun per via,
no 'l mira e non gli parla, e quasi tolto
   la favella e 'l veder par che gli sia;
ma fisso e intento ne l'amato volto
   tutt'altro e insieme sé medesmo oblia;
     e se pur scorge alcun, a lui novella
     richiede sol de la sua donna bella.

Mentre da' suoi martiri accompagnato   *11*
   camina pur, venir d'appresso sente
voce che sembra d'uom mesto e turbato,
   che gli fiede l'orrechie in suon dolente.
L'animoso guerrier verso quel lato
   sprona l'agil cavallo immantinente,
     forse anco scorto da speranza vana,
     che dagli amanti mai non s'allontana;

ed un vago e bellissimo garzone   *12*
   vide che sotto un pin steso giacea,
ed era di sua età nella stagione
   sacra e dicata a la ciprigna dea,
quando a sua voglia Amor di noi dispone:
   né del fiorir del pelo in lui parea
     pur segno alcun, ma netto e bianco il mento
     avea, qual terso avorio o puro argento.

Involto in pastoral candida pelle   *13*
   sparsa di nere macchie egli si stava,
e le chiome qualor lucide e belle
   mirto ed alloro in un gli circondava;
i ben formati piè, le gambe snelle
   sino al ghinocchio ricoprendo ornava
     di cuoio azuro, e quel con aurei nodi
     era da poi legato in mille modi.

Tal forse Endimione a Cinzia parve,   *14*
   qualor dal primo giro ella discese,
di sogni cinta e di notturne larve,
   e seco l'ore dolcemente spese.
Tal fuor de l'ocean sovente apparve,
   d'un candido splendor le gote accese,
     la stella cara a l'amorosa diva,
     che 'l giorno estinto innanzi tempo aviva.

Thus bent with care he rides from place to place,   10
    and if he meets a fellow traveler lets
no answering look or greeting slow his pace,
    seeming almost a madman as he frets,
who dreams his dream of the beloved face
    and all things else, even himself, forgets
        and, even if he speaks, only inquires
        for news about the queen of his desires.

While in this woeful state he rides his horse,   11
    he hears nearby a voice that seems to plead
as from a man in deep distress whose hoarse
    cries greet his ears with woe and need.
At once in the direction of its source
    the doughty warrior spurs his nimble steed,
        in part perhaps also by vain hope led
        that's never far from a fond lover's head,

and sees a boy of matchless beauty lie   12
    beneath a pine tree on a little hill,
young as the joyous season hallowed by
    the Cyprian goddess,[38] when her ringdoves fill
the air with moans and Amor's arrows fly
    to pierce or wound our hearts even as he will.
        No growth yet sprouted on his ivory skin,
        which glowed like white enamel[39] on his chin.

Swathed in a tunic made of white lamb's fleece   13
    spotted with black he lay. His curls trailed down
his back or twined up in a centerpiece
    of myrtle and laurel leaves to form a crown.
His shapely feet and legs up to his knees
    were wrapped in boots some craftsman of renown
        had fashioned of blue leather on which strings
        and knots of gold met in a thousand rings.

Like him the fair Endymion might seem   14
    to Cynthia descending from her sphere
escorted by dim shapes of shade and dream
    to embrace that shepherd whom she holds so dear.
Like him the star who hails with shining beam
    the coming day, the while with blushing cheer
        his mother[40] meets him, or who charms her sight
        when his bright candle greets approaching night.

In così dolci modi e sì pietosi   15
  si lamentava il pastorello adorno,
ch'avria commossi ancor gli orsi rabbiosi
  ove affetto gentil non fa soggiorno.
Avea le guancie e gli occhi rugiadosi,
  gli occhi ch'apriano quasi un novo giorno;
  e co' caldi sospir l'aria accendea,
  che dal profondo del suo cor traea.

— Lasso! dicea, perché venisti, Amore,   16
  Amor d'ogni mio bene invidioso,
con le tue fiamme a tormentarmi il core
  e turbar la mia pace e 'l mio riposo?
Deh! qual gloria te aspetti e qual onore,
  s'io tale schermo alcun non far pur oso,
  s'a pena l'arco steso, a pena accinto
  eri a ferir, ch'io mi rendei per vinto?

Chi crederia che gli tuo' strali infesti   17
  fussero a pastoral rustico petto,
non sendo quei di Giove unqua molesti
  a l'ignobil capanna, al basso tetto?
Ma poi che far, oimè! tu pur volesti
  così vil pruova in così vil suggetto:
  non dovevi il mio core in luoco porre
  u' senza speme ognor se stesso aborre.

Tu, perfido signor, tu disleale,   18
  che sotto ombra di ben copri il mal vero,
oggetto desti impare e diseguale,
  onde a pieno m'affliga, al mio pensiero.
Deh! mie stelle crudeli, or quando tale
  scempio fu visto e così strano e fero?
  Ché dove in altri amor da speme nasce,
  dal non sperar in me s'aviva e pasce.

Segue il rozo monton la pecorella,   19
  scorto da speme, per gli erbosi campi;
segue il colombo a la diurna stella
  la cara amica ed a' notturni lampi;
combatte il toro a la stagion novella
  da speme tratto, e par che d'ira avampi:
  sempr'è speranza, ov'è d'amor il foco,
  quella in me no, ma sì ben questo ha loco. —

Canto Five

Thus richly dressed, he in that solitude   15
    so sweetly did lament now and complain[41]
that even raging bears, whose native mood
    is never gentle, would have felt his pain.
His eyes, which opened like the dawn, bestrewed
    his rosy cheeks with drops of pearly rain,
        and the air grew warm with the hot, heaving sighs
        that from his heart's profoundest depth did rise.

"Alas! Ah, cruel Love!" so did he cry,   16[42]
    "Love, envious of all my happiness,
why have you set my heart on fire? Ah, why
    destroy my peace and fill me with distress?
What fame, what glory could you gain if I,
    not daring to oppose your might, confess
        that with your bow scarce bent I, scarcely hit
        by your sharp darts, surrender and submit?

"Who would believe it could be your intent   17
    to aim your shafts at a poor shepherd's breast,
for even Jove's great bolts are never spent
    on humble huts or break a peasant's rest?
But if you meant, as — woe! — indeed you meant,
    to put a lowly target to the test,
        you wronged by putting my heart in a place
        where it must ever feel shame and disgrace.

You, treacherous master and perfidious friend,   18[43]
    cloaking true wickedness in feigned good will,
work toward a disparate and conflicting end
    whereby — I swear — you do me deadly ill.
Ah — cruel stars! — whom did you ever send
    a shame so bitter and strange? All others still
        find that their hope feeds love, but my
        love feeds on lack of hope and grows thereby.

Hope makes the lusty ram follow the ewe   19
    through the green pastures. Thoughts of hope incite
cock-doves to chase their hen-doves as they coo
    under the day star or in star-lit night.
Afire with rage in springtime bulls pursue,
    drawn on by hope, their rival bulls and fight.
        Hope dwells wherever love burns, but in me
        the one does not; the other, certainly."[44]

Rinaldo

Mentre in soavi note ei si dolea,
    stava Rinaldo a le querele intento,
e la pietà che del fanciullo avea
    maggior in lui rendeva il suo tormento,
ch'a pensar ai suoi casi il conducea,
    al suo perduto bene, al gaudio spento.
      Poi che si tacque, a lui cortese disse,
      le luci avendo nel bel volto fisse:

— Vago garzon, che 'n sì bel modo fuora
    mostri l'alto dolor che in te s'asconde,
e ti lagni d'amor, ti lagni ancora
    de l'empie stelle a te poco seconde,
e nel tuo lamentar parte tallora
    tocchi de le mie piaghe alte e profonde:
      deh! se il ciel ed Amor ti sia cortese,
      la cagion del tuo duol fammi palese.

Io sono un cavalier cui similmente
    è il destino ed Amor crudo e spietato,
ché vivo ognora in mezzo 'l fuoco ardente,
    poco a me stesso e meno ad altri grato.
Narra dunque il tuo duol securamente
    ad uom che da egual pena è tormentato,
      perché recar ciascun dessi a guadagno
      ne le sventure sue trovar compagno. —

A quei detti cortesi il giovinetto,
    verso Rinaldo alzando il viso bello,
per cui rigando il puro avorio schietto
    scendea nel grembo un tepido ruscello,
gli disse: — Cavalier, s'hai pur diletto
    d'udir quanto Amor siami iniquo e fello,
      e quanto la Fortuna empia ed acerba,
      dal corsier scendi e posati in su l'erba;

ch'io te 'l dirò, poiché, qual dici, sei
    servo d'Amore, ed ei di te fa scempio.
Ma vedrai bene al fine che i casi miei
    son senza paragone e senza essempio,
e che quel duolo onde gir carco déi,
    è null'a par del mio gravoso ed empio.
      Ben caro avrò che tu mi narri poscia
      qual passion t'affliga e quale angoscia.

20

21

22

23

24

While in sweet accents he lamented so,   20
    Rinaldo listened, moved by his distress
and his compassion for the youngster's woe
    increased his own sense of unhappiness,
and the boy's sorrow made his own tears flow
    since he by perished joy was grieved no less.
        After a silence, he with courteous grace
        thus spoke, his eyes fixed on his lovely face:

"You lovely boy, who in this moving way   21
    lay bare the cruel pain you hide within,
who rail at Love and with such force inveigh
    against the stars whose grace you cannot win
and who somehow, in everything you say,
    touch on the agony myself am in,
        tell me at large, so heaven and Love again
        may show you grace, the reason for your pain.

I am a knight who also came to know   22
    how cruel and spiteful Fate and Love can be,
for the fire that I live in burns me so
    that others shun, and I grow tired of, me.
To me therefore securely bare your woe
    as to a man afflicted equally,
        since every suffering man should seek to find
        a friend who suffered in a similar kind."

The youngster, lifting at these words his fair   23
    countenance toward Rinaldo while a bright
trickle of tears streaked the pure ivory there
    and fell upon his bosom, said,[45] "Sir knight,
if you are truly pleased to learn what care
    Love heaped upon my heart and with what spite
        Fortune made all my days grow dark and drear,
        dismount and lie down on the grass to hear,

and I will speak, since — as you say — you are   24
    Love's servant and complain he treats you ill.
But you shall see that my misfortunes far
    excel those any others feel or will
and find your own grief nowise on a par
    with grief that I felt and I am feeling still.
        When I have done, I'll gladly hear the tale
        of the passion and the woe that you bewail.

Là dove già l'alta Numanzia sorse,   25
   ch'osò ben spesso al gran popol romano
co l'intrepido ferro audace opporse,
   e fe' del latin sangue umido 'l piano,
dove or per abitar usan raccôrse
   solo i pastor del territorio ispano,
      nacqui io, ma sotto stella iniqua e ria,
      del più ricco uom ch'in quelle parti sia.

Siede ivi un tempio a maraviglia adorno,   26
   ch'a Venere sacrar nostri maggiori,
dove sempre di maggio il primo giorno
   vengono cavalier, vengon pastori,
donne e donzelle dal vicin contorno
   a porgere a la dea solenni onori;
      né questo antiquo stil ponto è dismesso,
      perch'or s'adori il gran Macone in esso:

anzi premii son posti a qual più dotta   27
   gagliarda mano il pal di ferro tira,
a chi il nemico al gioco della lotta
   con maggior forza ed arte alza e raggira,
a chi con l'arco di più certa botta
   ferisce il segno, ov'altri indarno mira,
      a chi con ratto piè gli altri precorre,
      a chi la lancia più leggiadro corre.

Le donne poi, che son di basso stato,   28
   menano insieme vaghe danze a gara;
l'altre ch'in maggior grado ha 'l ciel locato,
   e che di stirpe son nobile e chiara,
si baciano a vicenda; e chi più grato
   il bascio porge, in ciò più dolce e cara
      a giudizio commun rapporta il pregio,
      ch'orna la sua beltà di nuovo fregio.

Soleano già, quando concesso ei n'era   29
   da' secoli miglior più libertate,
i giovanetti ch'a la primavera
   erano giunti di lor verde etate,
anch'essi intrar confusamente in schiera
   con le vaghe donzelle inamorate,
      e insieme gareggiar nel dolce gioco:
      ma ciò l'uso corresse a poco a poco.

In the land where once noble Numantia[46] rose 25
   whose people often against mighty Rome
lifted sharp swords and with their Latin foes'
   wet blood stained red their native loam,
a land which nowadays no dwellings shows
   but here and there some Spanish shepherd's home.
     There was I born, son of the richest man
     in those parts. There my ill-starred life began.

And there our forebears did a temple rear, 26
   sacred to Venus, glorious in view,
where on the first of May of every year
   knights, shepherds, lasses and great ladies, too,
in festive throngs gather from far and near
   to pay the goddess solemn homage due;
     nor has that ancient rite quite lost its sway,
     though great Mahoun[47] is worshipped there today.

"And there are games with prizes and acclaim 27
   for him who wields his javelin the best,
him who in wrestling puts his foeman's frame
   with greatest skill and power to the test,
for him who bends his bow with surest aim
   and makes his shafts fly farther than the rest,
     for him whose speed the runners' field commands,
     or him who thrusts most deftly with his lance.

Those women there who are of low degree, 28
   in contests of delightful dances meet,
while those heaven favored with nobility,
   high birth or famous ancestry compete
kissing[48] each other's lovely lips, and she
   whose kiss seems best, that is, most dear and sweet
     by general consensus gains the prize,
     which greatly makes her beauty's glory rise.

In earlier, better days there used to be 29
   a similar contest for young bachelors,
who in their green age were at liberty
   to take the field in games of skill or force.
These too, to please the girls they loved, made free
   to crowd into the lists and in due course
     to tussle in a kissing-match for men,
     but bit by bit that game has ceased since then.

Rinaldo

Avenne, ed or passato è il secondo anno,   30
    ché i dì non sol, ma l'ore in mente anch'aggio,
ch'al tempio venne per mio eterno danno
    la vaga Olinda il dì primo di maggio:
la vaga Olinda, mio gravoso affanno,
    c'ha bellissimo il volto, il cor selvaggio,
      Olinda ch'è del nostro re figliuola,
      di cui chiaro romor per tutto vola.

Lasso! non prima in lei gli occhi affisai,   31
    che per l'ossa un tremor freddo mi scorse.
Pallido ed aghiacciato io diventai
    allora, e fui de la mia vita in forse;
quasi in un tratto ancor poi m'infiammai,
    e contra il giel l'ardore il cor soccorse,
      spargendo il volto d'un color di fuoco,
      né dentro o fuor potea trovar mai luoco.

Non conobbi io l'infirmità mortale   32
    a segni, ohimè! ma nel bel volto intento,
misero! dava a l'amoroso male
    esca soave e dolce nutrimento.
Ben me n'avidi al fin, ma che mi vale,
    s'ogni rimedio era già tardo e lento,
      ed ogni sforzo van, ché 'l crudo Amore
      s'era in tutto di me fatto signore?

Conosceva il mio error, vedeva aperto,   33
    quanto a lo stato mio si sconvenisse
in donna di tal sangue e di tal merto
    l'insane voglie aver locate e fisse,
e che era ben per sentiero aspro ed erto
    fuggir pria ch'altro mal di ciò seguisse:
      ma mi sforzava il micidial tiranno
      gir volontario a procacciarmi danno.

Non così fonte di chiar'acqua pura   34
    a stanco cervo ed assettato aggrada,
né tanto al gregge il prato e la pastura
    piace ch'è sparsa ancor da la rugiada,
né tanto il rezo e la fresca ombra oscura
    a peregrin ch'errando il luglio vada,
      quanto sua dolce vista a me piacea,
      bench'ella fosse di mia morte rea.

It happened — it was two years to the day —   30
  the very hour is fixed within my mind —
that to the temple on the first of May
  Olinda came — ah, doom to me consigned! —
Olinda, who for grief makes me decay,
    fairest of face, but of a heart unkind,
      Olinda, our king's daughter, whose great name
      throughout the world is trumpeted by Fame.

Alas! I looked at her, and in a trice,   31
  cold trembling shook my bones, my face grew white
and every part of me as cold as ice,
  as if my very life were taking flight.
But then in one swoop a great flame did rise
    inside my heart and spread out with such might
      over my face as if intent to win
      space outside me and cramped for space within.

Heedless of signs that showed my health did fail,   32
  with eyes fixed on her lovely face — ah woe! —
I, wretch, fed the disease that made me ail
  sweet nutriment and fuel. Well did I know
what this would lead to, but to what avail?
    Already all physic was too late and slow,
      and every power vain, since cruel Love
      had breached my heart and was sole lord thereof.

I knew my error, knew it was insane   33
  and most unfitting to have fixed my will
on one whose blood and merit occupied a plane
  high above any station I could fill,
knew I should flee, no matter what the pain,
    and so perhaps avoid yet greater ill,
      but Love, that murderous tyrant, made me turn
      and hasten toward the fire in which I burn.

Less pleasure the pure water of the spring   34
  gives to the thirsty stag whom hounds pursue.
Less pleasure to the flock while pasturing
  holds the green meadow moist with morning dew,
and shady dells in June less pleasure bring
    to the wandering pilgrim when they come in view,
      than the delight that she brought to my eye,
      though but to look upon her meant to die.

L'ora de' giuochi era venuta intanto,   35
   ed al palo tirar si cominciava,
e già fra gli altri omai la palma e 'l vanto
   un gagliardo pastor ne riportava.
Siegue la lotta: io che mostrarmi alquanto
   al mio gradito amor pur desiava,
      corro al certame; e tal fu la mia sorte
      che giudicato fui d'ognun più forte.

Si giostrò poscia, e i giuochi anco si fèro   36
   de le donzelle; ed io che vidi allora
molte che baci a la mia donna diero,
   e che gli ricever più cari ancora,
arsi di dolce invidia, e col pensiero
   mi formai grate frodi ad ora ad ora,
      perché mi parve, inganno aventuroso,
      d'esser fra loro al bel gioco amoroso.

Ultimamente al corso poi si venne,   37
   di cui teneva Olinda il pregio in mano;
io m'accinsi al certame, e non ritenne
   il corpo stanco l'appetito insano.
M'aggiunse ai piedi Amor veloci penne,
   e mi rendè l'andar facile e piano,
      tal che gli altri precorsi, e giunsi dove
      sedean l'alte bellezze altere e nove.

Come fui sì vicino al mio bel sole,   38
   un gelato tremor tosto m'assalse,
tal ch'io mi dibattea sì come suole
   tenero giunco in riva a l'acque salse.
Quasi lasciò le membra vuote e sole
   l'alma, che gli occhi bei soffrir non valse.
      Al fin mi porse Amor cotanto ardire
      che 'n parte sodisfeci al mio desire;

e con sùbita astuzia, di cadere   39
   fingendo, nel bel sen quasi mi stesi.
Or chi potria mai dir quanto piacere
   e qual dolcezza in quel istante io presi?
Ma non deggio di ciò punto godere,
   da poi che fu cagion che più m'accesi:
      ché se caldo era pria, non fu in me dramma
      da indi in qua se non di fuoco e fiamma.

Meanwhile the games began. The javelin throw   35
   came first. Already amid joyous cries
a valiant shepherd lad with cheeks aglow,
   crowned with the palm and laurel, claimed his prize.
Wrestling came next, and I, eager to show
   myself somewhat to my beloved's eyes,
      ran to the contest, and my luck proved fair
      for I was judged one of the strongest there.

I also won the final joust. The game   36
   of damsels then commenced. Seeing them meet
and kiss my lady, who returned the same
   sweet kisses — nay, more exquisite and sweet —
I often, heated with fresh envy's flame,
   would wrap my thoughts in flattering deceit
      until, in bold imagination's prey,
      I seemed to join with them in amorous play.

Last came the footrace. At the distant goal   37
   Olinda stood, the trophy in her hand.
I girt myself. Nor could my love-crazed soul
   tire my body or slow it to a stand.
Love winged my feet, and under his control
   I easily outsped the runners' band
      and far ahead arrived in triumph at
      the stage where the enchanting beauties sat.

When I had drawn so close to my fair sun,   38
   chill tremors seized me and I stood a-daze
and shuddering like a rush that grows alone
   on shores that wind with icy droplets sprays,
in all my being so powerless and undone,
   that I could not endure that beauteous gaze.
      At last Love whispered to my daring heart
      a way to ease my plight, at least in part.

In a sly pretense, as if about to fall,   39
   I almost fell upon her lovely breast.
Now who could sum up all the joy and all
   the sweetness in that point of time compressed?
Still I should not take pleasure now to call
   that time a time when I was wholly blest,
      for if I burned before, now my entire
      self henceforth burned in unrelenting fire.

Poi tolsi il pregio, e lieve in tôrlo strinsi   40
    la man che quel tenea bianca e gentile,
e in questa di rossor le guancie tinsi,
    ed a terra chinai lo sguardo umile.
Or veder pòi quant'oltre io mi sospinsi,
    io di nissun valore uom basso e vile,
        verso dama sì degna e sì sovrana,
        e s'Amor mi rendea la mente insana.

Ma già dal ciel Apollo era sparito,   41
    onde ancor seco il mio bel sol spario,
ed io restai di tenebre vestito,
    preda del duol che soffro ognor più rio.
Oh pur, oimè! di queste membra uscito
    se 'n fusse allor l'infermo spirto mio,
        ch'a maggior pene ed a più fera sorte
        tolto m'avria quell'opportuna morte.

Quella inquieta notte in quanti e quanti   42
    angosciosi martir, lasso! passai;
quanti trassi dagli occhi amari pianti,
    quanti dal petto arsi sospir mandai,
non credendo i celesti almi sembianti
    e gli occhi belli riveder più mai:
        ma vietò questo per maggior mio male
        l'atrocissimo mio destin fatale.

Perciò ch'Olinda, a chi il paese piacque   43
    per lo ciel che temprato era e sereno,
per l'amene selvette e limpid'acque,
    e' bei colli che 'l fan vago ed ameno,
perché di caccie, a cui da ch'ella nacque
    ebbe il cor volto, è copioso e pieno,
        in un castel che signoreggia intorno
        tutto il paese, elesse far soggiorno.

E quinci ella uscia poi sovente fuori   44
    coi primi rai, con l'aura matutina,
allor che le verdi erbe e i vaghi fiori
    aprono il seno a la celeste brina,
cinta da cavalier, da cacciatori,
    e da schiera di dame pellegrina;
        ed or seguiva i lepri e i cervi snelli,
        or tendea reti ai semplicetti augelli.

I took the prize and so briefly retained   40
　　the white hand that had held it in my own,
then, with my cheeks by modest blushes stained,
　　I bowed and in all humbleness looked down.
Now see how far beyond my bounds I strained,
　　I of no worth, a common shepherd clown,
　　　　toward a sovereign maid so high above me
　　　　that it was mad to think that she could love me.

Apollo now had vanished from the sky,   41
　　when my fair sun did also seek her west
and left the world to darkness, so that I
　　lamented hour on hour without rest.
Would that my soul had then resolved to fly
　　the narrow confines of my feeble breast
　　　　though to more torments and more piercing grief!
　　　　Such death I would have welcomed with relief.

That restless night I spent in what untold   42
　　torments! In what unnumbered anguished cries!
What bitter tears from my eyes, uncontrolled,
　　then poured and from my breast what scalding sighs!
For I was sure I'd nevermore behold
　　that heavenly shape and those delightful eyes.
　　　　Yet even this my cruel fate denied
　　　　to have me by yet sharper tortures tried,

for fair Olinda, whom our country's air   43
　　pleased, since it was both temperate and serene,
with cheerful groves and clear springs everywhere
　　and lovely hills that made a pleasant scene,
and since it teemed with game, both bird and beast
　　(she always loved the hunt), decided there
　　　　to let a noble keep, whose lofty tower
　　　　commanded the wide plain, serve as her bower.

Thence she would often venture out to ride   44
　　by first rays of the sun, when day was new
and flowers and meadow grasses opened wide
　　their bosoms to receive the heavenly dew,
with a crew of knights and hunters at her side,
　　and a cheerful band of roving ladies, too,
　　　　to go in chase of stags and light-foot hares
　　　　or for poor wildfowl to spread nets and snares.

Rinaldo

Io c'ho tutti i miei dì cacciando spesi   45
    con quei che sono in ciò dotti e maestri,
e ch'era annoverato in quei paesi
    tra i più veloci e tra i più cauti e destri,
oltre che sapea i luochi ove son presi
    più facilmente gli animai silvestri,
        ne la sua compagnia tosto raccolto
        fui con grate parole e lieto volto.

Sempre era seco e gli pendea dal lato,   46
    e per felice allor mi riputava,
ch'avea il suo cane a lassa o l'arco aurato,
    o la carca faretra io le portava;
felicissimo poi se m'era dato
    toccar le veste ond'ella cinta andava.
        Così ne vissi insin ch'il solar raggio
        portò di nuovo il dì primo di maggio.

Ma 'l crudo Amor, ch'altrui piacer perfetto   47
    non fa sentire, insin ch'al fin s'arriva,
e traendo di questo in quel diletto
    l'uom, sempre in lui più il desiderio avviva,
mi sospinse a mortale infausto effetto,
    onde ogni mio tormento in me deriva,
        e 'l lume di ragion sì mi coperse,
        ch'egli dal bene il mal punto non scerse.

Deliberai, feminil vesta presa,   48
    tra le donzelle anch'io meschiarmi, quando
vengono insieme a placida contesa,
    l'una soavi baci a l'altra dando,
per poter poscia, oh temeraria impresa!
    cagion ch'or sia d'ogni mio bene in bando,
        congiunger con la mia la rosea bocca,
        onde Amor mille strali aventa e scocca.

E mi pensava ben poter ciò fare   49
    sicuramente, perché 'l pelo ancora,
che suol più ferma età seco apportare,
    non mi spuntava da le guancie fuora.
Vesti trovai d'oro fregiate e care,
    e molti altri ornamenti in poco d'ora;
        e solo il tutto ad un compagno dissi,
        con cui d'estremo amor congionto vissi.

I, who had all my life spent many a day   45
    with master huntsmen known throughout the land
and who was famed for speed in chasing prey
    and caution in pursuit and deftness and
as one who well knew where the quarry may
      most easily be found and made to stand,
          was often asked join her hunt and went
          whispering thanks and smiling with content.

Ever beside her, I would come and go,   46
    a happy man, delighted when I bore
her laden quiver or her golden bow
    or held her hound's leash or unlatched her door,
but happiest when allowed to touch and so
      to feel her warmth in garments that she wore.
          So I attended her until the day
          when the sun once more brought round
             the first of May.

But ruthless Cupid, who lets no man know   47
    perfect delight until the goal is won,
who yanks a man from joy to joy and so
    rouses more mad desires one by one,
plagued me with hapless, brooding thoughts, whence grow
      all torments I since then have undergone,
          and smothered reason's light in me until
          I saw no difference between good and ill.

I resolved by donning female garb[49] to try   48
    to mingle with the ladies and in this
disguise to join them in their revelry,
      giving in merry contest kiss for kiss
meaning — O bold attempt! and reason why
      I now am banished from my only bliss —
          to make my lips meet hers whose rosy glow
          breathes forth a thousand arrows from Love's bow.

I thought that, venturing thus, I might be bold   49
    since on my chin the attributes that grace
a riper age had not yet taken hold
    to warn of my approach to her dear face.
I found a gown adorned with precious gold
      and sundry other ornaments apace,
          and I confided in one friend alone
          who shared with me a passion like my own.

Così al tempio ne venni ove si féa   *50*
   l'amoroso duello, e già col volto
in un candido vel, quanto potea
   senza sospetto dar, chiuso ed involto.
De le donne lo stuol che concorrea
   insieme al dolce gioco era sì folto,
      che non fu chi 'l mio nome a me chiedesse,
      o in conoscermi pur cura prendesse.

Onde tra lor sicuro io mi meschiai,   *51*
   donna creduto da le donne anch'io.
Molte abbracciai di lor, molte basciai
   con poca gioia e con minor disio,
sin ch'ad Olinda al fin pur arrivai,
   stabile oggetto d'ogni pensier mio,
      cui com'edera tronco il collo cinsi:
      indi le labbra disiose spinsi.

Con voglia così ingorda affettuosa,   *52*
   con sì fervidi baci e con sì spessi,
spinto da forza interna ed amorosa
   ne le sue labbra le mie labbra impressi;
ch'allor quasi stupita e sospettosa
   ella fissò ne' miei gli occhi suoi stessi,
      onde io cangiai pur nel medesmo istante
      in color mille il timido sembiante.

Il che forse il sospetto a doppio rese   *53*
   maggiore in lei di quel che prima egli era,
tal che più fiso a rimirarmi prese,
   ed al fin mi conobbe, ahi, sorte fera!
onde le luci di furore accese.
   Disse con voce in un bassa ed altera:
      "Come a tal tradimento unqua pensasti?
      Come, falso villan, tant'oltra osasti?

Sgombra orsù via di qua, togliti ratto   *54*
   dal nostro regno, e più non t'accostarli;
e s'a l'audace o scelerato fatto
   quelle pene non do che dovrei darli,
e sì placidamente ora ti tratto,
   fo per non dar materia onde altri parli:
      ben la tua morte a me saria gradita,
      non meno, anzi via più de la mia vita."

Then I went to the temple that I knew   50
    was destined for that amorous competition
and with a veil managed to hide from view
    my face without arousing a suspicion.
So dense a press of ladies crowded through
    the temple's gates seeking to gain admission
        that none asked for my name or even took
        pains to take passing notice by a look.

Held for a lady among ladies, I   51
    mingled among them and was not found out.
I embraced, kissed many of them by and by —
    with little joy and less desire, no doubt.
But then Olinda came, my daystar, my
    one object, and I wound my arms about
        her neck, as ivy might an oaken trunk entwine,
        and, yearning toward her, let her lips meet mine.

With a will so glutted with desire, with such   52
    warm kisses and such frequent ones, so fast
propelled by amorous force, my lips so much
    battered against her lips that she at last,
like someone stunned, suspicious at my touch
    looked fixedly upon me and aghast,
        and in a trice I felt hot shame infuse
        my timid countenance with a thousand hues.

My look perhaps redoubled the surmise   53
    already dawning in her mind, and so
she began with closer looks to scrutinize
    my face and recognized me. Then — (ah, woe! —
with flames of fury kindled in her eyes
    she told me in a voice both proud and low:
        'How could you think such treason? How so far
        presume, being the peasant churl you are?

Make your way hence at once, and with all speed!   54
    Avoid our kingdom, nevermore return!
If for your felon and presumptuous deed
    I do not give the punishment you earn,
know that my grace and leniency proceed
    from a need to stop loose talk, else would you learn
        that, as in pleasure at my own life's breath
        nay more, I would take pleasure in your death.'

Ma perché, lasso! ti racconto a pieno   55
   quel che duro già fu tanto a patire?
E ch'or è duro a ricordar non meno,
   sì che 'l cor sento in mille parti aprire.
Uccider mi vols'io, ma pose freno
   a la man disperata ed al desire,
      dopo molta fatica e mille preghi,
      quel mio compagno a cui null'è ch'io neghi.

Ed a venir in Francia ei mi dispose,   56
   ov'è, se pur il ver la fama dice,
un antro a cui fra l'opre alte e famose
   null'altro al mondo oggi agguagliarsi lice;
ch'ivi a' suoi servi le future cose
   da un aureo simulacro Amor predice,
      e con certe risposte util consigli
      dà ne l'aversitati e ne' perigli.

Ed oggi a punto, allor che s'apre il giorno,   57
   tra via mi disse uom vecchio e peregrino,
che quinci presso sotto un colle adorno
   giacea lo speco, e m'insegnò il camino.
Or dimmi tu, guerrier, qual danno o scorno
   ti faccia Amor o 'l tuo crudel destino:
      ch'ambo da poi n'andremo al loco sacro
      per richieder consiglio al simulacro. —

Rinaldo i casi suoi più brevemente   58
   narrogli, e 'nsieme poi la via pigliaro;
né molto gir ch'altero ed eminente
   il colle e poi lo speco ancor miraro.
Occupava l'entrata un foco ardente;
   alta colonna di forbito acciaro
      gli stava a dirimpeto in terra fitta,
      e v'era tal sentenza in carmi scritta:

"A' leali d'Amor concesso è 'l passo,   59
   agli altri no, per mezo il vivo foco."
Era 'l colle d'un netto e vivo sasso,
   vago e lucente del color di croco,
opra d'incanto, e dimostrava al basso,
   tutte scolpite in apparente loco,
      le vittorie d'Amor, gli alti trofei,
      ch'egli acquistò contra celesti dei.

But why — alas! — do I at length retell   55
    the agony that I endured, which still
even in memory is a living hell
    that lacerates my heart? I turned to kill
myself, bidding both world and pain farewell,
      but stopped my hand and checked my desperate will,
        after my friend, whom I told all my cares,
        importuned me with countless, earnest prayers.

I then resolved to come to France to seek   56
    the famous cave, splendid beyond compare —
if Fame speaks truth — an edifice unique
    among the whole world's wonders, where
Love from a golden effigy is said to speak
    to lovers and their futures to declare
      and to give counsel in most apt replies
      to those whom misery and danger tries.

And on this very day, at dawn, along the way   57
    an aged pilgrim told me that nearby
beneath a leafy hill that cavern lay
    and pointed out the road there presently.
Do you, sir knight, now make me know, I pray,
    how you are plagued by Love or Destiny.
      When you have done, we will together seek
      the sacred cave to hear the image speak."

Rinaldo more succinctly told his woes   58
    then they set out together. By and by
they saw where in the distance proudly rose
    the green hill with its cavern and drew nigh.
Blocking the entrance, a fierce fire[50] glows
    and a pillar of bright burnished steel looms high,
      fixed in the spacious courtyard opposite,
      with this brief warning text engraved on it:

"Keep out! Love's loyal followers alone   59
    may pass this living fire by Love's grace."
A single slab of saffron-colored stone
    that seemed alive made up the hill's rock-face,
wrought by enchantment, and upon its base
    carvings depict, each in its proper place,
      the victories and trophies won by Love
      during his conquests of the gods above.[51]

Florindo, ch'il pastor tal nome avea,   60
    ch'era ne l'amor suo fido e leale,
sùbito entrò dove più il foco ardea
    con grand'ardire a la gran fede eguale;
ed andar per un aere a lui parea,
    sottilissimo e puro e forse quale
        è l'elemento men condenso e greve,
        ch'agli altri sorvolò spedito e lieve.

Il cavalier che rimirava intento   61
    de' favolosi dei gli antichi amori,
entrar vedendo senza alcun spavento
    Florindo tra le fiamme e tra gli ardori,
a seguirlo non fu pigro né lento,
    ma 'l feroce destrier lasciando fuori
        a Vulcan si credette: indi per quello
        entrò sicuro nel sacrato ostello.

Da tre leggiadri e vaghi sacerdoti   62
    ch'a la cura del loco erano eletti,
del faretrato arcier fidi e devoti,
    ambi furo raccolti i giovinetti,
ed a l'altar menati, u' preghi e voti
    dovean porger al dio con puri affetti,
        come da quei ch'ivi gli avean condutti
        erano a pieno ammaestrati e instrutti.

Ma il paladino in cui verace fede   63
    per rara grazia ognor cresce ed abonda,
ciò si sdegna di far, perché non crede
    che divin nume in sé quel or nasconda,
ma spirto aereo o de l'inferna sede,
    che narrando il futuro altrui risponda:
        onde in disparte alquanto ei si ritira,
        e 'l vaneggiar di quei tacendo mira.

E ben avria l'idol, sdegnato alquanto,   64
    ogni risposta al cavalier negato,
ma da Merlino allor, che fe' l'incanto,
    a risponder mai sempre ei fu sforzato;
e per simil cagion, tanto né quanto
    del ver tacer altrui gli era vietato:
        ché 'l saggio mago il tutto già previsto
        e similmente al tutto avea provisto.

Florindo — for such was the shepherd's name — 60
　　whose love was ever fervent, strong and true,
at once rushed where the fire's hottest flame
　　was burning with an ardor equal to
his faith and felt that the air he breathed became
　　subtler and purer like that ever-new
　　　　fifth element,[52] that light and swift and blest
　　　　substance, which hovers high above the rest.

The knight, whose eyes had meanwhile been intent 61
　　on the fabled loves of the old gods, now spied
how fearlessly his friend Florindo went
　　among the flames and their wild heat defied,
and seeing this he, no less confident,
　　followed him, leaving his fierce steed outside
　　　　and strode, trusting himself to Vulcan, through
　　　　the fire to gain the sacred chamber too.

Three charming, smiling acolytes, arrayed 62
　　in vestments destined for the chosen few,
the quivered archer's faithful servants, bade
　　a gracious welcome and conveyed them to
the altar where they vowed their faith and prayed
　　to love's great god in ceremonies due,
　　　　even as the guardians who led them there
　　　　taught them with all solemnity and care.

But the paladin, in whom by special grace, 63
　　True Faith grows daily, will not join in this,[53]
since he suspects that from that golden face
　　spoke, not the voice of heaven, but of Dis
or an airy sprite that tricks poor men to place
　　their trust in prophecies of bale or bliss.
　　　　He therefore steps a little out of sight
　　　　and silently observes the dubious rite.

The offended idol might well have withheld 64
　　the words it was to utter to the knight,
but that Merlin, in fashioning it, compelled
　　its answering voice by strong enchantment's might
and by the same charm forced the spirit that dwelt
　　in it to answer — when it did — aright:
　　　　for the sorcerer in his wisdom could foresee
　　　　all things and laid his plans accordingly.

Rinaldo

Un candido torel, che sotto 'l peso   65
    del grave aratro non gemeva ancora,
ed avea nuovamente il petto acceso
    di quel soave ardor che n'inamora,
sendo a giacer sovra l'altar disteso,
    sacrificaro al dio ch'ivi s'adora;
        ed a te poscia, o sua vezzosa madre,
        due colombe bianchissime e leggiadre.

Finito il sacrificio, ecco si scuote   66
    lo speco, e par che 'l suol dal fondo treme;
e con strano romor di voci ignote
    tutto d'intorno omai rimbomba e geme:
così s'Austro lo fiede e lo percuote,
    il mare irato orribilmente freme.
        Crolla la statua il capo e batte l'ali,
        sonangli a tergo l'arco e gli aurei strali.

Quinci il dio così poi la lingua scioglie: 67
    — Segui, Rinaldo, il tuo desir primiero
di venir chiaro in arme; e fia tua moglie
    Clarice allora, e pago il tuo pensiero.
Fu Malagigi, a ciò che più ti invoglie
    a l'onorato marzial mestiero,
        quel che sul carro te la tolse, e poi
        salva ed illesa l'ha renduta a' suoi.

E tu, Florindo, segui l'arme ancora,   68
    ché esse ti conduranno al fin bramato,
perché, se ben no 'l sai né 'l cognosci ora,
    sei di sangue reale al mondo nato. —
Ad oracolo tal rimase allora
    dubioso ognun di lor, ma consolato,
        e scacciò de' martir la schiera folta
        che intorn'intorno al cor se gli era accolta.

A white-fleeced yearling bull whose back no weight   65
    of yoke or ponderous plow ever oppressed,
and who had barely come to feel of late
    Love's first warm promptings stirring in his breast,
lay stretched out at the idol's feet, his fate:
    by death in Cupid's honor to be blest.
        This done, for you, the god's great mother,⁵⁴ they
        two perfect milk-white doves in homage slay.

The sacrifice is done — and lo! — the cave   66
    shakes and from chasms yawning underground
uncanny voices sigh and wail and rave
    while blasts and angry gusts burst all round.
Thus when rough Auster whips and strikes the wave
    the raging sea returns a thunderous sound.
        The god then nods his head and beats his wings
        and from his gold shafts a weird twanging rings,

while these words issue from his golden tongue: 67
    "Fulfill, Rinaldo, the first vow you made:
to earn your fame in arms. Clarice ere long
    will be your wife. Thus are your pains repaid.
It was Malagis, to keep your purpose strong
    in quest of honor in the martial trade,
        who took her in his chariot, and since then
        brought her back safe to home and kin again.

And you, Florindo, follow arms also.   68
    Knighthood will bring your long-desired good.
For you — though when or how you cannot know —
    were born into the world with noble blood."
Having heard the oracle, the two, although
    still somewhat doubtful and astonished, stood
        consoled and chased away the fitful starts
        of maddening pain that had besieged their hearts.

CANTO SESTO

Parton da l'antro i duo garzoni insieme, 1
  e prendon verso Italia il lor camino,
là ov'è già presso a le ruine estreme
  da Carlo astretto il campo saracino:
ch'ivi di fare eccelse imprese han speme
  dinanzi al gran figliuol del buon Pipino,
  e vuol Florindo da la regia mano
  tôr di cavaleria l'ordin sovrano.

Attraversando gir tutto 'l paese 2
  che Giulio ornò di molti fregi pria,
e superaro ancor l'Alpi scoscese,
  per cui s'aprì la malagevol via
con novo modo il gran Cartaginese,
  Roma, portando a te guerr'aspra e ria.
  Vider d'Italia poi l'almo terreno,
  ancor di riverenza e d'onor pieno.

— Salve, d'illustri palme e di trofei 3
  provincia adorna, e d'opre alte e leggiadre;
salve, d'invitti eroi, di semidei,
  d'arme e d'ingegni ancor feconda madre,
che estendesti agli Esperii, ai Nabatei
  l'altere insegne e le vittrici squadre;
  e d'ogni forza ostil sprezzando il pondo,
  e giusta e forte desti legge al mondo. —

Così Rinaldo va parlando, e 'ntorno 4
  intanto gira il guardo desioso,
ed ognor più vede il paese adorno
  di ricche ville e vago e dilettoso;
ma non trova ventura in quel contorno
  ov'ei col fatigar prenda riposo,
  ed ove mostrar possa il suo valore
  e la virtù del generoso core.

Canto Six

Leaving the cave, the two lads made their feet   1
   tread the high road to Italy, for there —
the Saracens now being in retreat,
   laid low by Charles — the youthful pair
hoped to accomplish many a daring feat
   in full view of good Pepin's mighty heir.
      Also Florindo meant in that fair land
      to be dubbed knight by the imperial hand.

They passed through the whole region that of yore   2
   Julius[55] adorned with trophies of high worth,
then crossed the rocky Alps that long before
   the hero who in Carthage had his birth[56]
opened in strange wise, waging bitter war
   against you, Rome, the mistress of the earth.
      At last they saw kind Italy's demesne,
      where reverent honor and high fame still reign.

"Hail, province crowned with oak and palm, great scene   3[57]
   of lofty works whose glories never cease!
Hail, fertile mother of heroes, sovereign queen
   of demigod subjects in both war and peace,
who from Hesperia[58] to the Nabatene[59]
   unfurled proud flags to blaze your victories
      and, scorning every power against you hurled,
      brought justice and strong law into the world!"

Thus spoke Rinaldo, riding, and all round   4
   glanced eagerly at everything in sight.
Wherever he looked he saw the land abound
   in dwellings of abundance and delight,
but no place in those pleasant precincts found
   where he could take his ease in some hard fight
      and exercise his skill in martial art
      or show the value of his generous heart.

Rinaldo

Gran parte trapassar d'Italia, e mai 5
   non potero incontrar ventura alcuna,
benché del lor camin fêssero assai
   al freddo lume de l'argentea luna.
Giunsero al fin co' matutini rai
   là dove 'l Franco e 'l Saracin s'aduna,
      e vider tremolar l'insegne altere
      al vento, e fiammeggiar l'armate schiere.

S'alzava il sol dal mar con l'ore a paro, 6
   né di nubi copria le gote ardenti,
e, ferendo per dritto il vario acciaro,
   mille formava in ciel lampi lucenti,
e con un corruscar tremulo e chiaro
   fêa non ingrata offesa agli occhi intenti,
      tal ch'il campo sembrava Etna qualora
      l'aer con spessi fuochi orna e colora.

Carlo in tre parti il campo avea diviso, 7
   ed ei tenea con una un picciol monte;
Namo s'era con l'altra al piano assiso;
   gli stava con la terza Amone a fronte.
L'essercito infidel dêmo e conquiso
   è cinto intorno e chiuso in Aspramonte;
      ben molti ancor vi son de' Saracini,
      che stan ne' forti luoghi ivi vicini.

Poi che 'l campo da lunge ebber mirato 8
   e sodisfatto al lor desire in parte,
Florindo, bene instrutto ed informato
   di quel che deggia far, da l'altro parte,
e dritto se 'n va dove attendato
   s'era il gran Carlo in elevata parte.
      Ma Rinaldo che gir seco non volle,
      si fermò giù nel piano a piè del colle.

Passa Florindo tra l'altere squadre, 9
   adorne di valor, di ferro cinte,
ed a varie fatiche, opre leggiadre,
   tutte le vede in util modo accinte.
Quinci l'anime vili, oscure ed adre,
   cui l'ozio piace, son scacciate e spinte;
      quivi Vener non ha né Bacco loco,
      né dado infame od altro inutil gioco.

They pass through much of Italy and yet   5
   find no adventure worth a sword or lance.
So they press on and, though the sun has set,
   by silvery moonlight through chill night advance,
until at dawn while grass with dew grows wet,
   they reach the tents of Frank and Moorish bands
      and see their pennants fluttering in the air
      and warlike armor glinting everywhere.

They see the sun then, with his Hours in train,   6
   his cheeks unstained by clouds, begin to rise,
see armored steel give back his light again
   like a thousand torches pointing at the skies
whose glittering greets with not unwelcome pain
   the youthful pair's intent and eager eyes,
      for the great camp like blazing Etna marks
      the dawn's haze with a thousand lively sparks.

In three battalions Charles defied the foe.   7
   First on a hillside, he himself led one;
Namo, the second in the plain below;
   the captain of the third was brave Aymon.
Outflanked and cowed, most Saracens long ago
   had fled to hide in Aspromonte undone,
      though there still lingered many a pagan band
      in strongholds scattered through the nearby land.

The youths gazed on the camp and gazed again   8
   until their eyes grew sated with delight.
Florindo then, stopping to ascertain
   the way, bade farewell to his fellow knight
and straight away rode up where Charlemagne
   with his attendants occupied the height.
      But since to join him did not suit his will,
      Rinaldo stayed behind below the hill.

Soon to Florindo the proud ranks appear,   9
   adorned with valor, clad in iron mail,
and he finds all engaged in high travail
   and in brave works with vigor and good cheer.
No nameless, feeble caitiffs who grow pale
   at slaughter or are pleased by sloth are here.
      Venus or Bacchus[60] this way never came,
      nor vicious dice nor other useless game.

Rinaldo

Quivi si vede sol chi dal forte arco   10
   aventi strai con certa aspra percossa,
chi di scudo coperto e d'arme carco
   poggi in loco erto con destrezza e possa;
chi porti il destro suo terreno incarco
   con lieve salto oltra ben larga fossa,
     chi mova a marzial feroce assalto
     gli aspri piombati cesti or basso or alto;

chi con robusta man la spada giri   11
   in fiammeggianti rote o l'asta vibri,
e chi lottando a la vittoria aspiri,
   e diverse arme paragoni e libri;
chi con gran forza il pal di ferro tiri,
   chi d'arte militar rivolga i libri,
     chi muova tutto armato il piede al corso,
     chi volga o lente ad un corsiero il morso.

Deh! come in tutto or è l'antica norma   12
   e quel buon uso e quei bei modi spenti!
Com'or nel guerreggiar diversa forma
   si serba, oimè! tra le cristiane genti!
Or chi celebri Bacco o inutil dorma,
   chi tutti aggia i pensieri al gioco intenti,
     chi ne' piacer venerei impieghi e spenda
     le forze, è sol de' campi in ogni tenda.

Che meraviglia è poi se 'l rio serpente,   13
   sotto cui Grecia omai languendo more,
orgoglioso minaccia a l'Occidente
   e par che 'l prema già, che già il divore?
Ma dove or fuor di strada inutilmente
   mi torcon giusto sdegno, aspro dolore?
     Dove, amor e pietà, mi trasportate?
     Deh! torniamo a calcar le vie lasciate.

Florindo, uno scudier tolto in sua scorta,   14
   si fa condurre al padiglion di Carlo.
Giunto a le guardie de la regia porta,
   prega ch'entro al signor voglian menarlo.
Come il re vide, con maniera accorta,
   chini i ginocchi al suol, prese a mirarlo;
     indi fatte le guancie alquanto rosse,
     riverente ed umil tai voci mosse:

Canto Six

See here the crossbow archer making trial   10
    of launching bolts with deadly power to hurt;
or him who scales a wall, swift and agile
    under his shield, though in full armor girt;
and him who lightly leaps a deep moat while
    his right arm bears a heavy load of dirt;
        or him whose cestus[61] fist, now high, now low,
        now here, now there, directs a shattering blow.

Here is he who, lance in rest, rides fore and aft,   11
    or trains his shining sword to slash and gore,
he who in wrestling learns both power and craft,
    he who tests weapons' heft or lets them soar;
he who with great force pulls the iron shaft,
    he who sits pondering texts of martial lore;
        he, armed and mailed, in a foot-race at full speed,
        or he, with bit and spur, checking his steed.

Ah! How such customs and that ancient rule   12[62]
    and discipline are everywhere now spent!
Now too for the Christian warrior there is a school
    of soldiering, but — alas! — how different!
Now he, a slave to sleep or Bacchus' fool,
    whom naught but dice and gaming can content,
        in whom venereal pleasures dull and cramp
        all strength, lolls in each tent in every camp.

What wonder then if the fell Dragon now,   13
    with dying Greece[63] still languishing in his claws,
threatens the West with overweening brow,
    ready to seize it in his brutal jaws?
But why do I thus bootlessly allow
    just wrath and bitter grief to make me pause?
        Where, Love and Pity, do you lead my mind?
        Let us resume the road we left behind.

Florindo, with one squire, presently   14
    seeks out great Charles' tent and entering
at its gate declares his urgent wish to see
    his majesty, praying the guards to bring
him to the throne. Once there, he courteously
    kneels to the ground, his gaze fixed on the king,
        and, with a faint blush glowing on his cheeks,
        in reverent and modest tones thus speaks:

— Sir, qui vengh'io da la tua fama tratto,   15
   che quasi un novo sol risplende e vaga,
per esser di tua man cavalier fatto:
   benigno adunque il mio desire appaga. —
Carlo del suo parlar ben sodisfatto,
   e de la nobil sua sembianza vaga,
      cavalier fello, ancorché non sapesse
      dirgli a pieno onde origine ei traesse.

Prega Florindo che la man d'Orlando,   16
   l'invitta man di Dio ministra in terra,
sia quella che gli cinga al fianco il brando,
   lieto e felice augurio in ogni guerra.
Il paladin di ciò gli è grato, usando
   detti cortesi, ond'egli umil s'atterra,
      ed al gran Carlo ed a lui grazie rende;
      indi di nuovo il dir così riprende:

— Un cavalier che qui vicin m'aspetta,   17
   ed io, che ambi d'Amor seguaci siamo,
per la sua face e per la sua saetta
   d'esser campioni suoi giurato abbiamo;
onde or de l'armi dando altrui l'eletta,
   al tuo cospetto mantener vogliamo,
      ch'ascender non può l'uomo a vero onore
      se non gli è duce e non gli è scorta Amore.

Dunque s'alcun de' tuoi guerrier si truova   18
   che nemico d'Amor si mostri e sia,
e ciò voglia negar, venga a la pruova,
   ch'a lui con l'arme in man risposto fia. —
Parve proposta tal leggiadra e nuova,
   e v'è chi contradirvi omai disia.
      Carlo vuol poi che sia l'alta proposta
      per un suo messo a' Saracini esposta.

Tosto di ciò si sparse fama, e molti   19
   che ne' lacci d'Amor non furon mai,
o che se 'n quelli pur vissero involti,
   ed aspri e duri gli provaro assai,
ed essendone già liberi e sciolti,
   fissi in mente tenean gli antiqui guai,
      disposer d'adoprar l'asta e la spada,
      perché d'Amor la gloria a terra cada.

"I've come here, sire, drawn by your great fame,   15
    which like a new sun shines and spreads delight,
with one desire in my heart: to claim
    by your most gracious hand to be dubbed knight."
Charles, pleased by the young warrior's gracious shame
    in speech and by his noble, handsome sight,
        agreed to knight him, though he did not know
        whether his ancestry was high or low.

Florindo asks then that the sword be by   16
    Orlando's hand, God's earthly minister,
girt to his side and sheathed upon his thigh,
    in sign of troth, whatever might occur.
The paladin nods with pleasure in his eye
    and so Florindo kneels while they confer
        knighthood upon him. He gives thanks and then
        in words like these begins to speak again:

"I and a knight who nearby waits for me   17
    both follow Love and in his service bow,
and by his torch and golden arrows, we
    have sworn to be his champions. Wherefore now,
giving the choice of weapons to the enemy,
    we will in arms and in your sight avow
        that no man rises to true honor's height
        unless controlled and guided by Love's light.

If therefore any knight here, in denial   18
    of this, profess himself, or be, Love's foe,
let him make ready to assay the trial
    at sword or lance point and be answered so."
At this brave dare, they ponder for a while,
    but none of them steps forward to say no.
        Charles forthwith makes a messenger speed thence
        to bear the challenge to the Saracens.

Fame of this swiftly spread. Men everywhere   19
    who never felt Love's chains, or if they did,
found them too bitter and too hard to bear,
    or who had burst their shackles to be rid
of pain, but, being released from care,
    deep in their hearts kept ancient grievance hid,
        were ready to wield lance and sword to prove
        they scorned the glory of the god of Love.

Rinaldo

Carlo già presso al piano era disceso,   *20*
   intorno cinto da' suoi duci alteri,
per risguardar come l'incarco preso
   sostenerian gli incogniti guerrieri.
Rinaldo, a cui toccava il primo peso,
   attendeva a la giostra i cavalieri:
      primo è a venir Gualtier da Monlione,
      e primo anco a lasciar scarco l'arcione.

Sorse vario parlar fra i circostanti,   *21*
   vedendo il fiero corpo inaspettato,
ma cessò tosto, perché fessi avanti
   Augiolin ch'era a vincer spesso usato.
Segnano i colpi a l'elmo ambo i giostranti:
   ecco si danno, ecco cader sul prato
      l'aventurier ch'a quel colpir non resse,
      e col tergo e col capo il suolo impresse.

Berlingier ch'Angiolino a terra ir vede,   *22*
   e ne vuol fare a suo poter vendetta,
la lancia arresta e 'l destrier punge e fiede,
   e veloce ne va come saetta.
Dal fren la mano e da la staffa il piede
   gli leva il colpo averso: ei pur s'assetta,
      e ferma in sella, e torna a giostra nuova;
      ma lunge dal cavallo al pian si trova.

Molti ch'eran d'Amor fidi e devoti,   *23*
   spinti da invidia e da pensier superbo,
vennero a giostra allor, ma lasciar vòti
   i cavalli al colpir grave ed acerbo.
Tu primiero col tergo il suol percuoti,
   benché sii di gran forza e di gran nerbo,
      o fier Riccardo; poi seguonti appresso
      Druso, Alcastus, Orion, Pulione e Bresso.

Tosto dopo costor giostra Gismondo;   *24*
   tosto è dopo costor sospinto a terra.
Cadde ancor seco Orin che furibondo,
   per voler troppo, il colpo falla ed erra.
Arban suo maggior frate ora è secondo,
   ch'Orin prima e poi lui Rinaldo atterra;
      bene Aldrimante, il terzo lor germano,
      venne terzo a cader disteso al piano.

Charles had already moved down to the plain,   20
   ringed by his retinue of dukes, to view
how well the unknown warriors would sustain
   the heavy task they were committed to.
They see Rinaldo, the first jouster,[64] gain
   the lists in readiness for the pagan crew.
      The first to come is Walter of Mollione,
      the first also whose mount comes back alone.

The chattering audience, lost in doubt and fear,   21
   having watched his huge hulk hug the ground and groan,
grows silent, seeing Angiolin appear,
   to whom all thought of failure is unknown.
Both jousters at the helmet aim the spear,
   and — lo! — he's struck, and — lo! — he's overthrown
      and will not rise again, for by that thrust
      hurled down, his head and back imprint the dust.

Berlingher, who sees Angiolin fall and bleed,   22
   bent on avenging him as best he might,
puts lance in rest, gives spur and whips his steed
   and charges swifter than an arrow's flight.
With hand from bridle, feet from stirrups freed
   his foe's shaft heaves him. Still he stays upright
      in the saddle and wheels to charge with better force,
      but hits the ground together with his horse.

Many there are whom envy and foul pride   23
   drives against Love's devout and faithful friends
and who ride out there, but no sooner ride
   than tumble when the bitter blow descends.
You first plunge from your saddle, terrified,
      though fierce of temper and of bulk immense,
         Richard; and you soon after, one by one,
      Alkast, Orion, Pulion, Druse, Bresson.[65]

Then in a trice see bold Gismond appear   24
   and in a trice behold his overthrow
and with it Orin's, when that furious peer
   falls trying too hard, misjudging a great blow.
Arban, his elder brother, is second here
   to Orin, whom Rinaldo first laid low.
      Drimant, of these three brothers third — how just! —
      is fated third to fall and bite the dust.

Rinaldo

Mentre Rinaldo fa sì agevolmente   25
 verso il cielo a costor volger le piante,
ecco a pugna venir chiaro e lucente
 di forte acciaro il saracino Atlante.
Sembra egli a l'apparir torre eminente,
 sembra il destrier c'ha sotto alto elefante;
  tutto di marzial sdegno s'accende
  il guerrier, come in lui le luci intende.

Senza parlar, senza pur dirgli "guarda!",   26
 ratto muove a l'incontro il fier pagano;
né men ratto di lui l'altro ritarda,
 ma l'asta indrizza, non mai corsa in vano.
De' circonstanti ognun sospeso guarda
 qual de' duo deggia roversarsi al piano;
  batte a quelli per dubio e per sospetto,
  per ira e brama a questi il cor nel petto.

Con quel vigor, con quelle voglie pronte   27
 con cui colpirsi Achille e 'l forte Ettorre,
là 've asconde tra nubi il sacro monte
 Ideo l'aerea testa, e 'l Xanto scorre,
con quelle o con maggior ne l'ampia fronte
 vengonsi questi al primo scontro a côrre:
  e fu 'l colpo crudel di tanta forza
  che gir tre volte o quattro a poggia e orza.

Si scontrano i cavalli, e 'l fier Baiardo,   28
 quanto minor, cotanto ancor più forte,
l'altro distende con urtar gagliardo,
 e dàllo in preda a la gelata morte.
Il pagan si drizzò, ma lento e tardo,
 ché gli presse il destrier le gambe a sorte;
  intanto il cavalier lui non offende,
  ma con l'integra lancia al pian discende.

Ride il superbo Atlante e lui minaccia,   29
 come da sella al pian disceso il vede,
e dal fodro Fusberta altero caccia,
 Fusberta il brando ch'ogni prezzo eccede.
Rinaldo verso quel volta la faccia,
 e inanzi il manco e dietro 'l dritto piede
  ben fermo in terra, e l'asta a mezzo presa,
  coraggioso si move a la contesa.

But while Rinaldo effortlessly strewed   25
    the field with fallen foes who groan and pant —
lo! to the fray, sheathed in bright steel, there rode
    great Atlas from the African Levant.
He stood like a high tower and bestrode
    a steed as massive as an elephant;
        and, burning with malignant rage, drew nigh,
        fixing Rinaldo with a baleful eye.

Without so much as an *en garde!* that great   26
    infidel speeds his stallion, giving rein,
nor with less speed the other, aiming straight
    his monstrous shaft and does not aim in vain.
The onlookers in high suspense await
    which of the two shall tumble on the plain.
        Hearts on one side beat fast with doubt and fright,
        and on the other, with desire and spite.

With such determination to subdue   27
    such boundless power and ferocious pride,
Achilles and strong Hector fought in view
    of Ida's cloud-capped peak by Xanthus' side.
Such is the force, or greater, of these two,
    who now rush toward each other and collide
        with a shattering impact, strong enough to turn
        both three times round, or four, from prow to stern.

Their chargers clash head-on and Bayard, though   28
    the smaller, proves the stronger steed, for he
kicks with all four hooves and bestows a blow
    that stuns and kills the other instantly.
The pagan scrambles up, but late and slow,
    since his dead horse is pinning down his knee,
        even as the knight, loath to exploit his chance,
        dismounts, holding his still-unbroken lance.

Proud Atlas with contemptuous laughter brayed   29
    to see him from his saddle thus alight
and drew Fusberta from its sheath, that blade
    of fame, priceless Fusberta, blazing bright.
Rinaldo turns to face him, undismayed,
    then firmly plants his feet, first left, then right,
        upon the ground, grasping the shaft midway,
        and moves with quiet courage to the fray.

Rinaldo

Tutto feroce l'African si lancia,   30
    ed a trovare il va con un mandritto,
ma in mezzo il corso da l'aversa lancia
    gli è tronco il calle e l'omero traffitto.
S'allegra tutto allor lo stuol di Francia,
    ma si conturba il Saracino afflitto:
        freme il gigante e di rabbiosa fiamma
        le guancie e gli occhi orribilmente infiamma.

E da la destra uscir si lascia il brando,   31
    ch'a catena di ferro avinto pende,
sì ch'afferrar può l'asta, e lei tirando
    quasi per terra il cavalier distende,
e di man gliela cava. Indi, gettando
    quella lontan, Fusberta altier riprende.
        Rinaldo, or che farai? Chi ti soccorre?
        Come potraiti inerme a morte tôrre?

Perde ei la lancia ben, non perde il core   32
    però, ma più che mai ratto e veloce
si sottragge, saltando al gran furore
    con cui giù dechinava il ferro atroce.
Scende il ferro con impeto e romore:
    pur al terren più ch'al nemico or noce,
        né sì presto il pagan l'alza che, mentre
        ciò fa, Rinaldo sotto lui non entre.

Entra Rinaldo e col pugnal percuote   33
    la mano ostil tra' nervi acerbamente;
poi gli elsi afferra de la spada, e scuote
    di lei la destra allor poco possente.
Il fier gigante contrastar no 'l puote,
    e la sua morte omai vede presente;
        vede, meschin, ne la sua spada istessa,
        l'acerba morte sua viva ed espressa.

Quei, ch'audace stimar via più che saggio   34
    il cavaliero a lor ancor novello,
perché 'l vedeano andar con disvantaggio
    senz'aver spada a l'orrido duello,
ora il senno stimar par al coraggio,
    tal destrezza e valor vedendo in quello:
        che sia Rinaldo alcun di lor non crede,
        benché sappiano il vanto il qual si diede.

All see the furious African advance   30
    and lunge to strike him with a right-hand blow,
to find in mid-course the opposing lance
    thrust toward him and slash his shoulder so.
Then shouts of joy come from the knights of France,
    but from the Saracens stifled groans of woe.
      The giant totters while chagrin and ire
      suffuse his cheeks and eyes with horrid fire,

and from his right hand drops the sword that's tied   31
    to its scabbard by a chain and reaches for
the lance and grasps it while he takes a sudden stride
    that almost pulls the knight down to the floor
and wrests it from his hold, hurls it aside
    and grips Fusberta by the hilt once more.
      Alas, Rinaldo! Who will help you? How
      can you escape from death, thus unarmed, now?

He has lost his lance, but not his courage and   32
    now leaps aside with a velocity
more than the speed with which the heathen's hand
    brings down the murderous steel, and — see! —
whistling the sword descends and strikes the sand,
    hurting the ground more than the enemy.
      The pagan stoops for it but, slow of limb,
      can't stop Rinaldo slipping under him.

He, slipping under him, hacks at his wrist   33
    with his sharp poniard till the sinews crack,
then wrests the sword's hilt from his wounded fist,
    now nerveless, drained of strength and growing slack.
The giant warrior, helpless to resist,
    knows that death's onslaught cannot be kept back,
      sees, pagan wretch, astonished and afraid,
      his own death mirrored in Fusberta's blade!

Those who had thought it was more bold than wise   34
    for a knight till then to them unknown,
an underdog, in that harsh enterprise
    to risk his person, swordless and alone,
now praised his pluck and wisdom to the skies
    after the skill and venture he had shown.
      But that this was Rinaldo none surmised,
      though of his young boast long ago apprised.

Rinaldo

Alza il guerriero intanto il suo robusto   35
   braccio per estirpar germe sì rio,
e dove il capo termina col busto,
   il gran corpo divise e dipartio;
da le gelate membra, inutil fusto,
   l'alma vermiglia involta in sangue uscio,
     e stridendo n'andò nel cieco Averno,
     là 'v'è 'l duolo, l'orrore e 'l pianto eterno.

L'asta raccolta, ascese in sul destriero   36
   Rinaldo, ma Fusberta il brando eletto
si cinse prima, poiché 'l voto altero,
   che già fece egli, or ha sortito effetto,
avendo tolto a forza ad uom sì fiero,
   da cui stat'era a dubii passi astretto,
     la ben guernita e ben temprata spada,
     di cui non è chi meglio punga o rada.

Otton, che si dolea che 'l pagan tronco   37
   il suo desio gli avesse e 'l luoco tolto,
vedendolol senza nome ignobil tronco,
   nel proprio sangue orribilmente involto,
sprona il destrier, arresta il grosso tronco,
   ma cadde, da Rinaldo in fronte colto;
     quindi poi fu da l'empio ferro estinto
     il buon Ugon, non che da sella spinto.

Questi il nimico in petto avea colpito,   38
   e quasi tratto al pian dal suo cavallo;
da l'altra parte il paladin, ferito
   sol l'aere e 'l vento, l'asta corse in fallo,
onde da l'ira e dal furor rapito
   poi l'uccise in brevissimo intervallo,
     e quasi in un istante a lui recise
     il capo, e 'l brando sino al cor gli mise.

Quel ferro ch'ad Ugon il cor traffisse,   39
   il cor traffisse insieme al magno Carlo,
perciò che lui, mentre in sua corte visse,
   cotanto amò che non potea più amarlo.
Or non vorria che invendicato gisse,
   e dentro è roso da mordace tarlo:
     da desir di vendetta ei dentro è roso,
     né puote il suo pensier tenere ascoso.

Meanwhile the knight with his strong arm proceeds   35
     to exterminate so criminal a race,
and where the neck to the vast ribcage leads
     divides the body just below the face.
From the carcass that grows ice-cold as it bleeds
     the soul, with crimson gore bathed, flees the place
         and shrieking sinks to blind Avernus, there
         to dwell in endless torment and despair.

Taking back his lance, Rinaldo mounts again,   36
     but first girds on Fusberta, that choice blade,
since the audacious vow that he swore when
     he came to manhood has now been obeyed,
and he has taken from that fiercest of men,
     unaided and by perils undismayed,
         the well-wrought and well-tempered sword,
           whose fierce
         edge knows no equal, be it to slash or pierce.

Otho,⁶⁶ grieved at the Saracen's mischance   37
     because it cheats him of both praise and prize,
seeing the corpse lie in a mortal trance,
     painted with its own blood in horrid wise,
gives spur and charges with his massive lance,
     but falls, struck by Rinaldo twixt the eyes.
         Next then the heathen sword transfixed and slew,
         though still erect upon his steed, good Hugh.

For he struck his opponent in the chest   38
     and almost made him topple from his horse.
But Rinaldo ran amiss with lance in rest
     wounding the wind and air with wasted force,
whereat, by sudden frantic rage possessed,
     he slew him there and then, without remorse,
         and almost in one instant cleft apart
         his skull and plunged his blade into his heart.

That sword that here transfixed Hugh's heart also   39
     transfixed with grief the heart of Charlemagne,
for Hugh, since he swore fealty long ago,
     had loved him best of any in his reign.
The king now aches for an avenging blow,
     stung by the serpent of his inward pain.
         His thirst for vengeance rankles in his mind
         and cannot long stay hidden or confined.

Rinaldo

Ma rivolto ad Orlando, il qual dal lato   *40*
   manco gli stava, a lui così ragiona:
— O da me qual figliuol nipote amato,
   o sostegno maggior di mia corona,
vedi ben tu com'empia man privato
   d'Ugone or n'have, e com'ei n'abbandona,
      quand'era la sua età nel più bel fiore,
      e in colmo i suoi servigi e 'l nostro amore.

Ahi quanto ardito fu, quanto fu forte,   *41*
   ahi quanto buono, ahi quanto a noi fedele!
Ed è ben dritto, oimè! ch'a la sua morte
   tutta Francia si lagne e si querele.
Ma chi per l'aspra sua spietata sorte
   sparger pianti e sospir, sparger querele
      de' più d'ambo duo noi, s'ambo duo noi
      deggiam più ch'altri ai gran servigii suoi?

Dunque un sì meritevol cavaliero   *42*
   morirà invendicato, e tu 'l vedrai?
Tu che 'l forte Troiano, Almonte il fiero
   vincesti, or di costui temanza avrai?
Deh! rompi omai l'orgoglio a questo altero,
   deh! fa' del nostro Ugon vendetta omai,
      e solleva qual pria l'onor di Francia,
      ch'abbattuto or si sta da l'altrui lancia. —

Con questi detti e con molti altri spinse   *43*
   il forte Orlando contra 'l forte estrano,
ché quegli prima a giostra non s'accinse,
   non essendo al pugnar facile e vano.
Né fello or volontier, né farlo ei finse,
   anzi il suo pensier disse aperto e piano;
      ma Carlo il prega, e contradir non giova,
      onde convien ch'al suo voler si muova.

Egli era armato, e sol l'ardita fronte   *44*
   non ricopria con l'onorato incarco,
ma fattosi recar l'elmo d'Almonte,
   tosto di quel si rese adorno e carco.
Rinaldo, ch'al quartier conobbe il conte
   ch'a scontrarlo venia, non fu già parco
      in allentar la briglia, oprar lo sprone,
      lieto di sì bramata occasione.

He to Orlando then, who silently   40
    stood on his left, says with a gloomy frown:
"Ah, nephew, like a son beloved of me!
    Ah, best support of my imperial crown!
Behold a villain's hand has treacherously
    robbed us of our dear Hugh and cut him down
        in the flower of youth and when none ranked above
        him in unswerving fealty and our love.

"Alas! How bold he was! How strong!   41
    Alas! How good! How loyal and how true!
Ah, woe is me! His slaughter is a wrong
    that rightly makes all France dissolve in rue.
But who could with more tears and sighs prolong
    his mourning for his murder than we two,
        since, from the time his services began,
        we owe him more than any other man?

And shall a knight of such great merit die   42
    all unavenged, with you nearby? Ah no!
You, who strong Troyan, fierce Almont defied,
    should you now fear an upstart, nameless foe?
Go then, and break his overweening pride!
    Go to wreak vengeance for our Hugh, and so
        raise back on high the fallen honor of France
        that now lies cast down by a stranger's lance!"[67]

In such words and in many more, he still   43
    goads on Orlando to attack and smite,
who had not earlier sought to try his skill,
    not being lightly moved or vain to fight.
Even now he is loath to joust or say he will
    and plainly states he feels it is not right,
        but since Charles bids him, he cannot refuse,
        though this is not a quarrel he would choose.

He had his armor on, but his bold brow   44
    was not yet graced by his illustrious casque.
He bade them bring him Almont's helmet now
    and quickly donned it to confront his task.
Rinaldo, seeing Orlando's shield avow
    the great count from afar, paused not to ask
        his name, but loosed his reins and spurred his steed,
        delighted at this chance Fate had decreed.

Rinaldo

Muse, or per voi s'apra Elicona, e 'l santo   45
  vostro favor più largo a me si presti,
onde con nuovo stil m'inalzi tanto,
  ch'al gran soggetto inferior non resti.
E tu, Minerva, ancor reggi il mio canto,
    come la man de' duo campion reggesti:
      ché non men puoi ne l'una e l'altra parte
      dar forza altrui, ch'Apollo insieme e Marte.

Non giamai negli ondosi umidi regni   46
  s'investon con furor sì violento
duo veloci nemici armati legni,
  spinti o da remi o da secondo vento,
che l'un ne l'altro imprime aperti segni,
  e ne rimbomba il liquido elemento,
    come costor ch'a colpi orrendi e crudi
    con spaventevol suon fendon gli scudi.

Fendersi i ferrei scudi e cadde a terra   47
  Brigliador prima e poscia ancor Baiardo;
tosto drizzarsi i duo folgor di guerra,
  né punto l'un fu più de l'altro tardo:
ognun ne l'armi si raccoglie e serra,
  adopra ogn'arte ed usa ogni risguardo,
    a ripararsi ed a ferir provisto,
    ché 'l valor già de l'inimico ha visto.

Si copre il petto con lo scudo Orlando,   48
  porto inanzi col ferro il braccio destro.
Rinaldo intorno a lui si va girando
  tutto veloce, tutto lieve e destro,
di farlo discoprir sempre tentando;
  ma sempre trova quel cauto e maestro:
    né per finte o per cenni unqua si muove,
    né cangia il passo o drizza il ferro altrove.

Ecco mentre Rinaldo aggira e tenta   49
  di poterlo ferir, ma sempre in vano,
scoperto alquanto il petto a lui presenta.
  Ratto egli spinge allor l'armata mano,
al capo accenna e mostra cura intenta
  di colpir quella parte al suo germano;
    poi declinando il ferro al petto giunge,
    trapassa ogni arma e lievemente il punge.

O Muses, open Helicon to me   45
    and by your grace now let my numbers glow
that in a new style I may soar, nor be
    too feeble for the theme you here bestow.
And you, Minerva, even as you see
    and guide the two knights, guide my song also
        till neither power from the other bars
        the sense that here Apollo joins with Mars.

Never in battle on the wave-tossed tide   46
    did two armed ships, which furiously careened
into each other, with such force collide,
    impelled by oars or by a favoring wind,
and mark with gaping holes each other's side
    through which the surge bursts thundering from behind,
        as now their shields with horrifying sound
        clash while their impact shakes the ground.

Their iron shields clash and their horses fall,   47
    first Brigliador and Bayard after him,
but lightning-fast the knights leap up withal
    for they were neither dazed nor slow of limb.
Each of his shield and armor makes a wall
    and summons all his skill and foresight, grim
        in expectation of the first stroke, for
        both sense they've glimpsed each other's might in war.

Orlando, covering with his shield his breast,   48
    stands rock-like, sword in hand, poised for the kill.
Rinaldo, turning toward him, tries his best
    by nimble leaps, by tricks of speed and skill
to shake his guard, and baits him without rest,
    but finds him masterful and wary still,
        unmoved, and by no feint or lunge dismayed,
        to change his posture or to lower his blade.

Lo! While Rinaldo tries his uttermost,   49
    shifting and turning for advantage, he
for an instant leaves his chest somewhat exposed.
    At this, his foe moves forward eagerly,
with sword upraised, pretending he proposed
    to strike his cousin's[68] head, then suddenly
        lowers his sword and, lunging swiftly in,
        stabs through his coat of mail and breaks the skin.

Quel, più che sangue allor dal petto, sparse 50
   ira dagli occhi, orribile in sembianza.
Non più schermir, non più con arte aitarse,
   ma ben vuol tutta oprar la sua possanza:
dove da l'elmo il cimier suole alzarse,
   fiede con forza, ch'ogni forza avanza.
      Orlando al colpo orrendo il capo inchina,
      co' piè traballa e quasi al pian ruina.

Pur si riave e poggia in tal furore 51
   che in sé non cape omai né truova loco;
gli occhi accesi travolge e manda fuore
   da la visiera un sfavillante foco;
fa co' denti fremendo alto romore.
   Che tanto dirò mai che non sia poco?
      Tal forse è Giove allor che 'l ciel disserra,
      e 'l folgor minacciando irato afferra.

Rinaldo, che venirsi adosso mira 52
   il fero conte in sì terribil faccia,
ne lo scudo si chiude e si ritira
   dal colpo ove opra Orlando ambe le braccia.
Così s'umido vento irato spira,
   ed inimica pioggia al suol minaccia,
      il peregrin che vede il nembo oscuro
      ver' quel schermo si fa di tetto o muro.

Ma per la troppo furia in man si volse 53
   al forte Orlando la tagliente spada;
pur di piatto lo scudo opposto colse,
   onde convien che rotto in pezzi cada.
Poi scese a l'elmo e 'l bel cimier gli tolse,
   chiuse ben l'elmo al suo furor la strada;
      Rinaldo sostenersi allor non puote,
      ma con ambo i ginocchi il suol percuote.

Pur tosto si drizzò, più che mai fosse, 54
   fiero e rabbioso il gran figliuol d'Amone,
e ne la spalla il suo cugin percosse,
   sì ch'indi il disarmò fino al galone;
e gli avria l'arme del suo sangue rosse
   fatte, ma gliel vietò la fatagione:
      ch'Orlando, quale Achille o Cigno, dura
      la pelle e contra 'l ferro ebbe sicura.

More dreadfully now wrath burns in his eyes   50
    than blood comes gushing from his wounded breast.
Dropping his guard, no longer he relies
    on art, but on his brute strength at its best,
and with a force that stuns and stupefies
    lands a huge blow near his opponent's crest.
        Orlando's head bobs at that buffet's thrust.
        He reels and nearly topples to the dust,

but soon recovers, and his giant frame   51
    seems insufficient to contain his spite.
His eyes, rolling in anger, are aflame,
    and from his visor fiery sparks alight.
He loudly grinds his teeth in wrath and shame.
    Can I find speech that will not seem too slight?
        Thus from his throne perhaps does furious Jove
        cleave with his dreaded bolt the clouds above.

Rinaldo, seeing Orlando near with those   52
    ferocious eyes set in a baleful glower,
retires behind his shield to ward the blows
    the count now deals him with two-handed power.
Thus when on high a gloomy rain cloud grows
    and threatens earth with a torrential shower,
        a pilgrim noting the approaching squall
        crouches beneath a sheltering roof or wall.

He then, with sharp sword at the ready, stands   53
    resolved to face the fury of his foe.
The flat side of Orlando's sword now lands
    upon his shield that, shattered, falls below,
next on his helmet that, though it withstands
    the impact, has its crest crushed by the blow.
        Rinaldo cannot stay erect. He reels
        and, both legs giving way beneath him, kneels.

At once recovering from his alarm,   54
    Aymon's great son, now fierce and battle-mad,
lunged with his blade and struck his cousin's arm,
    ripping the chainmail to the shoulder pad,
and would have bloodied it, but here a charm
    baffled his power, because Orlando had,
        as Achilles or as Cycnus[69] did, a skin
        no edge or point of steel could enter in.

Or chi narrar potrebbe a parte a parte   55
    le lor percosse orribili e diverse
onde di rotte piastre e maglie sparte
    tutto intorno il terren si ricoperse?
Chi accennar pur l'alta possanza e l'arte,
    a cui simile il ciel giamai non scerse?
        il ciel che de' mortali i fatti e l'opre
        or con mille occhi, or con un sol discopre.

L'essercito cristian e 'l saracino   56
    tutto stupisce a quel pugnar sì fiero;
tra sé rivolge il figlio di Pipino
    chi sia quel forte incognito guerriero.
Or Francardo l'estima ed or Mambrino,
    ora sovra Chiarello ei fa pensiero,
        de' quai l'alto valor con chiara tromba
        oltra l'Eufrate ed oltra il Nil rimbomba.

Rinaldo in questa ch'a se stesso vede   57
    ferito alquanto il destro fianco e 'l petto,
e conosce ch'Orlando indarno fiede,
    ché non ne segue alcun bramato effetto,
tenta novo partito, e certo crede,
    egli vien seco a guerreggiar più stretto,
        di superarlo al gioco de la lotta,
        tanto ha la mano essercitata e dotta.

Quegli ciò scorge e non si schiva punto,   58
    anzi mostra ch'a lui non manco piaccia;
ecco che l'uno a l'altro è già congiunto
    con le man, con le gambe e con la faccia.
L'afferra Orlando a mezzo il collo a punto;
    Rinaldo lui con ambedue le braccia
        sotto de' fianchi attraversando cinge:
        lo scuote e gira, lo solleva e spinge.

Ed or col destro piè gli avince il manco,   59
    ed or col mento l'omero gli preme;
or, perché 'l fiato pur gli venga manco
    lo stringe a' fianchi con le forze estreme.
Orlando a lui col core ardito e franco,
    l'arte accoppiando e la gran possa insieme,
        il collo calca sì pesante e greve
        che 'l tuo pondo, o Tifeo, forse è più leve.

Canto Six

Now who could tell or number one by one   55
    the terrible and varied blows here given,
by which the plain is strewn with mail undone
    and shattered plate of armor crushed or riven?
Who paint the strength and art here shown, like none
    that ever before that day was seen by heaven —
        heaven, which sees all actions from on high
        with a thousand eyes or with a single eye?

The Christian army and the Saracen   56
    both stand amazed at the fierce acts they see,
and Pepin's son is wondering deep within
    who this astounding unknown knight might be,
now thinks he might be Francard, now Mambrin,
    and now again great Clarel,[70] for all three
        were men whose fame for valorous deeds resounds
        beyond the Nile's, beyond Euphrates' bounds.

Rinaldo, who begins to feel some pain   57
    from wounds in his right flank and on his chest,
sensing he strikes Orlando all in vain,
    however hard or fast or without rest,
conceives a plan by which he might obtain
    the upper hand: to put him to the test
        in wrestling, feeling certain he would win,
        this being an art he is much practiced in.

The other is not slow to understand   58
    and his assent with a grim smile displays.
Behold how they are joined already: hand
    to hand and leg to leg and face to face.
For mid-neck then Orlando reaches and
    Rinaldo in a strong two-armed embrace
        grasps him beneath his flanks and lifts and twists
        and shakes and pushes him while he resists,

now with his left foot tries to trip his right,   59
    now with his chin jabs at his collarbone,
and now strains his great flanks with all his might
    to squeeze the breath from him and make him groan.
But brave Orlando makes his grip grow tight,
    using his cunning, not his strength alone,
        and pulls back on his nape with force so great
        that you, Typhoeus, would seem less in weight.

Non puote l'un l'altro gittar per terra,   60
    e quanto il vigor manca, il furor cresce;
pur anelanti l'ostinata guerra
    seguon, né lor disegno alcun riesce;
e già lo spirto lor si chiude e serra,
    già per tutto il sudor si spande ed esce;
        al fin tornan di nuovo al primo assalto,
        ed a girare il ferro or basso or alto.

Tornano al primo assalto, e 'l piano ancora   61
    torna a tremar con spaventevol suono;
manda l'aria percossa ad ora ad ora,
    qual da le rotte nubi orribil tuono.
Non più soffrir puote 'l gran Carlo allora
    ch'i duo guerrier, che 'nsieme a fronte sono,
        menino a certo fin la pugna incerta,
        poi c'hanno a pien la lor possanza esperta.

Egli deposto avea l'odio e 'l rancore   62
    che dianzi avea contra 'l guerrier strano,
sol per cagion de l'alto suo valore,
    ch'or ha veduto via più chiaro e piano:
ché se 'l frenare i sùbiti del core
    e' primi moti non è in nostra mano,
        può bene il saggio con miglior discorso
        porre agli affetti rei poi duro morso.

E sempre avien che così alberghi e regne   63
    l'amor de la virtude in nobil petto,
ch'a poco a poco al fin consuma e spegne
    d'ira e di sdegno ogni rabbioso affetto;
perché avinte fra lor son l'alme degne
    d'un legame d'amor sì forte e stretto,
        che se 'l caso talor pur le disgiunge,
        tosto quel le ristringe e ricongiunge.

Il saggio re, c'ha l'ira in amor volta,   64
    sospinge il corridor tra i duo guerrieri:
grossa sbarra partir così tal volta
    suol duo d'ira infiammati aspri destrieri.
Frena egli con l'aspetto, ove è raccolta
    divina maestà, gli animi alteri;
        indi con modi accorti a parlar mosse,
        e lor d'ogni rio sdegno ambi duo scosse:

Neither can make the other fall, and yet   60
     though their strength ebbs, their fury grows, and they
doggedly struggle with no rest or let,
     though neither strategy nor strength make way.
Already they are panting, soaked in sweat,
     with breaths so strained that scarce their limbs obey.
       At last they both draw swords just as before,
       pointing their blades now high, now low, once more.

Once more they try their first assault. All day   61
     the ground is trembling as they hack and smite.
Hour after hour the air echoes the fray
     as when a thunderstorm turns day to night.
But then great Charles no longer wished that they,
     thus locked in desperate conflict in his sight,
       should give uncertain fight a certain end,
       since now he knew how hard each could contend.

He had dispelled his hatred and disdain   62
     for the stranger knight, since now he felt arise
respect for his high valor, finding plain
     evidence of it right before his eyes:
for though we may be powerless to restrain
     the heart's quick stirrings when they first arise,
       yet can a wise man by due thought control
       a wicked impulse rising in his soul.

And verily love of virtue always dwells   63
     and reigns supremely in a noble mind,
so that at last it overrules and quells
     all promptings that are savage and unkind.
For the strong bond of love, unlike all else,
     will worthy souls so firmly join and bind
       that if they are wrenched by some mischance apart,
       it soon once more rejoins them heart to heart.

With anger turned to love, the thoughtful king   64
     now steps between the two in one great stride —
just so at times two stallions quarreling
     a high and sturdy barrier will divide —
and in his royal aspect mustering
     a godlike majesty, controls their pride,
       then speaks in words whose courtesy and skill
       cancel in both all rancor and ill will:

— Di sì lieve cagion nato, omai cessi   65
   lo sdegno, ed oltre più non vi trasporte;
e poiché mostro avete a segni espressi
   quant'ognun di voi sia pugnace e forte,
mostrate or di saper ancor voi stessi
   vincer, quando ragione a ciò v'esorte;
      e sendo chiara ormai la virtù vostra,
      date, vi prego, luogo a nuova giostra.

Abbracciatevi insieme, e così spero   66
   che tra voi le discordie or fian compite;
ciò concedete a me ch'in don ve 'l chero,
   vago di veder pace ov'era lite.
E tu dimmi anco, degno estran guerriero,
   c'hai le man forti quai le brame ardite,
      tuo nome e sangue, ond'io conosca aperto
      cavalier di tal pregio e di tal merto. —

Rinaldo allor: — Non già sostiene, o sire,   67
   tanto cognoscitor mio basso stato,
né senz'alto rossor ti potrei dire
   mio nome, tra guerrier nulla pregiato.
Nel resto poi son pronto ad esseguire
   quanto vedrò ch'a te fia caro e grato,
      e cedo volontier la palma e 'l pregio
      a questo invitto cavaliero egregio. —

Così dicendo, umile e riverente   68
   va per baciare al suo cugin la mano,
ma quegli la ritira e no 'l consente,
   anzi il raccoglie in cortese atto umano;
e di quella battaglia il fa vincente,
   e lieva al cielo il suo valor sovrano:
      ché, poiché in arme non può superarlo,
      almeno in cortesia tenta avanzarlo.

E sendogli recata un'armatura   69
   onde avea già spogliato un duce moro,
ch'era di tempra adamantina e dura,
   a scaglie fatta con sottil lavoro,
e sopravesta avea di seta azura,
   rigida ed aspra per argento ed oro,
      al cavalier estrano in don la diede,
      poi ch'indosso la sua rotta gli vede.

"Born of slight cause, let rage no longer grow;   65
   no longer feed your sense of enmity.
For now that you've made all and sundry know
   how warlike and how strong you both can be,
show all the world that you can overthrow
   yourselves as well. Let reason make you see
      that your great worth shines out as clear as day.
      You are champions both. Give over this joust, I pray.

Embrace! Be friends! After this desperate fight,   66
   let all discord between you two abate.
Grant me this gift, I beg you, and requite
   my longing to see peace where there was hate.
And you, moreover, worthy stranger knight
   with hands as strong as your desires are great,
      tell me your name and blood, and thus make known
      a man of such high merit as your own."

Rinaldo then: "Sire, I can't allow   67
   my low estate to be brought to your ear,
nor without blushing could I tell you now
   my name, being yet without distinction here.
As for the rest, without reserve I vow
   to do whatever service you hold dear
      and gladly yield the honors of the fight
      to this invincible and peerless knight."

This said, he bends down, meek and reverent,   68
   offering to kiss his cousin's hand, but he
draws back at once, surmising his intent,
   and folds him in his arms most graciously,
declares him winner of the fight, content
   to laud his sovereign valor, feeling free,
      though by the sword he could not win the field,
      by grace and courtesy to make him yield.

A suit of armor to him then was brought,   69
   which from a Moorish duke he seized of old,
its scale-plates joined with subtle art and wrought
   of tempered steel, a wonder to behold,
with a surcoat of blue stiffened silk that caught
   the light in inlaid threads of silver and gold.
      This gift he to the stranger knight presented
      whose own hung on his back all slashed and dented.

Ma né cortese in ciò punto mostrarsi   70
   di lui vol meno il gran figliuol d'Amone:
anzi dal suo scudiero una fe' darsi
   leggiadra spoglia d'african leone,
che bianchi peli avea tra fulvi sparsi,
   e già fu dono d'un gentil barone.
     Per le grosse unghie d'or, per l'aurea testa,
     e per li folti velli è grave questa.

Con tal dono ad Orlando il cambio rende   71
   de l'alta cortesia che gli ha dimostra.
Grifone intanto il Maganzese attende
   impaziente i cavalieri a giostra,
e sovra un gran cavallo intento rende
   ogn'occhio a sé con vaga altera mostra.
     Questi arrogava al suo valor cotanto,
     che si crede d'aver ne l'arme il vanto.

Già ver' costui Rinaldo si movea,   72
   ma Florindo il garzon vi s'interpose,
dicendogli ch'in arme ei fatto avea
   opre che sempre fian meravigliose,
e ch'ora il loco a lui ceder dovea,
   e curarsi le piaghe sanguinose:
     a lui che sin allor riguardatore
     stato era sol de l'alto suo valore.

Ecco, o Grifone, chi ti toglie omai   73
   di quel tant'orgoglioso tuo pensiero.
Misero! tu cadendo a terra vai
   al primo colpo d'un novel guerriero:
tu, che d'Orlando più ti pregi assai,
   per mano or d'un fanciul premi il sentiero.
     Florindo abbatte poscia anco Ansuigi,
     Avino, Avorio, Anselmo e Dionigi.

Solmon di Scozia, Alberto d'Inghilterra   74
   cadono ancora, e 'l parigin Vistagno,
ed altri molti dopo questi atterra
   Florindo, e fa di gloria alto guadagno.
Rinaldo a l'allegrezza il cor disserra,
   tai cose far vedendo al suo compagno.
     Intanto ha fine con la giostra il giorno,
     e Carlo al campo fa co' suoi ritorno.

Great Aymon's son is no less keen to win   70
 praise for his courtesy and power to please.
He therefore bids his squire to bring in
 for his new friend a Libyan lion's fleece
speckled with white hairs on the tawny skin,
 gift from a noble lord, a trophy piece:
  its massive golden claws, its golden head,
  and tousled mane rouse reverence and dread.

Such is the gift he gives in recompense   71
 for the great courtesy by Orlando shown.
Impatient for the joust to recommence,
 Maganzan Gryphon meanwhile sits alone
on his great steed. His proud self-confidence
 shows plainly in his posture. In his own
  prowess that warrior places absolute trust,
  thinking no mortal could abide his thrust.

Rinaldo, seeing him thus ready, came   72
 to face him, but Florindo stepped between
saying he had performed such feats as Fame
 would in eternal memory keep green
and now should tend to his still-bleeding frame
 and let him, who till then had only been
  an onlooker of his great prowess, vie
  by deeds to match it, or at least to try.

Look at him, Gryphon — him who evermore   73
 will empty you of all your arrogance.
Wretch! You are now sent tumbling to the floor
 by the first blow from this new warrior's lance.
You, who above Orlando thought to soar,
 here fall, pushed over by a mere boy's hands.
  These, after you, Ansuigi overwhelm,
  then Avin, Avor, Dennis and Anselm,[71]

make Scottish Solomon, English Albert fall,   74
 and Vistaing, knight of Paris, to their shame,
with countless others following, one and all
 thus amply bolstering Florindo's fame.
Rinaldo's heart leaps up to see them sprawl,
 delighted at his youthful friend's acclaim.
  Meanwhile the tourney ends as evening nears,
  and Charles returns to camp with all his peers.

Rinaldo

Ma prima ei tenta ben di ritenere
 i due guerrier per breve spazio almeno,
e di Rinaldo ancor tenta sapere
 la patria, il nome e 'l rimanente a pieno.
Ma non puote di ciò nulla ottenere,
 onde al desire ed al pregar pon freno,
  e d'ambo i cavalier le scuse accetta,
  e color quinci poi se 'n vanno in fretta.

But first he once again seeks to detain   75
    the champion pair if only for a while,
and once again attempts to ascertain
    Rinaldo's lineage, name and domicile,
but, recognizing that he sues in vain,
    he bridles his desire and with a smile
        accepts both their excuses in good grace,
        at which they mount and swiftly leave the place.

Canto settimo

Partonsi i duo guerrier poiché non hanno   1
    dove impiegar più quivi il lor valore,
perciò che i Mori entro al castel si stanno
    rinchiusi, ed a pugnar non escon fuore.
Nuove venture a ritrovar se 'n vanno,
    spinti da cura e da desir d'onore,
        ch'al petto e caldo stimolo pungente:
        né che stian neghitosi unqua consente.

Veggono intanto da facelle accese   2
    esser divisi largamente i campi,
e ch'a le cose lor sembianze han rese
    mal grado de la notte amici lampi;
senton l'orecchie da un lamento offese
    qual d'uom che d'ira e di dolore avampi;
        più sempre cresce il lamentevol suono,
        e già vicini i lumi ardenti sono.

Scorgono allora un uom già carco d'anni,   3
    giunto ove cader suol l'umana vita,
involto in neri ed angosciosi panni,
    con la faccia di duol colma e smarrita,
che in duro segno degli interni affanni
    e de la rabbia dentro il petto unita,
        geme, sospira ed altamente piange,
        batte il sen, squarcia il crine e 'l volto frange.

Era costui del morto Ugone il padre,   4
    che da paterno amor tratto seguio
col figlio insieme le francesi squadre,
    già vecchio ed al pugnar pigro e restio.
Ben ebbe in cielo stelle oscure ed adre,
    poiché con gli occhi proprii il caso rio
        venne a veder del misero figliuolo,
        e, vedendol, maggior fece il suo duolo.

Canto Seven

The two knights left the place since it displayed   1
   no fields where they could prove their might,
for all the Moors within their strongholds stayed
   walled up and did not sally out to fight.
They left to seek out new adventures, made
   eager by dreams of scaling honor's height
      that each of them felt burning in his breast,
      so that he never tired in the quest.

They see encamped as they start journeying thence   2
   the four great hosts,[72] whose flickering torches show
from far away the shapes of distant tents
   outlined in darkness by their friendly glow.
Anon their ears are met by wild laments
   as of a man gone mad with wrath or woe.
      Louder and louder sounds the piteous cry,
      and now they see the campfires blaze nearby.

There they behold a man who seems to be   3
   of an age when life is ready to depart,
garbed all in black, a pitiful sight to see,
   his face contorted by some grievous smart,
who in sure sign of dire agony
   and boundless sorrow raging in his heart
      sighs, beats his breast, tears his white locks and wails
      and tears his tear-stained countenance with his nails.

This mourner was the father of dead Hugh,   4
   whom his paternal love came to incite
to follow his son in the French retinue,
   himself being too old and weak to fight.
It was an evil star indeed that drew
   him there to greet his own eyes with the sight
      of his son's wretched death, of which to know
      was woe enough; to see it, utmost woe.

Rinaldo

Come egli scorge il tronco corpo amato,   5
    che par ch'in mezo un rio di sangue giaccia,
cader tosto si lascia, e sul piagato
    busto s'affige, e 'l prende infra le braccia:
lo cinge e stringe e nel suo manco lato,
    ove è ferito, più posa la faccia,
        e così stassi, fuor de' sensi uscito,
        sovra 'l morto giacendo il tramortito.

Al fin tornò lo spirto al suo ricetto,   6
    e seco il pianto ed i sospir tornaro;
spinse tai voci allor da l'egro petto
    con suono conveniente al duol amaro:
— Amato figlio mio, figliuol diletto,
    gradito figlio, figlio solo e caro,
        oimè! tu morto giaci, e quel ch'è peggio,
        per sì lieve cagion cotal ti veggio.

O voti a vòto fatti, o pensier miei   7
    fallaci, o preghi sparsi a sordi venti,
o decreti del cielo ingiusti e rei,
    se ciò dir lece, o Dio, com'el consenti?
Deh! ben felice per tua morte sei,
    tu, madre sua, ch'or nulla vedi e senti;
        io d'altra parte, oimè! vinto ho 'l mio fato
        per esser vivo a sì gran duol serbato.

Ma dove, lasso! or è? dove è, diviso   8
    dal busto, il capo? Ahi, forse alcun l'ha tolto?
Ahi! dunque non vedrò l'amato viso?
    Dunque non basciarò l'amato volto? —
Così dicendo mira intento e fiso,
    e lo vede tra sangue e polve involto:
        là corre impaziente e fuori il cava
        da l'elmo, il bascia e col suo pianto il lava.

Il nudo teschio dimostrava allora   9
    un non so che del fiero e dell'orrendo;
tiene in lui fissi gli occhi il padre ognora,
    e tra le man pietose il va volgendo;
se l'accosta a la bocca ad ora ad ora,
    nulla l'orror di quello a schivo avendo.
        Quanto, quanto sei grande, amor paterno!
        Sfoga intanto ei così l'affetto interno:

Canto Seven

He saw the dear child whom he once caressed   5
   prone in a pool of blood and to that place
hastened distraught and on his wounded breast
   collapsed, enfolding him in his embrace.
He hugged and strained him like a man possessed
   and on his bleeding left side laid his face,
     and thus remained as if bereft of breath,
     atop the dead man in a faint like death.

When sense at last returned to him, he cried   6
   and wailed in accents piteous to hear
and wrenched these harsh words[73] from his lips, his side
   heaving with groans mid many a bitter tear:
"O my belovèd son, my joy, my pride,
   my treasured son, my only son, my dear —
     woe! — you are dead, and worse, dead in a fight
     that claimed your young life in a cause so slight.

Oh, useless vows! Oh, empty thoughts that I'm   7
   deluded by! Oh, prayers prayed to air!
O heaven, can you permit so great a crime?
   Be it lawful then to call your doom unfair.
Ah! Blessed mother, to have died in time
   never to know the pain you now would bear,
     while I have been condemned by fate — ah woe! —
     to live to bear the torments I now know.

But where — alas! — where is it now? Where lies   8
   the severed head? Did someone take it? Must
I nevermore see those beloved eyes,
   or kiss those lips? Is heaven so unjust?"
Saying this, he looks round in frantic wise,
   then sees the head covered with blood and dust
     and picks it up and from its helmet clears
     the face and, kissing it, bathes it with tears.

The dead skull wears a blind, uncanny gaze   9
   on its repugnant, blood-smeared countenance.
The father, with his eyes fixed on its face,
   holds it and turns it in his loving hands,
and now and then lets his fond fingers trace
   its lips, showing no horror in his glance.
     How great you are, paternal love, how great!
     Then he goes on thus to bewail his fate:

Rinaldo

— Ove la luce de' begli occhi è gita? 10
Ove del vago aspetto il chiaro onore?
Come le guancie, oimè! come smarrita
    le labbia han lor vaghezza e lor colore?
Questa squallida fronte e scolorita
    è quella ond'io porgea tal gioia al core?
        Deh! quanto ei n'ebbe già diletto e gioia,
        tanto maggior or n'have affanno e noia!

Ecco, o figlio, ti fo gli estremi offici, 11
    ch'a me dovei tu far più drittamente!
Ecco che gli occhi omai con l'infelici
    man ti rinchiudo: or vale eternamente!
E se queste mie man non fiano ultrici
    de la tua morte, il ciel non lo consente,
        che con lungo girar l'ha già private
        del suo vigore e delle forze usate. —

Apre a pietà Rinaldo il nobil petto 12
    a quei lamenti, e raddolcir vorebbe
alquanto di colui l'amaro affetto,
    perché de l'altrui mal sempre gl'increbbe;
ma poi pensando che contrario effetto
    in quel meschino il suo parlar farebbe,
        se lui pur conoscesse, indi si toglie,
        dolente anch'ei de l'altrui gravi doglie.

D'un tetto pastoral schermo la notte 13
    fêrsi i guerrier contra l'algente luna.
Allora, poi che nell'oscure grotte
    da l'alba vinta ogn'ombra si raguna,
attraversando vie scoscese e rotte
    giunsero in selva solitaria e bruna,
        che mai, facendo a se medesma oltraggio,
        non riceve del sol l'amico raggio.

Per questa va con torto piede immondo 14
    serpendo un rio che da' vicin luoghi esce,
ch'a' riguardanti cela invido il fondo,
    né nutre in sen ninfa leggiadra o pesce.
Forma poscia di sé lago ritondo,
    e tutte l'acque in un raccoglie e mesce.
        Di sterpi e pruni ha le sue rive ingombre,
        e sol tassi e ginebri a lui fanno ombre.

"Where now has fled the light of these fair eyes? 10
   Where the clear honor of their gaze? And oh!
How from these cheeks the rosy radiance dies
   and from these lips their color and their glow!
Can I in this defiled brow recognize
   the brow that shone with joy not long ago?
      Ah! Much as once it spread delight and charm,
      so much the more it now brings grief and harm!

Lo! I, my son, now act that final rite 11
   that you should rather have performed for me!
Lo! Now forever on this fatal night
   I close your eyes. Farewell eternally!
And if my vengeful hands do not requite
   your death, let heaven bear the blame, not me,
      that has in time's irrevocable course
      deprived them of their wonted strength and force."

His lamentations reach Rinaldo's ear, 12
   whose heart and mind with gentle pity fill.
He thinks he ought to offer him some cheer,
   for he is always moved by another's ill,
but knowing that to offer solace here
   might have effects contrary to his will,
      if he were recognized, resolves to leave,
      much grieving as he feels the other grieve.

That night they sheltered from the moon's chill rays 13
   with a herdsman in a rustic neighborhood,
then, as the shadows fled the dawn's bright haze
   back to their caverns fathomless and rude,
set out again and by steep, craggy ways
   came to a dark and solitary wood,
      a wilderness that, in its own despite,
      never admits the warm sun's friendly light.

There courses through it from some spring nearby, 14
   too foul for nymph or fish, a murky rill,
its unplumbed bottom hid from every eye
   in twisting coils and turgid eddies till
it finds a round lake and is swallowed by
   the black and stagnant waters that its basin fill.
      Brambles and thorns the barren banks invade
      with ferns and stunted junipers for shade.

Rinaldo

Mirano i cavalier sospesi intorno,   15
    né cosa lieta lor s'offre a la vista;
nulla di vago v'è, nulla d'adorno,
    ogni parte per sé gli occhi contrista.
Qui sempre è fosco e tenebroso il giorno,
    sempre l'aria ad un modo oscura e trista,
        sempre orride le piante e torbo il rivo,
        sempre il terren di fiori e d'erbe privo.

Mentre pur se 'n vann'oltra i giovinetti,   16
    veggion d'apresso un'alta sepoltura,
e star intorno a quella in un ristretti
    molti guerrier con mesta faccia oscura,
che si squarciano i crin, battonsi i petti,
    quasi grave gli ingombri acerba cura;
        e fan con novo ed angoscioso pianto
        tutt'intorno sonar la selva intanto.

D'un così vivo sasso e trasparente   17
    era il sepolcro, che scopriva altrui,
qual sottil vetro o rio puro e lucente,
    ciò che avea dentro più riposto in lui:
sì che d'ambo i guerrier le luci intente
    penetrar tosto ne' secreti sui;
        e vi mirar, quasi incredibil cosa,
        donna leggiadra in vista ed amorosa.

Ella era morta, e così morta ancora   18
    arder parea d'amor la terra e 'l cielo,
e dal bel petto per la spalla fuora
    gli uscia pungente e sanguinoso telo;
sembrava il volto suo neve ch'allora
    scuota Giunon da l'aghiacciato velo:
        gli occhi avea chiusi e, benché chiusi, in loro
        si scopriva d'Amor tutto il tesoro.

Mentre i guerrieri a rimirar si stanno   19
    la bella donna che sepolta giace,
un di color che cerchio a l'arca fanno,
    e più degli altri in pianto si disface,
nel cor rinchiuso il suo gravoso affanno
    che s'ange più quando la lingua tace,
        s'armò la testa e in un cavallo ascese,
        ed in tal modo a ragionar lor prese:

The knights look round in horror and suspense   15
    while utter desolation greets their sight.
There is nothing lovely here, no ornaments
    of nature to bring comfort or delight.
The air is always noisome to the sense,
      the day forever gloomy as the night,
          the flood forever a foul, baleful mass,
          the ground forever bare of flowers and grass.

Looking for ways to cross these waters, they   16
    see on the shore a lofty sepulcher,
and near it, clad in sorrowful array,
    huge grieving throngs of knights, who tear their hair
and beat their breasts in sorrow and dismay,
      sobbing like creatures lost in deep despair,
          and make their wails of anguished grief resound
          in echoes through the forest all around.

The sepulcher was fashioned from a stone   17
    of strange transparency so fine and rare
that all things placed within it through it shone
    as if through glass or limpid spring or air,
so that its secret instantly was known
      to the intent gaze of the warrior pair,
          who saw a thing scarce credible to tell,
          the body of a beauteous damozel.

She was dead, but even in her death did show   18
    how Love for her might heaven and earth assail.
A sharp-tipped arrow, entering below
    her bosom, did her lovely breast impale.
Her face was white and radiant as the snow
      that Juno scatters from her frozen veil.
          Her eyes were closed, but closed seemed still to be
          brimming with riches from Love's treasury.

While the two knights looked down in silent gloom   19
    upon the lovely maid there laid to rest,
one of the crowd of mourners near the tomb,
    with face more marred by grief than all the rest,
having locked his woe in his heart's inmost room —
      sharp pain grows sharper when speech is repressed —
          put on his helmet, mounted a great steed
          and with this challenge bade them to take heed:

Rinaldo

— Signor, quest'acqua che qui presso stagna,   20
    gustar convienvi, ed ella ha tal valore,
ch'a qualunque uom le labbra indi si bagna,
    nuovo acerbo martir desta nel core;
onde convien ch'a pianger qui rimagna
    questa estinta donzella a tutte l'ore:
        dunque senza tardar di lei bevete,
        o morir di mia man pur v'eleggete. —

Rise Rinaldo in modo altero e disse: 21
    — Or su, vegniamo ormai, guerrier, a l'arme,
ché se tu brami inimicizie e risse,
    ch'abbi trovato uomo a tua voglia parme;
e se per le tue mani a me prescrisse
    il ciel la morte, or lei vien tosto a darme. —
        In questo dir voltaro ambo i destrieri,
        e corsero a ferirsi audaci e fieri.

Segnano al petto l'un, l'altro a la testa   22
    i colpi, ed ambo quei vanno ad effetto;
cadde Rinaldo a la percossa infesta
    che lo venne a ferir sovra l'elmetto:
ma la lancia fatal ch'ei poscia arresta,
    all'altro cavalier traffigge il petto,
        e lo distende dal corsier lontano,
        tutto tremante e sanguinoso al piano.

Rinaldo, d'ira e di furore acceso,   23
    leggierissimo s'alza e si solleva,
né riposar mai vuol se chi l'ha offeso
    prima di vita con sua man non leva.
Ma come vide quel meschin disteso,
    che nel suo sangue involto al pian giaceva,
        l'ira e 'l furor dal petto a lui fuggio,
        u' pietade in sua vece a por si gio.

Sopra gli va, l'elmo gli cava e slaccia,   24
    perché torni ne' sensi ond'era uscito.
Come da l'aria gli è tecca la faccia,
    aprendo gli occhi il cavalier ferito,
un profondo sospir dal petto caccia,
    onde a Rinaldo è 'l cor più intenerito;
        gli chiede nondimen perché mantegna
        quel rio costume e quella usanza indegna.

"Sirs, of the stagnant waters of this mere   20
    you needs must taste now, for they have the power
to make whoever sips them and draws near
    this tomb feel a strange pain his heart devour
that forces him to stay forever here
    lamenting this dead maiden hour by hour.
        Go kneel therefore and drink without delay
        or choose by this my hand to die today."

Rinaldo smiled in proud disdain and said,   21
    "Then let us go to arms at once, Sir knight.
Since you have called for buffets on your head,
    you've found your man in me, so try your might.
If it be heaven's will that I fall dead,
    let your hands do its bidding in this fight."
        At these words, each raised up his lance and targe
        and turned his steed to launch a furious charge.

One at the head, the other at the chest   22
    aims his fierce blow, and both achieve their ends.
Rinaldo falls, thrown by a thrust addressed
    to his helmet with the utmost violence,
but at that instant his own lance at rest
    pierces the other's armored breast and sends
        his body far behind his horse, to land
        bloody and quivering on the slimy strand.

Rinaldo, fired with fury and wrath, anon   23
    leaps back upon his feet and wheels around
and rushes murderously with sword drawn
    upon the man by whom he has been downed,
but seeing his wretched foe lie pale and wan
    in a pool of his own blood upon the ground,
        he exiles wrath and fury from his mind
        and, letting pity in instead, grows kind.

He ran to him and knelt down to undo   24
    his helmet's laces and his visor's ties.
Feeling the air caress his face anew,
    the wounded stranger opened wide his eyes,
while a great sigh convulsed him through and through.
    Rinaldo at this felt yet more pity rise,
        but asked him what had led him to coerce
        compliance with a custom so perverse.

Rinaldo

Ma quegli allor: — Perché servato or sia   25
  questo costume, a pien da me saprai,
se concesso da morte egli mi fia
  che mi sovrasta e mi rapisce omai;
e se pur ti parrà l'usanza ria,
  il mio crudel destin n'incolperai,
    che la prima cagion stata è del tutto,
    e m'ha fatto amator de l'altrui lutto.

Signor, ne' miei primi anni ebbi la sorte,   26
  ma per mio mal, sì destra ai miei desiri,
che tra mill'altre elesse in mia consorte
  questa dama ch'estinta or qui rimiri.
Er'io per cavalier gagliardo e forte,
  ella diva parea de' sommi giri,
    non donna umana; e col leggiadro viso
    ogni selvaggio spirto avria conquiso.

Non era alcun che gli occhi in lei volgesse   27
  senza infiammarsi d'amoroso ardore;
alcun non era ancor ch'a lei piacesse
  fuor che sol'io che fisso avea nel core.
Io d'altra parte, benché allor potesse
  goder di mille donne il dolce amore,
    lei solo amava, e in questo lieto stato
    ne vissi un tempo al mio parer beato.

Ma venne, lasso! dal tartareo fondo,   28
  a turbar la mia pace e la mia gioia,
quella peste crudel che suole al mondo
  recar sovente incomparabil noia,
che 'l sereno d'amor stato giocondo
  tutto col suo velen turba ed annoia:
    gelosia venne, e in forme strane e false
    di Clizia la mia donna il petto assalse.

Per usanza avev'io di gir sovente   29
  solo a cacciar per queste selve intorno;
ma quando il sol feria con più cocente
  raggio, qui mi schermia dal caldo giorno.
Quest'era un bosco allor diversamente
  d'alte vagghezze, d'ogni parte adorno,
    non già com'or che solo a prima vista
    con nuovo orror le menti altrui contrista.

He then[74]: "If there is time before I die —   25
    for even now I feel death's mastery
unman me — I will freely tell you why
    that custom was so long upheld by me.
Perverse you call it? Perhaps so. But I
    blame fate for what may seem perversity,
        my cruel fate, which first caused all my pain
        and made the grief of others seem my gain.

Sir, in my earliest manhood, Fortune's spite,   26
    which did to me like Fortune's boon appear,
gave me a matchless bride and made me plight
    my troth to her whom you see buried here.
I was a stalwart and courageous knight.
    She seemed a goddess from a higher sphere
        with eyes so lovely that they could control
        by gentle glances the most savage soul.

No man could look at her and not be swept   27
    away in hopeless storms of amorous flames.
And yet no man could please her eyes except
    myself, her heart of hearts and aim of aims.
I for my part, though I could well have kept
    in bonds of love a thousand other dames,
        loved her alone and, blessed with such a wife,
        long lived a joyous and contented life.

But then from deepest Tartarus — alas! —   28
    there came to vex my peace and to destroy
my bliss that monster that will bring to pass
    irreparable harm, apt to employ
noxious and false infections to harass
    love's faith and to wreak havoc on love's joy —
        the monster Jealousy I mean. It came
        to seize on Clytie. That's my lady's name.

It was my frequent wont to ride alone   29
    in these surrounding woods to hunt the deer,
but when the scorching sun most fiercely shone,
    to seek the shelter of some shadow here,
for in those days this forest was a zone
    replete with leafy loveliness and cheer,
        not yet as now, when its unnerving gloom
        fills every mind with thoughts of grief and doom.

Rinaldo

Solea meco ritrarsi in così vago 30
  bosco Ermilla, una ninfa anco talora,
che non le tele, la conocchia e l'ago,
  ma l'arco e i dardi audace adopra ognora;
e quando il cor di seguir Cinzia ha vago,
  tanto fugge la dea che Cipro onora.
    Ella è di belle membra e di bel viso:
    viso crudel, sì sua beltà m'ha ucciso.

Ma come spesso avien che 'l falso uom crede, 31
  e quel che crede osa affermar per vero,
è chi m'accusa di corrotta fede
  a Clizia, e di cor perfido e leggiero,
dicendo ch'io le rendo aspra mercede
  in cambio del suo amor puro e sincero,
    perciò che Ermilla a' maggior caldi estivi
    meco si gode nei piacer lascivi.

Clizia brama veder di ciò l'effetto, 32
  pria che meco ne muova altre parole;
e perché sa che sempre il mio ricetto
  questo luogh'era al più cocente sole,
molto prima vi viene, e nel più stretto
  bosco s'asconde, ov'aspettar mi vuole.
    Vi vengo io poscia e, già sudato e stanco,
    ne l'erboso terren distendo il fianco.

Quinci non molto poi moversi io sento 33
  un non so che dove s'allaga l'onda:
allor meschino acuto dardo avento,
  perché penso che fera ivi s'asconda.
Il dardo se 'n va ratto e violento,
  e tiene il suo camin tra fronda e fronda,
    sì ch'a Clizia nel petto al fin si mise,
    e lui piagando ogni mio bene uccise.

Cadde ella, ahi lassa! a la percossa atroce, 34
  solo un languido "ohimè!" mandando fuora.
Mi penetra nel cor l'amata voce,
  non già però ch'io la cognosca allora.
Là donde uscito è il suon corro veloce,
  e veggio, ahi! vista grave a l'alma ancora,
    la bella donna mia che debil langue,
    versando insieme con la vita il sangue.

At times there joined me at the noonday hour   30
   a woodland nymph, Hermilla, from these parts.
She never plied loom or needle in a bower
   but boldly in the woods used bows and darts
with a heart as keen to slay by Cynthia's power,
   as it was loath to ply Athena's arts.
      And she was fair, and her fair face — ah woe! —
      her cruel face brought on the pain I know.[75]

But all too often people will believe   31
   a lie and to its truth devoutly swear,
so now some man tells Clytie I deceive
   her faith and mock her love and wifely care,
repaying the sincere troth I receive
   with fraud that would, if known, bring on despair
      because Hermilla has been seen to toy
      with me at mid-day in lascivious joy.

Clytie, to be resolved how this can be,   32
   says nothing to me and since she well knows
the leafy nook where I invariably
   in flight from mid-day's torrid sun repose,
sets out one morning and there waits for me,
   concealed where a thick clump of bushes grows.
      Then I arrive and, bathed in sweat and hot,
      stretch out my spent frame in that grassy spot.

It is not long before I hear something —   33
   a rustling like waves on a shore — so now
I — wretch! — fit a sharp arrow to my string,
   thinking some beast lies hidden there somehow.
The shaft flies from my fingers and whistling
   with murderous speed crashes through bough and bough,
      until it plunges into Clytie's breast
      and, piercing it, kills all that I love best.

She falls — alas! — at the atrocious blow   34
   without a word except a faint 'Ay me!'
The piteous sound pierces my heart, although
   I am not yet aware that it is she.
Towards its source I hasten and soon see
   a sight that fills my soul with boundless woe:
      languishing feebly on the ground, my wife,
      spilling her blood together with her life.

Ratto m'inchino a lei, la prendo in seno,   35
    e con le mie le care labra accosto;
cerco di porre al sangue uscente freno,
    acciò ch'ella non mora almen sì tosto:
pria che l'alma gli venga in tutto meno,
    di voler favellarle io son disposto,
        e fo sì ch'essa scopre i lumi alquanto,
        ed ode il mio parlar, vede il mio pianto.

Vede il mio pianto che con larga vena   36
    più sempre par che 'l duol dagli occhi verse,
del qual non men ch'io m'aggia, ella ripiena
    n'have la faccia e le palpebre asperse;
ode questo parlar, al qual a pena
    ne l'uscir fuori stretta via s'aperse:
        "O cara, o dolce, o mia fedel compagna,
        qual da te rio destino or mi scompagna?

Deh! vita mia, deh! non fuggire, aspetta,   37
    ché teco correr voglio ogn'aspra sorte;
deh! non mi lasciar solo in sì gran fretta,
    empio ed odioso a me per la tua morte!
Mirami almen, mira la tua vendetta,
    ch'io far voglio in me stesso e giusto e forte:
        non mi negar il sol degli occhi tuoi,
        se punirmi così forse non vuoi!"

Ella tenendo il guardo in me converso,   38
    che passando per gli occhi al cor m'aggiunge,
dice: "Ben mio, poiché destin perverso
    così rapidamente or ne disgiunge,
non esser, prego, ai miei desiri averso:
    se pur di me qualche pietà ti punge,
        se l'amor mio premio sì degno or merta,
        fa' che di questo almen ne vada certa.

Fa' ch'a l'inferno almen vada sicura,   39
    che dopo ch'io sarò fredda e di ghiaccio,
Ermilla empia, cagion di mia sventura,
    non fia teco congiunta al sacro laccio.
Fallo, ti prego, o dolce unica cura
    di questo core." E qui stendendo il braccio,
        mi cinse il collo e chiuse i vaghi rai,
        per non gli aprir da poi, lasso! giamai.

I throw myself upon her, lift her to   35
    my breast and press her lips with mine and try
to staunch the bloody torrents that bestrew
    the grass. Knowing her time has come to die,
before her soul departs, one last adieu
    is all that I desire and, weeping, I
        implore her, not quite knowing if she hears,
        to open her fair eyes, to see my tears.

She sees my tears that ever ampler rise   36
    and on my cheeks their gleaming courses trace.
She feels the streams that issue from my eyes
    drop their warm moisture on her breast and face.
She hears my words that amid sobs and cries
    press through my lips as through a narrow place:
        'Ah sweet, ah dearest partner of my heart
        what evil destiny now makes us part?

Alas, my life! Wait, do not haste away.   37
    I'd share the bitterest torments for your sake.
Ah! do not leave me thus bereft, a prey
    to self-reproach, self-loathing and heart-ache.
If nothing else can make you stay here, stay
    to see the vengeance I myself will take
        on me. If you desire otherwise,
        don't rob me of the sunlight of your eyes!'

She fixed me with a look that, piercing through   38
    my eyes, convulsed my heart with pain and dread:
'My darling, since by doom perverse we two
    must now be parted in such haste,' she said,
'if any pity for me touches you,
    grant me one favor now at my death-bed,
        and if my love still seems a prize worth your
        seeking, at least of one thing make me sure.

Let me at least pass to the shades below   39
    with your sworn promise that when I am cold,
wicked Hermilla, cause of all my woe,
    shall never as your spouse cross our threshold.
Swear it, my sweet, I pray, and I will go
    in peace.' Then, lifting up an arm to hold
        my neck, she sighed and closed her eyes in pain,
        never — alas! — to open them again.

Grido io misero allor: "Vana temenza   *40*
   ti prese il core, o mia diletta moglie!
Deh! ch'un vano sospetto, un timor senza
   dritta cagione alcuna or mi ti toglie,
deh! ch'una sol falsissima credenza
   or mi porge cagion d'eterne doglie!
     Misera de' mortal vita fallace,
     s'ad ogni caso repentin soggiace!"

Parve che l'aere fosco asserenasse   *41*
   pel volto suo, Clizia tai cose udendo,
e che gioia e letizia alta mostrasse
   l'alma, da la prigion terrestre uscendo,
quanto fallace error pria l'ingombrasse
   nel mio vero parlar or cognoscendo;
     ma de la morte sua tanto i' mi dolsi,
     che quasi a me l'odiata vita io tolsi.

Pur ripensando poi che troppo leve   *42*
   fora pena cotale a tanto eccesso,
e n'andrebbe impunito il fallo greve,
   ch'uccidendo il mio bene avea commesso,
volsi che 'l duol, ch'in vita si riceve
   da chi vive inimico di se stesso,
     e la luce del sole aborre e sdegna
     fusse del mio fallir pena condegna.

E perché il mio dolor sempre crescesse,   *43*
   vedendo la cagion di lui presente,
oprai ch'un mago questa tomba fêsse
   di questo sasso vivo e trasparente;
e l'estinta donzella entro ponesse,
   così trafitta da lo stral pungente,
     sì che non mai per raggirar di cielo
     si corrompesse in lei la carne o 'l pelo.

Ma parendomi poi luogo difforme   *44*
   questo al mio duro stato ed angoscioso,
fei che quel mago lo rendeo conforme,
   ed oscuro lo fece e tenebroso,
togliendo a lui ciò che potea distôrme
   pur breve spazio dal pensier noioso,
     con gran poter ch'al suon de le parole
     muove la terra e 'l corso arresta al sole.

In anguish I cried out to her: 'Vain fear   40
  led your fond heart, beloved wife, astray!
Alas, that fancied injury and mere
    suspicion should thus take all joy away!
Alas, that one brief, heedless lapse should here
      undo me with eternal grief today!
          Ah, wretched and deluded mortal state
          laid low by each capricious trick of Fate!'

When Clytie heard these words it seemed the air   41
  about her face grew bright, as if her soul,
leaving its prison of terrestrial care,
    rejoiced to be released from the control
of the great falsehood that had held it there
      by the truth I spoke, to seek its heavenly goal.
          But I was at her death so much at strife
          with my whole self, I nearly took my life.

Yet I, considering that such punishment   42
  would be too lenient for my foul misdeed
and that my death would shorten or prevent
    penance that justice for my crime decreed,
decided that my hateful life be spent
      lamenting and admit no other need
          than grief and darkness. Thus my fault would be
          known to the world and punished fittingly.

To make my woe keep growing without rest   43
  and have its cause forever clearly shown
a sorcerer built this tomb at my request
    out of this living and transparent stone
and placed the damsel in it with her breast
      pierced by this dart. Her flesh has never known
          corruption, for the strong enchantments keep
          her skin so white and fresh, she seems to sleep.

But since this woodland then seemed quite unfit   44
  as a mourning place for her whom I had slain,
I asked the sorcerer to transfigure it
    into a scene of odiousness and bane,
charming away whatever might permit
      even a moment's respite from my pain.
          (That mighty magus by his spells could make
          the sun grow dark and hills and mountains shake.)

Volsi poi, per aver ne l'aspra sorte   45
  compagno alcuno e ne le acerbe pene,
e perché di costei la dura morte
  pianta ancor fusse quanto a lei conviene,
ch'incantasse quest'acqua di tal sorte
  ch'a qualunque uomo a gustar mai ne viene,
    per la pietà di chi qui morta giace
    nel cor destasse duolo aspro e tenace;

onde spinto da quel, fêsse soggiorno,   46
  meco piangendo la costei sventura,
come or gli vedi a questo sasso intorno,
  che miran sempre entro la sepoltura.
Io poi di stare ognor la notte e 'l giorno
  disposi in tutto in questa valle oscura,
    sforzando ogni guerrier che vi passasse
    che mai suo grado il rio liquor gustasse.

Ma il nuovo incanto di quest'acqua insieme   47
  col duro viver mio fia terminato;
ed ognun di costor che piagne e geme
  ritornarà nel suo primiero stato. —
Così diss'egli, e le parole estreme
  non bene espresse col mancato fiato.
    Non molto dopo spirò l'alma, e quella
    s'alzò volando a la sua pari stella.

Morto ch'ei fu, color che in mesti accenti   48
  disfogavano il duol chiuso nel petto,
posero fine ai queruli lamenti,
  liberi ancor dal grave interno affetto.
Alcun di lor non è che si ramenti
  a pien de la cagione ond'era astretto
    a lamentarsi, e l'un l'altro rimira
    dubio e sospeso, e 'l pensier volve e gira.

Rinaldo, ch'era assai doglioso e tristo   49
  del caso occorso al miser cavaliero,
molto si rallegrò com'ebbe visto
  liberi questi da l'incanto fiero;
e del lor dubio e del sospetto avisto,
  conto e chiaro lor fece il caso intiero.
    Quei gli resero allor grazie infinite,
    e per l'obligo lor gli offrir le vite.

Canto Seven

I then, desiring sharers in my hell   45
    of woe and fellows in my harsh ordeal,
and that her obsequies might fitly swell
    in numbers to lament her death and kneel,
asked him to bind these waters by a spell
    that made whoever tasted of them feel
        his heart beset by endless grief for her
        who lies entombed within this sepulcher.

Constrained by this enchantment here to moan   46
    forever, the great throng of knights you see
assembled on the shore around this stone
    gaze into it and weep unceasingly,
for each of them, having been overthrown
    by my hand, will he nil he mourns with me,
        and I compelled all warriors who drew near
        to taste the waters of this fatal mere.

But when I die, these foul spells will relent,   47
    the pain and woe they bring shall also cease,
and all who with me here weep and lament
    shall be as once they were and be at peace."
So said he, with his life's breath nearly spent,
    and presently expired to release
        his soul, that, as if beckoned from afar,
        ascended toward its predestined star.

No sooner was he dead than instantly   48
    the other mourners crowding round the tomb
ended their weeping and once more felt free
    of any inward sense of grief or doom.
Not one of them recalls the cause why he
    had let such sorrow his whole soul consume.
        They stare upon each other, gape and blink,
        puzzled, in doubt, scarce knowing what to think.

Rinaldo, who had grown extremely sad   49
    to hear the dying knight's unhappy fate,
when these poor knights regained their sense, grew glad
    to see their fierce bedevilment abate,
and finding them amazed and all but mad
    with doubt, did the whole truth relate.
        They rendered boundless thanks and vowed to be
        bound to his love in perpetuity.

Veggono, a dir mirabil cosa, intanto   50
    levarsi un gran sepolcro alto dal piano,
e in un momento a quel primiero a canto
    esser poi messo da invisibil mano.
Si maraviglia ognun del nuovo incanto,
    e gli par caso inusitato e strano;
        lo stupor crebbe, ché da lor fu scorto
        giacervi dentro il cavalier già morto.

Scorsero ancor del trasparente vaso   51
    lettre intagliate in apparente parte,
onde era esposto l'infelice caso
    de' duo miseri amanti a parte a parte.
Ma già nessun nel bosco è più rimaso,
    già l'un da l'altro si divide e parte,
        fatte di qua di là molte parole
        di cortesia, come al partir si suole.

Col gran figlio d'Amon sol vi rimane   52
    Florindo, a lui già d'amor sommo avinto;
e come cerca l'odorante cane
    le fere ognor per naturale istinto,
ne' cespugli, ne' vepri e ne le tane,
    così, da cura generosa spinto,
        cerca ognun di costor nova aventura
        or per monte, or per bosco, or per pianura.

Il terzo giorno, allor ch'il sol lontano   53
    da l'orto e da l'occaso è parimente,
videro il mar Tireno placido e piano
    il bel lito ferir tacitamente;
e si trovaro in un fiorito piano
    di tanti e più color vago e ridente.
        Di quante grazie adorno è 'l caro viso
        che m'have l'alma e 'l cor dęmo e conquiso.

Quivi si vede il bel garzon ch'estinse   54
    spietato disco, onde tal forma prese,
e quel cui folle errore a morte spinse,
    miser che di se stesso in van s'accese,
e chi di dolce amor t'arse e t'avinse,
    o bella diva, il cor molle e cortese,
        per cui tu Marte e 'l tuo Vulcan lasciasti,
        e con le selve il terzo ciel cangiasti.

They saw — a wondrous thing to tell! — meanwhile   50
   the sepulcher rise high up in the air
while unseen hands propelled the giant pile
   where lay the fallen knight and dropped it there.
That was a new enchantment. No denial!
   Amazement at that wonder made them stare,
      and their amazement grew when they espied
      the dead knight lying inside by his bride.

Above their crystal catafalque there stood   51
   displayed a tablet that in letters plain
of fine intaglio set forth and reviewed
   the dire misfortunes of the loving twain.
But soon no man remains within the wood.
   The company disbands. Now and again
      a courteous fare-thee-well rings out, until,
      the customary greetings done, the place grows still.

Only Florindo stays, his one desire   52
   to please great Aymon's son, whom he loved well.
And as a hound by kind will never tire
   to search, excited by his sense of smell,
for savage beasts in bush or cave or briar,
   so with an eagerness no pain could quell
      these two now seek adventure, be it found
      in hills or forests or on level ground

On the third day, with the sun about to gain   53
   the mid-point twixt its east- and westward door,
they saw afar the blue Tyrrhenian main
   with placid wavelets strike the tranquil shore
and found themselves within a blossoming plain
   of such unnumbered smiling hues and more
      that its fair face, decked with such grace and art,
      might well have ravished both my soul and heart.

There blooms the fair youth whom the discus slew   54
   whereby he took such shape as now he shows,
and he who by vain error came to view
   the charming form toward which he bent too close,
and he who, fairest goddess, lit in you
   the flames of gentle love, so that you chose
      to leave great Mars and your own Vulcan's bed
      and from your third sphere to a greenwood fled.[76]

Quivi il nardo, l'acanto, il giglio e 'l croco   55
   veggonsi il vago crin lieti spiegare,
ed altri fior di cui null'altro luoco
    volle giamai l'alma Natura ornare;
tra' quai con mormorar soave e roco
    se 'n va limpido rio serpendo al mare,
        pieno il bel corno di coralli e d'auro,
        onde Teti non ha maggior tesauro.

Quivi non querci e pini, abeti o faggi,   56
   ma lauri, mirti e vaghi altri arbuscelli
difendono il terren da' caldi raggi
    con gli odorati lor verdi capelli;
quivi nei cor più duri e più selvaggi
    destan dolce pensier vezzosi augelli,
        che scherzando su' rami e su le fronde
        soavemente a l'un l'altro risponde.

Mentre rimiran questi il luoco adorno,   57
   pensando che tal forse esser doveva
il bel giardin dove già fêr soggiorno
    i gran nostri parenti Adamo ed Eva,
sentir poco lontan sonar un corno
    che dolcemente l'aria percoteva,
        e vider poi venir due damigelle,
        vaghe, leggiadre, a maraviglia belle.

Ha l'una i bei capelli al capo avolti,   58
   partiti in treccie in maestrevol modi,
e poi gli tiene in sottil rete accolti,
    che di fin auro e perle ha sovra i nodi;
l'altra ad arte ir gli fa negletti e sciolti,
    e quasi par ch'ivi se stessa annodi
        l'aura ch'or gli alza, or gli rincrespa e gira,
        e sempre in lor più dolcemente spira.

Purpurea seta testa a gigli d'oro   59
   le belle membra a quella asconde e cela;
gonna, ch'è del color del sacro alloro
    sparsa di gemme, a questa il corpo vela;
ambo candidi sono i destrier loro,
    adorni sin ai piè d'argentea tela;
        tutti i loro scudieri a la divisa
        con vesti vanno d'un'istessa guisa.

Citron, acanthus, lily, crocus here   55
   with swelling buds adorn the verdant lea,
along with blooms that nowhere else appear
   but in this place by Nature's kind decree.
Through them with rustlings that delight the ear
   a limpid stream meanders toward the sea
      over corals branching on its golden floor
      than which all Thetis[77] holds no richer store.

No oaks or firs, beeches or pines here rise,   56
   but myrtles, laurels, trees of slender girth
from the hot rays of the unclouded skies
   shelter with their fresh verdant locks the earth.
Here even in hardest hearts all rudeness dies,
   and gay-plumed birds engender pleasant mirth,
      flitting from branch to branch in amorous play,
      each answering each in a soft roundelay.

While the two knights admired this charming place,   57
   thinking that such perhaps was long ago
the garden that the parents of our race,
   Adam and Eve, came with delight to know,
they heard, as though resounding in some space
   not far away, a dulcet horn-blast blow
      and saw two gracious maidens drawing near
      of slender shape and beauty without peer.

One wears her blond hair piled high on her head,   58
   bound up in braids that intricately twirl
beneath a subtle net of finest thread
   knotted in artful loops of gold and pearl.
The other walks with loosened locks outspread
   to the breeze, which seems to fondle curl on curl,
      lifts them and turns them, gently lets them fall
      and breathes refreshing sweetness through them all.

Fine purple silk adorned with filigree   59
   of golden lilies hides the limbs of one.
The other wears gem-studded drapery,
   green as the sacred laurel, finely spun.
Both ride white palfreys swathed down to the knee
   in cloth of silver sparkling in the sun
      and a young squire walks by either maid,
      in garb of matching preciousness arrayed.

Rinaldo

Giunte queste ai guerrieri, ad ambo pria   60
  fanno inchin riverente e grazioso;
poi richieggiono un dono il qual non fia
  ad alcun di lor duo grave o noioso.
Rinaldo allor: — Chi dono a voi potria
  negar, e sia quant'esser può dannoso?
    Vostro è, signore, il comandarne, e poi
    deggiam quel ch'imponete esseguir noi. —

Ed elle a loro: — Il don che noi chiediamo,   61
  e che voi di concederne affermate,
è che un nostro palagio ove alberghiamo
  de la vostra presenzia oggi degniate;
indi, signor, non molto lungi siamo,
  ch'è quel che dirimpetto or rimirate
    là su la cima del piacevol colle,
    che vagheggiando intorno alto s'estolle. —

Così dicendo ancor, si fêro scorta   62
  de' cavalier ch'a lor se 'n vanno a paro,
i quai però quanto il dover comporta
  di tanta cortesia le ringraziaro.
Prendon la strada ch'è più vaga e corta,
  sin che al colle vicin tosto arrivaro,
    al bel colle dipinto il tergo e 'l seno,
    cui lava i vaghi piedi il mar Tireno.

Pausilippo quest'è, dove s'avanza   63
  natura ed ha de l'opre sue stupore,
ove è di Clori la perpetua stanza,
  ov'ha Pomona il suo tesor maggiore;
ove menan le Grazie eterna danza
  in compagnia di Venere e d'Amore,
    c'hanno l'antiquo Cipro in lui cangiato,
    come in più degno albergo e più pregiato.

Come a la cima fur del vago monte,   64
  dolce sonar di nuovo un corno udiro.
Indi calossi del palagio il ponte,
  onde molte donzelle insieme usciro.
Han tutte vaghe membra, amabil fronte,
  abito eletto e d'artificio miro;
    cortesi in vista son, ma nel bel volto
    han virginal decoro insieme scolto.

They halted near the warriors by and by,   60
    bowed to them both with gravely courteous cheer
and said they came to ask a boon whereby
    none should feel troubled or have cause to fear.
Rinaldo then: "Who is it could deny
    a gift to such as you, however dear?
        Be it what it may, you, ladies, must impose
        the task. We'll gladly do all you propose."

And they to them: "The boon we crave is this: 61
    be pleased to honor us — do not say nay! —
at one of our splendid palaces
    with your distinguished presences today.
It stands nearby, my lords, quite hard to miss.
    You see it even now, not far away,
        on yon fair hill, which from its lofty ground
        surveys the spacious prospect all around."

This being said, they formed an escort and   62
    guided the knights toward their new sojourn,
who both, however, as duty gave command,
    thanked them for their high courtesy in turn.
They took the shortest, best road toward the strand
    till they could clearly the fair hill discern,
        the green hill, blossoming front and rear, whose feet,
        washed by Tyrrhenian waves, the sea surge meet.

This is Posillipo,[78] where Nature excels   63
    herself, astonished by what she can do,
where Chloris in perpetual blossom dwells
    and fair Pomona never fades from view,
where dancing Graces[79] weave their deathless spells
    accompanied by Love and Venus, who
        from ancient Cyprus[80] to this place have come
        as to a worthier, more beloved home.

Arrived at the fair mountain's top, once more   64
    they heard a horn resound, now quite nearby.
The drawbridge fell, and through the open door,
    a crowd of maidens issued from on high.
Their limbs, their brows, the garments that they wore
    bespoke nobility of mind and eye.
        Their looks were open but did not forget
        the chaste decorum of true etiquette.

Una di loro, a cui la schiera bella 65
    tutta portar parea maggior rispetto,
raccolse con benigna umil favella
    i cavalier e con cortese aspetto:
e l'un con questa man, l'altro con quella
    preso, gli addusse dentro il real tetto,
        ricco e superbo per materia ed arte
        in ogni sua men degna e nobil parte.

Giunsero, ascesa pria la regia scala 66
    ch'era di pietra alabastrina e viva,
in spaziosa e ben formata sala,
    che scopre il piano e la tirena riva;
quivi da più fenestre il fiato esala
    verso là dove il dì more o s'avviva,
        verso settentrione e verso dove
        cinto di pioggia i crini Austro si move.

S'alza a punto nel mezo ornato altare, 67
    ricco d'oro e di gemme a maraviglia,
ove di donna un bel ritratto appare
    che sol se stessa e null'altra simiglia;
veggonsi in lei grazie divine e rare,
    sguard'uman, chiara fronte, allegre ciglia,
        aria gentil, benigno onesto riso,
        e par ch'accoglia ognun con grato viso.

Tiene aperte le mani in modo tale 68
    che si mostra al donar pronta ed usata;
l'attraversa per mezo un motto, il quale
    ha tal sentenza in lettere d'or segnata:
"Tra le figlie di Dio nata immortale
    son io, non men d'ogni vertù pregiata:
        né senza aver di me ripieno il core
        ascender può mai l'uomo a vero onore."

Pendon dopoi da le pareti belle 69
    molte imagin ritratte in tutti i lati;
di sesso e volto son diverse quelle,
    e gli abiti tra loro han variati;
né so se tai le avria già fatte Apelle,
    o se tai le fèsse oggi il Salviati,
        che coi colori e col penello audace
        scorno a Natura, invidia agli altri face.

One who of all that lovely company   65
    seemed most respected met the warrior pair
with a fine curtsey, smiling courteously
    and humbly bade them cordial welcome there.
Taking their hands, stepping between them, she
    led them inside, ascending stair by stair
        through spaces furnished with huge wealth and art
        down to the humblest and least noble part.

They climbed the regal staircase, which was all   66[51]
    fashioned of living alabaster stone,
and reached a spacious, well-proportioned hall
    that overlooked the whole Tyrrhenian zone.
On all four sides fine casements, wide and tall,
    opened where first and last daylight is shown,
        and northward toward Boreas and again
        where Auster shakes his hoar head crowned with rain.

A shrine stood raised in that hall's center, made   67
    of shining gold with jewelry inlay,
on which a lady's picture was displayed,
    incomparably fine in every way.
Rare, godlike charms the painter there portrayed —
    kind brow, bright eyes, dark lashes soft and gay,
        a kind and chaste smile on a candid face
        seeming to welcome all with pleasant grace.

She holds out open hands as if to show   68
    that she will ever give most eagerly.
On the frame beneath her, golden letters glow
    in an inscription plain for all to see:
"I, too, among God's deathless daughters go
    prized for the power that resides in me.
        The man whose heart is unmoved by my name
        will never rise to honor or true fame "

On all four walls, more images were hung   69
    of varying persons, next each window sill,
diverse in sex and look, both old and young
    diversely clad, depicted with such skill
as to Apelles[52] might of old belong
    or as Salviati[53] now commands who still
        with bold pen and bright hues makes Nature keep
        in her own bounds and other painters weep.

Come nel bel de le dipinte carte 70
    la vista i cavalier hanno appagata,
e de la regia sala a parte a parte
    la mirabil ricchezza ancor mirata,
chiedono a lei che gli divide e parte,
    sendo tra l'uno e l'altro in mezo intrata,
      di chi l'imagin sia che rende adorno
      l'altare, e di chi l'altre appese intorno.

L'esser suo chiedonle anco, e di coloro 71
    che fan seco dimora in compagnia,
e come il feminil leggiadro coro
    così da' cavalier sevro si stia.
Ella, a que' detti rispondendo loro,
    disse: — Il saprete allor che tempo ei fia. —
      Poscia in stanza men grande indi gli mena,
      ove apparata è la superba cena.

Gareggia insieme il nobil drapelletto 72
    in far allor servigio a' duo baroni:
chi scarca lor de la corazza il petto,
    chi di spade e pugnale ambi i galloni;
altra l'elmo e lo scudo e 'l braccialetto,
    altra il resto lor trae fino agli sproni;
      altri le mani lor da vasi aurati
      sparge di liquor varii ed odorati.

Vinti donzelle ne la mensa a canto 73
    s'assidono ai guerrier; vint'altre han cura
di farla ricca e lieta, a pien di quanto
    produce grato al gusto uman natura.
E spumante liquor di Bacco intanto
    meschian vint'altre ancor con acqua pura,
      ed altre tante ai lor vocali accenti
      rendon concordi i musici stromenti.

Come coi cibi fu, come coi vini 74
    dèma la sete e l'importuna fame,
e si scoprir, levati i bianchi lini,
    i bei tapeti adorni d'aureo stame,
disse ver' lor, rivolta ai pellegrini
    baron, colei che fra quelle altre dame
      maggior sembrava: — Ora, signor, saprete
      quel che poco anzi a me voi chiesto avete.

But when the knights had at full length admired,   70
   sating their gazes with repeated view,
those works, and with delight that never tired
   the hall's great treasures one by one run through,
they turned unto their escort and inquired,
   for she was still standing between them, who
      it was whose image the high altar crowned
      and whose the panels hanging all around.

And they inquired who she was and those   71
   who kept her company, and why a throng
of graceful maids would chose to be without
   a knightly escort to guard them from wrong.
She answered them, "All this you shall find out
   in good time and be satisfied ere long,"
      then led them to a smaller chamber where
      a banquet stood prepared of lavish fare.

A group of maids now hastens toward each guest   72
   to serve him as he readies for the meal.
One loosens the hard cuirass from the chest,
   or from its sheath removes the mortal steel,
or takes the shield and helmet with its crest,
   or helps to slip the spur from off the heel,
      or with a golden ewer ready stands
      to pour sweet-scented streams to wash the hands.

With twenty maidens ranged along their side   73
   the knights are seated. Twenty more take heed
to serve them at the table and provide
   drink and delicious nourishment at need.
Another twenty with glad hands provide
   water to temper merry Bacchus' speed,
      while yet another twenty maids commence
      to sing and play on tuneful instruments.

When the exquisite wines had quenched their thirst   74
   and their importune hunger had been fed,
and their gaze fell on fine carpets interspersed —
   the table cloth being off — by golden thread,
then she who of these ladies seemed the first
   looked blithely at the errant knights and said:
      "Dear Sirs, the time has come for you to know
      the truth for which you asked a while ago.

Rinaldo

Di Napoli, città che 'n riva al mare 75
   siede quindi vicin, già resse il freno
donna che fu de le più degne e rare
   virtuti adorna e copiosa a pieno,
che sopra tutto non trovò mai pare
   in cortesia, sì n'ebbe il cor ripieno;
      ed in ciò vinse i più lodati essempi
      che giamai furo negli antiqui tempi.

Costei, vaga d'oprar cosa ch'ognora 76
   la memoria di lei viva serbasse,
tai che, sì come in vita, in morte ancora
   l'alta sua cortesia si celebrasse,
fece con l'arte maga, ond'essa allora
   a pena ritrovò chi l'aguagliasse,
      questo palagio in cima a questo colle,
      ed a la cortesia sacrare il volle.

Sendo a la cortesia poscia sacrato, 77
   chiamollo Albergo de la Cortesia,
e l'imagin di lei sovra l'ornato
   altar drizzò, dove ad ogni or si stia;
ritrasse poi ciascun che mai sia stato
   raro tra' più cortesi o che pur fia,
      ed i ritratti loro intorno appese,
      sì che il muro più vago indi si rese.

Lascia da poi che in cortesia si spenda 78
   in questo albergo tanto argento ed oro,
che ve 'n fia sempre, benché il sol risplenda
   mille volte or nel Cancro ed or nel Toro;
né crederò ch'a cotal pregio ascenda
   altro cui re possegga ampio tesoro;
      e vuol che le ricchezze e 'l luoco istesso
      sia governato ognor dal nostro sesso:

da donzelle però d'alti parenti 79
   ne l'Italia felice al mondo nate,
le quali a note ed ad ignote genti
   non sol ricetto dar siano obligate,
ma cercar anco co' pensieri intenti
   deggian ch'ad albergar sempre menate
      sian qui donne e donzelle e cavalieri,
      del paese così come stranieri.

Canto Seven

Naples, which lies quite near here on the sea,   75
    in olden times was ably governed by
a queen endowed with every quality
    that mind or soul could be ennobled by,
but none throughout the world in courtesy
    could match her, for she valued it so high
       that she excelled each woman and each man
       known for that virtue since the world began.

She, much desiring that her courteous ways   76
    should by unending fame be crowned,
so that in death, even as in life, her praise
    for noble courtesy should still resound,
by potent sorcery — and in those days
    few who could match her in that art were found —
       raised up this hill-top palace for divine
       Courtesy's monument and hallowed shrine.

She named the place you visit now the Inn   77
    of Courtesy. Moreover, it was she
who had that splendid image placed within
    the spot where now it stands for all to see.
She then had painted all who had ever been
    renowned for courtesy, or soon would be,
       and had their portraits hung to deck each wall
       facing the altar that commands the hall.

She left for our inn's maintenance and care   78
    silver and gold enough to make it last
to the end of time and keep it standing there
    when a thousand suns the Crab and Bull[54] have passed —
a price, I think, more than a king could spare
    out of whatever riches he amassed —
       and she ordained this wealth and place to be
       ruled by our sex in perpetuity —

yes, women only, but noble ones, home-grown   79
    Italian maids whom high-born parents bore.
We are charged to lodge all comers, be they known
    or unknown, and not merely to wait for
chance guests but eagerly from every zone
    to summon maidens, ladies, knights — the more
       the merrier — and to make all who come,
       neighbors or foreigners, here feel at home.

Vuol anco ch'ognor vada a questo effetto   80
   una copia di lor là presso il lito,
la qual tenti condurre al suo ricetto
   ognun che passa con cortese invito.
E perché non le punga al cor sospetto
   de l'onor suo, che non le sia rapito,
      incantò il monte e intorno ancor sei miglia
      con nuova ed incredibil meraviglia:

che s'alcun donna ingiurioso offende   81
   ne l'aver, ne la vita o ne l'onore,
d'invisibile ardor tutto s'accende,
   sì che miseramente al fin ne more.
Ma sì come l'incanto ognor difende
   chi serva in fatto il virginal suo fiore,
      così qual donna il macchia e 'l tiene a vile
      quinci discaccia con perpetuo stile.

Come il mar scaccia d'uom le membra estinte,   82
   come scaccia pastor le infette agnelle,
così con forza non veduta spinte
   da questo spazio son le damigelle,
che da l'amore o dal gran premio vinte
   misere furo al proprio onor rubelle;
      e quinci avien che i padri nostri poi
      non han, mentre stiam qui, cura di noi.

Fe' da poi la regina, Alba nomata,   83
   per mostrarsi cortese in ogni cosa,
e per farsi a coloro amica e grata
   che van cercando ogni ventura ascosa,
una barca mirabile incantata
   ch'ella chiamò la barca aventurosa;
      perciò ch'ognun che in lei di gir si fida,
      sempre a qualche aventura in breve guida.

Senza nocchier, sol da l'incanto scorta,   84
   se 'n va la barca per l'ondoso mare,
e gli erranti guerrier securi porta
   là dove il lor ardir possin mostrare,
come, se 'l vostro core a ciò v'essorta,
   voi potrete, signori, ancor provare,
      ché la barca tegniam quinci vicina,
      dove col nostro lito il mar confina.

Canto Seven

Our founder also bade that with this aim 80
    a pair of us at intervals should ride
down to the shore to ask whoever came
    in courtesy to walk up by their side.
And so that virtue's claims, for fear of shame
    or ravishment, be met and satisfied,
        she in a strange enchantment's power bound
        this mountain and six miles of circling ground,

by which whoever harms a lady in 81
    her goods, her honor or her life will sense
a sudden heat erupt beneath his skin
    and slowly burn to death for his offense.
But as this spell protects her who has been
    faithful in guarding virgin innocence,
        so she who scorns or sullies it is sent
        disgraced into perpetual banishment.

For as the limbs of dead men by the sea 82
    and tainted lambs by shepherds are cast forth,
so by an unseen force are made to flee
    all ladies who betray their maiden worth
for love or gain, for they irrevocably
    have robbed themselves of honorable birth.
        And this is why our fathers without fear
        or worry about us let us sojourn here.

Lastly, that great queen — Alba she was named — 83
    to show herself in all things courteous
and to give aid to any man enflamed
    by ventures daring and mysterious,
cast one last magic spell by which she framed
    a vessel called the Ship Adventurous."
        Whoever enters her and trusts her sail
        she speeds to new adventure without fail.

Without a pilot, guided by a charm, 84
    that bark sails out upon the wave-tossed sea
and carries daring warriors safe from harm
    to places of extremest jeopardy,
and if your hearts can face without alarm
    such prospects of adventure, Sirs, feel free
        to board her, for she rides not far away
        from here at anchor in a little bay.

Or l'ordin che tra noi serbar sogliamo 85
    riman che sol vi dica, ed egli è questo,
ch'ogn'anno tra noi tutte una eleggiamo,
    ch'abbia a regger poi l'altre il pensier desto.
A quant'ella n'impon tutte obidiamo,
    pur che comandi il licito e l'onesto.
        Io che per nome Euridice son detta,
        al degno grado fui poco anzi eletta.

Fu Guilante il leggiadro padre mio, 86
    e in Capua dominò mentre che visse. —
Qui tacque alquanto, indi il parlar seguio,
    e de l'altre la stirpe e 'l nome disse.
Ma perché tinta già d'oscuro oblio
    sorgea la notte, fe' ch'ognun si gisse
        a riposar su l'addagiate piume,
        sin ch'in ciel si mostrasse il nuovo lume.

One thing remains to tell you: in our throng   85
    there is always one who is accounted best,
for every year we meet to choose among
    our numbers one to govern all the rest.
We must obey all her commands so long
    as they pass honesty's and virtue's test.
        I'm called Eurydice and was — I'll have you know —
        picked for this office a short while ago.

My father was Guilant, a great burgess   86
    who, while he lived, held Capua in thrall."
She paused, then gave, after a brief recess,
    the others' names and their descents withal.
But now that, dyed in dark forgetfulness,
    night was advancing, she ordained that all
        on downy beds provided spend the night
        until the sky displayed the new dawn's light.

CANTO OTTAVO

Già svegliata l'Aurora al dolce canto   1
    de' lascivetti augei vaga sorgea,
e con le rosee mani il fosco manto
    de la notte squarciava e dissolvea;
i suoi tesori vagheggiando intanto,
    l'aria, l'acqua, il terren lieto ridea,
        e giù versava dal bel volto il cielo,
        formato in perle, il matutino gielo;

quando i guerrier, lasciato il pigro letto,   2
    vestir le membra di lucente acciaro,
e 'n compagnia del nobil drappelletto
    a rimirar quei bei ritratti andaro,
ché brama ognun di lor che gli sia detto
    di quelli eroi futuri il nome chiaro;
        de' quai, ciò ch'ebbe Alba di dire in uso,
        di bocca in bocca poi s'era diffuso.

Così di bocca in bocca era discesa   3
    di quei cortesi eroi l'istoria vera,
ch'Euridice l'aveva anch'ella intesa
    e render ne sapea notizia intera;
onde per appagar la brama accesa,
    che di par giva in quella coppia altera,
        or ne' ritratti, or ne' suoi volti fisse
        le luci avendo, al fin così le disse:

— Dei duo che là su stanno, a cui lucente   4
    porpora sacra il sacro capo adorna,
questi Ippolito fia, da l'Occidente
    noto sin dove il sol nasce ed aggiorna,
Ercol Gonzaga quel, ch'unitamente
    potranno a l'eresia fiaccar le corna,
        ed atti ad alte imprese, a grave pondo
        regger insieme con la Chiesa il mondo.

Canto Eight

Aurora, waking to the melodies   1
   of merry birds, already rose in view,
and with her rosy fingers[86] by degrees
   the inky veil of gloomy night withdrew,
and gazing on her treasury, the breeze,
      the waters and the earth were smiling while
         the sky began from its fair face to strew
         in pearly drops the early morning dew,

when from their idle beds the warriors rose   2
   and sheathed their limbs in shining steel to go
with the maiden band to view those fine tableaus
   of courteous men and women, and also
eager to learn the glorious names of those
      exemplars future times would know,
         whose fame would fly — Alba was pleased to say —
         from mouth to mouth, growing day after day.

From mouth to mouth, foreknowledge in the past   3
   of future courteous heroes had come down.
Eurydice knew it all and now at last
   could bring new listeners word of their renown,
wherefore she, acting the encomiast,
      turns to the eager warriors and makes known,
         the persons pictured there,[87] while her bright gaze
         now on the knights, now on the portraits stays:

"Of this pair here," she says, "whose brows display   4
   the sacred purple's reverend majesty,
one is Ippolito,[88] to be famed one day
   from the far orient to the western sea,
the other, Ercole Gonzaga.[89] They
      in time will crop the horns of heresy
         and, apt to greatly dare and deeply probe,
         with Mother Church together rule the globe.

Rinaldo

Mirate quel che da le più vicine   5
   parti presso l'altar sacrato pende,
a cui non men di lucido ostro il crine
   e di regal onor la faccia splende.
Adorneran costui virtù divine,
   e quel che più simile a Dio l'uom rende,
      del sangue estense fia, Luigi detto,
      giovene ancora a sommi gradi eletto.

Ma fra tutti gli alteri e degni pregi,   6
   che sempre luceran qual fiamme accese,
nullo sera che più illustri e fregi
   de l'alta cortesia, ch'ogn'or palese
farà con mille e mille fatti egregi
   in mile occasioni, in mille imprese:
      Onde darà soggetto a bronzi, a marmi,
      a dotte prose ed a vivaci carmi.

Volgete gli occhi a quel che in vista pare   7
   figliol di Marte, anzi pur Marte istesso.
Or chi potrà costui tanto lodare,
   ch'ai suoi merti divin giunga mai presso?
Per questo il Po n'andrà più lieto, e 'l mare,
   non solo i fiumi, inchinaransi ad esso.
      Sarà il secondo Alfonso, e 'l ricco freno
      di Ferrara terrà felice a pieno.

L'altro, severo il volto e grave il ciglio,   8
   e adorno sì di maestà regale,
del gran Maria Francesco serà figlio,
   maggior del padre in pace, in guerra eguale,
sotto 'l cui saggio impero unqua in periglio
   Urbin non fia d'alcun dannoso male,
      ma fiorirà per l'alme sue contrade
      una lieta, felice ed aurea etade.

Da tanto genitor prodotto al mondo   9
   fia quel garzon ch'in volto è così fiero,
che sosterrà di mille guerre il pondo
   e d'eserciti mille avrà l'impero:
fulgor de l'armi a null'altro secondo,
   prudente duce, audace cavaliero;
      né mai morrà, se mai non muor colui
      che ne' cuor vive e ne le bocch'altrui.

Now look on him whose image hangs most near   5
    the sacred shrine. The form those pigments trace
no less adorned with purple rises here
    nor with less splendor shines that regal face,
yet what adorns the part of him most dear
    to God, most like to God, is virtuous grace.
        Of Este born — Luigi[90] is his name —
        he'll rise, while still a youth, to highest fame.

"But of all men whose skill or valor feeds   6[91]
    the blaze of honor's beacon evermore,
none in transcendent courtesy exceeds
    or matches him, for it provides the core
of thousands upon thousands of his deeds,
    a thousand thousand times displayed, wherefore
        in bronze or marble, learned prose or verse,
        he'll be a subject men will long rehearse.

And here behold a man who seems to be   7
    a son of Mars, or Mars himself. Ah, say
what tongue has words to praise sufficiently
    his godlike excellence? For him some day
the Po shall flow more gladly, him the sea
    itself, not only rivers, shall obey:
        Alfonso[92] second of that name, whose reign
        will gladden great Ferrara's rich terrain.

The next you see, whose brow shows such austere   8
    majesty, wisdom and unflinching will
is great Maria Francesco's[93] son, his peer
    in deeds of war, but in peace greater still.
Urbino under him shall never fear
    danger or want but, governed by his skill,
        shall smile with joy and wonder to behold
        his scepter usher in an age of gold.

This exemplary father shall beget   9
    the youth[94] depicted here who looks so grim.
He'll bear of countless wars the grief and fret
    and countless armies shall be led by him,
a blazing soldier-sun who'll never set,
    sage strategist, peerless of mind and limb.
        He'll never die: death has no claim on one
        who in men's hearts and mouths lives on and on.

Rinaldo

De' duo quindi lontan, giovani in vista,   *10*
    la sacra mitra ha l'un, l'altro ha la spada:
Un, Annibal di Capua, onde di trista
    convien che lieta Roma un tempo vada;
l'altro, che la fortezza al senno mista
    vendo al ciel si farà larga strada,
        é Stanislavo, di Tarnovio conte,
        che star potrà co' più famosi a fronte.

Fia quel nel cui benigno e vago aspetto   *11*
    splende di cortesia sì chiaro lume,
Scipion da Gazuol, fido ricetto
    d'ogni virtù, d'ogni gentil costume,
che sevro dal vulgar stuolo negletto
    al ciel s'inalzerà con salde piume:
        a Minerva, a le Muse, a Febo amico,
        de' buon sostegno, a' vizii aspro nemico.

Quel che mostra desio di gloria aperto   *12*
    nel volto, e aperta ha l'una e l'altra mano,
serà Fulvio Rangone, il cui gran merto
    lo farà noto al prossimo e al lontano;
l'altro ch'al vero onor per camin certo
    n'andrà, raro scrittore e capitano,
        Ercol Fregoso al mondo noto; e quello
        che par sì uman, fia Sforza Santinello.

Or rimirate da quell'altro canto,   *13*
    ov'il bello del ciel tutt'è raccolto,
sì ch'il sol non ne vide unqua altretanto,
    il sol cui nulla di mirare è tolto.
Colei c'ha ducal cerchio e ducal manto,
    ma reali maniere e real volto,
        Vittoria fia del gran sangue Farnese,
        magnanima, gentil, saggia e cortese.

"Lucrezia Estense è l'altra, i cui crin d'oro   *14*
    lacci e reti saran del casto amore,
ne le cui chiare luci ogni tesoro
    del cielo riporrà l'alto Fattore;
per cui Minerva e di Parnaso il coro
    non so se loda o biasmo avran maggiore:
        loda, perché da lei fiano imitate,
        biasmo, sendo poi vinte e superate.

These two men further off, youngsters by sight,   10[95]
    one with a miter, the other with a sword,
are Hannibal of Capua,[96] who shall fight
    to make Rome pass from hardship to reward,
and he whose wisdom joined with martial might
    shall blaze an ample highway heavenward,
        great Stanislaus, the count of Tarnow,[97] who
        in fame shall match all others, or outdo.

He there, whose generous and smiling eyes   11
    shine with such candid rays of courtesy,
Gazzuolan Scipio[98] shall epitomize
    all virtue and civility for aye,
destined aloof from vulgar crowds to rise
    soaring on mighty pinions to the sky.
        Minerva, Phoebus and the Muse shall know
        him as a friend, Vice, as a bitter foe.

This one who stands — see how his face displays   12
    desire for fame! — with both hands open wide
is Fulvio Rangon,[99] destined for praise
    both near and far, in every virtue tried.
This other, who shall rise by fated ways
    to honors that both sword and pen provide,
        is Ercole Fregoso, and his fellow,
        who smiles so kindly, Sforza Santinello.[100]

Now turn and on the opposite wall see shown   13
    a sphere of beauty, radiant and serene,
a dizzying sun of splendor and renown
    too bright to be by mortal gazers seen.
She pictured there with ducal cape and crown,
    but with the face and manner of a queen,
        shall be Victoria,[101] of Farnese's blood,
        wise and magnanimous, gracious and good.

Lucrezia d'Este[102] is next, in whose chaste womb   14
    and golden ringlets love waits to be born,
whose eyes the high Creator shall illume
    and with the treasures of his grace adorn,
Minerva's and the Muses' handmaid, whom
    I know not whether they shall praise or scorn:
        praise, since through her their tasks shall be completed;
        scorn, since their charms shall be by hers defeated.

Rinaldo

Le due fian sue germane e belle e saggie,   15
  e d'ogni raro ben ricche ed altere,
per queste de' mortai fallaci piagge
  scorte di gire a Dio fidate e vere.
L'altra, che par che l'aria intorno irragge,
  onde Amor se medesmo accende e fere,
    Claudia Rangona fia, che non gli altrui,
    ma faran chiara i proprii scritti sui. —

Qui fu da lei fine al suo dire imposto,   16
  che destò nei guerrier diletto eguale.
Quelli, che già tra loro avean disposto
  di solcar lo spumante ondoso sale,
chieggiono umili al vago stuol che tosto
  lor si conceda in grazia il pin fatale;
    né ciò fu sol da quelle a lor concesso,
    ma cari doni ancor largiti appresso.

Ebbe Rinaldo, onde se 'n vada ornato   17
  il suo Baiardo, sella e fornimento
di spesse gemme sparso e tempestato,
  sì ch'ogn'occhio rendea pago e contento.
Il morso a la gemina è lavorato,
  le staffe ancora, e son di puro argento;
    de l'istesso metallo è 'l grosso arcione,
    vago d'intagli ad ogni paragone.

Diero a Florindo ancor, perché gli copra   18
  l'arme, vaga e mirabil sopravesta,
ch'ai più ricchi lavor se 'n gia di sopra
  di vario stame, in varii modi testa.
Né forse Irene bella unqua fece opra,
  non ch'Aragne o Minerva, eguale a questa:
    ivi pinto con l'ago han mani industri
    de la suora del sol l'imprese illustri.

Quel che con maggior arte e maggior cura   19
  quivi il saggio maestro intesto avea,
era di Niobe la crudel sventura,
  tal ch'opra naturale altrui parea.
Piangeva i figli nel cui volto oscura
  morte viva ed espressa si vedea,
    le man stringendo e con doglioso affetto
    al ciel volgendo il minacciante aspetto.

This pair[103] shall be her sisters, who'll abound,   15
   in knowledge, wisdom and profound insight
and shall from this fallacious earthly ground
   toward God's celestial truth direct our flight.
Last, see emitting radiance all around,
   burning and wounding Love himself with light,
      Claudia Rangoni,[104] destined for renown
      not by another's pen, but by her own."

She says no more, and the young warrior pair   16
   muse with delight on the account she gave,
but now, since they are of one mind to dare
   a quest upon the foaming salt-sea wave,
they to the lovely band make humble prayer
   to grant them the enchanted prow they crave.
      Their wish being granted, they receive as well
      gifts of great price before they bid farewell.

Rinaldo gets to grace his Bayard's back   17
   a saddle and trappings. On its burnished seat
many a jewel and many a golden tack
   disposed in ravishing devices meet.
Gems stud the bit, gems glitter on the black
   bridle and spurs in silver, trim and neat.
      Of silver, too, is the great saddle-bow
      incised with masterly intaglio.

They then gave to Florindo to enfold   18
   his armor a great surcoat richly wrought
with varying designs both fine and bold
   in sundry fabrics with such cunning fraught
it might have made Irene's[105] hand of old
   or Arachne's or Minerva's[106] seem ill-taught.
      It shows, by the industrious needle done,
      the exploits of the sister of the sun.[107]

The master has used fine embroidery   19
   with such transcendent skill and consummate care —
his theme, the cruel fate of Niobe[108] —
   that Nature seems the only artist there.
You see the queen bewail her dead sons, see
   her face in living death dark with despair.
      She wrings her hands and with a dreadful cry
      lifts up her face in menace to the sky.

Scorgesi altrove in abito succinto,   20
    con faretra pendente al manco lato,
con crine sciolto e parte in nodi avinto,
    tender l'arco la dea curvo e piegato:
par ch'ondeggi il capel, da l'aura spinto,
    ch'ella piova furor dal volto irato,
        ch'orribilmente fischi e ch'ali metta,
        mentre fendendo il ciel va la saetta.

Stan le figlie di Niobe in viso smorte   21
    davanti a lei, sovra i fraterni petti,
qual di duol, qual di tema e qual di morte
    scolti avendo negli atti i vari affetti.
Una ch'apre le labbia onde conforte
    la madre forse con pietosi detti,
        riceve in questa il dardo in bocca, e pare
        fermarsi a mezzo, tronco il suo parlare.

Ad un'altra che stende il braccio dritto,   22
    quasi dar voglia a la sorella aita,
si vede quello e 'l petto ancor trafitto
    d'un dardo sol con doppia aspra ferita.
Col ferro entro in un fianco ascoso e fitto
    giace la terza languida e smarrita,
        cui da strale è confissa una in quel modo
        che legno a legno suol da saldo chiodo.

Mostra la quinta aver timore immenso,   23
    la man tendendo in mesto atto e dimesso;
col piede alzato e 'l corpo in aria estenso,
    l'altra sorella il suo fuggire espresso.
Si scorge in Niobe duol grave ed intenso,
    mentre nasconde col suo corpo stesso
        l'ultima figlia, che tremante sembra
        coprir le sue con le materne membra.

Se 'n vanno al lido i due guerrieri insieme,   24
    e rendon quivi il fatal legno carco.
Quel, come sente il pondo il qual lo preme,
    si move quasi stral ch'esca da l'arco.
Frangesi l'onda e mormorando freme
    tutta spumante sotto 'l curvo incarco;
        intanto fugge e si dilegua il lito,
        sì che dagli occhi omai tutt'è sparito.

There swathed in a short tunic you could see   20
    her quiver at her left, her golden strands
part loose, part knotted up, the deity,
    stringing her curving bow with practiced hands.
Her tresses wave, lashed by the breeze, and she,
    her countenance raining scorn and fury, stands
        while bursts of horrid whizzing fill the skies
        and cleaving through the clouds her arrow flies.

Niobe's daughters, deathly pale and weak,   21
    stand near her while their brothers sprawl below.
Despair's numb lull, fear's quivering, terror's shriek —
    all symptoms of distress are here on show.
One girl runs openmouthed as if to speak
    some piteous words, seeing her mother's woe,
        when an arrow speeds between her rosy lips to reach
        her throat, so stopping both her tongue and speech.

Another holds out her right arm to lend —   22
    too late, in vain — her falling sister aid,
as the goddess lets another shaft descend
    and makes twice-bitter pain her breast invade.
An iron shaft, buried from end to end
    in her white flank, piercing the third young maid,
        proceeds the fourth she lies on to impale
        as plank to plank is hammered with a nail.

The fifth seized by wild panic and dismay   23
    in meek entreaty lifts her hands and eyes.
The sixth strains feet and trunk to get away
    and claws the air around her as she flies.
Niobe, to extremest anguish prey,
    to save her youngest with her body tries
        to hide the girl, who cowers half-concealed,
        as if to make her mother's shape her shield.

But now the pair of warriors hasten straight   24
    down to the shore and board the fated prow.
The craft no sooner than it feels their weight
    casts off swift as an arrow from a bow.
The waves rush by, the timbers crepitate
    and foam churns white beneath the speeding bow.
        Swiftly the shore flies off, and from their eyes[109]
        all objects vanish except seas and skies.

Già tutto mare e cielo è d'ogni canto,   25
   ché quanto cala il suol, tanto il mar poggia.
Tien dritto il suo camin la barca intanto,
   senza alternar la vela ad orza o poggia;
se 'n va per l'alto mar, mossa da incanto,
   con ratto corso e non usata foggia,
     passando d'uno in altro equoreo seno,
     tal ch'uscita ella è già dal mar Tireno.

Volgeasi omai, di mille fregi adorno,   26
   tacito e muto il cielo, e, tolto il sole,
col tôrci il volto suo, n'aveva il giorno,
   quando sentiro un suon qual di parole,
qual d'uom a cui vien fatto oltraggio e scorno,
   che di ciò con le strida alto si duole.
     La barca verso 'l suon ratta si drizza,
     sì che più ratto mai delfin non guizza.

Vider, come fur presso i due guerrieri,   27
   due legni in un congiunti ed abbordati,
e d'uno in altro poi da masnadieri
   varii arnesi esser messi e trasportati;
e insieme ancora donne e cavalieri,
   ma sciolte quelle van, questi legati.
     I vincitori lor sembianza accusa
     per corsari e per gente al mal sempre usa.

Tra lor si scaglia, dal garzon seguito,   28
   Rinaldo, e sgrida e gli minaccia forte.
Un che più sembra di lor tutti ardito
   e duce de la barbara coorte,
disse: — Avete mai più, compagni, udito
   ch'uom vada a ricercar la propria morte?
     Or vedetelo in questi, i quai non sanno
     come altramente procacciarsi danno. —

Indi, volto a Rinaldo: — Or su, meschino,   29
   tratti quest'arme e datti a me prigione:
così fuggirai forse il tuo destino,
   ch'è 'l mio volere, e fia ch'io ti perdone. —
Per parole parole al Saracino
   già non rendette il gran figliol d'Amone,
     ma nel petto, dov'ha l'anima albergo,
     cacciògli il ferro e fello uscir da tergo.

There is sea and sky on all sides since the more   25
  earth falls away, the more the sea prevails.
The ship, which all the while straight onward bore,
  veers neither left nor right, nor changes sails,
moves by enchantment far from any shore
  with an uncanny speed that never fails
    from sea to sea in unimpeded motion
    and soon has left the blue Tyrrhenian ocean.

Ere long, when myriads of bright gems adorn   26
  the cloudless stillness of the sky, and day
has gone with the sun, some hours before morn
  they hear what seems a voice from far away,
as of a man who meets outrage or scorn
  and loudly cries in protest and dismay.
    Toward the sound the magic vessel drives
    more rapidly than any dolphin dives.

The bark drew near, and in the morning sun   27
  the knights saw two joined ships at anchor ride,
and men from one into the other run
  with gear and harness, dragging by their side
two bands of knights and ladies, of which one
  walked unbound and the other chained or tied.
    The victors, by their looks, were — plain to see —
    corsairs inured to every villainy.

Rinaldo, followed by his friend, leaps in   28
  their midst with threatening cries. Their leader, who
seems bolder than the rest, turns with a grin
  and in these words speaks to his barbarous crew:
"You've heard, men — have you not? — that it's a sin
  to seek one's own death. Look upon these two,
    fools that they are, who do not seem to know
    another way to their own overthrow."

Then, turning on Rinaldo: "Wretch!" he cries,   29
  "Lay down your sword, surrender to me, lest
much worse befall you. Do it, if you're wise,
  and I may spare you. Yield now, you were best!"
To his words with no words Aymon's son replies
  but thrusts his blade into the Saracen's breast,
    even where the soul is lodged, with an attack
    so strong it cleaves right through and out his back.

Rinaldo

Come s'aventan susurrando al viso   *30*
  l'irate pecchie insieme unitamente
al villanel ch'aggia il re loro ucciso,
  per vendicarlo di morir contente:
così contra Rinaldo a l'improviso
  muove gridando la villana gente;
    e se fu tarda a la colui difesa,
    tarda non è per far a questo offesa.

Miseri! dove gite, a tôr la pena   *31*
  forse che merta il vostro oprar sì torto?
Quest'impeto a morir tutti vi mena
  e non a vendicar il duce morto.
Rinaldo quanta ha forza e quanta ha lena,
  quanto ha valor qui dimostra scorto,
    e fa l'istesso il suo Florindo ancora,
    vago ei non men che sì ria gente mora.

Man, gambe, busti e sanguinose teste   *32*
  già si veggion per l'aria andar balzando;
s'addoppian sempre le percosse infeste,
  lampeggia e tuona l'uno e l'altro brando.
Elmo o scudo non è che quelli arreste,
  qual volta ratti in giù vengon calando;
    né solo arma non è ch'a lor resista,
    ma non gli può soffrire ancor la vista.

Il gran figliol d'Amone otto n'occise   *33*
  con l'otto prime orribili percosse;
poi con la nona ad un l'elmo divise,
  e le chiome gli fe' sanguigne e rosse.
Quel, ritirato, al crin la man si mise
  per veder s'ampia la ferita fosse;
    ma mentre ei tocca la primiera piaga,
    novo colpo maggior la man gli impiaga.

Florindo il sovragiunge, e d'un riverso   *34*
  l'alzata mano a lui troncando taglia;
quel furioso e ne la rabbia immerso
  allor contra 'l baron ratto si scaglia:
tira gran colpi a dritto ed a traverso,
e tutto si discopre e si sbaraglia.
    Cauto il guerrier di punta il ferro vibra,
    gli aggiunge al cor, né lascia sangue in fibra.

As bees will fling themselves with furious spleen   30
   joined in a buzzing swarm against the brow
of a rude peasant who has killed their queen,
   content to die in her revenge, so now
against Rinaldo suddenly careen
   the villains all at once. But if somehow
      their chief in his defense had been too slow,
      Rinaldo in offense now was no less so.

Cretins! Why in such haste? Are you so keen   31
   to pay for crime as you deserve? Your spite
beckons you all to death, not as you ween
   to vengeance for your fallen leader's plight.
For in a few, brief moments here is seen
   all of Rinaldo's courage, skill and might.
      Florindo no less eagerly shows why
      such criminal and barbarous folk must die.

Hands, legs, chests, bloodied heads, flung through the air   32
   bounce on the deck where wounded wretches crawl.
The fearsome buffets of the youthful pair
   in ceaseless thunder crash down and appall
the pack. Nor shield nor helmet helps them there.
   Like rats caught in a trap they scurry and fall.
      Nor does Rinaldo's blade alone make space
      all round him, but they flee his very face.

With his first eight blows, good Aymon's mighty son   33
   kills eight of his attackers instantly,
then with the ninth cuts through the helm of one,
   making his hair drip red. Astounded he
falls backs and gropes, sensing his warm blood run,
   his skull to feel how grave the hurt might be,
      but as his hand touches his first wound — lo! —
      it is slashed by a still heavier second blow.

Florindo runs in and with a backward slash   34
   lops off the upraised, wounded hand.
Meanwhile another makes a furious dash
   toward Rinaldo from the villain band.
He strikes wide sweeping blows and in his rash
   speed drops his guard. Rinaldo sees it and,
      with sword-point aimed at the undefended part,
      thrusts home and makes his life-blood leave his heart,

Uccise poi Lico, Euribante e Orgolto: 35
    divise il primo da la spalla al fianco,
al secondo partì per mezzo 'l volto,
    recise al terzo il drito braccio e 'l manco.
Avrebbe Alferno ancor di vita tolto,
    ma gliel vietar Folerico e Lanfranco,
        che, dar volendo al lor compagno aita,
        con la morte comun gli porser vita.

Sembrano i due campion strali ch'al basso   36
    irato aventi fulminando Giove:
a quel alto furore, a quel fracasso,
    a quelle rare e non più viste prove,
già quasi ogni pagan di vita è casso,
    né più l'armi dannose indarno move;
        e chi fruisce ancor l'aura vitale
        si crede al mar com'a men grave male.

Già di tutto il villan barbaro stuolo   37
    solo un vivo ne' legni era rimaso,
e verso lui se 'n gia Rinaldo a volo,
    per mandar la sua vita anco a l'occaso;
ma lo sottrasse a quell'estremo duolo
    improviso consiglio, anzi pur caso,
        ch'impetrò breve spazio a la sua morte
        con atti umili e con parole accorte.

Dopoi dice: — Signor, vostro destino   38
    col morir nostro quel di voi procura,
e v'induce a far onta al gran Mambrino,
    al più fort'uom che fêsse mai Natura,
al maggior re del popol saracino,
    c'ha di noi qual di servi amica cura,
        e vorrà farne in tutto aspra vendetta,
        qual a l'offesa, al suo valor s'aspetta.

Noi suoi ministri aveamo a forza prese,   39
    per condurle a lui poi, queste donzelle,
ch'ei manda a corseggiare ogni paese
    sol per averne di leggiadre e belle;
or come avrà de le mortali offese
    che tutti estinti c'ha, vere novelle,
        non vedrà suo desir contento e sazio
        sin che di noi non aggia fatto strazio.

then kills Orgolt, Lycus and Eurybas.   35
    The first he hews from neck to shoulder blade,
of the second splits the middle of his face
    and cuts off both arms of the third. Unstayed,
he struck Alphernos fourth, but in his case
    Lanfranc and Foleric his death forbade,
      who sped to his assistance in the strife
      and with their joint demise procured his life.

Like lightning bolts the two young champions strive   36
    that Jove hurls down in fury from on high.
Their actions are disasters none survive
    or tests no sane man would be tested by.
Few of their enemies are left alive,
    and fewer left to fight, or even to try,
      and those who still draw breath leap overboard,
      deeming the sea less cruel than the sword.

At last of all the ship's barbaric press   37
    just one man now remains, and toward him
Rinaldo leaps with savage eagerness
    as if intent to hew him limb from limb,
but he, instructed by extreme distress,
    suddenly found his wits and even a dim
      hope of delaying for a while his end
      by humble act and speech as of a friend.

Therefore he says: "My lord, it is your fate   38
    to have with our deaths procured your own,
for you have shamed Mambrin, surnamed 'the Great,'
    the strongest man Nature has ever known,
the mightiest Saracen king, to whose estate
    we freely our fondest fealty own.
      He'll wreak such bitter vengeance in short time
      as shall befit his valor and your crime.

We are his slaves and have at his command   39
    carried off these ladies. This is what we do.
For he makes pirates seize in every land
    the noblest maidens, loveliest to the view.
He'll know of this and come to understand
    who here has caused the death of his whole crew.
      Nor will he rest or feel content at all
      until he has fully avenged our fall.

Ei ben saprà la nostra avversa sorte,   40
    bench'uccida or qui me la vostra mano;
saprà non men chi n'abbia posto a morte,
    sia di Cristo seguace o sia pagano,
perch'un gran mago che gli alberga in corte
    il tutto gli farà palese e piano.
        Ma se da voi lasciato in vita io sono,
        spero impetrarvi a tanto error perdono. —

Qui gli tronca Rinaldo il suo parlare,   41
    e gli dice: — La vita or ti dono io,
perché tu possa al tuo signor narrare
    degli altri suoi ministri il caso rio;
e s'ei di lor vorrà vendetta fare,
    e di combatter nosco avrà desio,
        digli che siam guerrier del magno Carlo,
        ch'in ciò pronti saremo ad appagarlo.

Questi Florindo, io son Rinaldo detto   42
    di Chiaramonte, e son figliol d'Amone,
che lui non temo, e ne vedrà l'effetto
    quando venirà meco al paragone.
E chi temer deve uom da cui negletto
    sia, qual da lui, l'onesto e la ragione?
        Or su, prendi il tuo legno e quinci parti,
        poi c'ha voluto a morte il ciel sottrarti. —

Si volge poi con più serena faccia   43
    dove le dame e i cavalier si stanno,
e dal lor petto ancor dubbioso scaccia
    con cortesi parole il grave affanno.
Indi le man con le sue man dislaccia
    a coloro ch'a tergo avinte l'hanno;
        e fa l'istesso il buon Florindo ancora,
        sì ch'ogni nodo è sciolto in poco d'ora.

Intesero ambo poi come si chiame   44
    di quelli ogni guerriero, ogni donzella;
e che colei che fra tutt'altre dame
    riportava la palma in esser bella,
possedeva d'Arabia il gran reame,
    figlia di Pandion, detta Auristella;
        e ciascun d'essi a la comun preghiera
        diede non men di sé notizia intiera.

He is sure to know our fate, though you may quell   40
    my life with your own hand right now. He'll know
who it is that sent us to our deaths as well,
    Christian or a pagan, nobly born or low,
for a great sorcerer at his court can tell
    by magic all things done by friend or foe.
        But, should you let me live, I may succeed
        in begging his forgiveness for your deed."

Rinaldo here cut off his words and said: 41
    "I'll let you live to tell your lord that we
are the cause why his vile henchmen now lie dead
    as their misdeeds amply deserved. If he
seeks vengeance for this and is not in dread
    to fight such as we are, let him feel free.
        Say that we serve great Charles. Bid him prepare
        to get prompt payment in this whole affair.

This is Florindo. I'm Rinaldo, born   42
    of Clairmont stock, good Aymon's youngest son.
We fear him not. Yea, he will come to mourn
    the day he comes for me, when all is done.
And who could fear a man that holds in scorn,
    as he does, reason and honesty? So run
        to tell him this, and take your ship. You know
        you're lucky to be still alive. Now go."

Then with a face less grim he turned around   43
    to the knights and ladies who stood doubtfully
nearby to reassure them as they frowned
    and ease their fears and their uncertainty,
and went to work to undo the ropes that bound
    the knights' hands to their backs and set them free.
        Thus, with Florindo busy at his side,
        it was not long till all knots were untied.

Then they inquired the birth, degree and name   44
    by which each of these maids and knights was styled
and learned that in the former group, a dame
    who with transcendent beauty blushed and smiled
was Araby's heir a princess of high fame
    called Auristella, Pandion's noble child.
        And upon further questioning, all the rest
        their names and states made freely manifest

Dopo lungo parlar i due baroni   45
   tornar di nuovo a l'incantata barca,
e ricusar de la regina i doni
   ch'ella dar lor volea con man non parca.
Il legno com'al fianco aggia gli sproni,
   ratto si move e 'l mar solcando varca;
     e fatto gran camin volge a la terra
     il corso, e con la proda il lito afferra.

Come cadente peso al centro giunto   46
   tosto si ferma ed ivi il moto affrena,
così più non si mosse il legno punto,
   avendo tecco il salso lido a pena;
smontano i cavalier dov'è congiunto
   l'estremo mar con la minuta arena,
     e cavar fanno ancor dagli scudieri
     fuor di barca insellati i lor destrieri.

Non pria dal legno ognun fu dismontato   47
   che quel ratto lasciò la terra a tergo,
e da l'incanto per lo mar guidato
   tornò veloce ne l'antiquo albergo.
Veggiono intanto i cavalieri alzato
   d'un vago piano in sul fiorito tergo
     un padiglion che, qual palagio grande,
     superbo intorno si dilata e spande.

Verso l'altera e ricca tenda i passi   48
   la bella coppia immantinente torse:
giunto u' per larga porta entro in lei vassi,
   gli occhi per tutto raggirando porse,
e di lucenti alabastrini sassi
   un gran pilastro in mezzo alzato scorse,
     sovra del qual scolpita in treccia e 'n gonna
     si vedea vaga e giovinetta donna.

Quivi gran sacrificio allor si fèa   49
   com'era stil del popolo asiano,
che sovente onorar, stolto! solea
   con vani sacrifici un idol vano.
Tra le velate corna il bue cadea
   ferito, e fèan di sangue umido 'l piano
     le simplici agne e l'umil pecorelle,
     trafitte ne la gola e queste e quelle.

The two knights, their inquiries satisfied,   45
    board their charmed vessel once more presently,
refusing gifts the grateful princess tried
    to bestow, of no mean generosity.
The ship, as though she felt spurs prick her side,
    speeds off and, skimming lightly over the sea,
        sails day and night toward a distant land
        and there halts when her prow touches the strand.

As a falling weight, striking some obstacle,   46
    stops in its course and suddenly lies still,
so now their vessel does not move at all
    but hovers as if held by its own will.
They go on land where dying breakers fall
    and over the sand in foaming channels spill.
        Their mounts are saddled and the squires are told
        to lead the horses shoreward from the hold.

Scarce have they disembarked, when suddenly   47
    their ship turns round from prow to stern and then,
piloted by enchantment through the sea,
    speeds back to its old anchorage again.
Meanwhile the two knights riding inland see
    in a blossoming meadow on a pleasant plain
        a great pavilion whose palatial pride
        and splendor dominates the countryside.

Toward that enormous and luxurious tent   48
    the two youths at a gallop made their way,
and, having reached its lavish entrance, went
    riding inside, and there found on display,
made of pure alabaster stone, a monument
    on which, high on a splendid column, they
        beheld the sculpted image of a maid
        with braided hair and sumptuously arrayed.

Just then a ritual was in process here,   49
    conducted in the way that Asians prize,
who still preserve the custom to revere —
    fools! — their vain idols with vain sacrifice.
Struck between garland-covered horns, the steer
    falls to the axe's blow, and sharp blades slice
        the throats of lambs and kids, till all around
        the monument's base the red blood wets the ground.

Da viva fiamma uscian chiari splendori, 50
    ond'era adorno e risplendente il loco;
né men ch'accesi raggi, arabi odori
    spirava in fumo accolti il sacro foco.
Salendo il fumo al ciel, con varii errori
    si meschiava ne l'aria a poco a poco.
      Ne l'imagin Rinaldo i lumi gira,
      e la conosce tosto e ne sospira.

Conosce gli occhi onde aventogli Amore 51
    il primo stral ch'ancor gli punge il petto,
ed onde mosse insieme il dolce ardore
    ch'ognor l'infiamma d'amoroso affetto;
conosce i crin, co' qual gli avinse il core
    sì ch'anco egli è tra sì bei nodi stretto,
      la chiara fronte e l'aria del bel viso,
      la bocca e 'l dolce lampeggiar del riso.

Mentre fiso contempla il gran campione 52
    l'amato oggetto d'ogni suo pensiero,
un cavalier di quei del padiglione,
    c'ha grandissimo corpo, aspetto altero,
atti superbi e sguardo di leone,
    e inquieto sembra, audace e fiero,
      volta a Rinaldo l'orgogliosa faccia,
      con tai detti lo sgrida e lo minaccia:

— Villan guerrier, perché d'arcion non scendi, 53
    e non adori la divina imago?
Come a la mia presenza audacia prendi
    di rimirar così l'aspetto vago?
Or su, poiché 'l tu' error chiaro comprendi,
    se pur non sei de la tua morte vago;
      scendi, e scenda anco il tuo compagno teco,
      e fate sacrificio insieme or meco.

Vo' che confessi ancor che tra' mortali 54
    d'amar cosa sì degna io solo merto,
e ch'alcun altro per bellezze tali
    degno non è d'aver pene sofferto. —
— Chi sei tu, disse allor Rinaldo, e quali
    sono i tuoi merti? Or di ciò fammi certo,
      ch'in quanto al primo teco io già m'accordo,
      ma nel secondo sin ad or discordo. —

The sacred flames with lively sparks illume   50
    the chamber, brightening by degrees,
and with their smoke Arabian perfume
    mingles a scent of myrrh and ambergris.
Incense in rising ringlets fills the room
    with sweetness wafted on a gentle breeze.
        Rinaldo's gaze upon the image turns
        and, knowing its subject instantly, he burns —

burns for those bright eyes from which Cupid's dart   51
    first issued to transfix his aching breast
and lodged in it to make the pleasing smart
    of amorous yearning rankle without rest,
burns for that hair in which his willing heart
    captive in golden shackles lay oppressed,
        for that white forehead, that fair face, that smile,
        whose artless candor does his soul beguile.

As the great champion freezes to behold   52
    his idol and her lineaments to trace,
one of the knights there, villainous and bold,
    immense of stature, arrogant of face,
with a hungry lion's eyes, restless and cold,
    that seem to search for prey in every place,
        contemptuously blocks Rinaldo's path
        and in loud words gives utterance to his wrath:

"Base villain, wherefore do you not descend   53
    from your saddle and revere what I revere?
How dare you while I'm standing by pretend
    to know that lovely face and have no fear?
Get down, you knave, confess your fault and mend,
    unless in search of your own death you're here.
        Dismount, and make your friend dismount, too! Kneel
        and sacrifice with me or taste my steel.

Confess, first, that of all men only I   54
    could hope to merit such a lady's kiss,
and second, that no other man should try
    to gauge such beauty's worth in pain or bliss."
"Who are you?" said Rinaldo then, "and why
    do you claim such merit? Make me sure of this.
        For though about your last point, I agree,
        your first point is a lie. That's plain to see."

Rinaldo

— Se no 'l sai son Francardo, e son signore   55
  d'Armenia, e basti ciò — colui riprese.
Al gran figlio d'Amone intorno 'l core
  fervendo il sangue allor tosto s'accese;
indi al volto poi corse e d'un colore
  di viva fiamma rossegiante il rese,
    sì che fe' del pagano a la preposta
    altera e convenevole risposta:

— Io dirò ben che sei più d'altro indegno   56
  di locar in tal luoco i pensier tuoi;
e te 'l dimostrarà con chiaro segno
  questa mia spada or or, s'or or tu vuoi. —
Non così rode tarlo arido legno,
  come quel rose l'ira a' detti suoi;
    onde imbracciato il manto in lui si scaglia,
    e sol col brando corre a la battaglia.

Ride Rinaldo pien di sdegno e dice: 57
  — Va', t'arma pur; né ti pigliar tal fretta. —
E quelli a lui: — Questa mia spada ultrice
  basterà sola a far la mia vendetta. —
— Ahi!, risponde Rinaldo, ei si disdice
  così pugnar ad uom ch'onor n'aspetta. —
    L'altro più non attende e 'l ferro tira,
    ma Baiardo da parte ei ratto gira.

Indi dice: — Guerrier, teco giamai   58
  non pugnarò se tu primier non t'armi.
Cavaliero sono io, né tu potrai
  con la tua villania villano farmi. —
Il Saracino a lui: — Tu falli assai,
  se tu credi in tal modo unqua placarmi. —
    E 'n questo tanto colpi orrendi mena,
    sì che Rinaldo se 'n difende a pena.

Non può Florindo allor ciò più soffrire,   59
  ma di giusto disdegno arma il coraggio,
e gli dice: — Pagan privo d'ardire,
  che vantagio cerchi or nel disvantaggio?
Volgi, volgiti a me, s'hai pur desire
  di dar del tuo valor sì chiaro saggio:
    ché tu non merti ch'il tuo corpo cada
    per la costui sì degna invita spada. —

236

"If you don't know it, Francard is my name,   55
    Armenia's lord. And so, enough!" he said
At this, Rinaldo's blood boiled as it came
    from the furnace of his burning heart and sped
toward his countenance until a flame
    dyed both his cheeks and brow a ruby red,
        so that to chasten the foul pagan's pride
        he thus in words of apt disdain replied:

"I say your words reveal a soul too low   56
    for a theme of which you have no right to speak,
a truth my sword shall plainly make you know
    now if a quarrel is the thing you seek."
No dry wood ever burned with ruddier glow,
    than, at these words, the pagan's brow and cheek.
        With cloak wound round his arm, he rushes toward
        the combat, armed with nothing but his sword.

Rinaldo smiles in scorn, with this rebuff: 57
    "Why in such haste? Go, don your armor first."
And he: "My matchless sword is quite enough
    to make my wrath and vengeance do their worst."
"Ah!" said Rinaldo, "I am not so rough
    as to flaunt honor's rule and be accurst."
        Heedless, his foe attacks, intent to slay,
        but he makes Bayard nimbly wheel away,

and once more cries out: "Arm, for knighthood's sake!   58
    No foe unarmored shall be struck by me.
I am a knight. You should not try to make
    me act the villain by your villainy."
The Saracen then: "You're making a mistake
    to think you can escape by sophistry,"
        and wields his blade in strokes so fast and grim
        Rinaldo scarcely can stay clear of him.

Florindo then, impatient to stand by,   59
    with indignation rising in his breast,
cries out: "You coward unbeliever! Why
    seek vantage thus in disadvantage? Test
your sword against me, if you wish to try
    its edge and make your courage manifest.
        Your life is much too vile to be unmade
        by his invincible and priceless blade."

Rinaldo

Qual orso che colui che l'ha percosso   60
   di sbranar con gli unghion rabbioso tenta,
s'altri in questa lo fiede, ei tosto addosso,
   il primiero lasciando, a lui s'aventa;
tale il pagan verso Florindo mosso,
   la destra ch'era a l'altrui danno intenta,
      contra lui drizza e 'l crudo ferro inchina,
      che con novo furor in giù ruina.

Florindo al brando ostil lo scudo oppone,   61
   e quel ne taglia poi quanto ne prende;
giunge al braccio e l'impiaga, ed a l'arcione
   quinci ogni arme rompendo orribil scende.
A quel colpir sì grave il fier barone
   d'ira il cor, di rossore il volto accende;
      su le staffe s'inalza e 'l ferro stringe,
      e con un gran fendente il cala e spinge.

Parte del colpo su la spada tolse   62
   il re pagan: non però vano il rese,
ché quel per dritto a meza tempia il colse,
   e di piaga mortal quivi l'offese.
Gocciando il sangue in rosso smalto volse
   il verde, ed ei tremando al pian si stese,
      con quel romor che suol ben grave sasso
      che d'un monte si spicchi e caggia al basso.

Color che da la tenda erano intenti   63
   a rimirar la perigliosa guerra,
ad armarsi non fur pigri né lenti,
   giacer vedendo esangue il re per terra.
Altri lancie, altri spade, altri pungenti
   spiedi con ratta man sùbito afferra;
      altri l'arme si veste a sua difesa
      per far sicuro a l'inimico offesa.

Tutti precorre il forte re Chiarello,   64
   ch'era con gli altri allor nel padiglione;
fu cugin di Francardo e fu fratello
   del superbo Mambrin questo campione.
Conducea seco a par d'irsuto vello,
   coperto e fiero in vista, un gran leone,
      sanguigno i denti e i crudi unghion rapaci,
      cui lucon gli occhi com'ardenti faci.

As a bear, while mauling with ferocious claws   60
     a man who has wounded him, may suddenly feel
another at his back and without pause
     leave off the first and on the second wheel,
so now the pagan from one man withdraws
     and rushes at the other with his steel
         raised in his fist, hearing Florindo's call,
         and with new ruinous fury makes it fall.

It strikes Florindo's lifted shield, cuts through,   61
     slashing his arm and with horrendous force
rips through his chain-mail and continues to
     shatter his saddle-bow and graze his horse.
Seeing this, the baron[110] feels his rage renew
     and blames his sloth and blushes with remorse.
         He rises in his stirrups, sword held high, to bring
         it down upon his foe in one great swing.

In part the pagan king parries the blow   62
     with his own blade, but it has already found
a passage to the center of his brow
     and, piercing through, has caused a mortal wound.
His enameled hilt turns red with blood, and now
     he drops all pale and quivering to the ground
         with a crash such as a heavy boulder makes,
         which in its fall a mountain gulley shakes.

The pagans in the tent see with alarm   63
     the perilous fight, and when in their full view
their king first falters and then comes to harm
     and at last falls lifeless there, the savage crew
hastily snatch their weapons up and swarm,
     some wielding swords, some spears, toward the two,
         while others put on armor to oppose
         with plate and chain-mail their ferocious blows.

In front sped strong King Clarel, who had been   64
     in the pavilion worshiping with the rest.
He was King Francard's cousin, brother to Mambrin,
     and a fierce champion famed from East to West.
He led by his side a lion, tawny of skin
     and shaggy-maned, a terrifying beast
         with sharp teeth dripping blood from gaping jaws
         and eyes that glowed like coals and knife-like claws.

Egli avea già la generosa fera   65
    vinta con l'arme a dubbia pugna atroce,
e con lusinghe la natura altera
    poi di lei dǫma e l'animo feroce;
ond'ella sempre fida al fianco gli era,
    e l'obbediva a cenni ed a la voce.
        Perciò dagli stranier, perciò da' suoi
        il guerrier dal leon fu detto poi.

Rinaldo ver' costui sprona Baiardo,   66
    pria ch'ei con gli altri il buon Florindo assaglia.
Da l'altra parte il Saracin gagliardo
    con un ferreo baston viene a battaglia.
Non è 'l leon ad aiutarlo tardo
    ma sovra il paladin ratto si scaglia,
        e muove contra lui l'acute branche;
        poi co' denti il destrier prende ne l'anche.

D'un riverso Rinaldo al leon tira,   67
    e 'n cima de la fronte il fiere e punge;
poi contra il fier Chiarello il brando gira,
    e d'un fendente sovra l'elmo il giunge:
raddoppia il colpo con più sdegno ed ira,
    e lo scudo per mezo apre e disgiunge;
        passa oltra il ferro e 'l braccio ancor colpisce,
        e se ben non l'impiaga, ei lo stordisce.

Si rinfranca Chiarello, e poscia offende   68
    con due percosse al paladin la faccia;
e le branche il leon di novo stende,
    e di piagarlo con l'unghion procaccia.
Rinaldo a costor noce e sé difende,
    e quando fiere l'un l'altro minaccia;
        presto ha l'occhio e la man, presto il destriero,
        securissimo il cor, saldo il pensiero.

Sempre che cala il colpo il fier pagano,   69
    egli a schivarlo è già parato e 'ntento;
Baiardo quel leon si tien lontano
    con calcitrar continuo e violento;
e, pronto a lo speron, pronto a la mano,
    salta di qua di là qual fiamma o vento,
        tal che de' colpi suoi la maggior parte
        commette a l'aura il saracino Marte.

That royal creature he had once defied   65
    and conquered in a fight on desert sands,
and afterwards had tamed its savage pride
    by tricks no generous nature understands,
until, forever faithful at his side,
    it knew his voice and leapt at his commands.
        He as the Lion Knight was thenceforth known
        in other lands as well as in his own.

Toward him Rinaldo now makes Bayard race,   66
    seeing him charge Florindo with the rest.
The Saracen, armed with a huge iron mace,
    wheels round to face him like a man possessed,
even as his lion hurls himself apace
    upon the paladin, clawing at his breast
        with his talons before turning on his steed
        with savage bites that make his haunches bleed.

With a quick backward thrust Rinaldo made   67
    a gash upon the lion's brow, then wheeled
upon fierce Clarel brandishing his blade,
    and by a feigned jab at his crest concealed
the advent of the blow that followed, laid
    squarely upon the middle of his shield,
        which cleft it through and through to meet his arm,
        and, though not wounding, stunned him with alarm.

Recovering, Clarel with blows of force immense   68
    twice at the paladin's visor seeks to hack,
while from huge paws the lion again extends
    his claws, intent to leap upon his back.
Rinaldo strikes at both in strong defense,
    with a fierce frown confronting their attack.
        His steed is quick, and quick his hands and eyes,
        his heart secure, his mind alert and wise.

Each blow the pagan aims against him, he   69
    anticipates and beats aside or parries.
Bayard meanwhile the lion furiously
    with violent kicking from his hind legs harries
and leaps like wind or fire, glad to be
    now spurred, now reined in by the man he carries.
        The Saracen Mars strikes out, now here, now there
        but wastes the great part of his blows on air.

Rinaldo

Ma s'avien mai che l'inimico coglia,   70
    spezza ogni acciar, la carne e l'ossa pesta.
Rinaldo lui ferir puote a sua voglia,
    e l'have già piagato in petto e 'n testa;
tuttavia d'arme e di vigor lo spoglia,
    e con nove percosse ognor l'infesta,
        onde quel morto al fin cadde per terra,
        qual torre cui di Giove il telo atterra.

Il fier leon, che del suo sangue tinto   71
    giacer nel piano e morto esser lo scorse,
da grand'amor, da gran furor sospinto
    per vendicarlo immantenente corse;
ma tosto fu con due stoccate estinto.
    Ei morendo il terren rabbioso morse,
        e fe' con alto orribile muggito
        risonar l'onde e l'arenoso lito.

Da indi in qua fu del barone impresa   72
    sempre un fulvo leon d'orrendo aspetto;
la pantera lasciò ch'avea già presa
    a portar ne lo scudo e su l'elmetto.
Florindo intanto fa crudel contesa,
    da molti cavalier cinto ed astretto;
        e folgorando intorno il ferro gira,
        e coraggioso a la vittoria aspira.

Il drappello per mezo era omai scemo   73
    quando tra loro il paladin si mise,
e con possanza e con furore estremo
    quattro capi partì, cinque recise.
Son dal valor di questi eroi supremo
    tosto le genti saracine uccise;
        e s'alcun vivo pur rimane, al piede
        la sua salute e la sua vita crede.

Come Rinaldo vòto il campo scorge,   74
    dal pilastro la statua svelle e piglia,
ed a lei mille baci ardenti porge,
    spinto dal vano error che lo consiglia.
Del dilettoso inganno ei non s'accorge,
    perché la miri con immote ciglia,
        ché vivo crede e vero il falso e l'ombra:
        oh dolce froda che gli amanti ingombra!

His sword has lost its aptitude to kill 70
    or even to pierce the flesh or pound the bone,
whereas Rinaldo cuts and pounds at will
    at breast and head and not at these alone.
He dulls his weapons, saps his strength until
    a last rush makes his enemy, with a groan,
        crash to the ground and crumple like a tower
        lightning has struck for challenging Jove's power.

The fierce lion, seeing him thus expire 71
    blood-stained and ignominiously downed,
impelled by fervent love and vengeful ire
    leaps at his slayer with a furious bound,
but two stabs to his heart soon quench its fire.
    Writhing in wrath the great beast bites the ground
        and, dying, makes the sea and sandy shore
        resound with a last, terrifying roar.

From that time onward the great baron bore 72
    as his device-in-arms that tawny beast
and not the leopard[111] he displayed before
    on his escutcheon and his helmet's crest.
Florindo meanwhile fought a furious war,
    by countless knights surrounded and oppressed.
        Like lightning his blade glints and leaps, for he
        aspires undauntedly to victory.

He had shrunk their swarm already to half its size 73
    when the paladin charged into that heathen hive
and, feeling his strength opposed and fury rise,
    decapitated four and wounded five.
Soon each time that they strike, an enemy dies,
    till scarce a Saracen is left alive,
        or if he is, entrusts his life and weal
        to his legs and drops his weapon and turns heel.

Rinaldo, finding that the field is clear, 74
    takes down the statue from its pedestal
and fondles it with many a joyful tear
    and many a kiss in fond delusion's thrall
nor notes her fixed gaze and unvarying cheer
    nor how her lashes do not move at all.
        For him the image lives, the feigned is true.
        Ah! Sweet deceit that dims a lover's view!

Se n'avvede al fin poi, né già gli è grato   75
    di conoscer il vero, anzi se 'n duole.
Ma spenti nel profondo umor salato
    sendo i vapori onde si forma il sole,
del ritratto un destrier prima aggravato,
    segue il compagno che partir si vole
        a ricercar albergo ov'ogni piaga
        la medica gli curi o l'arte maga.

Poi che Florindo fu del tutto sano,   76
    per molte parti gir de l'Asia errando,
opprimendo il malvagio ed il villano,
    ed il cortese e 'l buon sempre esaltando,
con la lingua agli afflitti e con la mano
    ora consigli ed or aita dando,
        tal che lor nome a l'uno e a l'altro polo
        se 'n gì su l'ali de la fama a volo.

Brunamonte il superbo e Costantino   77
    il falso allor Rinaldo a morte pose,
di Chiarello germani e di Mambrino,
    agli uomini ed a Dio genti odiose.
Tendea questi al mal cauto peregrino
    sotto grate accoglienze insidie ascose;
        quegli con forza aperta altrui la vita
        toglieva, o pur la libertà gradita.

He at last knows his error and indeed   75
    is glad to know it, though it grieves his heart.
But then, since over the sea the mists recede
    through which the last few rays of sunlight dart,
he, having laden the image on a steed,
    follows his friend who hastens to depart,
        seeking some shelter where his wounds might be
        tended by physic or by sorcery.

When good Florindo was all healed, they made   76
    their way through many an Asian neighborhood,
confronting evildoers unafraid
    and succoring the courteous and good,
by speech or action tendering now aid,
    now counsel in peril or incertitude
        so that from pole to pole their glorious name
        is borne to high and low by wingèd Fame.

Proud Brunamont and lying Constantine   77
    were slain in combat by Rinaldo then,
Clarel and Mambrin's brothers, a pair of swine
    guilty of crimes abhorred by God and men.
By hidden malice, seemingly benign,
    one lured incautious travelers to his den.
        By open force the other thrived, for he
        murdered his prey or sold to slavery.

Canto nono

Tonda due volte avea la faccia adorna   *1*
    mostrata a noi la dea che nacque in Delo,
ed altretante con l'argentee corna
    era apparita men lucente in cielo;
duo segni scorsi avea colui ch'aggiorna
    il mondo, indi sgombrando il fosco velo,
        da che Florindo e 'l gran figliuol d'Amone
        uccisero i guerrier del padiglione;

quando in un vago piano, ove da colte   *2*
    piante scendea l'ombra soave e grata,
ritrovar vaghe dame in schiera accolte,
    che tenean di guerrier scorta onorata.
Molte eran le donzelle, poi di molte
    rare eccellenze era ciascuna ornata,
        e degli abiti l'arte e la ricchezza
        congiunta aveano a la natia bellezza.

Una però così tra tutte loro   *3*
    come Diana infra le ninfe splende,
qual volta in care danze il vago coro
    guida e per Cinto il passo altera stende,
che spiega a l'aure liete i bei crin d'oro,
    e la faretra agli omeri sospende:
        Latona intanto un tacito dolzore
        correr si sente per le vene al core.

Come da lunge in sì superbo aspetto   *4*
    apparir costei vede i duo baroni,
che ben ciascun d'esser guerrier perfetto
    sembra, e cui rado alcun si paragoni,
mandagli ambo a pregar per un valletto
    che si voglian provar co' suoi campioni,
        perch'ella veder brama a chiara giostra
        s'è 'l lor valor qual la sembianza mostra.

CANTO NINE

Twice had the goddess born on Delos[112] shown   1
     her radiant face, with dimmer light each time
decking her silver horns while she, upon her throne,
     moved her resplendent chariot in its climb;
two signs the god had passed[113] who makes day known
     to the world and rids the skies of gloom and grime
         since Aymon's great son and Florindo brought
         the pavilion's knight and all his crew to naught,

when on the wide plain of a pleasant land   2
     in a shaded arbor of well-tended trees
they saw fair damsels gathered in a band,
     who beckoned them with generous courtesies.
They were many, and many were the graces and
     the charms they showed to fascinate and please,
         and their ingenious opulence of dress
         worthily matched their native loveliness.

But one especially in that beauteous throng   3
     shines like Diana when she leads the dance
of wood-nymphs on Mount Cynthus and their song,
     or when she proudly passes seas and lands
and, with her quiver over her shoulder slung,
     spreads to the jocund breeze her golden strands.
         Latona meanwhile feels her heart and head
         from all her veins with silent sweetness fed.

She from afar beheld the warrior pair   4
     high on their steeds, so proud and confident,
they seemed like perfect knights, beyond compare.
     As they drew near she by a valet sent
a message asking them if they would care
     to be her champions in a tournament
         and there by open trial make men know
         the valor their appearance seemed to show.

Rinaldo

Vanne il valletto u' la donzella il manda,   5
  e l'imbasciata ai duo guerrieri espone.
Gli dà grata risposta e gli dimanda
  chi sia la dama il buon figliuol d'Amone.
E quegli allora: — A noi costei commanda
  ed a la Media freno e leggi impone:
    Floriana si noma, e sin ad ora
    marital nodo non la stringe ancora. —

Ciò detto, a la regina egli rapporta   6
  che i duo baron son di giostrar contenti.
La dama allora i suoi guerrieri esorta,
  e desta in lor brame di gloria ardenti
con dolci detti e con maniera accorta,
  ch'al cor son caldi stimoli pungenti:
    tal ch'a gara onorata ognun di questi
    primo esser tenta che la lancia arresti.

Galasso il poderoso e 'l destro Irnante   7
  si mosser prima al fin di questa parte,
ma tosto rivoltaro al ciel le piante
  per man de' duo stranier più cari a Marte.
Dopo costoro Albernio ed Odrimante,
  venuti onde le piagge il Tigre parte,
    stampar la terra con le spalle: e colto
    fu sotto 'l petto quel, questi nel volto.

Eran quivi fra gli altri Argo ed Androglio,   8
  compagni in guerreggiar d'alta possanza,
ma d'alterezza tal, di tanto orgoglio,
  ch'assai cedea la forza all'arroganza.
Questi avean ne lo scudo orrido scoglio
  che frange l'onde e sovra 'l mare avanza,
    intorno a cui scritto era in auree note
    un cotal motto, "Rompe chi il percote";

volendo indi inferir che 'l lor valore   9
  ad ogni incontro fier saldo restava,
e che, più ch'al ferito, al feritore
  de la percossa il danno al fin tornava.
Ahi! qual superbo, ahi! qual fallace errore
  il lume di ragion loro adombrava,
    ché, vinti or da Florindo e da Rinaldo,
    debil pianta sembrar, non scoglio saldo.

At once the obedient valet speeds from view   5
   and to the noble pair declares his embassy.
Aymon's good son, in courteous words and few,
   agrees, then asks who that fair maid might be.
"That," says he, "is our gracious mistress who
     rules and gives laws to Media's realm,[114] and she
       is known as Floriana and to this day,
       unbound by nuptial ties, has here held sway."

He posts back to his mistress to declare   6
   that the two barons are content to fight,
and she, when they arrive to greet her where
   she sits enthroned, bids them to scale the height
of fame and glory in words gracious and fair,
     which like sharp spurs their ardent hearts incite,
       so that each, to put his valor to the test,
       wants to be first to put his lance in rest.

Massive Galassos and nimble Hyrnas strive   7
   against them first, and fiercely each attacks
but soon laments to heaven, scarce left alive
   by the strangers dear to Mars. Right in their tracks
Albernio and fierce Odrimant arrive
     from the banks that Tigris parts. Both with their backs
       imprint the earth —one with his chest pierced through,
       the other with his face —and bid the world adieu.

Androlius and Argos next arrayed   8
   their limbs in arms, war-comrades of great power,
but of such pride and arrogance that it made
   all praise their strength might else deserve turn sour.
These on their shields a horrid cliff displayed
     that loomed by wave-tossed seashore like a tower
       round which in golden letters there was writ
       the motto, "This hurts him who strikes at it,"

to signify their valor could withstand   9
   all force, however fierce, and never fall,
and was so proof to blows that any hand
   that dared to strike against it struck a wall.
Ah, fire of fallacy, by folly fanned,
     which their poor wit caused them play withal!
       For at Rinaldo's and his friend's first pass
       they seemed, not hard as rock, but soft as grass.

Lucindo e Floridan, duo cavalieri   *10*
    per giovenil bellezza a dame grati,
insieme furon poi dagli stranieri
    lunge da' lor cavalli al pian gettati;
e lor fèr compagnia molti guerrieri,
    de la corte i più degni e più pregiati,
        onde sol degli estrani ogni donzella
        con meraviglia e con onor favella.

Ma sovra tutti la gentil regina   *11*
    è d'ammirarli e d'onorarli vaga:
ogni cosa ch'è in lor le par divina,
    e 'n tutto pienamente ella s'appaga.
Pur a Rinaldo più l'affetto inchina,
    di quel ch'avenir dee quasi presaga,
        e più le sembra del compagno destro,
        più forte ed in ferir meglior maestro.

Come uom cui già novella febre algente   *12*
    deggia assaltar tra breve spazio d'ora,
un lieve freddo non continuo sente
    scorrersi per le membra ad ora ad ora:
così costei ne l'alma e ne la mente
    prova de l'amor nuovo, ignoto ancora,
        i leggieri principii, i primi affetti,
        ch'oprano a volta in lei diversi effetti.

Ella, e non bene la cagion n'intende,   *13*
    d'ogni bel colpo suo lieta diviene,
e se tal volta alcun lui punto offende,
    il sangue se l'aggiaccia entro le vene:
sempre nove bellezze in lui comprende,
    sempre più fisso in lui lo sguardo tiene,
        e sol brama veder se corrisponde
        a quel ch'appar, quel che l'elmetto asconde.

Ma diè Fortuna al suo desire effetto,   *14*
    ché l'ultimo guerrier che al pian conquiso
cadde, a Rinaldo fe' sbalzar l'elmetto,
    rompendo i ferrei lacci a l'improviso.
Al sùbito apparir del vago aspetto
    parve che le s'aprisse il Paradiso,
        e vide entro lo spazio d'un sol volto
        quanto in mill'altri è di beltà raccolto.

Next Floridan and Lucindo, who excel   10
    in chivalry, for youth and charm renowned,
are they whom the two strangers now compel
    to fall far from their chargers to the ground,
followed by countless other knights as well,
    the worthiest and most famous to be found,
      and soon all talk among the damozels
      is of the stranger knights and no one else.

But above all the gentle queen's eyes start   11
    fondly to dwell on the victorious pair.
Both seem almost like gods in every part,
    both please her by their grace and manly air,
but most Rinaldo, and she thinks her heart
    has had presentiments of his coming there.
      He seems somehow more dexterous than his friend
      stronger somehow, more able to contend.

Like a man asleep who, suddenly struck ill,   12
    is seized by a burning fever in the night
and feels a faint and intermittent chill
    shaking his limbs, making his face turn white,
so she feels now in mind and soul a thrill
    of nascent love, till then unknown, the slight
      first symptom of the thing she least expects
      soon to be followed by diverse effects.

She — and she scarcely understands the cause —   13
    delights at every blow he gives or feigns,
and if sometimes a blade strikes him and draws
    blood, feels her own blood freezing in her veins.
She greets his deeds with ever more applause
    and ever more fixedly upon him strains
      her gaze, deeming his visor must conceal
      beauty to match the grace his acts reveal.

Fortune favors her eager eyes and slakes   14
    their thirst: the last man falling in the fight,
grazing by chance Rinaldo's visor, breaks
    a strap. He, feeling it no longer tight,
removes his helmet and so doing makes
    all paradise lie open to her sight,
      for in his face her one quick glance found more
      delight than in a thousand seen before.[115]

Rinaldo

Sembrava a lei ch'Amor quivi spiegato   *15*
   tutte le sue vittrici insegne avesse,
e quale in carro suol di palme ornato
   trionfator alter lieto sedesse;
pareale ancor che nel suo manco lato
   tutte l'auree quadrella indi spendesse,
      e l'annodasse al collo un forte laccio,
      grave insolito sì, ma caro impaccio.

Bionda chioma, neri occhi e nere ciglia,   *16*
   lucidi e vivi quelli e queste arcate,
fronte ben larga adorna a meraviglia
   d'alterezza viril, di maiestate;
guancia leggiadra in un bianca e vermiglia,
   piume nascenti allor crespe ed aurate,
      naso aquilin, de' regi segno altero,
      traggon tutti in stupor del cavaliero:

oltre ciò larghe spalle ed ampio petto,   *17*
   braccia lunghe, snodate e muscolose,
ventre piano, traverso, ai fianchi stretto,
   gambe diritte ed agili e nerbose,
mobil vivacità ch'in giovinetto
   grazia aggiunge e decoro a l'altre cose,
      grata fierezza, altero portamento,
      unite con mirabil tempramento.

Qual meraviglia è poi se la regina,   *18*
   in cui brame gentil sol trovan loco,
già fatta omai d'Amor preda e rapina,
   esca diviene di sì nobil foco?
Sent'ella farsi il cor nuova fucina,
   e crescervi la fiamma a poco a poco;
      pur come sia del suo mal propio vaga,
      d'arder più sempre e di languir s'appaga.

Non può soffrir la giovinetta amante   *19*
   ch'indi il suo caro ben faccia partita;
ma con benigno e placido sembiante
   a seco rimaner ambo gli invita.
Preghiere aggiunse poi sì calde e tante
   ch'ella, da loro al fin pur obbedita,
      s'invia ver' la citate, e per lo freno
      gli conduce Rinaldo il palafreno.

Canto Nine

It seemed to her the god of Love had spread   15
    all his victorious banners in that face
and sat enthroned with palm leaves garlanded
    on his triumphal car in pomp and grace.
It seemed that, having toward her bosom sped
    all of his golden darts, he rose to place
        a leash around her neck, which made her fear
        as never before and yet was somehow dear.

Blond curls, black eyes with lashes jet-black too,   16
    fringes to orbs that shine out frank and free;
a spacious, noble brow that greets the view
    with manly loftiness, with majesty;
cheeks of mixed ivory and vermilion hue
    sprouting a crisp down's golden filigree;
        an eagle nose, sign of imperial might:
        all fill her with amazement at the knight.

Thereto add massive shoulders, a deep chest,   17
    long arms where finely-knotted muscles meet,
a belly flat and tapering toward the breast,
    straight, sinewy thighs and legs and nimble feet,
the whole imbued with liveliness and zest
    and grace and fine decorum, made complete
        by a noble bearing, fiercely confident
        and a most amiable temperament.

What wonder if the queen, for whom to yearn   18
    in soft desire was only natural,
born for Love's prey and plunder, should now turn
    into fuel for his noble fire and fall?
She feels her heart like a great furnace burn
    with growing heat that soon spreads over all,
        and though she guesses at her peril, she
        delights in flames from which she cannot flee.

The loving girl could scarce endure the thought   19
    that the dear man should ever leave her side,
and with benign and pleasant mien besought
    the friends to stay, and when they faltered, plied
them both with pleas so frequent and so hot
    that she, her wish at last being gratified,
        toward the nearby city took her course,
        holding the bridle of Rinaldo's horse.

Il palagio real fra tanto adorno 20
 con magnifica pompa a pien si rende:
chi razzi aurati per le mura intorno
 a l'eburnee cornici alto sospende;
chi bei tapeti, che potriano scorno
 far a tutt'altri per le soglie stende;
  chi loca al lume suo dipinti quadri,
  vivi ritratti degli estinti padri.

La mense altri apparecchia, e i bianchi lini 21
 stesi per lungo poi vi mette sopra;
vi mette vasi preciosi e fini,
 ma varii di materia e varii d'opra,
ove dei re di Media i pellegrini
 fatti, perché atro oblio lor non ricopra,
  veggonsi impressi in puro argento ed oro
  con ordin lungo e con sottil lavoro.

Giunta al tetto real, di sella tolta 22
 fu la regina dal figliuol d'Amone,
e fu per troppa gioia al core avolta
 sorgiunta ancor da nova passione,
quasi allor se n'uscio l'alma disciolta
 da la terrestre sua bella prigione;
  ma qual più dolce e più soave morte
  le potea dar benigno cielo in sorte?

Floriana ad ognor cortese stile 23
 usava di serbar con gli stranieri,
ma più che mai cortese e più gentile
 or si dimostra ad ambo i cavalieri.
Amor il fa che, s'è 'l cor basso e vile,
 desta in lui nobil brame, alti pensieri;
  ma s'è regio e sovran, via più l'accende
  a virtù vera, e più pregiato il rende.

L'istesso fanno i suoi baroni ancora, 24
 né sembra d'onorargli alcun restio,
perciò che il lor voler dipende ognora
 da quel di lei, come da fonte rio.
Ma venut'era omai la solita ora
 che ne conduce natural desio
  a ristorar con cibi il corpo stanco,
  perché al lungo digiun non venga manco.

And now the royal palace comes in sight,   20
    where wealth, magnificence and art abound.
Here fixed to ivory rods at ceiling height
    fine golden arrases hang all around.
Here carpets of a workmanship to spite
    all other workmanship cover the ground.
        Here paintings glow in torch-lit corridors,
        the living portraits of dead ancestors.

The tables are prepared, and over them   21
    white linen stretched, on which they place
salvers and cups, studded with many a gem,
    and wrought of finest stuff with art and grace
that show, embossed or etched on rim or stem,
    the feats of Media's nomad royal race
        and wrought in gold or purest silver strive
        to keep their memory and their fame alive.

Arriving at the royal gate, the queen   22
    was lifted from her steed by Aymon's son,
which seized her heart with a new joy so keen
    that she felt by her passion quite undone,
as if her soul had of a sudden been
    from its fair prison by that touch withdrawn.
        What sweeter death or easier could be
        vouchsafed by heaven as her destiny?

Floriana always treated every guest   23
    and stranger with true, courteous good will,
but now the courtesies that she addressed
    to her two visitors were kinder still.
Love even in a low-born, common breast
    will high desire and noble thought instill,
        but all the more in those of royal birth
        he kindles virtue that confirms their worth.

Her courtiers, following her example, then   24
    showed them all honor too and took
pains like her own, for the wills of all her men
    moved with her will like currents in a brook.
But now there struck the wonted hour when,
    prompted by natural appetite, men look
        for nourishment to ease their limbs' travail,
        lest hunger long prolonged cause them to fail.

S'assidono a le mense, e Floriana   25
    ponsi a l'incontro il suo gradito amante;
e come suol nocchier la tramontana,
    mira i begli occhi e 'l dolce almo sembiante,
e d'un'esca d'amor fallace e vana
    pasce la mente afflitta e l'alma errante:
        il corpo no, ch'ov'è un maggior desire,
        l'altro minor non fassi allor sentire.

Museo fra tanto al suon de l'aurea cetra   26
    scioglie la dotta lingua in dolci accenti,
e, col favor ch'egli da Febo impetra
    dona principio ai musici concenti,
soave sì ch'un cor d'orsa e di pietra
    avria commosso e raffrenato i venti,
        allor che 'l sasso cavo Eolo disserra,
        e desta l'ira in lor, gli accende a guerra.

Canta egli come da la massa informe   27
    trasse Natura il seme de le cose,
e come in vaghe e ben composte forme
    il mondo qual veggiam tutto dispose,
dando perpetue leggi e certe norme
    a fuoco, ad aria, a terra, ad acque ondose,
        in un giungendo con discorde pace
        quanto appar fuori, e quanto ascosto giace.

Segue ch'essendo ormai l'età de l'oro,   28
    de l'argento e del rame ite in disparte,
per dar Giove a' mortal giusto martoro
    fe' sommerger la terra in ogni parte;
e che da Pirra e dal consorte foro
    le fatal pietre dopo 'l tergo sparte,
        onde il genere uman fu ricovrato,
        stuol duro, a le fatiche avezzo e nato.

Né tacque le tue fiamme, o biondo dio,   29
    né le piaghe ch'Amor ti fe' profonde,
e qual cangiò lungo il paterno rio
    Dafne le braccia, e i crin in rami e 'n fronde;
come in giuvenca poi fu convers'Io,
    come giunse del Nilo a l'alte sponde;
        d'Argo non meno e di Siringa disse
        l'aspra sorte che loro il ciel prescrisse.

The banquet ready, Floriana went   25
    to sit across from her new love and, blind
to all else, like a pilot on the pole star, bent
    her gaze on those fair eyes, so sweet and kind,
and with the vain, illusive nutriment
    of love fed her lost soul and troubled mind —
        and fed on nothing else, for a great desire
        will make all lesser ones wait or expire.

Meanwhile Musaeus[116] tunes his lyre of gold   26
    and makes his learned tongue intone
the dulcet harmonies he learned of old
    from Phoebus' self. A bear's heart or a stone
his music would have softened or controlled
    or stilled the raging winds that howl and groan
        when Aeolus unlocks his rocky caves
        to make a storm wage war among the waves.

He sings how Nature from a formless mass   27
    caused the first seeds of being to increase
and into ordered, lovely forms to pass
    and make the world we know, in which she frees,
constrained by limits nothing may trespass,
    air, water, earth and fire, joining peace
        and strife by laws immutable and sure,
        some plain as day, some hidden and obscure.[117]

He sings how, when the age of gold had passed   28
    and those of silver and of brass gone by,
Jove sent, to punish human crime at last,
    a universal deluge from the sky;
and then how Pyrrha and her consort cast
    the fated stones behind their backs, whereby
        a new mankind sprang from the barren soil,
        a rugged race, born and inured to toil.

Nor is he silent of your fires, blond god,[118]   29
    of the Love that wounded you and of your woe
when Daphne paused, feet rooted in the sod,
    arms turned to twigs and hair to fronds; of how,
transformed into a heifer, Io trod
    the ground where far-off Nile's great waters flow;
        nor of the bitter fortunes fails to tell
        that Argus or that Syrinx once befell.

Tai cose ancor, ma con più dolce canto,   *30*
  ho già, Veniero, a te spiegar sentito,
e visto uscir del salso fondo intanto
  i marin pesci ed ingombrare il lito;
e, quasi astretti da ben forte incanto,
  i varii augei per appagar l'udito
    ne l'impeto maggior frenare il volo,
    e fermartisi intorno a stuolo a stuolo.

Trae, già cenato, de la notte l'ore   *31*
  Floriana in parlar vario e giocondo;
e non men per l'orecchie il lungo amore
  bee che per gli occhi, e 'l manda al cor profondo.
Molte cose or di Carlo, or del valore
  chiede d'Orlando, sì famoso al mondo;
    de' propi fatti suoi chiede non meno,
    ch'ei l'esser suo l'avea già detto a pieno.

Dolce lo prega: — Deh, se non vi pesa,   *32*
  ditemi quel ch'ancor fanciullo essendo
fêsti di vostra madre a la difesa,
  l'onor quasi perduto a lei rendendo;
io già sentii parlar di questa impresa,
  se pur con la memoria al ver m'apprendo,
    anzi il mio genitor, da un cavaliero
    ch'allor tornava a noi dal franco impero. —

Rinaldo a lei: — Benché non punto sia   *33*
  di sì degni uditor degno il soggetto,
per me narrato il tutto ora vi fia,
  poiché sono a ciò far da voi costretto.
A la mia volontade, a l'età mia
  risguardo aggiate voi, non a l'effetto:
    ch'assai picciolo fu, ma pur allora
    scorsi i tre lustri io non aveva ancora.

Ginamo di Baiona il Maganzese   *34*
  già fu rival del mio parente Amone,
ch'ambo avean l'alme per Beatrice accese
  allor che l'uno e l'altro era garzone.
Costor dopo diverse altre contese
  vennero insieme a singolar tenzone,
    dove Ginamo, da vil tema spinto,
    cesse ad Amon l'amata e diessi vinto.

Canto Nine

Such things I heard you, Venièr,[119] also sing   30
    one day, but in far sweeter notes, wherefore
out of the salty deep each fish-like thing
    swam up to hear and crowded near the shore,
and flock on flock of wild birds on the wing,
    as if compelled by sorcery, ceased to soar
        aloft and swooped down earthward in mid-flight
        to gather round you, listening in delight.

Floriana, having dined, while daylight fails,   31
    sits down in pleasant colloquy, spellbound
by all that meets her ears, while Love assails
    her heart with beauties that her eyes have found.
She asks for many things — for news, for tales
    of Charles or of Orlando, world-renowned,
        or of himself and his own deeds of glory,
        though she, in fact, already knows the story.

"I would," she sweetly asks, "take great delight   32
    to be told how, when you were young and new
to arms, your mother felt a villain's spite
    and how her honor was restored by you.
I heard of it, if memory serves me right,
    some years ago, as did my father, too,
        from a knight who then was passing through by chance
        returning from the emperor's court in France."

Rinaldo then: "A noble listener's mind   33
    may deem the story trivial and uncouth,
but I will tell it to you, since I find
    that you command me, and I'll tell the truth.
But hearing me, I trust you will be kind.
    Judge not my deeds, but my good will and youth,
        for I was very young, of untried worth,
        with fewer than three lustra[120] since my birth.

Maganzan Ginam of Bayonne[121] became   34
    my father Aymon's rival long ago.
Both felt their souls enkindled by the flame
    of love for Beatrice when mere lads, and so,
after long disputes and dissensions, came
    to fight a duel. Without striking a blow,
        Ginam in craven fear preferred to yield
        his claim to Aymon and to quit the field.

Ma l'odio contro Amon serbò rinchiuso   35
    sempre, che al cor gli fu continuo tarlo,
e, com'è di sua stirpe invecchiato uso,
    cercò di vita a tradimento trarlo:
pur sempre il suo desir restò deluso.
    Al fin dopo gran tempo il magno Carlo
        nel suo natal corte bandita tenne,
        facendo alcuni dì festa solenne.

Il re mirando la fiorita corte,   36
    un dì ch'a caso a mensa ritrovosse,
a nova voglia aprio del cor le porte;
    indi così ver' gli altri a parlar mosse:
"O de' miei fidi schiera invitta e forte,
    arme e sostegni miei, mie guarde e posse,
        vorrei ch'alcun di voi qui si vantasse
        d'alcuna cosa ch'a mio pro tornasse."

Ciascun di quei baroni allor si diede   37
    un vanto, altri superbo, altri modesto.
Sorse il mio genitor fra quelli in piede
    per sé vantare, e 'l vanto suo fu questo,
d'aver tre figli in cui di già si vede
    nobile spirto a fatti eroici desto,
        che fian sempre con lui fida difesa
        del franco Impero e de la santa Chiesa.

Fu di mio padre il vanto a Carlo grato,   38
    e bene a tutti il fe' palese e piano,
ch'il vaso ov'era el sol di bere usato
    porse cortese a lui di propria mano.
Da quest'atto sentissi il cor piagato
    profondamente il reo cugin di Gano,
        Ginamo, ch'in mal far seco concorse,
        ch'allor, sendo presente, il tutto scorse.

Non può soffrir l'iniquo e fraudolente   39
    ch'ad Amon più ch'a lui si faccia onore,
tal che più cresce e più diviene ardente
    per novell'esca il vecchio odio e 'l rancore;
e gli è tanto accecata al fin la mente,
    voler di Dio, da l'ira e dal furore,
        che con maligno sùbito consiglio
        così parla ad Amon, turbato il ciglio:

But rankling hatred for good Aymon wrought   35
    on Ginam's heart like a sharp thorn, and he,
as is his race's ingrained custom, sought
    to take away his life by treachery.
Yet all his guile and malice came to naught
    until, long after, Charlemagne's decree
        was issued for a great feast held at court
        with pageants, games and jousts of every sort.

At banquet there one day the king surveyed   36
    his gathered band of knightly conquerors
and, feeling that his heart's gates opened, swayed
    by a new desire, was thus moved to discourse:
'O faithful vassals, ever undismayed,
    props to my throne, my best defense, my force,
        I long to hear a boast from some of you
        of what on my behalf you'd dare to do.'

The barons one by one rose to compete,   37
    boasting, some proudly, some more modestly.
My father heard them, then leapt to his feet
    to make his own boast, and thus boasted he:
'I have three sons[122] whose hearts already beat
    with longing for high deeds of chivalry.
        All three, like me, are sworn to one endeavor:
        to fight for France and Holy Church forever.'

My father's boast pleased Charles. He made this clear   38
    by giving him the cup that he alone
drank from, with gracious thanks for all to hear,
    and the hand that tendered it was his royal own.
At this one man grew pale and lost all cheer:
    Ginam, kinsman of vicious Ganelon,
        vicious like him, for he was present there
        and saw it all and writhed in envious care.

This false and shameless man cannot abide   39
    that Aymon should be honored more than he,
so that this injury to his touchy pride
    fuels the fire of his malignancy.
At last his mind grows so preoccupied
    with hate that, blinded by mad fantasy —
        as God wills — he in sudden fury now
        turning to Aymon says with clouded brow:

Rinaldo

"*Amon, non vo' ch'altero e glorioso*   40
    tu ne vada di quel che non è tuo:
sappi che sempre al mio voler bramoso
    ebbe Beatrice ancor conforme il suo,
e diemmo spesso effetto di nascoso
    a quel ch'era il voler d'ambo noi duo,
        sì ch'inde nacquer poi quei tre garzoni
        che miei sono; e tua moglie or mi perdoni.

Perdoni a me se t'ho la cosa aperta   41
    e di quanto è tra noi narrato il tutto,
e tu perdona a lei, che ben lo merta,
    poiché n'è nato così nobil frutto.
E s'unque hai la d'amor possanza esperta,
    sai ch'a tai falli a forza è l'uom condutto.
        Ti prego ancor ch'a me tu renda i miei
        figli, ché loro omai nutrir non déi.

E se non che sin qui m'ha ritenuto   42
    di non turbar altrui giusta cagione,
tu da me stesso avresti ciò saputo
    già molto prima in altra occasione.
Pur or, più d'ogni cosa, ha in me potuto
    paterno affetto e degna ambizione."
        Così disse egli, e 'l suo dir molto spiacque
        al saggio re, che non però si tacque.

Ma più ch'ad altro penetrar ne l'imo   43
    petto queste parole al padre mio;
pur gli rispose irato: "Io falso estimo
    quanto tu dici, e te malvagio e rio.
Né questo, o conte, è 'l tradimento primo
    ch'uscir da Maganzesi ho vedut'io,
        ed ad oltranza, quando più t'aggrada,
        ciò ti vo' mantener con questa spada."

"*Ah!, rispose colui, l'uom saggio deve*   44
    ogni cosa tentar prima che l'arme;
e chi non serva ciò, più stolto e lieve,
    né credo errar, che coraggioso parme.
Io, benché a te serà noioso e greve,
    già non vo' rimaner di discolparme,
        e dimostrar che son leale e vero,
        qual conviensi a mio pari, a cavaliero."

'Aymon, it pains me that you should go hence   40
     made proud and glorious by what is not yours.
Know then I once found my concupiscence
     welcomed by Beatrice and my overtures
secretly gratified in every sense,
        for mutual will a mutual joy secures.
          And from this union sprang these boys, all three.
          They are mine. I hope your wife may pardon me,

and may you pardon me if I've been too   41
     hasty in speech rather that keeping mute.
And pardon her, for pardon is her due,
     since she has born such fine and noble fruit.
And if you know what strong desire can do,
        you know all men at times will play the brute.
          I also pray you: yield my sons to me.
          They do not now befit your custody.

Had I not feared, and rightly feared, the wrong   42
     my mentioning this earlier might wreak,
you would yourself have heard it from my tongue
     long before now. Perhaps I was too weak.
But now, moved by my love of these my young
        sons and my care for their success, I speak.'
          He ceased. The wise king then in no small measure
          displayed his consternation and displeasure,

but Ginam's words had nearly burst   43
     my father's heart, his honor being hit,
and he cried out in wrath: 'Villain accurst,
     you lie. Your speech is slander, all of it,
nor is this loathsome treason, count, the first
        that I have known Maganzans to commit.
          This I with this my sword, in your despite,
          will maintain to the death if you dare fight.'

'Ah!' said the other then, "a wise man should   44
     sift all the facts before he comes to blows.
A fool is he who thinks this does no good,
        though he brawl like a brave man. But who knows?
I, though you call it coward turpitude,
        will not stay here to squabble in vain shows
          of loyalty and truth, but claim my right
          of equal hearing as befits a knight.'

Così disse, e mostrò poscia al cospetto   45
   di tutti quei baron due ricche anella
ch'avea fatto a Beatrice, ad altro effetto,
   credo, involar per una sua donzella.
Indi, stendendo quei, con lieto aspetto
   guarda il mio genitore e gli favella:
      "Amon, conosci questi? Eccoti il segno
      che del suo amor mi fa Beatrice degno.

Questi, no 'l puoi negar, già fur tuo dono,   46
   allor che lei mal grado tuo sposasti,
e questi chiari testimoni sono
   ch'a torto menzonier tu mi chiamasti.
Or l'oltraggio commune io ti perdono,
   e credo ben che ciò per pena basti.
      Misero, a che riguardi? Eccoli, prendi,
      mirali bene, e 'l vero ormai comprendi."

Qual divenisse Amon, quale il suo core   47
   fosse, chi dirà mai? Si parte tosto,
e come 'l tira il sùbito furore,
   ad uccider la moglie ei va disposto.
Ma da più messi in breve spazio d'ore
   di ciò quella avisata è di nascosto,
      la qual, noi tre fratei menando seco,
      si sottrasse a quel primo impeto cieco.

Gissene presso il padre, ove si stesse   48
   dal non giunto furor d'Amon sicura,
fin che con chiare prove ella potesse
   mostrargli la sua fe' candida e pura,
e quel error ch'in lui sì fermo impresse
   lingua maligna e perfida natura.
      Venne a trovarla Malagigi poi,
      ch'era nipote a lei, cugino a noi.

La dispose ed indusse egli a mandarmi   49
   co' miei germani insieme a la reale
corte, acciò ch'ivi io provocassi a l'arme
   Ginamo come falso e disleale.
Ella volse però prima giurarmi
   d'esser stata ad Amon sempre leale,
      chiamando in testimonio il Re del cielo,
      e tenendo la man su l'Evangelo.

Having spoken thus, he held out in full view   45
    of all the court two rich rings he had made
a girl in Beatrice's retinue
    under some pretext steal. He then displayed
the shining pair as if in triumph to
    my baffled father, smiled at him, and said:
        'Look, Aymon! Do you know these rings? They prove
        that Beatrice thought me worthy of her love.

To her — can you deny it? — you once gave   46
    these rings when, much against your will,
you wedded her — which makes self-evident
    that you were wrong to call me liar. Still,
I pardon your offense, because of punishment
    you have by now, I dare say, had your fill.
        Look at them now, you wretch! Why stand aghast?
        Look well, and understand the truth at last.'

What now can Aymon do, hearing this scoff?   47
    What thoughts torment his heart? What can he say?
Possessed by sudden wrath, he rushes off,
    intent to kill his wife that very day.
But she by messengers had heard enough
    to cause her to seek safety in some way
        and, taking us three brothers, in great dread
        of the first blind impulse of his anger, fled.

She fled back to her father's, where she stayed   48
    secure from Aymon's fury for a while,
awaiting some clear proof that would persuade
    her spouse to cease in his denial
of her pure faith, so monstrously inveighed
    by a false tongue and a cunning villain's guile.
        Malagis, her nephew and our cousin, she
        next visited in her adversity.

He counseled her — and she agreed — to send   49
    me and my brothers to the royal court,
where I should charge, and challenge to that end,
    Ginam with treasonable false report.
She sent us forth, but first made me attend
    her gospel oath that never, in any sort,
        had she been false to Aymon heretofore,
        nor ever could, by heaven. This she swore.

Rinaldo

Giunto a la corte, quel fellon sfidai,   50
   che qual figliuol accôr già mi volea;
ma lo rispinsi indietro e gli mostrai
   nel volto aperto quel che 'l cor chiudea.
Ei, che mi vide sì fanciullo omai,
   de la mia morte dentro si godea,
     ma pur sotto diverso e finto volto
     l'interno affetto suo teneva occolto.

Io, cui troppo spiaceva ogni dimora,   51
   prendo l'ordin dal re di cavaliero,
e similmente i miei fratelli allora
   il degno grado da lui dar si fêro.
Indi torno a sfidar Ginamo ancora,
   ed a chiamarlo falso e menzogniero:
     ond'ei, come di me molto gli caglia,
     mostra venir sforzato a la battaglia.

Drizzò la lancia: a me resse la mano   52
   la ragion che m'empiea d'alto ardimento.
A quel debile il braccio e 'l colpo vano
   rese il gran torto e 'l fatto tradimento,
tal che ferito a morte ei va sul piano:
   resto in sella io, né pur la lancia sento.
     Ahi! giustizia di Dio, com'opri spesso
     ch'il ver risorga, e resti il falso oppresso!

Per ucciderlo allor corro veloce: 53
   come lo veggio tal per terra steso,
mi richiede Ginamo in umil voce
   d'esser da tutti anzi che mora inteso.
Io, poiché l'indugiar nulla mi noce,
   in concerderli ciò non sto sospeso,
     perché inanzi il morir confessi e dica
     sé traditor, Beatrice esser pudica.

E 'l fece ben, perché 'l suo rio trattato   54
   e' modi suoi fur da lui tutti espressi.
La genitrice mia ne l'onorato
   suo primo nome allor così rimessi.
Io giurai poi, sendo dal re lodato
   che senza brando oprar ciò fatto avessi,
     non oprar brando, no 'l togliendo a forza
     a guerrier di gran fama e di gran forza. —

Arrived at court, the villain greeted me 50
    as if I were his son, but I defied him
and from his welcoming embrace broke free
    with a look that showed that I could not abide him.
He, seeing how young I was, smiled inwardly.
    The thought of my sure death much gratified him,
        although his outward face seemed calm and kind
        and hid the malice seething in his mind.

Impatient of delay, I begged the king 51
    to dub me knight, and so it pleased his grace.
My brothers, too, on the same evening
    received their knighthoods in that very place.
Once more I turned on Ginam then to fling
    a charge of foul high treason in his face,
        and he, perhaps deeming the danger slight,
        at once declared his readiness to fight.

He aimed his lance. For me, my hand was made 52
    firm by the courage a good cause implants.
For him, treason and manifest guilt betrayed
    his arm and made his first blow go askance.
So down he went, mortally hurt. I stayed
    in the saddle and did not even feel his lance.
        Justice of God! How often will your frown
        let truth rise up and bear vile falsehood down!

Seeing him fall, pierced by my lance, and lie 53
    stretched on the ground, I run up for the kill.
Ginam then begs me not to make him die
    till I knew all the grounds for his ill-will.
He can no longer harm me, therefore I
    restrain my hand and let him speak until
        he has, at point of death, defeated and disgraced,
        declared himself a traitor, Beatrice chaste.

And so he did, for freely he confessed 54
    all his devices, devious and abhorred.
Thus peace returned to my dear father's breast,
    and thus my mother's honor was restored.
And when the king said that what he liked best
    in my deed was I never used my sword,
        I vowed I'd use no sword henceforth to fight
        until I seized one from some man of might."

Così dicea Rinaldo, e la donzella   55
    pendea dal suo parlar con dolce affetto.
Poi che chiuse le labbra a la favella,
    sorse essa in piè, cangiato il vago aspetto,
e da lui pur si svelle al fine, e 'n quella
    sentio svellersi il cor da mezzo il petto.
        Misera! mentre dal suo ben si parte,
        lascia a dietro di sé la miglior parte.

Del suo lungo viaggio il terzo almeno   56
    trascorso già l'umida notte avea,
e 'n maggior copia da l'oscuro seno
    sonni queti e profondi a noi piovea;
la regina però, cui rio veleno
    tacito per le vene ognor serpea,
        non dava gli occhi stanchi in preda al sonno,
        ché le cure d'amor dormir non ponno:

ma rivolgea ne l'agitata mente   57
    del novo amator suo l'alma beltate,
e 'l valor così raro ed eccellente
    in così verde e giovenile etate,
le grazie sì diverse unitamente
    per meraviglia giunte ed adunate.
        Fra tai pensieri ancor le sovenia
        quel che già le predisse una sua zia.

Costei ch'era gran maga, e degli aspetti   58
    del cielo cognoscea tutti i secreti,
prevedendo i maligni e i buoni effetti
    che in noi deggiano oprar gli alti pianeti,
le disse già che d'amorosi affetti,
    senza che mortal cura unqua ciò vieti,
        arder dovea per un baron cristiano
        d'alta bellezza e di valor sovrano;

e che sarebbe a quel larga e cortese   59
    del suo fior virginal non pria toccato,
sì ch'indi poi, compito il nono mese,
    ne saria doppio e nobil parto nato,
duo gemelli ch'a chiare e nuove imprese
    già destinava il lor benigno fato:
        maschio l'un, ma viril femina l'altra,
        ne l'arte militar perita e scaltra.

So speaks Rinaldo, and she hears, aglow   55
    with sweet emotion, constantly reborn,
and when his lips close, she prepares to go
    but lingers, looking puzzled and forlorn.
At last she tears herself away and — oh! —
    she feels her heart out of her bosom torn.
        Poor girl! She parts from him, only to find
        she has left the best part of herself behind.

One third or more of her long voyage now   56
    the damp night had traversed and come to rain
deep sleep from her dark bosom to endow
    men with new vigor and reprieve from pain,
and still the queen, awake and sensing how
    the silent venom crept through every vein,
        could not submit her weary eyes to slumber.
        They do not sleep whom thoughts of love encumber.

She tossed and turned and felt her troubled mind   57
    from thought to thought about her new love race.
She thought how brave he was, how good, how kind,
    how wise and yet how young and smooth of face,
and how all qualities in him combined
    to make a miracle of manly grace.
        So musing, she remembered what of old
        her aunt had in a prophecy foretold.

That aunt, a sorceress of great power, knew   58
    all secrets that the heavenly signs conceal,
foreseeing what the stars on high would do,
    be it to wreak our harm or for our weal.
She had told her it was fated to come true —
    and no man could prevent it — that she'd feel
        a burning passion for a Christian knight
        of sovereign loveliness and matchless might

and that to him she'd yield her virgin flower,   59
    untouched before by any man on earth,
and after nine months in a fateful hour
    would bring forth at a noble double birth
twins destined by auspicious Fortune's power
    for enterprises of renown and worth:
        one male, one female but soon famous for
        her man-like skill in strategy and war.[123]

Rinaldo

Mentre priva la mente è di riposo,   60
   prive di quello son le membra ancora.
Sempre le tiene in moto, e del noioso
   letto cerca ogni parte ad ora ad ora.
Drizza ai balcon sovente il desioso
   guardo, onde veggia s'anco appar l'aurora,
     e se tra le fissure entra alcun lume,
     tanto a noia le son le molli piume.

Come il ciel si comincia a colorare,   61
   e le ferisce gli occhi il novo giorno,
non vuol gli altrui servigi ella aspettare:
   da sé si veste e rende il corpo adorno,
troppo ogni dama sua pigra le pare,
   e le fa dolce ma pungente scorno;
     e la compagnia loro a pena aspetta,
     ch'a ritrovar se 'n va gli ospiti in fretta.

Qual parer suol tra le minori piante,   62
   ricco di nove spoglie, alter cipresso,
ch'alzando sovra quelle il verdeggiante
   crine, vagheggia il bel ch'orna se stesso;
tale a lei parve il suo gradito amante,
   tra molti in mezzo passeggiando messo,
     che col bel volto sovra ognun s'ergea,
     e mille rai di gloria indi spargea.

Ella dolce il saluta e 'l mena poi   63
   per Acatana, sua real cittade.
Gli mostra i tempii che gli antiqui eroi
   ornar di palme ne la prisca etade,
i gran sepolcri de' maggiori suoi,
   i bei palagi e le diritte strade,
     le mura, l'alte torri e le fortezze,
     e tutto il suo potere e le ricchezze.

Ma il cieco mal nutrito ognor s'avanza,   64
   tal ch'ella a morte corre e si disface;
né più regger d'amor l'alta possanza
   puote, o da lui trovar pur breve pace.
Si cangia d'or in or ne la sembianza,
   apre a parlar la bocca e poi si tace,
     e la voce troncata a mezzo resta,
     gli occhi travolge, e move or piedi or testa.

But all the while, her mind deprived of peace,   60
    her limbs of rest, turning her head
now this way and now that, without surcease,
    she shifts in her uncomfortable bed.
Time and again she, aching for release,
    stares at her casement for a hint of red,
        that dawn's first light might greet her eyes
        and from her noisome pillow let her rise.

The sky begins to color and new day   61
    bursts at long last upon her eager sight.
She does not wait for help but right away
    dresses herself in garments of delight
then chides her ladies for their long delay
    in words of sharp but somehow charming spite
        and nearly leaves them all behind her when
        she hastens off to find her guests again.

As a lofty cypress above lesser plants,   62
    adorned with trophies of the year renewed,
lifts his green locks in springtime radiance
    assured that beauty is beatitude,
even so her new-found lover now enchants
    her eyes as in the courtly multitude
        he walks and his fine face above them all
        lights with a thousand glorious rays the hall.

She gently greets him and then leads the way   63
    through Hamadan,[124] the high seat of her crown,
shows him its fanes reared in an earlier day,
    adorned with palms by heroes of renown,
its great tombs where her ancient forebears lay,
    its gorgeous halls, the wide streets through the town,
        its walls and mighty bastions, tower on tower,
        and all its sights of pomp and wealth and power.

But her blind illness, ever nourished, grows   64
    and of her very life makes cruel sport,
while Love's high power, which no man can oppose,
    denies all hope of peace of any sort.
She changes hue, now deathly white, now rose,
    opens her mouth, then stops with speech cut short,
        and, moving restless eyes from place to place,
        now shifts upon her feet, now turns her face.

Rinaldo

Sovente ancor con interrotto suono 65
    profondamente sin dal cor sospira;
le lacrime talor sugli occhi sono,
    ma vergogna le affrena e le ritira;
or quasi fuor di sé col volto prono
    stassi, or quasi sdegnosa il ciel rimira;
      ma s'induce a la fin quell'infelice
      a scoprir il suo male a la nutrice.

— Cara Elidonia mia, tu che già desti 66
    a le mie membra il nutrimento primo,
e col tuo sangue aita a me porgesti,
    cui, non avendo io madre, in madre estimo:
tu mi soccorri or che novelli infesti
    desir se 'n vanno del mio core a l'imo,
      e 'l non ben noto male è in me sì forte
      che m'ha condutt'ormai vicino a morte.

Misera, tutto 'l male in me procede 67
    da l'un de' duo stranier, ma dal maggiore:
non vedi tu quanto in bellezza eccede
    ciascun mortale e in grazia ed in valore?
Ahi! come, oimè! di lui l'imagin siede
    ed affissa si sta dentro 'l mio core,
      come ogn'atto di lui mi sta presente,
      come il suo dir mi sona or ne la mente!

Sol l'orecchie appagate e gli occhi miei 68
    son dal dolce parlar, dal vago aspetto:
madre, te 'l dirò pur, madre, vorrei
    spenger la sete de l'acceso affetto.
Ma che dico io? La terra s'apra, e 'n lei
    nel suo fondo maggior mi dia ricetto,
      anzi, santa onestà, ch'a te faccia onta,
      e se poi morir deggio, eccomi pronta. —

Qui dà fine al parlar, raffrena il pianto, 69
    onde avea pregni i lumi, e 'l viso inchina.
L'antica donna tra sé volge intanto
    ciò che già detto fu da l'indovina,
e ben cognosce a varii segni or quanto
    immenso sia l'amor de la regina.
      Muta e sospesa sta breve ora, e poi
      così dolce risponde ai detti suoi:

And now she heaves as if out of some place 65
 deep in her inmost heart a wrenching sigh,
now feels her tears well up, but fears disgrace
 and holds them back, proud and ashamed to cry,
now stands as in a trance with downcast face,
 now as in outrage glowers at the sky.
  At last the hapless girl must speak, and she
  to her old nurse confides her malady:

"Beloved nurse, dear Helidonia, who 66
 first fed my infant limbs and who once swore
to shed your blood for me: I honor you
 as a mother, since my mother is no more.
Ah! Help me now, for yearnings strange and new
 rack my poor bosom to its inmost core,
  and the strange malady has grown so strong
  I fear my hour of death will not be long.

This plague — alas! — that makes my senses spin 67
 from the elder of these guests of ours I caught.
Look at his matchless strength, his flawless skin,
 his valor and his grace without a spot!
Ah, wretched me! How, deeply seated in
 my heart, his image rules my every thought.
  I dote upon his every act and find
  each word he speaks re-echoed in my mind!

My ears are pleased, my eyes are gratified 68
 by his fair speech, by his fair face alone.
Mother, I tell you, mother, all my pride
 is this great thirst that makes me burn and moan.
What am I saying? Let earth open wide
 on the abyss of doom. Let me be thrown
  into the depths of hopelessness, for I,
  rather than blot chaste maidenhood, would die."

She says no more, and pent-up tears commence 69
 to fill her eyes as she inclines her face.
The ancient dame already had a sense
 of what her mistress said was taking place.
She had seen by countless tokens how immense
 the queen's love was and pitied her sad case.
  So now, after a silent pause to seek
  for words of comfort, she began to speak:

— *Figlia e signora mia, che tal ti tegno,*   70
    non puote opporsi al ciel forza mortale,
più che de' venti a l'orgoglioso sdegno
    in mezo il mar pin disarmato e frale;
né d'un sol punto mai passare il segno
    che le prescrive il suo destin fatale.
        Parlo così, ché 'l variar de' tempi
        di ciò m'ha mostro mille e mille essempi.

Quando tu possa de l'amor novello   71
    sveller dal petto il radicato germe,
ed a desir più glorioso e bello
    volger la mente e le speranze inferme,
fallo, sottrati a questo iniquo e fello
    tiranno, ancidi il velenoso verme
        che attoscar la tua onestà procura,
        senza cui di beltà poco si cura.

Ma se non puoi, come a più segni espresso   72
    veder già parmi, a che t'affligi in vano?
Se di sforzar il ciel non t'è concesso,
    questo è difetto del poter umano;
e poiché n'è per un error promesso
    da la verace maga un ben sovrano,
        non invidiare a te medesma, a noi,
        quei duo, che nascer denno, illustri eroi. —

Così diss'ella, e con que' detti sciolse   73
    a la regina di vergogna il freno;
le diè speranza e di timor la tolse,
    crescer la fiamma e 'l duol fe' venir meno:
onde tosto a pensar allor si volse
    di far il suo desir contento a pieno,
        e di mandar per alcun modo un poco
        nel figliuolo d'Amon del suo gran foco.

Fa pria tentar, ma con maniere accorte,   74
    di trarre il paladin ne la sua fede,
con promesse di tôrlo in suo consorte,
    e di locarlo ne la regia sede;
ché quando giunse il re suo padre a morte,
    libera autoritate in ciò le diede:
        ma poi che ciò colui punto non muove,
        cerca novi partiti e strade nove.

"My daughter and my queen, I see your pain.   70
   No mortal power can heaven's will oppose
any more than a frail keel lost on the main
   can thwart the billows when the tempest blows.
None by a jot can alter or detain
   the fatal destiny the stars disclose.
      I speak from long experience, and I know
      by countless instances that this is so.

If from your breast you can expunge the seeds   71
   of this new love, if you somehow
can turn your mind and your weak hope to deeds
   and thoughts that virtuous glory will allow,
do it. Pluck out the evil, for it leads
   to shame. Go kill the tyrant serpent now
      whose poisons your fair chastity assail
      without which beauty is of small avail.

But if you cannot, as I seem to see   72
   by more than one clear sign, why vainly fret?
If it is heaven's will, then let it be
   by human frailty. And do not forget
what sovereign good your old aunt's prophecy
   predicted that your yielding would beget.
      Don't make yourself, don't make us all forlorn
      of those two heroes fated to be born."

So she concludes, causing to disappear   73
   the reins of shame that the queen's love repress.
She gives her hope and takes away her fear
   and feeds her fire and makes her grief grow less,
who thereupon studies with altered cheer
   how to crown avid craving with success
      and tries all ways on Aymon's son to turn
      the power of the flame that makes her burn.

She first tries in a tactful, courteous way   74
   to hint unto the paladin that she
might make him her prince-consort any day
   to share with her the throne and regency,
for when the Median king, her father, lay
   dying, he left her this authority.
      But when that offer fails in its intent
      she turns to other forms of blandishment.

Cerca d'accrescer con lo studio e l'arte 75
    la natural beltà ch'in lei risplende:
l'auree chiome in vago ordine comparte,
    ed adornarsi il rimanente attende;
poi lieta si contempla a parte a parte
    ne l'acciar che l'imago al vivo rende;
        così augellin dopo la pioggia al sole
        polirsi i vanni e vagheggiarsi suole.

Ella mostra or co' guardi, or coi sospiri 76
    al cavalier le piaghe sue profonde,
e quai ferventi Amor caldi desiri
    dai begli occhi di lui nel cor le infonde,
onde Rinaldo in amorosi giri
    le luci volge e 'n parte a lei risponde:
        ché se ben altro ardor gli accende il petto,
        d'amar donna sì bella è pur costretto.

Nel palagio reale era un giardinoq 77
    ove ogni suo tesor Flora spargea;
da le stanze ivi sol del paladino
    e da quelle di lei gir si potea.
Quivi sovente il fresco matutino
    Floriana soletta si godea:
        la porta uscendo e intrand'ognor serrava,
        ché star remota a lei molto aggradava.

Mentre una volta al crin vaga corona 78
    tesse ella quivi d'odorate rose,
e presso un rio che mormorando suona
    se 'n giace in grembo a l'erbe rugiadose,
e seco intanto e col suo ben ragiona,
    dicendo in dolci note affettuose:
        — Ahi! quando serà mai, Rinaldo, ch'io
        appaghi ne' tuoi baci il desir mio? —,

sorgiunge il paladino ed ode a punto 79
    i cari detti de la bella amante.
Ahi! come allora in un medesmo punto
    cangiar si vede questo e quel sembiante;
ben ciascun sembra dal disio compunto,
    e mira l'altro tacito e tremante:
        lampeggia, come 'l sol nel chiaro umore,
        negli umidi occhi un tremulo splendore.

She undertakes by study and by art   75
    to ornament her inborn loveliness.
She makes her hair in golden ringlets start
    and takes great care in elegance of dress.
With pleasure she surveys her every part
    and in her mirror checks on her success.
        So after rain a little bird will play
        and wash his wings, pleased by the brightening day.

She then by glances or by sighs made known   76
    her aching wound to her beloved knight,
and by Love's power her desire shone
    into his heart's depth with her fair eyes' light.
Soon toward her avid gaze Rinaldo's own
    was partly drawn in amorous delight.
        For though his ardent soul was pledged elsewhere,
        he could not help but love a face so fair.

There was a garden by the royal court   77
    where Chloris spread out all her flowery treasure.
It was forbidden to the common sort,
    though the paladin could use it at his leisure.
There often Floriana would resort
    alone in the fresh dawn to take her pleasure.
        On entering she always locked the gate
        to keep her solitude inviolate.

There she one morning, after gathering   78
    sweet-smelling roses for her lovely hair,
stretched out her limbs next to a bubbling spring
    in a lap of flowering grass, and lying there,
lost in lovelorn and fond imagining,
    she cried out loudly to the empty air:
        "Ah, when, Rinaldo, shall I quench this fire
        and in your kisses smother my desire?"

Just then the paladin passes by. He hears   79
    her loving words and hurries up apace.
Ah, how in both their faces hopes and fears
    flicker but then to wild desire yield place!
Shame wakes, but in an instant disappears.
    Both stand enraptured, silent, face to face,
        while, as in bright pools mirroring sunlit skies,
        a trembling splendor shines in their moist eyes.

L'un nel volto de l'altro i caldi affetti   *80*
 e l'interno voler lesse e comprese:
rise Venere in cielo, e i suoi diletti
 versò piovendo in lor larga e cortese;
e forse del piacer de' giovinetti
  sùbita e dolce invidia il cor le prese,
   tal che quel giorno il suo divino stato
   in quel di Floriana avria cangiato.

Il paladino in così dolce vita   *81*
 trasse più dì con la real donzella,
tal che l'antica fiamma era sopita,
 e sol gli ardea il cor l'altra novella.
Al fin l'astrinse a far quinci partita
 strana ventura che gli avenne in quella,
  la qual il primo ardor di nuovo accense,
  ed il secondo quasi a fatto spense.

L'alma stella d'Amor in ciel spiegava   *82*
 cinta di rai l'aurata chioma ardente,
e 'l sol di nova luce il crin s'ornava
 per mostrarsi più bello in oriente,
quando a Rinaldo, che col sonno dava
 dolce ristoro ai membri ed a la mente,
  apparve in sogno giovinetta donna,
  dogliosa agli atti e involta in bianca gonna;

ma splendor tal l'ornava il mesto viso,   *83*
 così la fronte avea vaga e serena,
che ne la prima vista ei fugli aviso
 veder l'Aurora che 'l bel dì rimena;
pur dopoi rimirando in lei più fiso,
 benché 'l suo lume sostenesse a pena,
  esser Clarice sua certo gli parve,
  vera e non finta da mentite larve.

Crede vederne i rai del viso, e crede   *84*
 de la favella udir le dolci note:
quel, secondo gli par, la vista fiede,
 questa così l'orecchie a lui percote:
— Ahi! che sincero amor, che pura fede
 di cavalier, se tal nomar si puote
  chi le parole sue commette al vento,
  fraude usando in chi l'ama e tradimento!

Each reads the other's warmth and inward will 80
    and every secret wish and fancy knows.
Great Venus smiles and hastens to instill
    in them the virtue she alone bestows
and even feels perhaps a secret thrill
    of envy at their pleasurable throes,
        tempted to change divinity that day
        for earthly bliss in Floriana's clay.

The paladin in such soft joy sojourns 81
    for some time with his queenly counterpart,
so that the ancient flame[125] no longer burns,
    and the new fire takes hold of all his heart.
At last a strange event befalls that turns
    his mind toward the thought that he should part,
        which sets the earlier flame ablaze anew
        and makes the later die and fade from view.

Love's gentle star was gleaming in the sky 82
    with rays of gold circling his shining head
and in the east, prepared to rise on high,
    the sun had donned his garb of flaming red,
when good Rinaldo, who asleep did lie
    with rested mind and limbs on his fine bed,
        saw in a dream a damsel greet his sight,
        bowed as in grief and clad in dazzling white,

but such huge splendor decked her countenance, 83
    such lovely light did in her sad brow show,
that he at first sight thought he saw advance
    Aurora summoning back the day, but no,
a closer look and a more fixèd glance —
    though he could scarce endure the blinding glow —
        told him this was his Clarice, even she
        herself, not some delusive fantasy.

He knows her by the fierce look in her eyes, 84
    he knows whose voice is speaking when he hears —
feels that the one his guilty eyes defies;
    and that the other thunders in his ears:
"Alas, where now is love or truth," she cries,
        "when a knight grows so unworthy of his peers
        as to make windy vows the servants of
        deceit and treachery against his love?

Rinaldo

Dunque, Rinaldo, t'è di mente uscita　　　　　　　85
　　chi te sempre ritien fisso nel core?
Dunque hai d'altra beltà l'alma invaghita,
　　e sprezzi il primo via più degno amore?
Deh! torna, torna a me, dolce mia vita,
　　ch'io tua mercé languisco a tutte l'ore.
　　　　　Queste lacrime, oimè! questi sospiri,
　　　　　segno ti sian degli aspri miei martiri.

Ma se 'l mio duol non curi, e non t'aggrada　　　86
　　l'amor, crudele, il proprio onor ti muova:
ahi! si dirà Rinaldo in Media or bada,
　　e lascivi pensier ne l'ocio cova,
e per una pagana e lancia e spada
　　posto in non cale, ei preso ha legge nova. —
　　　　　Così detto, a sua vista ella si tolse,
　　　　　e meschiata ne l'aria si dissolse.

Svegliasi il cavaliero, e gli occhi intorno　　　87
　　per veder la sua dama indarno gira;
s'infiamma intanto di vergogna e scorno,
　　ed apre il petto a nobil sdegno ed ira;
face il desir primiero in lui ritorno,
　　e quell'altro si fugge e si ritira;
　　　　　le veste e l'arme insieme in fretta prende,
　　　　　ed adorno di lor tosto si rende.

Di Clarice il ritratto ecco veduto　　　　　　　88
　　a caso viene al paladino in questa;
egli lo sguarda e sta pensoso e muto,
　　e come sia di pietra immobil resta.
Dopo gran spazio al fin, qual rinvenuto
　　da lunga stordigion l'uomo si desta,
　　　　　tal con sùbito moto egli si scosse,
　　　　　e la voce e le mani insieme mosse:

— Come, o mio ben, come ho potuto io mai　　89
　　fare al tuo tanto amore torto cotale?
Deh! poiché in merto io ti cedeva assai,
　　esser deveati almeno in fede eguale;
ma, ché 'l tuo fallo non punisci omai,
　　cavalier traditore e disleale?
　　　　　Ahi! qual pena maggior posso soffrire,
　　　　　che 'l duol che nasce in me dal mio pentire? —

Has she, Rinaldo, quite slipped from your mind   85
   whose heart to yours eternally is bound?
Has some new beauty's witchcraft made you blind
   to the earlier and worthier love you found?
Come back! Come back to me, sweet life! Be kind!
   I lie forsaken. Lift me from the ground.
      Let these my tears, these groans — ah woe is me! —
      attest my anguish and my agony.

But if my pain or true love cannot sway   86
   your soul, hear Honor's voice to make you well.
Rinaldo lolls in Media, people say,
   besotted by a pagan damozel.
He has put his warrior lance and sword away
   and turned from Christian knight to infidel."
      She said no more and vanished from his sight,
      her form dissolving in the dawn's first light.

The knight, awakening in the brightening morn,   87
   looked up to see his love, but looked in vain,
but then he, kindled with hot shame and scorn,
   opened his breast to wrath and proud disdain,
for now his first desire was reborn,
   and the other died, never to rise again.
      He snatched his clothes up, quickly armed and laced
      his helmet on, intent to leave post-haste.

He chances, gathering up his gear, upon   88
   Clarice's image from the pagan tent.
He sees it and grows motionless and wan
   and stares at it in blank astonishment.
At last, like one by sudden impulse drawn
   out of a spell of long bedevilment,
      he reaches to embrace it where it stands
      and moves his voice even as he moves his hands:

"How, my best self, could I be so perverse   89
   as to offend your love? Yea, though I knew
that I in my deservings am much worse,
   I should at least in faith have equaled you.
Yet am I now a man whom you must curse
   as a foul traitor and a knight untrue.
      Ah woe! Is there a more severe ordeal
      than anguish that my guilt will make me feel?"

Così detto, il compagno in fretta chiama,   90
    e fallo armar de la ferrigna spoglia;
indi lo prega che per quanto ei l'ama
    allor allor con lui quinci si toglia.
Quel, che servirlo e compiacerlo brama,
    si mostra obediente a la sua voglia;
        ben dolce il prega a dirgli la cagione,
        né glien'è scarso il buon figliuol d'Amone.

Come accorto nocchiero i dolci accenti   91
    fugge de le Sirene, e tutte sciôrre
fa le sue vele dispiegate ai venti,
    ed ogni remo appresso in uso porre,
così quei cari preghi e quei lamenti,
    che lo potrian dal suo pensier distôrre,
        schiva Rinaldo, e tacito se n'esce,
        ma pur di Floriana assai l'incresce:

ché, benché quel ardor già spento sia,   92
    non è però ch'egli non l'ami ancora;
e l'alta sua beltà, la cortesia,
    e l'altre sue virtù pregia ed onora;
e ben quel duolo mitigar vorria,
    ch'assalir délla in breve spazio d'ora;
        ma perciò ch'in se stesso ha poca fede,
        parte sì ch'altri allor non se n'avede.

Canto Nine

This said, he wakes his comrade and, pale-faced,   90
  bids him to arm himself from helm to greave
and, whispering that there is no time to waste,
  begs him for love of him with him to leave.
He readily obeys and arms in haste,
  eager to please his friend and loath to grieve,
    but gently asks, "Why part so out of season?"
    and Aymon's son does not withhold the reason.

As a wise pilot, conscious of the lure   91
  of Siren song, at once will hoist full sail
and speed the oars, make every hatch secure,
  and, rather than the temptress, brave the gale,
so though he loves no more, but is not sure
  that her complaints and tears will not prevail,
    Rinaldo from Floriana steals away
    although it grieves him more than he can say.

For, though his ardor is completely spent,   92
  it is not that he does not honor still
and love her grace and worth, her high descent,
  her beauty and her courteous goodwill.
And dearly would he comfort the lament
  that in an hour would from her bosom spill,
    but knowing his will is weak, his mind unfit,
    he leaves so that she does not notice it.

Canto decimo

Ma 'l fero Amor, che al fin discopre e vede   *1*
  gli occulti fatti, ancorché d'occhi privo,
a la regina chiari indizii diede
  del partir de l'amante fuggitivo,
lasciando lei d'acerbi affanni erede,
  e fuor per gli occhi in lagrimoso rivo
    ogni gioia scacciando: ond'egro il core
    rimase in preda al sùbito dolore.

Di sì grave nimico afflitto geme   *2*
  il cor, già presso a l'ultima sua sorte;
ma tosto in suo favor s'arma la speme,
  e schermo gli è da la vicina morte:
raduna il duolo a l'altrui danno insieme
  lo stuol de' sensi impetuoso e forte,
    e la speranza in quell'assalto crudo
    la ragion chiama, e di lei fassi scudo.

Mentre or la speme il duol preme ed atterra,   *3*
  or quasi vinta fugge e si ritira,
Amor risguarda la dubbiosa guerra,
  né qua né là col suo favore aspira.
Ma Floriana intanto apre e disserra
  a' lamenti la via, piange e sospira:
    talor sì ne' pensier giace sepolta,
    che non vede, non parla e non ascolta.

E se non ch'anco di vergogna il freno,   *4*
  benché sia rotto, non è rotto in tutto,
né quel animo altier venuto è meno
  che la puote ritrar da simil lutto,
onta farebbe al vago crine e al seno,
  né lasciaria di sangue il volto asciutto;
    pur mentre splende in ciel raggio di giorno,
    per la real città s'aggira intorno.

CANTO TEN

Imperious Love, whose ever-watchful sense 1^{126}
    will in the end all hidden deeds discover,
soon gave the queen abundant evidence
    of the departure of her fleeing lover,
whereat the air fills with her loud laments
    and streams of tears with their hot moisture cover
        her cheeks as Disappointment and Dismay
        and sudden Grief make her poor heart their prey.

Her heart, unnerved by these atrocious foes, 2
    trembles, convinced its final hour draws near,
but Hope at once gets ready to oppose
    savage Despair and paralyzing Fear.
Numberless crowds of grievances and woes
    protest the loss of all that she holds dear,
        while Hope to meet their onset stands resigned
        and summons Reason to defend her mind.

While Hope seems now to conquer Grief and now 3
    to own defeat or falter and give ground,
Love sees the dubious fight nor will allow
    either to triumph. Meanwhile a profound
gloom settles on poor Floriana's brow.
    Her hot tears flow, her heaving sobs resound,
        and she lies prostrate, nerveless and undone,
        nor sees, nor hears, nor answers anyone.

The reins of shame, though sadly strained, still held, 4
    not utterly broken yet, but, had they not,
or had that haughty spirit failed her that impelled
    her to keep grief in check, she would have wrought
havoc on hair and bosom or compelled
    her nails to score her face. But now, distraught,
        she quits her bed and until dusk's last rays
        wanders the royal city in a daze.

Rinaldo

S'aggira intorno, e non con grave passo,   5
    qual si conviene a donna ed a regina,
ch'a ciò punto non guarda, e 'l corpo lasso
    dal furor trasportato oltre camina:
onde non manco egli di lena è casso
    che sia di gioia l'anima meschina;
        e non trovando questa o tregua o pace,
        né quello anco in riposo unqua si giace.

Così a punto suol far chi alberga e serra   6
    in sé rio spirto ad infestarlo intento,
dal qual soffre continua interna guerra
    sì che non ha di posa un sol momento;
e, mentre scorre furioso ed erra,
    porta seco ad ognora il suo tormento.
        O possanza d'Amor, come ne' sforzi,
        come in noi del giudizio il lume ammorzi!

Pur si risveglia ed eseguisce intanto   7
    ciò ch'a la vita sua giovevol sia,
ché per mare e per terra in ogni canto
    molti guerrier dietro l'amante invia,
i quai per ricondurlo oprin poi quanto
    d'eloquenza e di forza in lor più fia;
        e quel che non potran co' detti umani,
        almen si faccia con l'armate mani.

Con dubbia mente e con tremante petto   8
    de' suoi guerrieri aspetta ella il ritorno,
qual prigioniero in cieca fossa astretto
    a la sentenza il destinato giorno;
e ben si legge nel pensoso aspetto
    quai cure entro nel cor faccian soggiorno:
        gli atti dolenti e 'l parlar rotto danno
        segno non men del grave interno affanno.

In questa di fortuna atra procella,   9
    cui tempesta maggior seguì da poi,
trasse più giorni la real donzella,
    aspettando qualcun de' guerrier suoi.
Ahi! che 'l lungo aspettar fora per ella
    il meglio assai, bench'or così l'annoi:
        vivi, vivi meschina in questo stato,
        e ti sia l'aspettar soave e grato!

Then she turns back, but not with such a gait   5
    as might befit a lady and a queen,
for she, oblivious of a monarch's state,
    walks with her frame enfeebled by her spleen.
Her body stripped of vigor, a dead weight,
    her soul deprived of joy, so that between
        the one and the other, she finds neither peace
        nor motion, neither rapture nor release.

Even as a madman rages, forced to hide   6
    the evil spirit preying on his soul
and feels a never-ending war inside
    his thoughts, his acts, his very life control,
so she now runs and errs about, blear-eyed,
    unhinged by grief that no man can console.
        O power of Love, what dreadful ways you find
        to quench the light of judgment in the mind![127]

At last she finds sufficient sanity   7
    to hit upon a plan or last resource:
for in pursuit of her lost lover, she
    dispatches warrior bands by sea and horse
with orders to convey him instantly
    back to her court by eloquence or force,
        and, if their gentle speech did not prevail,
        to see to it their valor did not fail.

With dubious mind and trembling breast she now   8
    waits for her troops of warriors to come back —
so in his cell a convict wonders how
    soon he will face the gallows or the rack —
too well her pallor and her troubled brow
    display what cruel cares her heart attack.
        Her languid mien and broken speech no less
        show her anxiety and deep distress.

So in a tempest of internal war,   9
    soon to be followed by a greater storm,
the royal dame spent several days before
    the news comes to appall her or inform.
Ah! That the tedious wait would please her more,
    which makes her mind with nameless terrors swarm!
        Live, wretched girl! Live in your clueless state,
        and fill your life with sweetness while you wait!

Rinaldo

Ecco che 'l terzo dì sei di coloro,   *10*
   che dietro 'l paladin furon mandati,
ritorno fêr poi che la speme loro
   in tutto al fin gli aveva abbandonati:
ché da Rinaldo al primo assalto foro
   vinti ed in molte parti ancor piagati,
      con lor volendo, mal suo grado, trarlo,
      perch'egli in cortesia negava farlo.

Giunti a l'alta donzella i sei baroni,   *11*
   sciolse un d'essi la lingua in queste voci:
— Regina, noi trovammo i due campioni
   che giano al lor camin pronti e veloci;
e prima con benigni umil sermoni,
   e dopoi con parole aspre e feroci,
      ultimamente con l'armata mano
      tentamo ricondurli, e sempre in vano.

Al cortese parlar cortesemente   *12*
   il figliolo d'Amon diede risposta,
e con modo efficace ed eloquente
   purgò l'error de la partita ascosta.
Soggiunse ch'a lasciarvi era dolente,
   e ch'al ritorno avea l'alma disposta,
      ma che 'l forzava un caso repentino
      gir prima in Francia al figlio di Pipino.

Né meno ancor si dimostrò cortese   *13*
   alle nostre minaccie il cavaliero,
perché placidi detti egli ne rese
   in cambio del parlar acro e severo.
Ma ben di sdegno e di furor s'accese,
   e conoscer si fe' tremendo e fiero,
      quando assalito fu; tal ch'indi in breve
      parve ogni nostro sforzo al sol di neve.

Ne disse, poi ch'in suo poter ridutti   *14*
   n'ebbe, e tolto il fuggire e 'l far difesa,
ch'egli certo n'avria morti e distrutti
   in pena sol di sì arrogante impresa;
ma perché troppo avea di servir tutti
   i servi vostri la sua mente accesa,
      volea, dando perdono al nostro ardire,
      far pago in qualche parte il suo desire. —

Lo! Three long days have passed when six of those   10
    she sent out to pursue the paladin,
return to her and their demeanor shows
    all hope is lost. When they first tried to win
Rinaldo over, seeking to impose
    her will on his, he spoke them fair and in
        all courtesy refused, but when defied
        to arms, his blade their utmost valor tried.

The six knights now approached the royal chair,   11
    and one of them loosened his tongue to say,
"Your majesty, we found the champion pair
    while they were swiftly riding on their way
and bade them, first with humble speech and fair,
    then with harsh words of anger, to obey,
        and last by force of arms to turn again
        back to this court, but all attempts proved vain.

To courteous prayers Aymon's son returned   12
    replies of comparable courtesy,
and from his eloquent response we learned
    he rued his having left so secretly.
He added he was loath to leave — yea, burned
    with a desire to come back presently —
        but for one task most needful to be done:
        to go to France in search of Pepin's son.

And no less courteous was his reply   13
    when we began to threaten, for he wooed
our kind good will and begged us not to try
    to change his mind by bitter speech and rude,
but showed at last, when wrought to fury by
    our show of violence, a far fiercer mood
        for, once provoked, he with such force assailed
        that all our strength like snow in sunlight failed.

Having reduced us to his power, bereft   14
    of all hope of defense or flight, he said
he had been sorely tempted to have cleft
    our skulls, and we would certainly be dead
had not fond memories of the love he left
    and the wish to serve you still prevailed instead
        and made him spare your servants and forgive,
        to serve you thus by suffering us to live."

Per l'orecchie que' detti a la donzella   *15*
   girno il core a ferir nel petto allora,
qual da giust'arco spinte aspre quadrella
   nel segno il punto a colpir van talora.
Slargati i lacci suoi, l'anima bella
   in quel tempo volò dal corpo fuora;
      pur, dopo lungo error, con tarde penne
      ne la vaga prigion mesta rivenne.

Allor la dama aprì le luci, e 'ntorno   *16*
   quelle con guardo languido converse,
e ch'al secreto suo caro soggiorno
   l'avean portata sovra 'l letto scerse,
e le sue damigelle a sé d'intorno
   vide non men di caldo pianto asperse;
      onde, quasi posar dormendo voglia,
      fa ch'ognuna di lor quinci si toglia.

Come sola rimase, e 'l seno e 'l volto   *17*
   scorse d'amare stille aver rigato;
l'infermo spirto in un sospiro accolto
   spinse da l'imo del suo cor turbato;
congiunto palma a palma indi, e rivolto
   in se medesma il fosco guardo irato,
      disse: — Ahi, che fo? chi questo pianto elice?
      Deh! ch'a regina il lagrimar disdice.

Lascia a l'ignobil alme, ai bassi petti,   *18*
   Floriana sfogar piangendo i guai;
tu mostra con alteri e degni effetti
   il regal sangue onde l'origin trai.
Mentre arrise Fortuna ai tuoi diletti,
   né provasti inimico il ciel giamai;
      mentre ti fu la castità gradita,
      già vivesti onorata e lieta vita.

Or ch'è morto l'onore onde vivevi,   *19*
   e t'è contrario il cielo e la fortuna,
mori! mori, infelice, e non t'aggrevi
   uscir di vita dolorosa e bruna:
ché quanto averla pria cara dovevi,
   quand'era senza nota e macchia alcuna,
      tanto ora esser ti dee noiosa e schiva,
      de' suoi primi ornamenti orbata e priva.

These tidings pierced the lady's ears with woe   15
  and reached her heart, which shook with sudden pain.
So will a bolt shot from a well-aimed bow
  sometimes the center of the target gain.
Her soul, freed of its chains, took flight to go
  from her body's prison cell, but then again,
    on tardy wings, though wandering far, turned back
    to writhe in torment on her sorrow's rack.

Opening her eyes, she turned their languid gaze   16
  upon her maids and grew aware that they
had carried her, while lying in a daze,
  to the bed she once had used in amorous play
and saw them all, alarmed by her malaise,
  in tears no less than she, stand in dismay,
    wherefore she, whispering with a stifled moan
    she needed sleep, begged to be left alone.

Left to herself, feeling the teardrops part   17
  her face and bosom with their bitter flood,
she let her spirit from her inmost heart
  heave a huge sigh and then leapt up and stood
palm joined to palm and with an angry start
  said in a voice of outraged womanhood:
    "What am I doing? Who sheds these tears? Not I.
    Tears are for milkmaids. Queens must never cry.

Let vulgar souls, Floriana, vent their woe   18
  in tears. Let petty breasts lament, forlorn.
Do you by proud and noble actions show
  the royal blood with which you have been born.
While Fortune smiled at you, you did not know
  that there are joys that heaven holds in scorn.
    While chastity was dear to you, you had
    honor and lived without a care and glad.

That honor that once gave you life is dead.   19
  Fortune now frowns, and heaven is your foe.
So die, unhappy woman, die instead
  of clinging to a life of shame and woe!
For just as life was dear to you when led
  without a blemish or a stain, even so
    the life that now remains should make you sorry,
    stripped and despoiled of what was once its glory.

Tu, sommo Dio, ch'ascolti i miei lamenti,   20
  e sin dal cielo il mio dolor rimiri,
s'a le tu' orecchie onesti preghi ardenti
    penetrar mai sovra i superni giri,
se ti mosser giamai devote menti
    a dar effetto ai lor giusti desiri,
      fa' che 'l crudel cagion de la mia morte
      pena condegna in premio ne riporte.

Fa', giusto Re, ch'a fera donna il core   21
  doni, che prenda i suoi lamenti a gioco,
e si veggia preposto altro amadore
    men degno e ch'arda in men vivace foco!
Questo picciol conforto al gran dolore
  chieggio. Padre pietoso, ahi! chieggio poco:
    altra pena, altro scempio, altra vendetta
    al suo peccare al mio morir s'aspetta.

Tu che ben sai, Signor, quanto far déi,   22
  punisci lui secondo il suo fallire,
perch'unqua imaginarmi io non saprei
    strazio eguale al suo merto, al mio desire.
Ma perché meno in lungo i detti miei?
    Di parlar no, ben tempo è di morire:
      pongasi al dire, al far togliasi il morso,
      tronchisi omai de la mia vita il corso. —

Così detto un pugnale in furia prende,   23
    ch'al gran figlio d'Amon già tolto avea,
e 'n lui lo sguardo fissamente intende,
    in lui che nudo ne la man tenea.
In questa di rossor le gote accende,
    ch'intrepido furor quivi spargea,
      e con fermezza non più vista altrove
      di novo ancor queste parole move:

— O di crudo signor ferro pietoso,   24
    il mal ch'ei femmi, a te sanar conviene:
ei mi trafisse col partir ascoso
    il cor ch'aspro martir per ciò sostiene;
tu con aperta forza il doloroso
    uccidi, com'uccisa è già sua spene;
      ché quanto il primo colpo a lui fu grave,
      tanto il secondo, e più, gli fia soave.

You, God on high, who hear my lamentation   20
    and from your skies look down upon my grief,
if ever ardent and sincere oration
    attained your sphere and met with your belief,
if ever hearing a just accusation,
    you granted victims vengeance and relief —
        ah! — make my downfall's cruel causer pay
        with condign torments for his deed one day.

Let him bestow, just king, his heart upon   21
    some cruel girl who makes his woe her sport
and who in lust is to another drawn,
    of a far duller, far less worthy sort!
Merciful Father, for what I've undergone
    grant this small justice from your heavenly court!
        With other plagues and vengeance in due time
        let my own death afflict him for his crime.

Lord, you well know what ill he came to do,   22
    smite him in keeping with his fault, for I
cannot conceive a torment equal to
    his merit or to my desire. But why
do I in vain words thus my pain renew?
    This is no time to babble, but to die.
        Let speech be bridled, action feel the goad,
        and take at once the black and fatal road."

This said, she grasped a dirk that she one day   23
    in sport had taken from Rinaldo's side
and stared at it in a peculiar way
    watching the light along its keen edge glide.
A flush overspread her whole face to betray
    her outraged passion and her injured pride,
        while she with strength not seen before addressed
        thus the sharp dagger pointing at her breast:

"Kind blade that once a cruel master bore,   24
    the wound he made you now must heal again.
His clandestine departure struck and tore
    my heart to make it suffer untold pain.
Now you with open force must strike once more
    that suffering heart when all its hope lies slain.
        As sharp as was the first blow it did meet,
        so much and more the second will be sweet.

Quegli già lo privò d'ogni dolzore.   25
   ch'il ciel con larga man versava in lui,
ma questi gli torrà tutto il dolore
   che lo fanno invidiar le pene altrui.
Tu, caro letto, che d'un dolce amore
   testimon fusti mentre lieta io fui,
      or ch'è cangiata in ria la destra sorte,
      testimonio ancor sii de la mia morte.

E come nel tuo sen prima accogliesti   26
   le mie gioie, i diletti e i gaudii tutti,
ed or non meno accolti insieme hai questi
   sospir dolenti e questi estremi lutti,
così accogli il mio sangue, e in te ne resti
   eterno segno. — E qui con gli occhi asciutti
      alzò la man per far l'indegno effetto,
      e trapassarsi, oimè! l'audace petto.

Ma 'l ferro, più di lei benigno e pio,   27
   lasciò di sé la man cadendo vòta;
il balcon in quel punto ancor s'aprio,
   quasi repente gran furor lo scuota.
Sovra un gran carro allor tosto appario,
   tratto da quattro augei di forma ignota,
      un'antiqua matrona all'improviso,
      venerabile gli occhi e grave il viso.

Era costei Medea l'incantatrice,   28
   sorella al genitor de la regina,
che per darle venia, fida adiutrice,
   in tanto mal remedio e medicina;
ché già del caso occorso all'infelice
   e dell'empia sua voglia era indovina,
      e per giunger a tempo in suo soccorso
      avea su questo carro il ciel trascorso.

Come entra e vede la real nipote,   29
   che di nuovo il pugnal volea ritôrre,
adosso le si stringe, onde non puote
   ai suo crudel disegno effetto porre.
La spruzza alquanto poi gli occhi e le gote
   con un liquor ch'al suo martir soccorre;
      e mentre a lei di sonno i lumi aggrava,
      d'ogni soverchio affanno il cor le sgrava.

Canto Ten

The first blow robbed it of all sweetness shed 25
    upon it once by heaven's bounteous hand.
The second blow shall grant to it instead
    peace from distress no true heart can withstand.
And you, dear witness of our love, sweet bed,
      while joy and pleasure were at our command,
        now that Fate changes all our good to ill,
        be witness to my end, and I'll be still.

For just as your soft bosom first received 26
    my throes of transport, my delighted cries,
just so, while I writhe hopeless and bereaved,
    you heave now with my sobs and anguished sighs.
Let my blood now, the mark of love deceived,
      forever stain your sheets." This said, with eyes
        wept dry, she swiftly raised her hand and pressed
        the dagger's point to her undaunted breast.

But lo! The blade, more pious and kind than she, 27
    dropped from her hand as of its own accord.
Her balcony doors flew open suddenly
    by a gust of violence shattered and unbarred
and through them a huge chariot, strange to see,
      drawn by four birds of monstrous aspect, soared,
        steered by an ancient dame whose countenance
        commanded reverence with every glance.

This was Medea, the great sorceress 28
    and sister to the father of the queen,
who had come, a faithful helper, to redress
    her wrongs and for her pangs bring medicine,
for she, divining the poor girl's distress,
      had long her impious purposes foreseen,
        and now, to comfort her in wondrous wise,
        had in that chariot traversed the skies.

Arrived, she sees her royal niece intent 29
    to grasp the dagger once again and throws
her arms about her shoulders to prevent
    the cruel act, then, to allay her woes,
sprinkles her eyes and cheeks with an emollient,
      which, plunging her into a sudden doze,
        weighs down her lids and lightens the sore smart
        of feelings overmastering her heart.

La maga, che sapea le più secrete   30
　　cose, né l'era alcun sentier conteso,
l'incantato liquor dal fiume Lete
　　a questo effetto prima avea già preso,
il qual potea con dolce alma quiete
　　le membra ristorar e 'l cor offeso.
　　　　Ma la regina sopra 'l carro pose,
　　　　come dormendo i rai degli occhi ascose.

La pon sul carro ed ella ancor v'ascende,   31
　　e di sua propria man regge la briglia.
Quel rato vola e l'aria seca e fende,
　　e dov'essa l'indrizza il camin piglia:
né sì veloce in giù si cala e scende
　　l'augel che tien nel sol fisse le ciglia,
　　　　né sì veloce al ciel sospinto sale
　　　　razzo dal fuoco, o pur da l'arco strale.

Giace un'isola in mar oltra quei segni,   32
　　che per fin pose a' naviganti Alcide,
ove agli audaci ed arrischiati legni
　　Calpe in due parti l'ocean divide,
in cui par che la gioia e 'l gaudio regni,
　　così d'ogni vaghezza adorna ride;
　　　　in cui scherzando co' fratelli il Gioco,
　　　　rende più bello e dilettoso il loco.

Quivi alcun narra che de' chiari eroi   33
　　le stanze sian da Giove a lor concesse,
poscia che l'alme degli incarchi suoi
　　sgravate sono, ond'eran dianzi oppresse.
Quivi null'è che l'uom mai punto annoi,
　　lieto divien ciascun che vi s'appresse;
　　　　e perché il luogo fa sì strano effetto,
　　　　l'isola del Piacer egli vien detto.

La maga a questa parte il carro inchina,   34
　　e come giunta v'è, tosto l'arresta,
e posa sovra l'erbe la regina
　　che dal salubre sonno era omai desta.
Non più la punge l'amorosa spina,
　　non più 'l perduto ben or la molesta:
　　　　ben fisso in mente tien l'avuto danno,
　　　　ma non però ne può sentir affanno.

The sorceress, adept in secret lore   30
    and undeterred by pathways of the deep,
had earlier from infernal Lethe's shore
    taken that liquid, knowing it would keep
pain from her niece's spirit and restore
    her limbs to health by tranquil, blessed sleep.
        Into the chariot then she brings queen,
        who lies in slumber, passive and serene.

She puts her in the chariot, which takes flight   31
    upon the instant, its reins guided by
her hands. It cleaves the air, now left, now right,
    wherever she directs it through the sky.
The bird whose eyes endure the sun's pure light[128]
    does not on swifter pinions heavenward fly,
        nor with more speed do bright sparks spin aglow
        from a great blaze, or arrows leave the bow.

Beyond Alcides'[129] signposts that restrain   32
    the foolish mariner's audacity,
far from where Calpe parts the bounding main,
    a lovely island rises from the sea
where everlasting peace and gladness reign
    with blessed beauty and serenity.
        There Joy and his young brothers day by day
        make merry sport and sing and dance and play.

There lie, they say, the mansions destined by   33
    Jove for illustrious heroes when their souls
shake off their former weight and thither fly
    to find new life that gladdens and consoles.
There all are happy, for no sorrows tie
    their spirits down, no rage their minds controls.
        And since that island knows nor grief nor guile
        nor misery, it is called the Joyous Isle.

Here the great sorceress makes her chariot rest   34
    and here descends from it to lay the queen
upon the grass, whose mind is still possessed
    by healthful sleep though it is plainly seen
that Love's sharp thorn no longer pricks her breast
    and that her heart no longer aches with spleen,
        for now, though her wronged love can still be brought
        to mind, she feels no sorrow at the thought.

In questo luoco a cui benigno il cielo
    con man più larga le sue grazie infonde,
a cui d'intorno il gran signor di Delo
    rai più temprati e bei sparge e diffonde,
ove fioriscon gemme in aureo stelo,
    d'argento i pesci e di cristal son l'onde,
        Medea ritenne la nipote amata
        seco, ch'ivi era d'albergar usata.

Intanto al suo camin pronto e veloce
    va con Florindo il gran figliuol d'Amone,
avendo vinto già lo stuol feroce
    ch'osò di venir seco al parangone;
e perché 'l vecchio amor lo scalda e coce,
    di tornar in Europa ei si dispone,
        lasciando Media e le contrade a tergo,
        ove genti infideli han loro albergo.

Verso Armenia costor prendon la via,
    poi c'han tutta la Media attraversata;
verso Armenia maggior, che 'n cruda e ria
    pugna avean dianzi del suo rege orbata.
Passan quella ed Assiria, ed in Soria
    giungon, che Siria fu già pria nomata;
        quivi a Baruti in nave al fin intraro,
        essendo il mare e 'l ciel tranquillo e chiaro.

Scorsero, poi che si fidaro a l'acque,
    e le spiegate vele ai venti apriro,
l'isola vaga che già tanto piacque
    a l'alma dea che regge il terzo giro;
e quella ov'il gran Giove in culla giacque,
    e la Morea non lunge indi scopriro,
        con la Sicilia, ove l'aeree fronti
        stendon su l'onde i tre famosi monti.

Mentre ne vanno al bel camin contenti
    i cavalier, gli occhi girando intorno,
tien l'accorto nocchiero i lumi intenti
    nel cheto ciel di mille fregi adorno:
mira egli i duo Trioni, astri lucenti,
    ed Orione armato a l'altrui scorno,
        e con l'Iadi poggiose il pigro Arturo,
        sovente a' naviganti infesto e duro.

35

36

37

38

39

And here, where heaven's bounteous hand makes flow   35
    from more than generous springs its ample grace,
where the great lord of Delos comes to show
    with mildest and most temperate rays his face,
where jeweled blooms on golden branches glow
    and silvery fish through crystal waters chase,
      Medea stayed with her beloved niece,
      for here she often earlier dwelt in peace.

On his swift way meanwhile Aymon's great son   36
    flies with Florindo, having bravely faced
the fierce band sent to fetch him, having won
    the fight they dared, leaving them all disgraced,
and, by his ancient flame[130] once more drawn on,
    he back to Europe' realms his steps retraced.
      They left Hamadan's countryside behind,
      where they do none but heathen dwellers find,

and having crossed all Media, took the road   37
    into Armenia — Armenia the Great,
upon whose king[131] they earlier had bestowed
    the punishment decreed for him by Fate.
They passed into Assyria, and thence rode
    to Soria, renamed Syria of late,
      and boarded ship at Beirut, setting sail
      under a cloudless sky and favoring gale.

Having embarked upon their watery way,   38
    their sails filled with the breeze, and they passed near
the lovely isle where once was pleased to stay
    the goddess of the third celestial sphere[132]
and the isle where great Jove in a cradle[133] lay,
    then watched afar the Morea[134] appear
      and Sicily, which from its three cliffs[135] braves
      with lofty brow the tempests and the waves.

While thus the knights pursue in great content   39
    their journey, scanning the great sea's confines,
the skillful pilot keeps his eyes intent
    on the calm sky, which with bright jewels shines.
He sees Orion, with his great bow bent,
    and the two Wains, lucent and trusty signs,
      and slow Arcturus near the Hyades,
      portent of woe to those who sail the seas.

Contempla il volto de la luna ancora,   40
    e rosso il vede e tutto acceso in vista:
tal parve forse per vergogna allora
    ch'ignuda fu ne le fresch'onde vista:
onde il nocchier si turba e si scolora,
    e ne rende la mente afflitta e trista;
        d'oscura nube intanto ella si vela,
        e le bellezze sue nasconde e cela.

Ecco precipitose ir giù cadendo   41
    più stelle, e 'l lor camin lasciar segnato,
come razzi talor, ch'al ciel salendo
    caggion da poi che l'impeto è mancato.
Allor grida il nocchier: — Lasso! comprendo
    che ne sfida a battaglia Eolo turbato. —
        In questa per l'ondoso umido mare
        guizzante schiera di delfini appare.

Egli l'orecchie ad ogni suono intente   42
    porge, e raccolto in sé sospira e tace,
e fremer l'onda dal più basso sente,
    sì come fiamma suol chiusa in fornace,
che, mentre esalar cerca e violente
    scorre, il luogo di lei non è capace.
        Strider strepito egual s'ode non meno
        di Giunon per l'oscuro aereo seno.

Ma già l'atra spelonca Eolo disserra,   43
    scioglie i venti, gli instiga e fuor gli caccia;
vago ognun di costor d'orribil guerra
    primo essere a l'uscir ratto procaccia;
trema al furor tremendo, e par la terra
    che d'immobile omai mobil si faccia;
        e, qual tra gli elementi or nasca amore,
        il tutto involve un tenebroso orrore.

Sin dal suo fondo il mar sossopra è mosso,   44
    e vien spumoso, torbido e sonante;
l'aer da varie parti allor percosso
    si veste un novo orribile sembiante.
Il nocchier, che venir si vede adosso
    tanti fieri nemici in un istante,
        s'arma e s'accinge a la dubbiosa impresa,
        ed invita i compagni a far diffesa.

He studies then the countenance of the moon   40
    and finds it stained with a faint ruddy gleam
like that fair blush when she one afternoon
    was spied on bathing naked in a stream.[136]
The troubled pilot watches her and soon
    finds all his mind with sad misgivings teem,
        while she with darkening clouds obscures her rays
        and hides her beauty from his fearful gaze.

Lo! In that instant falling meteors streak   41
    the gloomy vault of heaven all around
like rockets that, when their ascent grows weak,
    plunge into darkness or back toward the ground.
The helmsman cries: "Now Aeolus shall wreak
    havoc, for all his minions are unbound!"
        The great deep churns, and rising to its face,
        dolphins in splashing crowds cavort and race.

Alert to the uncanny sounds that keep   42
    striking his ears, he waits in silent care
and feels a tremor rising from the deep,
    even like a flame that, reaching for the air,
from a imprisoning furnace seeks to leap
    but finds no outlet and throbs fiercely there.
        A horrid shrieking makes the sea and sky
        resound no less than outraged Juno's cry.[137]

Then from his dark caves Aeolus lets break   43
    a thousand winds and sends them forth to cleave
the waves, each readier than the next to wake
    fierce war, each vying to be the first to leave,
till, like the earth when plains and mountains shake
    and cliffs and forests move, the waters heave
        and all the elements Love joined[138] of yore,
        in horrid chaos fall apart once more.

The bottom of the sea rears up, a black   44
    hulk on whose crest a frothy whiteness glows.
Great roaring clouds of spume both front and back
    in ghastly shapes both stern and prow oppose.
The pilot, sensing imminent attack
    by such great multitudes of cruel foes,
        braces for labors dubious and hard
        and shouts unto his crew to be on guard.

Tosto l'ignavo stuol, ch'a nulla è buono,   45
   e i marinar col suo timor offende:
ove non veda il mar, non n'oda il suono,
   poi che gli è commandato, al basso scende.
Altri i lini maggior, che sciolti sono,
   cala, e solo il trinchetto il vento prende;
      altri col fischio altrui commanda e legge
      gli impon, sì ch'a sua voglia ognun si regge.

Ma che più giova omai l'industria e l'arte?   46
   Sì sempre cresce il verno impetuoso,
e l'onda il pin da l'una a l'altra parte
   scorre qual capitan vittorioso,
e fuor seco trarrebbe a parte a parte
   gli uomini tutti nel suo fondo algoso,
      se per non esser preda a l'acque sorde
      non s'afferrasser quelli a legni, a corde.

Il tempestoso mar sovente in alto   47
   cotanto spinge i flutti suoi voraci,
che par ch'al re del ciel movano assalto
   Nettun superbo e gli altri dei seguaci.
La barca allor con periglioso salto
   portata è in su presso l'eteree faci;
      scorge, da l'onde poi spinta al profondo,
      tra duo gran monti d'acqua il terren fondo.

Né men de' venti è formidabil l'ira,   48
   né men l'afflitta nave urta e conquassa,
la qual di qua di là sovente gira
   come sovente ancor s'alza ed abbassa.
Borrea a la fin con tal fierezza spira
   che l'arbore maggior rompe e fracassa,
      e qual gelido egli è, tal manda al core
      de' naviganti un gelido timore.

Ahi! chi narrar potrebbe i varii effetti   49
   che fanno i venti e fan l'onde sonanti?
Deh! chi mai dir potria gli interni affetti
   de' mesti e sbigotiti naviganti?
Tutti rivolgon nei dubbiosi petti
   quella morte crudel c'hanno davanti,
      e veggon lei ch'in spaventosa faccia
      orribil gli sovrasta e gli minaccia.

His tone of fear alarms them and makes pale   45
    the common sort of passengers, so he
orders below deck all whose spirits fail,
    where they can neither see nor hear the sea,
then bids some others douse the mainmast sail,
    which has torn loose, but let the bowsprit be.
        The rest await his orders or his shrill
        whistle, and all are governed by his will.

But what's the use of all his toil and skill?   46
    Ever more fierce the impetuous tempest grows.
From prow to stern the monstrous breakers spill
    like a marauding horde of conquering foes
and would have hurled all men into the chill
    abyss below with their relentless blows,
        had not a few, to shun the battering streams,
        clutched at and clung to rails and ropes and beams.

The raging sea heaves ravenous waves so high   47
    among the clouds that through the welkin fling,
it seems that Neptune and his sea gods try
    from towers to lay siege to heaven's King.
The ship one moment leaps, yea seems to fly,
    and sees the ethereal torches glimmering
        but sees an instant later, as it falls,
        the bottom yawning between watery walls.

The winds no less than the wild waters shake   48
    the fragile bark and leave her crew aghast.
They hurl, now at her prow, now from her wake,
    now port, now starboard, blast and counterblast.
Boreas at last makes all her timbers shake
    with an icy gust that breaks and fells the mast,
        causing the crew's hearts at that sign of death
        to feel a chill as icy as his breath.

Ah! Who could tell the countless kinds of harm   49
    wrought by the winds, wrought by the raging sea?
Who could describe each seafarer's alarm,
    terror, despair and shuddering fantasy?
All contemplate their certain death and arm
    their hearts and minds to bear its cruelty.
        They see it loom already overhead,
        threatening horrors from a face of dread.

Sospira altri la moglie, altri il figliuolo,   50
   in cui solea già vagheggiar se stesso;
altri il suo genitor, che vecchio e solo
   lasciò, né men da povertade oppresso;
altri de' cari amici il fido stuolo,
   ch'anzi il suo fin veder non gli è concesso;
      altri, cui cura tal punto non preme,
      piange sé solo e di sé solo teme.

Molti con menti poi devote e pure   51
   giungon le palme e levan gli occhi al cielo
ma lor l'han tolto, oimè! le nubi oscure,
   e 'l disteso d'intorno orrido velo.
Sorgon tal volta in lor nove paure,
   e gli scorre per l'ossa un freddo gielo,
      s'avien che quel si mostri in vista acceso,
      quasi egli abbia i lor preghi a sdegno preso.

Rinaldo fatto avea nel palischermo   52
   de' marinari il più sagace intrare,
ch'in quel volea, come a l'estremo schermo
   col suo compagno andarsi egli a salvare,
perch'indi a l'elemento asciutto e fermo
   si credea breve spazio esser di mare,
      e s'era trasportato in quel primiero
      la spada, il bel ritratto e 'l buon destriero.

Ma il marinar, che più che 'l paladino   53
   e che 'l compagno assai se stesso amava,
temendo pur che di soverchio il pino
   carco non fusse s'altri ancor v'entrava,
sì che cedesse a l'impeto marino,
   tagliò la fune ond'egli avinto stava,
      e col battel si fe' tosto lontano,
      pregar lasciando e minacciarsi in vano.

La nave intanto il dritto lato e 'l manco   54
   aperto mostra al gran colpir de l'onde;
entran quelle per l'uno e l'altro fianco,
   ed a le prime sieguon le seconde.
Viene ogni marinar pallido e bianco:
   pur, a ciò che 'l naviglio non s'affonde,
      o tenta d'impedir la strada al mare,
      o 'l legno vòta pur de l'acque amare.

One mourns his wife, another his dear son   50
    in whom he took such huge delight one day,
another his father, age-worn and undone
    by poverty and doomed to slow decay,
another mourns his boon companions, won
    in olden times and now a world away,
        and yet another, by such cares unknown,
        fears for himself, weeps for himself alone.

Many of them, grown pious and devout,   51
    lift up their suppliant hands toward the skies
but find — ah woe! — that clouds have quite put out
    all light to let a horrid darkness rise,
and novel terrors fill their minds with doubt
    as through their bones an icy shiver flies.
        They feel that heaven that here meets their sight
        holds, as it were, all piety in spite.

Rinaldo had most wisely gained access   52
    unto the pilot-boat, in which he meant
at last resort to flee from his distress
    and with his friend, the sea's rage being spent,
by chance or skill to reach — such was his guess —
    safely a dry and firmer element.
        In it he stowed to serve at future need
        his sword, his true love's image and his steed.

But now its mate, who loves himself much more   53
    than he loves the paladin and his friend, afraid
the boat might not sustain the weight it bore
    if by two further passengers down-weighed,
so that the tempest, raging as before,
    would make the waters its poor shell invade,
        slashes the rope and pushes off, while they
        entreat or curse in vain, and rows away.

Huge gashes meanwhile in the hull appeared,   54
    both on the windward and the leeward side.
Now here, now there through shattered timbers sheared
    the monstrous surges of the raging tide.
The battered vessel pitched and yawed and veered,
    as white-faced sailors desperately tried
        to dam the flow of waves that inward rolled
        or clear the salt bilge from the flooded hold.

Rinaldo

Ecco che d'Aquilon l'orribil fiato   55
 fa che di timon privo il legno resta,
ed è dal mar rapito e fuor gettato
 l'infelice nocchier, percosso in testa.
Lasso! non gli giovò l'esser legato,
 con tal forza lo trasse onda molesta;
  seco lo trasse nel suo fondo, e 'nsieme
  trasse nel fondo la comune speme.

Or che dee fare in mezo l'onde insane,   56
 privo del suo rettor, legno sdruscito?
Vani i rimedii e le speranze vane
 forano omai, ché 'l caso è già seguito.
Ciascun de' naviganti allor rimane
 oppresso da la tema ed invilito,
  e par che fredda mano al cor gli stringa,
  ed aspro ghiaccio il corpo induri e cinga.

Tu solo, altera coppia, isgomentarti   57
 vista non fusti ne l'estrema sorte
ché tal ti piacque in volto allor mostrarti
 qual anco eri nel core invitta e forte.
Ma già spinto ad un scoglio e in mille parti
 spezzato il legno, espon gli uomini a morte:
  s'ode in quel punto in suon flebile e tristo
  invocar Macon altri, ed altri Cristo.

Rari, e que' rari in vari modi allora   58
 veggonsi i notator per l'ampio mare:
quegli alza un braccio sol de l'onda fuora,
 questi col sommo de la fronte appare;
altri mostra le gambe e in breve ancora
 scorgonsi quelle poi sott'acqua intrare;
  s'afferra altri a lo scoglio, altri ad un legno,
  altri fa del compagno a sé ritegno.

Ma de' guerrier l'invitta copia avea   59
 asse ben lungo e largo allor pigliato,
e con la destra a quella s'attenea,
 con l'altra ributava il flutto irato;
ed a la forte man sempre aggiungea,
 sospinto a tempo fuor, gagliardo fiato;
  stender anco in quel punto in largo i piedi,
  poi giunti in uno a sé raccôr gli vedi.

Canto Ten

See now the vessel spinning helplessly   55
    caught in the dreadful breath of Aquilo,
and the doomed coxswain by the raging sea
    swept overboard when his head receives a blow.
Alas! Though tethered to his tiller, he
    is yanked off by the waves and pulled below.
        Pulled to the bottom, see him drown and fall
        and drown with him the last faint hope of all.

A shattered shell caught in a hurricane,   56
    what can the ship do now with none to steer?
Vain is all hope. All effort now is vain.
    The final doom is not to come, but here.
The sailors, as if paralyzed, remain
    inert, each feeling seized by coward fear,
        as if a cold hand squeezed his heart, and ice
        held every limb in a relentless vise.

You only, valiant pair, without dismay   57
    face these extremities of Fortune's wrong.
For both your countenances well display
    the calm of hearts indomitably strong.
The ship now strikes a rock and splits straightway,
    flinging its men into the flood headlong,
        and soon the roars of crashing surges drown
        their prayers, some to Christ, some to Mahoun.

They sink from view. Now and again   58
    some arms or legs or backs or heads appear
bobbing upon the frothing wave and then
    are seen no more. But still the waters near
the foundering vessel teem with desperate men:
    some gasp out cries for help that none can hear,
        some clasp the rock, some clasp a timber's end,
        and some seek life by clinging to a friend.

But meanwhile the undaunted warrior pair   59
    had seized a spar, glimpsed by a sudden gleam,
and each of them, with one hand fastened there,
    beat back with the other hand the raging stream.
They drew strong breaths in tandem and took care,
    with hands joined firmly on the floating beam,
        to stretch legs out in unison, before
        pulling them back in unison once more.

307

Rinaldo

Gran pezzo andaro i duo guerrieri uniti,   60
   rompendo a forza l'impeto marino:
da vasto monte d'acqua al fin colpiti
    si separar Florindo e 'l paladino;
ma perde quegli il legno, ond'ambo arditi
    erano in tal furor di reo destino,
       né con mani o con piedi oprar può tanto
       che di nuovo afferrar lo possa alquanto.

Da l'altra parte il buon figliuol d'Amone   61
   per aitarlo e forza ed arte adopra,
e sovente se stesso in rischio pone,
    ma riesce al desir contraria l'opra:
ché 'l mare al suo disegno ognor s'oppone,
    e par che quello ormai nasconda e copra,
       onde in Rinaldo il duol cotanto cresce
       che quasi la sua vita omai gli incresce.

Quasi si diede in preda a l'acque salse,   62
   l'ira e lo sdegno in se stesso rivolto;
ma l'amica ragione in lui prevalse,
    e 'l sottrasse al desir crudele e stolto.
Come il consiglio oppresso in lui risalse,
    tutto il suo gran vigor in un raccolto,
       franse col forte petto i flutti insani,
       oprò le gambe e 'l fiato, oprò le mani.

Già da lunge apparisce umil la terra,   63
   che par che sotto l'onde ascosa giaccia;
allora ad ogni tema il petto serra,
    e con più forza i piè move e le braccia.
Ecco ch'il molle estremo lito afferra,
    e, chinati i ginocchi, alta la faccia
       leva con guardo riverente al cielo,
       e Dio ringrazia con devoto zelo.

Ma quando gli sovvien che restò morto   64
   in mezzo l'onde il suo compagno caro,
e c'han voraci invidi flutti absorto
    sì sovrana beltà, valor sì raro,
men de la vita sua prende conforto
    che prenda duol de l'altrui fine amaro;
       e partiria col morto i giorni suoi,
       qual già fèr, Leda, i duo gemelli tuoi.

Long thus together the two warriors brave   60
    the raging sea amid the tempest's din.
At last, struck by a mountainous ocean wave,
    Florindo is parted from the paladin.
His hand slips from the beam to which he clave,
    the whirling currents set his trunk a-spin
        and, as he struggles to swim back, defeat
        the utmost efforts of his hands and feet.

For his part, Aymon's son, to aid his friend,   61
    musters all strength and skill, does all he can
and puts himself at risk, but in the end
    the furious billows foil his every plan
with the reverse of what he did intend
    and pull away or hide the other man.
        Rinaldo's grief at his friend's futile strife
        makes him almost feel grieved by his own life.

He almost let the salt flood bear him down,   62
    turning upon himself his scorn and ire,
but friendly reason would not let him drown
    and checked his cruel and insane desire.
At last he, taking counsel, with a frown
    made resolution once more grow entire,
        parted the waves with strong breast and employed
        legs, arms and breath in combat with the void.

Soon he saw, far away, what seemed like land,   63
    so low it scarcely rose above the sea,
and at that sight out of his bosom banned
    all coward fear and swam on valiantly.
He reached at last the barren shore's soft sand
    and raised his face and upon bended knee,
        in prayers of gratitude and reverent zeal,
        thanked God for his escape from his ordeal.

But when he calls to mind that his best friend   64
    had drowned, that all his beauty now decayed
in the briny deep, he grieves that Fate could send
    such valor into depths where monsters preyed.
He loathes his own life, weeping at the end
    of the dear man, and would have gladly stayed
        in the abyss with him forevermore,
        as one of your twins, O Leda, did of yore.

Mentre tra sé si duol, vede un castello,   65
    ch'indi vicin la fronte a l'aria alzava;
gliel mostra il Sol che dal celeste ostello,
    serenando le nubi, omai spuntava.
I passi il paladin drizza ver' quello,
    i cui piedi il Tireno irriga e lava,
        e fuvi accolto dal signor cortese,
        e d'esser giunto presso Roma intese.

Fu d'arme, di cavallo e di scudiero   66
    non men provisto il buon figliuol d'Amone,
e tutto ciò ch'a lui facea mistiero
    ebbe anco in dono dal gentil barone.
Tolto commiato poi, prese il sentiero
    verso la Francia, ove d'andar dispone,
        e trovò presso un fonte il terzo giorno
        un cavalier di lucid'arme adorno.

Questi ad annoso pin tenea legato   67
    per l'aurea briglia il suo destrier gagliardo,
e nel medesmo tronco era attaccato
    vago ritratto ov'ei fissava il guardo.
Fu da l'invito eroe rafigurato
    tosto l'amata imago e 'l suo Baiardo;
        poi, risguardando il cavalier non manco,
        vide Fusberta a lui pender dal fianco.

Quel marinar che sul battel fuggito   68
    de l'irato Nettuno avea lo sdegno,
abbandonando il paladin schernito
    in periglio maggior, nel maggior legno,
come salvo fu giunto al molle lito,
    di vender il suo furto ei fe' disegno;
        e poi del prezzo con costui convenne
        col quale a caso a riscontrar si venne.

Rinaldo a lo straniero allor richiese   69
    gli arnesi suoi con parlar dolce umile.
Quelli, ch'era superbo e discortese,
    disse: — Il far doni è fuor d'ogni mio stile.
S'elle son tue, con l'arme il fa' palese,
    ché l'adoprar parole è cosa vile. —
        L'altro, intendendo ciò, punto non bada,
        scendendo in terra ad impugnar la spada.

Canto Ten

As he thus inwardly laments, he sees   65
   a nearby castle on a rocky hill.
For now the storm yields to a gentle breeze,
   the sun shines once again, and all grows still.
The paladin gains entrance there with ease
   at a gate with the Tyrrhenian at its sill.
      Its courteous owner bids him feel at home
      and lets him know he has arrived near Rome.

Aymon's good son is given sword and lance,   66
   a horse, a suit of armor and a squire
by his kind host who generously grants
   all that a knight unfurnished might require.
He bids farewell and takes the road toward France,
   drawn thither by his amorous desire,
      and finds, after some three days' journeying,
      a knight in shining armor by a spring.

He had tied his fine steed to a knotty pine   67
   by a golden bridle and had placed likewise
against the trunk of that-same tree a fine
   image on which he gazed with amorous eyes.
At once Rinaldo knew that form divine
   and his own Bayard, and to his surprise,
      when looking at the knight more closely, spied
      his own Fusberta hanging at his side.

That sailor who had on the cockboat fled   68
   from Neptune's fury, and who, once afloat,
had left behind the paladin in his stead
   in greater danger on the larger boat,
unto the kindly shore had safely sped.
      There for his stolen goods he took good note
      of likely buyers and by good fortune met
      this man who bought them at the price he set.

Rinaldo now besought the stranger knight   69
   for what was his in mild, humble speech,
but he replied, full of discourteous spite,
   "I'm in no mood to give, but if you'd teach
me how, come use your blade and fight.
      Cowards use words for claims beyond their reach."
      At this, the other, quick to understand,
      leapt nimbly to the ground with sword in hand.

Scese egli del corsier, ché non vorrebbe   70
    avere in pugna alcuna alcun vantaggio,
sapendo che colui non mai potrebbe
    spingere il suo Baiardo a fargli oltraggio.
Allor ne lo stranier lo sdegno crebbe,
    e l'aversario suo stimò mal saggio,
        poi ch'ardisce affrontarsi a paro a paro
        con lui sì forte e sì ne l'arme chiaro.

Rinaldo prima 'l brando in opra mise,   71
    ma schivò 'l colpo il cavaliero estrano;
poscia alzando la spada aspro sorrise,
    e disse: — Or guarda chi ha più dotta mano. —
La percossa crudel ruppe e divise
    lo scudo, e mezzo ne mandò sul piano;
        poi dichinando ne la manca coscia
        gli fe' quivi sentir gravosa angoscia.

Non a tanta ira è mai Nettun commosso,   72
    se lui Maestro od Aquilon percote,
in quanta salse il paladin percosso,
    sì ch'accese di sdegno ambe le gote.
Divien lo sguardo ardente e l'occhio rosso,
    ch'altrui sol di timore atterrar puote;
        or che farà quel formidabil brando,
        che con impeto tal vien giù calando?

A forza apre la strada al colpo orrendo   73
    l'elmo, e 'n due pezzi o 'n tre riman partito;
si riversa l'estrano al pian cadendo,
    piagato no, ma ben de' sensi uscito.
Disse Rinaldo allor: — Chiaro comprendo
    ch'abbiam questa battaglia ormai fornito. —
        Indi Fusberta e 'l bel ritratto prese,
        e sul caro destrier d'un salto ascese.

Quelli lieto il riceve, e del su' amore   74
    mostra con l'annitrir segno evidente,
e con mille altri aperti indizii fuore
    scopre il piacer che dentro 'l petto sente.
Così fa can fidele al suo signore,
    il qual di lusingarlo usi sovente,
        che d'intorno li salta, e con la bocca
        e con la coda dolce il bacia e tocca.

He left his saddle, having no desire   70
    for unfair vantage, since full well he knew
that his opponent never could inspire
    his own Bayard to be to him untrue.
At which the stranger, in contemptuous ire,
    thinks him a feeble foe, and foolish, too,
        to risk, unmounted, mortal combat with
        a foe of such renown and warlike pith.

Rinaldo first put his good sword in play,   71
    but the alert antagonist dodged its blow
and, smiling dourly, lifted his to say,
    "Now which of us strikes better we shall know,"
and cleft Rinaldo's upraised shield straightway,
    sending its two halves to the ground below.
        The blade bore down to slash his thigh and made
        sharp pangs of grievous pain his frame invade.

Neptune shows not more furious chagrin   72
    when Aquilo's or the Mistral's[139] gusts resound
than now overtakes the wounded paladin.
    His blazing eyes shoot lightning all around,
and his whole visage, red from brow to chin,
    spreads terror enough to strike men to the ground.
        What will that blade he swings with all his might
        do now, impelled by such prodigious spite?

The horrid blow by sheer force makes its way   73
    through the stranger's casque, who wheels around
feeling the crack and falls in great dismay,
    unwounded but unconscious, to the ground.
Rinaldo murmurs softly: "I dare say
    this fight is done," and at a single bound
        snatches the image, grasps Fusberta and then
        with a leap mounts his beloved steed again.

Gladly the horse received him, making known   74
    his ardent love by loud neighs, and expressed —
the rider on his back once more his own —
    by countless signs the pleasure in his breast.
So will a faithful dog with whimpering moan
    flatter his master or with muzzle pressed
        against his body kiss him or zig-zag
        leap round him joyfully with tail a-wag.

Rinaldo

Già si partia Rinaldo, allor che scorse   75
    lo scudo suo per mezzo esser diviso,
onde il destrier di novo in dietro torse,
    là 've giaceva il cavalier conquiso;
e fe' che 'l suo scudier quello gli porse
    del superbo baron, ché gli er'aviso,
        che fino fosse e là temprato dove
        Bronte sopra l'incude il braccio move.

Era quivi intagliata una donzella   76
    da così dotta e maestrevol mano,
che giamai non fu vista opra sì bella:
    divin pareva e non sembiante umano.
Viva rassembra, e 'l moto e la favella
    mancava solo a l'artificio strano;
        ma se non parla ancor, se non s'è mossa,
        par che non voglia, e non che far no 'l possa.

Sì vivo in quello il finto al ver somiglia,   77
    benché di spirto sian le membra casse,
ch'altri mirando in lei si meraviglia
    ch'ella non parli, più che se parlasse.
Allor il vago scudo il guerrier piglia,
    e meglio era per lui che no 'l pigliasse,
        ch'ove solo lo tolse a sua difesa,
        gli fe' poi, lasso! al cor mortal offesa.

Tolto lo scudo, il cavalier s'accinge   78
    prontissimo di novo a la sua via;
e così caldo Amor lo sferza e spinge,
    che non si ferma mai né si disvia
mentre ch'Apollo il mondo orna e dipinge,
    o per tornare o per partir s'invia.
        Sol quando è d'aurei fregi il ciel contesto,
        posa, né dorme ben, né bene è desto.

In pochi giorni scorse il bel paese   79
    che quinci il mare e quindi l'alpe serra.
Indi, varcando i monti, al pian discese,
    e vide lieto la natia sua terra;
poi, giunto omai presso Parigi, intese
    ch'il magno re co' suoi mastri di guerra,
        e con le dame sue l'alta regina,
        avean la stanza lor molto vicina.

Scarce on his way, Rinaldo brought to mind   75
   that his shield lay shattered by his foeman's ire,
wherefore back where that conquered knight reclined
   he once more turned his horse and made his squire[140]
take up that baron's shield. Its metal was refined
   to hardest temperament in Etna's fire
      and shaped on Brontes'[141] anvil — so Fame tells —
      where Vulcan with Cyclopean helpers dwells.

On it was limned a lady or a queen   76
   by such a consummately skillful hand
that never lovelier workmanship was seen.
   She seemed a goddess, not a woman, and
with such a graceful port and smiling mien,
   did wordlessly and motionlessly stand
      that, though suspended, it seemed that she could
      both move and speak at any time she would.

For so much truth shone in that fancied thing,   77
   although it lacked a soul, it made you stare
in marvel at its features, wondering
   that no words issued from a face so fair.
That shield the warrior now lifts by its sling
   and shoulders it. Ah, had he left it there!
      For what he deemed defense from scathe and smart
      would soon — alas! — wound mortally his heart.

With that shield on his back, the knight sets out   78
   upon his quest once more without delay,
and Love goads him so hotly that without
   rest or digression he pursues his way
hour by hour, so long as round about
   Apollo brightens and adorns the day
      and only rests when stars and planets throng
      with golden dots the sky, nor rests for long.

He soon attains the lovely land that ends   79
   here at the Alps, there at the Western sea,
and from the mountains to the plain descends
   hailing his native country joyfully
and soon learns as he toward Paris wends
   that Charlemagne with all his lords-in-fee
      and his high queen and her fair retinue
      is lodged at a place just coming into view.

da la città duo miglia o tre lontano   80
   luogo u' la cacciagion sempre abbondava,
sovra un fiorito e dilettevol piano,
   cui lucido ruscel dolce irrigava;
e ch'ivi contra ogni guerriero estrano
   ch'o suo conseglio o sorte là guidava,
      alcun franco baron veniva a giostra,
      di sé facendo a dame altera mostra.

Come fu presso, il pian ripieno scerse   81
   D'illustri cavailier e di donzelle,
I quai d'oro, d'acciaro e di diverse
   Sete ornavan le member altere e belle;
Alter vermiglie, alter turchine or perse,
   Candide queste e verdiggianti quelle;
      E l'sol, che reflettendo indi splendea,
      Di nova iride vaga il ciel pingea.

Ma sendo visto il paladin Rinaldo   82
   sul gran Baiardo in sì feroce aspetto,
che ne venia sì ne la fronte baldo
   che mostrava l'ardir chiuso nel petto,
e sì sovra 'l destrier fondato e saldo
   che parea muro in terra soda eretto,
      vario parlar tra quei di Carlo nacque,
      e ciascuno il lodò, ch'a ciascun piacque.

Ma 'l superbo Grifon, che difendea   83
   per amor di Clarice a tutti il varco,
sentendo ciò ch'altri in su' onor dicea,
   contra gli andò quanto trarebbe un arco;
e perché nel pensier prefisso avea
   di far tosto di lui Baiardo scarco,
      gridò: — Giura, guerrier, ch'a la mia dama
      cede in beltà qual ha più pregio e fama! —

Grifon già per amor avea servito   84
   gran tempo inanzi d'Olivier la suora,
ma 'l foco suo negletto ed ischernito
   fu da l'altera giovinetta ognora;
onde per longa prova al fin chiarito,
   ch'accôr tentava in rete il vento e l'ora,
      stolto! a servir Clarice egli avea preso,
      né potea ciò Rinaldo avere inteso;

Here, two or three miles from the city wall,   80[142]
  upon a blossoming and delightful plain,
where game abounds and splashing waters fall
  in limpid rivulets to feed the Seine,
French nobles wait in proud display to call
  into the joust with them each wandering swain,
    by luck or daring thither drawn, to show
    the ladies how a champion meets his foe.

Approaching, he took in the splendid scene   81
  of famous knights and ladies whose array
of arms and garments glittered with a sheen
  of gold and steel and silk in a display
of purple, turquoise, vermeil, gold and green
  and snowy whiteness, which the sun's pure ray
    projected toward the heavens through the air
    like a new rainbow glowing everywhere.

But seeing Rinaldo to the lists proceed   82
  on giant Bayard, all appear spellbound,
for his undaunted brow displays indeed
  the flames that in his valiant heart abound.
Seated so hale and firmly on his steed,
  he seems a wall rising from solid ground.
    Talk spreads through Charles' court in various ways,
    but all who find him pleasing sing his praise.

Only proud Gryphon, ready to attack   83
  all men for Clarice's love, being nearby,
and hearing them commend him, taken aback,
  with greater speed than any arrow can fly —
intent to topple him from Bayard' back —
  now rides against him with this threatening cry:
    "Swear, knight, that my own lady far excels
    in beauty and in worth all maidens else!"

This Gryphon formerly had hotly yearned   84
  for Oliver's sister's love, but she had met
his heat with coldness and had nobly spurned
  his pleas, so that at last, to his regret,
after much labor, he had plainly learned
  that he tried to catch the wind within a net
    and now — the fool! — as Clarice's champion fought.
    Rinaldo of all this suspected naught

onde rispose: — Vil timor non deve   85
    giamai la lingua altrui torcer dal vero,
né periglio o fatica, ancorché greve
    si convien d'ischivare a cavaliero.
Dico dunque ch'oltraggio il ver riceve
    da te non poco, e ciò mostrarti spero:
        bella è la dama tua, ma molto cede
        a chi fe' del mio cor soavi prede. —

A l'arme, ai fatti orrendi al fin si venne   86
    da le minaccie e da l'altere voci:
di qua, di là le due massicie antenne
    vengon portate da le man feroci.
Par ch'abbiano i cavalli al fianco penne,
    così a l'incontro van ratti e veloci;
        l'aria si rompe, e trema ancor la terra
        al primo cominciar de l'aspra guerra.

Pose il suo colpo a vòto il Maganzese   87
    incauto troppo, e corse l'asta in fallo;
ma lui Rinaldo a mezzo scudo prese,
    e lo sospinse fuor del suo cavallo.
Sendo percosso e 'l suol premendo, rese
    alto rimbombo il lucido metallo,
        come suol squilla che sonando invita
        a sanguinosa guerra ogn'alma ardita.

Rinaldo allor dal degno stuol è cinto   88
    e supplicato a tôrsi via l'elmetto,
tal che da' prieghi lor forzato e vinto
    di compiacerli è mal suo grado astretto.
Si scioglie al fin que' lacci ond'era avinto
    l'elmo, e scopre la chioma e 'l vago aspetto:
        né men bello e leggiadro or si dimostra,
        ch'apparso sia possente e forte in giostra.

Tosto fu conosciuto il cavaliero   89
    al discoprir del volto e del crin d'oro,
e chiare voci di letizia diero
    con replicato suon l'amico coro,
ché già del suo valore il grido altero
    era giunto a l'orecchie a tutti loro.
        La gloria sovra lui si spazia intanto,
        battendo l'ali d'or con dolce canto.

and so replied: "Vile fear should never wrest   85
   a man from truth, and no good knight should fly,
however much by toil or danger pressed,
   from truth's detractors whom he should defy.
I here maintain and will prove by the test
   of arms that you have outraged truth. You lie.
      Your lady is fair, but far less fair, I say,
      than she who makes my willing heart her prey."

From threatening words and insults they proceed   86
   to deeds, to acts of furious war at last.
From this side and from that they fiercely speed,
   each strong fist grasping a horrific mast.
Wings seem to grow upon each rider's steed,
   so eagerly they press on and so fast.
      Earth trembles and the air makes a great jar
      at this first onset of their bitter war.

The rash, heedless Maganzan puts his lance   87
   in rest and misses when he runs his course,
but Rinaldo's finds his shield, and in a trance
   he plummets to the earth far from his horse.
Blinded and stunned he meets the ground and pants,
   as his armor, struck with his fall's sudden force,
      rings like the tocsin signaling brave men
      to find the bloody field of war again.

Then in a crowd the noble lookers-on   88
   run to Rinaldo and beg him to unlace
his casque, until, by their entreaties won,
   he — will he, nil he — needs must do them grace,
and, when his helmet's fastenings are undone,
   shows them his golden locks and lovely face,
      nor does he seem less blithe and handsome than
      he had seemed dreadful when the joust began.

His face and tresses being thus displayed,   89
   at once all recognize the knight and fall
upon his neck in joyous accolade
   and his great deeds throughout the world recall
for Fame by now has of his exploits made
   a loud report unto the ears of all.
      Glory meanwhile, beating her golden wings,
      hovers above his head and sweetly sings.

Rinaldo

Ad onorar Rinaldo ognun s'accinge,   90
    e di farsegli grato ognun procaccia:
altri la man gli tocca, altri gli cinge
    il collo e il petto con amiche braccia;
altri, cui caldo amor più innanzi spinge,
    pien d'un dolce disio lo baccia in faccia;
        ma il padre Amone al petto alquanto il tiene,
        e sente alto diletto ir fra le vene.

Lasciato il padre il cavaliero invitto,   91
    de' suoi regi a bacciar se 'n va la mano;
quei, mostrando l'amor nel volto scritto,
    l'accoglion lieti e con sembiante umano.
Fan le donne tra lor dolce conflitto
    in onorare il vincitor soprano;
        e in quanto è lor da l'onestà concesso,
        gli mostra ognuna il suo voler espresso.

An eager crowd surrounds Rinaldo, and 90
    all men to pay him homage do their best.
Some fall upon his neck, some grasp his hand
    with theirs, or tap his shoulder or his chest
and some, heeding affection's hot command,
    kiss his fair face. But happiest and most blest,
       his father Aymon in that jubilant train
       clasps him and feels delight in every vein.

Released by his father, the victorious knight 91
    ascends to kiss the royal couple's hands.
Gladly the two receive him with delight
    and love expressed in either countenance.
To show him grace, the ladies sweetly fight:
    each honors him as best she understands
       and, insofar as modesty allows,
       shows her good will by curtseys and by bows.

Canto undicesimo

Ma trattasi in disparte alto sospira   *1*
   Clarice, e gelosia sol n'è cagione:
tra sé fremendo l'accoglienze mira
   che fan quell'altre al gran figliol d'Amone,
e s'arma incontro lui di sdegno e d'ira
   per l'onta in suo disnor fatta a Grifone,
     e per veder che ne lo scudo il volto
     d'ignota dama porta impresso e scolto.

— Non ti basta, crudel, dice in se stessa,   *2*
   romper la fede e far torto al mi' amore,
se non mi scopri la cagione espressa
   del tuo grave fallir, del mio dolore?
Poiché viva non puoi, mi mostri impressa
   la donna, oimè! che ti possiede il core,
     ed onde io più mi doglia, ahi! perché questo?
     a la mia gloria sei con l'arme infesto.

Lassa! qual sotto i fior l'angue è celato,   *3*
   tal sotto cortesia, sotto bellezza,
s'asconde in te perfido cor spietato,
   che l'altrui fede e 'l puro amor disprezza.
Fuggite, donne, oimè! fuggite il grato
   sembiante e 'l guardo umil pien di dolcezza,
     che promettendo vita altrui dan morte,
     e son d'un fido cor mal fide scorte.

Ma stolta, a che sospiro? a che mi doglio?   *4*
   Se 'l più dolermi e 'l sospirar non vale,
s'egli è perfido e lieve, io, come soglio,
   ancor dunque serò ferma e leale?
Ahi! non fia ver ch'a lui scoprir mi voglio
   ne la costanza e ne la fede eguale. —
     Così detto tra sé, prese consiglio
     di mostrare a Rinaldo irato il ciglio.

Canto Eleven

But Clarice, fretting inwardly, withdrew,   1
    and jealousy was what made her fret, for she
beheld with inward spleen the welcome due
    bestowed on Aymon's son so copiously.
She was filled with scorn, incensed with wrath and rue
    by Gryphon's fall and much repined to see
        how graven on Rinaldo's shield there shone
        the image of a maid to her unknown.

"Cruel man," she cried out, "did it not suffice   2
    to break your troth and scorn my love, but must
you thus parade before my very eyes
    the cause of your betrayal and my distrust?
Though absent, plainly on your shield's device
    she smiles for whom I'm spurned. Ah, is this just?
        What's more — and this completes my grief
        and shame —
        you have come in arms to denigrate my fame.

Ah! Like a flower with a snake below   3
    your beauty hides the conscience of a liar,
a foul and treacherous heart, ready to throw
    my pure love for some stranger's in the mire.
Flee, ladies, flee those outward charms — ah woe! —
    those humble gazes full of sweet desire
        that promise life, delivering death instead,
        faithful attendants of a heart misled.

But, foolish me, why should I sigh? Why weep   4
    and lose myself in tears? To what avail?
If he is fickle, should I seem to keep
    firm as a rock and loyal without fail?
Nay, if I'm true, he shall not hold it cheap,
    nor shall my countenance ever tell the tale."
        So saying she deliberated how
        to greet Rinaldo with a frowning brow.

O di tema e d'amor figlia crudele,   5
    figlia che 'l genitor sovente uccidi,
a l'alte sue dolcezze amaro fele,
    peste ch'infetti l'alme in cui t'annidi:
torna a l'inferno omai tra le querele,
    tra l'aspre pene e tra gli eterni stridi!
        Né più turbar sì puro e casto foco,
        ch'ivi non merta aver tuo giaccio loco.

Il paladin che sempre gli occhi porse   6
    sin da principio a la sua dolce amata,
sì come lampo in ciel turbato scorse
    folgorar l'ira ne la faccia irata,
non già de la cagione allor s'accorse
    che la rendesse incontro lui sdegnata.
        Pur cheto disse: — Lasso! or chi m'oscura
        il seren de l'angelica figura?

Dunque sarò per così lunga via   7
    morte venuto a tôr così noiosa?
Ché mi dà morte l'inimica mia,
    quando m'appar superba e disdegnosa.
Qual fora, oimè! se fusse umile e pia,
    s'è tal, sendo crudel ed orgogliosa.
        Deh! come soffri, Amor, ch'ingiusto sdegno
        turb'i begli occhi, ov'è 'l tuo albergo e 'l regno? —

Fra tanto Carlo ver' le regie mura   8
    vol che la nobil schiera il camin prenda.
Spogliar si vede allor la gran pianura,
    prima di quella e poi di questa tenda,
ed ogni cavalier cui dolce cura
    per dama de la corte il petto accenda,
        pigliare il freno del destrier di quella,
        ma con bel modo pria riporla in sella.

Si reca ancor Rinaldo infra le braccia   9
    Clarice, e la ripon sul palafreno;
ma quella da' bei lumi e da la faccia
    piover rassembra allor sdegno e veleno;
e benché con la lingua immobil taccia,
    è 'l suo tacer d'aspre querele pieno,
        e ciò ch'a lui non vietan le parole,
        negar con gli atti e con gli sguardi vole.

O cruel demon, daughter born of Fear   5[143]
    and Love, daughter who kill your father, you
who hate his noble sweets and who besmear
    with plagues the souls you cling unto,
return to hell, and there remain to hear
    perpetual howls of the infernal crew!
       Ah, cease to vex a flame so pure and chaste,
       which with your ice you now seek to lay waste!

The paladin, who had from first to last   6
    upon his sweet beloved fixed his eye,
saw glints of scorn that over her visage passed
    like bolts of lightning over a troubled sky,
and her displeasure rendered him aghast.
    She seemed affronted, and he knew not why.
       "Alas!" he thought, "What clouds do here advance
       to darken that angelic countenance?

Has the long road that I have come to trace   7
    but led me to my deathbed and a shroud?
For she gives death if, leaving pity and grace,
    she lets such scorn her gentle features cloud,
yeah, death, if she, once so benign of face,
    becomes like this, so cruel and so proud.
       Ah, Love! Will you allow unjust disdain
       to dim those eyes in which you live and reign?"

Great Charles meanwhile bid all his retinue   8
    to make return toward the royal wall.
Throughout the plain there soon faded from view
    first one tent, then another. At last all
the knights who loved their ladies drew
    near them, not waiting for their beck or call,
       to hold their stirrups, grasp their reins and see
       them safely mounted with all courtesy.

Rinaldo, too, extends his hand and tries   9
    to lift fair Clarice to her seat but — lo! —
her once so mild and gracious face and eyes
    rain hatred and with venomous anger glow.
She is silent, but her very silence cries
    disgrace and outrage at some horrid woe.
       Checked by no word of hers as he advances,
       he is checked by silence and her chilling glances.

Rinaldo

Il cavalier, ch'audace in tali imprese 10
   costume innato e cald'amor rendea,
mentre per gli occhi al cor fiammelle accese
   dal caro amato oggetto egli traea,
qual uomo in amar cauto, il tempo prese
   ch'ascosamente a lui già si togliea,
     e mostrando di fuor gli interni affetti,
     sciolse l'accorta lingua in questi detti:

— Ahi! quant'empio è colui ch'ad uom mendico 11
   de le lunghe fatiche il frutto invola!
quanto crudele e di pietà nemico
   chi negli affanni il miser non consola!
Quest'or, signora, a voi piangendo dico,
   perché del mio penar la dolce e sola
     mercè mi si contende, e mi si toglie
     ogni conforto in sì gravose doglie.

L'affanno dunque in lungo error sofferto, 12
   e quanto sol per voi ne l'arme oprai,
avrà per degno e per estremo merto
   sdegno, ch'al cor mi mandi acerbi guai?
sdegno, ch'in questo amaro stato incerto
   de' bei vostri occhi oscuri i dolci rai?
     da' quai prende vigor l'anima stanca,
     ed al duol si sottragge e si rinfranca.

Misero, e qual cagione? — E quivi il corso 13
   volea di sue parole oltre seguire,
ma sua lingua frenò con duro morso
   Clarice allor, così prendendo a dire:
— Diavi nel vostro mal, diavi soccorso
   chi vi diè contra me forza ed ardire,
     il cui volto non sol nel cor portate,
     ma fuor ne l'arme impresso ancor mostrate! —

Tu, fero Amor, tu che gli strai di queste 14
   voci drizzasti al cor del giovinetto,
narra non men l'acerbe piaghe infeste,
   onde tua forte man gli aperse il petto:
ché farle in qualche parte or manifeste
   a la mia musa è disegual soggetto,
     né potrebbe cantando alzarsi al vero,
     ov'alzar tu sol puoi l'altrui pensiero.

Yet undeterred the knight decides to speak,   10
    guided by innate tact and loving fire,
for, though his eyes receive the looks that wreak
    havoc within his heart, though wounded by her,
he, wise in love, somehow grows bold to seek —
    seizing the chance as she is drawing nigher —
        to lay his feelings bare to her and in
        this courteous manner ventures to begin:

"Ah! What a crime to let a beggar feed   11
    on hopes of alms and then refuse all aid!
What cruelty to find a wretch in need
    and pitilessly watch his fortunes fade!
I say this to you, lady, for indeed
    your mercy is all for which I ever prayed,
        and now without relief you let me mourn,
        denied all comfort, unloved and forlorn.

Could all woes that I, wandering long, endured,   12
    and all I did in arms only for you,
in final payment only have procured
    disdain? — disdain for all I dared to do? —
disdain, by which your sweetness is obscured,
    which dims those rays that make my course stay true,
        those rays that let my weary soul grow strong
        and free me from all pain when suffering wrong?

Ah, wretched me! But why?…" He was about   13
    to add more words, when Clarice cut him short,
for she was in no mind to hear him out
    and curbed his tongue with this whispered retort:
"To her whose power and influence you flout
    for aid in your affliction make resort,
        whose face not only in your heart you wear
        but blazon plainly on the arms you bear!"

Do you, who aimed these sharp-edged words, cruel Love,   14
    into the young man's bosom, now make known
with what harsh wounds your strong hand clove
    his breast to cause him boundless moan,
for that's a theme beyond my reach, above
    the strength of inspiration like my own,
        nor could my song rise to the truth, where you
        alone can soar to bring it into view.

Rinaldo

Nel fosco senso de le voci irate   15
    ben tosto penetrò l'accorto amante,
benché fossero fuor quelle mandate
    oscuramente e in suon basso e tremante;
ed a far conta a lei sua lealtate
    già si moveva con umil sembiante,
        ch'era verace testimon del core,
        e certo segno de l'incerto amore.

Ma Clarice, al suo dir la via troncando,   16
    lo schernì, lasso! con astuzia ed arte,
ch'a sé chiamò cortesemente Orlando,
    lo qual da tutti gli altri iva in disparte,
ed a lui di parlar materia dando,
    al suo mesto cugin la tolse in parte;
        da poi, giunti a Parigi, ancor gli tolse
        la dolce vista, ond'ei non men si dolse.

Misero cavaliero, ingiustamente   17
    di Fortuna e d'Amor prova l'offese,
e per l'aura del duol nel petto sente
    gir più crescendo ognor le fiamme accese;
e, qual da poco umore acciar rovente
    più fervido che pria talor si rese,
        tale in lui da piacer fugace e breve,
        l'ardore e 'l duol maggior forza riceve.

Quel sì breve piacer che talor prende   18
    dal caro oggetto e da l'amata vista,
col suo dolce licor via più raccende
    il foco e 'l rio dolor ne l'alma trista:
ché l'un contrario maggior l'altro rende,
    e 'l mal dal ben vigore e forza acquista,
        ch'ove lieve sarebbe, essendo ignoto,
        s'aggrava al paragon col farsi noto.

Sei volte il sol de la fosca ombra scosse   19
    de la gran madre antiqua il duro volto,
ma dal mesto amador già non rimosse
    le tenebre del duolo ond'era involto.
Pur ei sì con Clarice intanto oprosse
    ch'ella amante il tenea fervido molto,
        se non leale, e nel suo casto petto
        già rallentava l'ostinato affetto.

Yet the quick-witted lover by and by   15
    surmised the dark sense of her angry speech,
though uttered softly with a hasty sigh
    and its plain meaning somewhat out of reach.
He therefore set about at once to try
    to prove his loyalty and to beseech
      her faith and grace with a humility
      that showed both love and love's uncertainty.

But Clarice, cutting short his words — alas! —   16
    by an astute pretense quickly withdrew,
calling Orlando to her side, who was
    leaving just then in the king's retinue,
to chat with him about what came to pass,
    and touching his sad cousin's fortune, too.
      In Paris afterwards she kept once more
      aloof, which pained her lover as before.

Poor knight, unjustly tried, you writhe and reel,   17
    while Love and Fortune your true merit spurn!
In your heart, fanned by storms of woe, you feel
    the kindled flame ever more fiercely burn,
and as some drops of water make hot steel
    blazing within a forge yet hotter turn,
      so now sparse drops of joy, fleeting and brief,
      magnify both your ardor and your grief.

The rare and short-lived pleasure that he takes   18
    when her dear countenance comes by chance in view,
though sweet, is fuel to his pain and makes
    the fire of his torment blaze anew,
for a hint of one contrary sometimes wakes
    its opposite. Bliss can make bane ensue.
      A thoughtless woe is lightly borne, but joy
      may bring thoughts that all happiness destroy.

Six times the Sun had chased the gloomy shade   19
    from the great ancient Mother's stony face,
yet could not cause the shades of gloom to fade
    from the lover's soul thus lingering in disgrace,
but meanwhile worked on Clarice's mind and made
    her look at him and see more than a trace
      of ardent, if not loyal, love in him,
      wherefore she grew by slow degrees less grim.

Non però di color conforme il molle   20
   animo veste e 'l placido pensiero:
anzi lo sdegno, che dal petto tolle,
   ripon negli occhi e nel bel viso altero,
onde 'l foco e 'l martir molto s'estolle
   ne l'innocente afflitto cavaliero,
     ch'oltra la scorza non penetra dove
     face in su' aita Amor pietose prove.

Ma fra tanto pomposa e nobil festa   21
   nel suo stesso palagio il re prepara:
la gente tutta a tai diletti desta
   la notte aspetta, e gli è la luce amara;
chiama quella Rinaldo atra e molesta,
   chiama la sera poi lucida e cara.
     Oh stolta de' mortai fallace mente,
     che cieca il suo peggior brama sovente!

Già la notte, stendendo umida l'ali,   22
   gli almi ed eterni fochi in cielo accende,
là donde il bene e 'l mal tra noi mortali
   con varia sorte ognor deriva e scende;
già soave armonia per le reali
   stanze altamente risonar s'intende,
     e concorde a' soavi e dolci accenti
     va misto al cielo il suon degli istromenti.

D'alti guerrier, di donne adorne e belle   23
   il palagio real tosto è ripieno,
e come suol tra le men chiare stelle
   splender Vener e Giove in ciel sereno,
così tra' cavalier, tra le donzelle
   Clarice e 'l suo amator splende non meno;
     e da' bei lumi lor fiammelle aurate
     escon, d'empia dolcezza avvelenate.

Non già Rinaldo ne l'amato viso   24
   pietà vede però del suo martoro,
né ver' lui lampeggiar quel dolce riso
   che gli scopre d'Amor tutto 'l tesoro.
Al fin dispone, ahi! duro infausto aviso,
   ch'Alda componga le discordie loro:
     Alda la bella invitar vole a danza,
     poi c'ha locato in lei la sua speranza.

But still she hesitates and deems it best   20
   not to relent forthwith, but to advance
the scorn that she has banished from her breast
   once more into her eyes and countenance,
wherefore the knight's mind is the more oppressed
   by a sense of searing torment and mischance,
      nor penetrates beneath the surface where
      Love favors him but plots more grief and care.

Meanwhile the king ordains that his great hall   21
   be readied for a great feast held by night.
Impatient for that splendid night, soon all
   his subjects wish for day to fade from sight.
Rinaldo in his turn feels moved to call
   day dark and foul and nightfall dear and bright.
      Ah! foolish and deluded human mind,
      drawn to the worse, to better Fortune blind!

Already night, spreading her dewy wings,   22
   lights the eternal torches in the sky
from which all good and all ill-fortuned things
   derive for us who live below and die.
Already through the royal halls, the strings
   of tuneful lutes and viols commence to ply
      their mingled harmonies with dulcet sound,
      which mounts to heaven while echoing all around.

Anon the royal hall is crowded by   23
   a host of fair maids and proud cavaliers,
and as among the lesser stars on high
   Venus and Jupiter blaze from their spheres,
so Clarice and her lover draw the eye
   of everyone who in that press appears.
      She smiles, and in her golden glances
      a dangerous and envenomed sweetness dances.

Rinaldo, gazing at her face, can see   24
   no pity in it for his pain. He knows
that surely it is not for him that she
   puts on that smile in which Love's treasure glows.
At last — ah, hapless plan! — in Alda he
   decides to place his hope and therefore goes
      to ask her for a dance: an act — alas! —
      by which yet harsher discord came to pass.

Egli costei con puro zelo amava,⁣⁣⁣ 25
  ed era amato con eguale affetto,
perché quando altre volte in corte stava,
  con lei nudrito fu da fanciulletto.
Sapeva poi ch'apriva ella e serrava
  di Clarice a sua voglia il duro petto
    e con bei modi e con parlar soave
    dolcemente di quel volgea la chiave.

Ver' lei dunque si mosse e le richiese⁣⁣⁣ 26
  di ballar seco, ed ella era a ciò presta;
ma fu dal forte Anselmo il Maganzese
  nel punto istesso a danza ancor richiesta.
Alda, che 'l doppio invito a un tempo intese,
  chinò a terra lo sguardo e l'aurea testa,
    né quel né questo col parlar ricusa,
    ma tacendo si sta dubbia e confusa.

Vedendo Anselmo ciò, l'altera fronte⁣⁣⁣ 27
  ed insiem'il parlar ver' l'altro torse:
— Cedi, garzon: se non, da' gridi a l'onte,
  e da l'onte s'andrà più inanzi forse. —
Non men altero quel di Chiaramonte
  a lui tai detti rispondendo porse:
    — Cedi pur tu: se non, verrassi tosto
    più oltre ancor, ch'io già ne son disposto. —

Anselmo, folgorando il torvo sguardo,⁣⁣⁣ 28
  ad aspro riso allor la bocca mosse,
e disse: — Se tanto osa un vil bastardo,
  che poi farebbe se mio pari ei fosse? —
Or ben tal detto fu pungente dardo
  ch'al nobil giovanetto il cor percosse:
    come leon ferito in ira salse,
    e 'l suo sdegno frenar punto non valse.

Con la sinistra mano al collo stringe⁣⁣⁣ 29
  quel superbo, e 'l trar fiato a lui contende,
e con l'altra il pugnal di punta spinge,
  e trapassando il petto il cuor gli offende.
Di rosseggiante smalto il suol dipinge
  tiepido rio che da la piaga scende,
    e col sangue esce ancor lo spirto insieme,
    sì che 'l corpo cadendo il terren preme.

His love for her was pure and innocent, 25
    and she with blameless candor loved him too,
for he, while still a boy, when first he went
    to Charles' court, had found her kind and true.
Knowing her nature, he felt confident
    her gentleness would soon gain access to
        Clarice's stony heart and turn its key
        to let Love in and banish Cruelty.

So thinking he approached her to request 26
    a dance, and she was following where he led,
when mighty Anselm of Maganza pressed
    between and claimed the dance with her instead.
Fair Alda blushed and, puzzled and distressed
    by the twin offer, bowed her golden head
        nor gave assent to either nor refused,
        but stood in silence, doubtful and confused.

At this, proud Anselm fixes haughty eyes 27
    upon his rival and thus speaks his mind:
"Leave off, Sir boy. If not, your coward cries
    will soon be heard, and worse may come behind!"
But he of Clairmont instantly replies
    in accents of no less defiant kind:
        "Leave off yourself, or else you'll quickly learn
        what follows when a man like me you spurn."

Anselm then, glowering grim as the abyss, 28
    his grimace twisted in a bitter leer,
replies, "Though a vile bastard speaks like this,
    what could he do to me, were he my peer?"
These words like sharp and poisoned arrows hiss
    and pierce the youth's heart as they piece his ear.
        He, like a wounded lion, eyes afire,
        leaps up, and nothing now can check his ire.

Seizing his foe's throat with his left hand, he 29
    choked off his breath and made his right hand guide
his dagger to his heart, and instantly
    a gaping breach was opened in his side
from which a stream gushed, horrible to see
    that all the ground with red enamel dyed.
        And with his blood, his spirit issued forth
        even as his falling body struck the earth.

Rinaldo

Come sanguigno in giù cader tremando
   il maganzese cavalier fu visto,
intorno per la sala ir risonando
   strepito udissi di più voci misto,
qual fremer s'ode ancor negli alvei, quando
   le pecchie infesta morbo orrido e tristo;
     e qual ne' boschi, allor ch'in lor serrati
     spiran d'Austro e di Coro i primi fiati.
30

Si vider lampeggiar mille lucenti
   ferri in quel punto ancor, qual fuochi accesi,
e quinci correr d'alta rabbia ardenti
   contra Rinaldo Gano e gli altri offesi;
e quindi poscia al suo soccorso intenti
   i suoi fratelli opporsi a' Maganzesi,
     e col fior de' guerrier di Chiaramonte
     l'invitto cavalier ch'uccise Almonte.
31

Le pavide donzelle i bei colori
   smarriro, oppresse da la fredda tema,
come soglion talor vermigli fiori
   s'avien che troppo giel gli asconda e prema.
Pallide i volti e palpitanti i cori,
   quelle col piede, che mal fermo trema,
     si ristrinsero intorno a la regina,
     quale in porto dal mar fragil carina.
32

Carlo, tutto di sdegno acceso in volto,
   altri tiene e riprende, altri minaccia,
e di spegner in lor l'orgoglio stolto
   con gli atti e col parlar tenta e procaccia.
Ma Rinaldo, col manto al braccio avolto,
   con tardi passi e con sicura faccia,
     verso la porta il piè va ritirando,
     e tiene nella destra ignudo il brando.
33

I Maganzesi, che sì audaci in prima
   gli erano adosso corsi a fargli offesa,
come vider risorti oltre ogni stima
   tanti feri campioni in sua diffesa,
l'ira frenaro e quella furia prima,
   pentiti omai di sì dubbiosa impresa;
     pur col mover de l'armi e con le voci
     si mostravan da lunge assai feroci:
34

When the Maganzan knight was seen to fall   32
   covered with gore and quivering on the ground,
among the nobles in the crowded hall
   half-stifled gasps and groans passed all around,
as, when alarmed, a swarm of bees makes all
   the hive with an increasing buzz resound,
      or as, when Auster and Corus lash the leaves
      a forest thicket rustles, moans and heaves.

A thousand blades, like fires newly lit,   31
   rose high aloft then, flashing in the air,
as Ganelon and his kinsmen in a fit
   of sudden anger rushed Rinaldo there,
whose brothers[144] saw the fray and joined in it,
   ready to fight Maganzans anywhere
      while on the Clairmont side, prepared to fight,
      stood Almont's slayer,[145] undefeated knight.

On the fair ladies' cheeks the ruddy glow   32
   yields to chill fear and is no longer seen,
as when, weighed down by crusts of frost or snow,
   fair crimson blossoms droop and lose their sheen.
With faces pale and throbbing hearts they go
   in trembling haste to huddle round their queen
      like fragile boats that to a sheltering port
      from perils of the open sea resort.

King Charlemagne, wrath flaming in his face   33
   at the scene of violence that greets his sight,
restrains some, threatens others with disgrace
   and seeks by word and deed to stem the fight.
Meanwhile Rinaldo, with deliberate pace,
   his cloak wrapped round his left hand and his right
      gripping his naked sword, defies all hate
      and slowly inches backward toward the gate.

The Maganzans, who at first had been so bold   34
   to rush upon him, in the meantime found
reasons for pause when they came to behold
   so many dangerous champions ring him round.
Misgiving chilled their courage and controlled
   their rage, until they started to give ground,
      though they still made their shouts and weapons jar
      fiercely enough while threatening from afar.

così di can timido stuol sovente,　　　　　　　　　　35
　　ch'incontra 'l toro, arda di sdegno e d'ira;
corre per assalirlo e poi si pente,
　　e latrando lo sguarda e si ritira,
mentre in feroce aspetto alteramente
　　quel move i passi e gli occhi intorno gira;
　　　　e dov'ei volge il tardo e grave piede,
　　　　la vile schiera paventando cede.

Poté salvo ed illeso a la sua stanza　　　　　　　36
　　dai nemici ritrarsi il giovinetto,
ma 'l suo soverchio ardire e la baldanza
　　lascia di sdegno a Carlo acceso il petto:
troppo, troppo gli pare alta arroganza
　　ch'abbia tanto oltre usato al suo cospetto,
　　　　sì che, di Gan seguendo il rio consiglio,
　　　　di Francia al fin gli diè perpetuo essiglio.

Or che far deve l'infelice amante,　　　　　　　　37
　　non al suo re, non a sua donna grato?
Partirà dunque, e 'l dolce almo sembiante,
　　ond'egli vive, a lui sarà celato?
Ahi! Fortuna crudel, per quante e quante
　　fatiche a sì rio fin l'hai tu guidato:
　　　　quand'ei trovar credea breve conforto,
　　　　l'hai con un colpo sol trafitto e morto.

La carta ei prende e ciò ch'Amor gli ditta　　　　38
　　scrive a l'amata in umil note espresso;
poi che la lettra ebbe composta e scritta,
　　la manda a lei per un secreto messo.
Ma colei l'un minaccia e l'altra gitta,
　　crudel forzando il suo volere istesso:
　　　　gelosia n'è cagion, che 'l cor ripieno
　　　　un'altra volta l'ha del suo veleno.

L'aver dianzi veduto Alda la bella　　　　　　　　39
　　dal cavaliero a se stessa preporre,
quando ei voleva in sua presenza quella
　　prima di tutte l'altre a danza tôrre,
e che per non lassar poi la donzella
　　volse più tosto Anselmo a morte porre,
　　　　l'era a l'acceso innamorato core,
　　　　lassa! nova cagion d'alto timore.

So sometimes will a pack of dogs who meet   35
    a great bull fling against him in their ire,
but then turn tail when his horned temples greet
    their sight and force them, yelping, to retire,
while he moves on ferociously, his feet
    stamping the dust, his threatening eyes afire.
        And every time he turns his bulk, the pack
        of coward mongrels scatters and falls back.

The youth soon reached his chamber, hale of limb,   36
    and in no peril from the enemy,
but meanwhile Charlemagne's bosom seethed with grim
    anger, to whom his outburst seemed to be
beyond the pale, a bold affront to him,
    breach of the peace in plain sight. Therefore he,
        prompted by Ganelon, pronounced this stern
        verdict: "Leave France and nevermore return."

What now should the unhappy lover do,   37
    made outlaw by his king and in disgrace
with his dear lady? Must he leave her who
    means life for him and never see her face?
Ah, cruel Fate, you've chased him long! Do you
    now chase him from his only resting place?
        He looked to find brief solace in his woe,
        and you've transfixed him with a single blow.

Upon a snatched-up sheet he writes to say   38
    what Love dictates, humbly and ardently,
then bids a trusty messenger convey
    the letter to her hands in secrecy,
but she rebukes the one and throws away
    the other with self-wounding cruelty.
        Jealousy made her do so, which once more
        filled all her heart with poison as before.

For having earlier seen her knight prefer   39
    fair Alda to herself and struck with shame
when in her presence he requested her
    to dance and not some other, lesser dame,
and seeing him afterwards meet Anselm's slur
    with mortal blows rather than quit his claim,
        she now — alas! — felt novel grounds for fear
        in her deluded, lovesick heart appear.

Tra sé dicea: — Deh! come ascondi il vero   *40*
  con umil voce, e dimandar mercede?
Ahi crudo, ahi disleale, ahi lusinghiero,
  dunque ciò merta la mia pura fede?
Dunque così s'inganna un cor sincero?
  Ben stolta ed infelice è chi ti crede:
    ma chi non crederebbe a que' sospiri
    ed a quel volger gli occhi in dolci giri?

Amo, tu dici a me con l'occhio, ed ardo,   *41*
  con l'occhio ch'è in amar mal fido duce.
Misera! io 'l credo, ma 'l soave sguardo
  d'Alda la bella ad arder ti conduce.
Deh! benché spesso al discoprir sia tardo,
  fuor l'affetto de l'alma al fin traluce;
    e s'a' guardi, al parlar non ben risponde,
    più chiaro appar quant'al fin più s'asconde. —

Sospeso il paladin fra tanto attende   *42*
  il messo ch'a Clarice avea mandato;
ma quel tornando a lui di nova offende
  e profonda ferita il cor piagato.
Com'il meschin l'empia risposta intende,
  riman tra vivo e morto in dubbio stato:
    non parla o piange, e non sospira, e tolto
    have ogni varco al duol ch'è dentro accolto.

Qual suole spesso chiuso umor fervente   *43*
  in cavo rame a cui sott'arda il foco,
con rauco suon, con gorgogliar frequente
  girsi sempre avanzando a poco a poco,
poi con impeto ratto e violente
  versarsi, uscendo da l'angusto loco:
    tal versossi in lamenti il rio dolore,
    di cui non era più capace il core.

Accolto ne' lamenti e ne' sospiri   *44*
  fuor esce il duolo, e 'l cor si sfoga intanto;
ma quando sotto il fascio de' martiri
  poté al fin l'alma respirare alquanto,
facendo dura forza ai suoi desiri,
  Rinaldo, ogni indugiar posto da canto,
    solo ed armato sul cavallo ascese;
    indi, a ventura errando, il camin prese.

Within herself she cried out:"Do you hide   40
 the truth in humble words, yet sue for grace?
Ah, cruel man, ah, flatterer! How you lied!
 Does my pure faith merit return so base?
Do you in breaking of true hearts take pride?
 A wretched fool is she who trusts your face —
  yet who is there that would not trust those sighs
  and the sweet motion of those pleading eyes?

Those eyes protest,'I love! I burn!' I know   41
 eyes are suspicious guides in love, and yet
wretch that I am, I trust them, though
 they burn for Alda. Ah! Do not forget
that love, though its discovery may be slow,
 shines in the end through every ruse or let,
  and when the eye speaks louder than the tongue,
  pretense at last must fail, however strong."

Meanwhile the paladin waits in suspense   42
 for his messenger to Clarice to return,
and as he sees him coming, doubt torments
 his mind, but when at last he comes to learn
of her response, he feels all outward sense
 freeze while his inward senses reel and churn.
  He does not speak, nor weep, nor sigh, denied
  all outlets for the grief pent up inside.

But even as, boiling in a copper pot   43
 above a white-hot flame, a liquid will
bubble and gurgle as it grows more hot
 and start to churn, then churn more strongly still,
until it makes a seething spurt or clot
 from out its narrow confines gush and spill,
  so from his lips laments in torrents pour
  at last, though dammed up in his heart before.

His grief pours out in floods of sighs and wails   44
 unburdening his heart, and as the weight
of torment lifts, his spirit no longer fails,
 and his exhausted powers resuscitate.
Desire once bridled, a calmer mood prevails,
 and Rinaldo, uninclined to stay or wait,
  arms, mounts his steed alone at break of day,
  and, choosing paths at random, rides way.

Rinaldo

Mentre d'ogni piacere ignudo e casso 45
   camina il cavalier muto e pensoso,
giunge ove Sena il fondo ha via men basso,
   e con piè corre al mar più strepitoso.
Quivi ei raffrena il suo veloce passo
   e 'l collo sgrava de lo scudo odioso;
      dal collo il cavalier lo scudo tolse,
      e 'l guardo e le parole in lui rivolse:

— O nemico crudel d'ogni mio bene, 46
   o turbator del mio stato giocondo,
scudo infausto, infelice, onde mi viene
   l'aspro martir ch'a nullo oggi è secondo:
tu, ch'al cor mi recasti acerbe pene,
   tu quelle porta or teco insieme al fondo;
      ma lasso! tu n'andrai nel fiume or solo,
      ché da me separar non puossi il duolo.

Vattene, e quivi omai t'ascondi altrui, 47
   quivi ti copri infame odiosa peste;
onde, com'io da te, crudel, già fui,
   così altro amante offeso ancor non reste. —
Qui tacendo diè fine a' detti sui,
   e quei seguir le man veloci e preste;
      frangesi l'onda, e giù se 'n cala ratto
      lo scudo al fondo, dal suo peso tratto.

Quinci Rinaldo poi si parte e piglia 48
   altro camin, né sa dov'ei si vada,
e mentre ch'otto volte in ciel vermiglia
   l'Aurora apparse, candida rugiada
versando dai crin d'oro e da le ciglia,
   errò per varia e per incerta strada;
      al fin vide il dì nono ombrosa valle
      a cui si gia per dritto e piano calle.

Quivi era un uom d'assai strana figura, 49
   che sostegno del braccio al mento fèa,
e con sembianza tenebrosa e scura
   gli occhi pregni di pianto al ciel volgea.
In ogni atto di lui gravosa cura
   e duol profondo impresso si vedea;
      la bocca apriva e queruli lamenti
      quindi spargeva in dolorosi accenti.

While, lost in thought and bowed by silent pain,   45
   the knight rides swiftly westward, he
arrives where in a shallower bed the Seine
   with noisier wavelets rushes toward the sea.
There, slowing his speed, the paladin draws rein,
   dismounts, casts down his shield impulsively —
      that hateful shield — and looks at it and sighs
      and bitterly invokes it in this wise:

"O cruel enemy of all my joy!   46
   O fell disturber of my blessed state!
O shield ill-omened, fated to destroy,
   all hope through undeserved, unheard-of hate!
Oh that you, who with grief my heart annoy,
   could take grief with you where hell's waters wait.
      But you — alas! — must drown alone, for no
      power on earth can part me from my woe.

Away with you! Down to the depths! There hide,   47
   the hateful infamy you caused. There stay,
lest others shall so cruelly be tried
   as I once was by you some other day!"
His tongue ceased, and his ready hands supplied
   the consequence in action straight away.
      The wave was broken by the shield in flight,
      which, drawn by its weight, sank swiftly out of sight.

Rinaldo quits the shore and sadly makes   48
   his way elsewhere, not caring whitherto.
He keeps on wandering while Aurora shakes
   eight times out of her golden locks the dew
in skies that blush vermilion. He forsakes
   all trodden roads for paths untried and new,
      and on the ninth day spies a gloomy vale
      and makes his way there by a level trail.

Within that vale a man[146] of aspect grim   49
   with chin on hand is sitting all alone.
Immersed in gloom, he raises eyes that brim
   with tears to heaven, making endless moan.
His every act and utterance shows in him
   a mind by dire misfortune overthrown,
      and from his open mouth his sorrow streams
      in sobs and whimpers and half-stifled screams.

Quanto a la valle ria più s'avicina   50
    il cavalier, più cresce in lui la pena,
tal ch'oppressa dal duol l'alma meschina
    reggersi e respirar puote a gran pena;
ma pur senza arrestarsi egli camina
    per l'ampia strada che là dritto il mena,
        sin che, giunto a quell'uomo, in lui mirando
        sente il martir nel petto irsi avanzando.

Giace la valle tra duo monti ascosa,   51
    da' quali orribil ombra in lei deriva;
l'aria ivi 'l giorno appar sì tenebrosa,
    sì colma di squallor, di gaudio priva,
com'altrov'esser suol quando nascosa
    Febo tien la sua luce ardente e viva;
        la terra ancor di spoglie atre e funeste
        la fronte e 'l tergo suo ricopre e veste.

Sorgon con fosche e velenose fronde   52
    quivi piante d'ignota orrida forma,
ed in quelle s'annida e si nasconde
    di neri infausti augelli odiosa torma,
e l'un stridendo a l'altro ognor risponde
    con suon ch'a luogo tal ben si conforma:
        quel noioso a ferir va l'altrui core,
        sì che ben par la valle del dolore.

Rinaldo com'ivi entro ha posto il piede,   53
    sente che quasi il cor per duol gli scoppia,
sì che discende dal cavallo e siede,
    traendo fuor sospiri a coppia a coppia.
Dovunque volge i torbidi occhi ei vede
    cosa ch'il grav'affanno in lui raddoppia;
        mai non può rimirar lunge o dappresso
        ch'il duol non veggia in vera forma espresso.

— Lasso!, diceva, io luogo ho pur trovato   54
    ove dorrommi ognor meco a bastanza;
ahi quanto, ahi quanto al mio penoso stato
    conviensi quest'oscura orrida stanza!
Io qui vivrò, ché così vole il Fato,
    lo spazio che di vita ancor m'avanza:
        qui de' corbi morrò preda infelice,
        sol per amarti troppo, empia Clarice! —

Now as the knight approached that grisly dell   50
     he sensed his own soul's agonies increase,
until his grief seemed too immense to tell,
     and he could scarce draw breath. All hope of peace
seemed lost, yet, as if drawn on by a spell,
     he followed the wide road and did not cease
         until he reached that man and, seeing his woe,
         felt yet more torment in his own breast grow.

Two towering peaks that loom on either side   51
     plunge that deep valley in perpetual shade,
so that it seems more gloomy at noontide,
     more joyless and more drearily arrayed
than when at dusk Apollo's beacons hide
     from mortal eyes and cause all light to fade.
         Upon the dismal hillsides all around,
         the earth with graveyard spoils attires the ground.

There plants of nameless kinds and horrid shape   52
     lift their envenomed twigs in twisted prongs
in which there nest, with loathsome beaks agape,
     black and ill-omened birds in countless throngs,
and the hoarse shrieks that from their craws escape,
     well suited to the place, fill it with songs
         that pierce the heart of anyone who hears,
         so that it verily seems a Vale of Tears.

Rinaldo setting foot there feels as though   53
     his heart stopped beating for excess of pain,
and he dismounts, and sitting down below
     a tree, he sighs and sighs and sighs again.
Wherever he casts his tearful glances, woe
     is mirrored back and chills his every vein.
         However near or far he looks, he sees
         true images of grief's extremities.

"Ah!" said he, "I at last have found a place   54
     where all things woeful like myself appear.
How well — alas! — how well these tracts retrace
     the bleakness in my soul, so dark and drear!
Here shall I live, while Fortune makes me face
     the dregs of life still left in me, and here
         I'll die — cruel Clarice! — prey to crows, forlorn,
         because my too-great love has earned your scorn."

Tutto quel giorno e tutta notte ancora   55
    spese il mesto guerriero in tai lamenti,
apparendogli innanzi ad ora ad ora
    varie forme d'orrori e di spaventi;
ma quando ai rai de la vermiglia aurora
    si dileguaro l'umid'ombre algenti,
        un cavalier da presso armato scorse,
        ch'a Baiardo la man nel freno porse,

dicendo: — Or meco vien, ché 'l tuo signore   56
    pur troppo indegno è di sì bon destriero,
poiché soggiace al senso ed al dolore
    qual donna vil non già qual cavaliero. —
Così parlando, da la valle fuore
    ratto il menò l'incognito straniero,
        onde ver' lui Rinaldo irato mosse,
        bench'in grave dolor immerso fosse.

Non avrebbe però potuto mai   57
    tenerli dietro per la valle oscura,
non potendo anco con la vista omai
    penetrar molto di quell'aria impura;
ma quel così fulgenti e chiari rai
    spargea fuor de la lucid'armatura,
        che n'eran l'ombre in parte scosse e rotte,
        ed illustrata la profonda notte.

Rinaldo per sentier ch'alluma e pinge   58
    lo splendor che da l'armi ardendo uscia,
velocissimo il passo affretta e spinge,
    non mai torcendo da la dritta via;
sì che dal luogo uscio ch'intorno cinge
    e sovr'ammanta nube oscura e ria,
        ed in questa sentì de l'aspra salma
        discarca alquanto sollevarsi l'alma.

Fermossi allor quell'uom di luce adorno   59
    che così presto a lui volgea le spalle,
e disse: — Il destrier togli, e più ritorno
    non far ne la dogliosa infausta valle;
vanne a man destra, ch'a miglior soggiorno
    tosto ti condurrà quest'erto calle. —
        Indi per quello stesso a gir si pose,
        sì che ratto a sua vista ei si nascose.

All day and all the following night he spent 55
    lamenting in this pitiable wise,
while hour after tedious hour sent
    visions of dole and dread to greet his eyes,
but when the next night's veil of damp was rent,
    and the vermilion dawn began to rise,
        an armed knight, seizing Bayard's bridle, led
        the horse away and, as he did so, said:

"Come with me, since to such a worthy steed 56
    as you your master now has lost all right,
for he lets passion and brief sorrow lead
    him on, like some weak girl, not like a knight."
This said, he with the horse behind made speed
    to quit the vale and vanished out of sight,
        wherefore Rinaldo, though sunk in his mood
        of woe, was moved to anger and pursued.

However, he could not have found a way 57
    to keep behind him in the valley's gloom,
where impure murk — for it was not yet day —
    lay heavy as the haze within a tomb,
had not at times a swift uncanny ray
    from the stranger's armor glinted to illume
        the path and parted shadows here and there,
        sketching his fleeing outline on the air.

Led by that armor, which by magic force 58
    shimmered before his eager sight and glowed,
Rinaldo hastened after man and horse,
    but never left the straight and narrow road,
and as he thus continued on his course
    away from his malignant last abode,
        he felt his soul somewhat resuscitate,
        unburdened of its grim and corpse-like state.

At last that armored man adorned with light, 59
    who had so swiftly fled from him, stood still
and said: "Take back your horse. Keep up your flight
    away from those abysmal depths that kill.
To find a better dwelling-place, turn right
    and take the narrow path to yonder hill."
        And, handing over Bayard's reins, anon
        he turned about and in a flash was gone.

Rinaldo

Per lo sentier Rinaldo i passi move 60
   ch'avea tenuto il cavalier estrano,
e 'l vede ognor più di bellezze nove
   vago e adorno, e più facile e piano;
speme ed ardir fra tanto infonde e piove
   ne lo suo cor benigna ignota mano.
      Giunse alla fine a piè d'un picciol colle,
      ch'il verdeggiante capo a l'aura estolle.

Da quel scendea con piè distorto e lento 61
   lucido e cheto rio tra l'erbe e i fiori,
ed ogni occhio rendea lieto e contento
   con le bellezze sue, co' suoi tesori.
D'oro l'arene, i pesci avea d'argento,
   le sponde adorne de' più bei colori,
      e col soave suon de' suoi cristalli
      parea ch'altri invitasse a dolci balli.

Rinaldo a l'alto, ov'il piacer l'alletta, 62
   il passo indrizza, dal desir sospinto,
e vede il suol di viva e fresca erbetta
   colmo, e di fiori poi sparso e distinto;
oltra ciò da vaghissima selvetta
   intorno intorno coronato e cinto:
      sì verde è l'erba e sì la selva è verde,
      ch'ogni color vi si smarisce e perde.

L'aria d'almo candor quivi si veste, 63
   raccesa già da' lieti rai novelli,
ed or su quelle frondi ed or su queste
   forman dolce armonia dipinti augelli:
sì che rapito dal cantar celeste
   oblia Rinaldo i pensieri egri e felli,
      e la speme e l'ardire ognor ravviva
      grazia che largamente in lui deriva.

Mentre di sì gioconda e sì gradita 64
   vista cibava gli occhi il cavaliero,
e quindi egli porgeva a l'alma aita,
   e rischiarava il torbido pensiero,
donna vi scorse che se 'n gia vestita
   di verde, e sovra 'l colle aveva impero:
      tien quella i lumi e 'l volto al ciel supino,
      quasi attenda di là favor divino.

Rinaldo in glad haste sets out to go   60
    toward that hill. Upon the grassy floor
each glance shows some new blossom's lovely glow.
    Each step seems easier than the one before.
He feels, instilled by unseen hands, the flow
    of hope and daring in his heart once more.
        At last, reaching a gentle slope, he sees
        the hill lift up its green head to the breeze.

From it, a limpid stream makes its descent,   61
    meandering peacefully through flowers and grass,
and every eye is filled with sweet content
    that sees its crystal waves in triumph pass
over sands of gold, with fish of silver pent
    in the clear depths like jewels under glass.
        The tuneful murmuring of that stream's advance
        seems like the summons to some joyous dance.

Rinaldo to the summit makes his way,   62
    where pleasure seems to wait for him, and sees
a plain covered by verdure fresh as May
    and strewn with flowers dancing in the breeze
and in the distance ringed round by a gay
    copse of far-branching, newly-budding trees.
        Green grass, green woods — a green world
        greets his view,
    all colors else here hide or lose their hue.

A gentle, balmy breeze springs up among   63
    the sunlit boughs and moves from tree to tree,
while, flitting here and there, a lively throng
    of brightly colored birds makes melody.
Rinaldo, ravished by their heavenly song,
    forgets all thoughts of former misery,
        feeling that music with each note impart
        new hope and courage in his grateful heart.

While thus the knight allowed his eyes to feast   64
    upon the charms of this enchanting scene
by which his soul was solaced and released
    from all dark thoughts, he saw, arrayed in green,
a lady walking towards him from the East
    who of that shining hill was sovereign queen.
        And as she walked, she turned her eyes and face
        on high like one who trusts in heaven's grace.

Rinaldo

È serena, ridente e lieta in vista,   65
    e nel tacere espresse ha le parole;
mostrano alta baldanza a speme mista
    gli occhi ch'apron lucenti un novo sole;
ed indi fugge ogni cura egra e trista,
    come da Febo ancor la nebbia suole.
      Rinaldo, in lei mirando, al cor profondo
      manda per larga via piacer giocondo.

Ei fa varii pensieri, e già gli sembra   66
    d'aver Clarice in suo poter ridutto,
e già ne le leggiadre amate membra
    raccôr di sua fatica il caro frutto;
e se pur tra sé volge e si rimembra
    il colei sdegno, a lui cagion di lutto,
      contempra in parte la presente noia
      con la futura imaginata gioia.

Poi ch'appagati ha gli occhi, egli non meno   67
    la fame appaga, e 'l corpo ciba e pasce
di quel che dal fecondo almo terreno
    sovra i vaghi arboscei produtto nasce;
e del dolce ruscel gustando a pieno
    fa che l'arida sete in tutto il lasce.
      L'orecchie a lui percosse intanto sono
      da strepitoso d'arme orribil suono.

Affamato leon, che l'unghie e i denti   68
    insanguinato già più dì non s'abbia,
s'ode il muggito de' cornuti armenti,
    desta nel fero cuor desire e rabbia;
fiamma riversa da' torvi occhi ardenti,
    fumo dal naso e spuma da le labbia;
      batte la coda e 'l folto crin rabbuffa,
      e lieto corre a sanguinosa zuffa:

così al fero rimbombo appar focoso   69
    Rinaldo in volto, e 'l cor move e raccende,
ch'avido di pugnar, l'ozio e 'l riposo
    già lungo troppo a noia e sdegno prende;
senza punto tardar, sul poderoso
    destrier saltando leggiermente ascende,
      e là donde quel suono a lui ne viene,
      volge il cavallo e dritto il corso tiene.

She smiled, serene and gay of countenance. 65
 She did not speak, but —oh! — her silence spoke.
Hope mixed with noble boldness from each glance
 of her kind eyes like dawning sunlight broke.
Care fled from them and Terror of mischance,
 as Night flees Phoebus wrapped in her black cloak.
  Rinaldo gazed and, cheered beyond all measure,
  felt summoned to a path to boundless pleasure.

Cheered by a thousand happy thoughts, he dreams 66
 that he has Clarice once more in his power
and in her arms, after his long toil, seems
 to pluck already the much-longed-for flower,
and even when he thinks of the extremes
 of woe her wrath once caused him hour by hour,
  he tempers memories that his heart annoy
  with thoughts of an imagined future joy.

Having fed his eyes, he senses he must feed 67
 his body too and so finds fruit to still
its hunger, which, as if to meet his need,
 hangs from each branch upon that bounteous hill.
He then drinks from that clear stream and is freed
 at once of parching thirst by its sweet chill.
  Anon he hears rough voices shout and cry,
  and weapons clash with thunderous noise nearby.

Even as a starving lion who has not 67
 bloodied his claws and teeth for many a day
will summon rage and freeze upon the spot,
 hearing a horned herd low not far away,
and then, with reeking maw and eyes blood-shot
 and foam-flecked lips, rush forth to seize his prey.
  Tail lashing and mane bristling, with a roar
  he leaps, intent to stain the ground with gore.

So now Rinaldo at that fierce noise feels 69
 his face aglow and his great heart aflame,
eager for war, while over his spirit steals
 at his too-long repose a sense of shame.
He mounts at once and on his charger wheels
 in the direction whence the hubbub came
  and at a gallop, never changing course,
  toward the sound of battle spurs his horse.

Vide, disceso al basso, ad aspra guerra   70
     star un sol cavalier con molti armati,
ch'otto di lor n'avea già posti a terra,
     altri del tutto morti, altri piagati.
Ahi! come destro ei si rinchiude e serra
     sotto lo scudo ai color colpi irati;
         come possente poi, come feroce
         fulmina orribilmente il ferro atroce!

Or tutt'alzato sovra un gran fendente   71
     disnoda il braccio con destrezza e possa;
di punta or vibra il brando suo tagliente,
     e col corpo accompagna la percossa.
Rinaldo in lui stupisce, e l'alma sente
     da novo amor verso 'l guerrier commossa,
         ché la virtù non sol ne' fidi amici,
         ma s'ama negli ignoti e ne' nemici.

Disponsi al fine, e con gran cor s'accinge   72
     a dare al franco cavalier soccorso:
cogli sproni Baiardo al fianco stringe,
     ed a l'impeto suo rallenta il morso.
Quel, come stral cui curvo acciar sospinge,
     move il piè ratto a furioso corso,
         e tra' nemici va con quel furore
         che tra' minori augei rapace astore.

Rinaldo il ferro sin al mento pose   73
     tra lo spazio che parte ambe le ciglia;
al primo ed al secondo entro, ascose
     nel ventre, là dov'il nutrir s'appiglia:
caggiono ambo color qual piante annose,
     e fan la terra nel cader vermiglia.
         Non qui Rinaldo la sua furia affrena,
         ma passa inanzi e costor guarda a pena.

Era quivi fra gli altri un giovanetto   74
     che di peli disgombra avea la guancia.
Questi, vedendo che dannoso effetto
     fèa ne' compagni il cavalier di Francia,
di generoso sdegno armato il petto
     sopra gli va con l'arrestata lancia,
         e con immenso ardir lo preme e 'ncalza,
         e 'l fiere a punto ov'il cimier s'inalza.

He sees, after descending from the height, 70
    a single knight attacked by many foes.
Already eight of them, felled by his might,
    lie wounded at his feet or in death's throes.
And — ah! — how nimbly, as the rest unite,
    he ducks behind his shield to ward their blows,
        and then how dreadfully against their rout
        with flashing, lethal blade he sallies out!

Now rising high with a great swashing blow, 71
    he severs one man's arm with skill and force,
now with his blade's point quickly thrusts below
    and with his body's weight follows its course.
Amazed, Rinaldo feels his whole heart glow
    with love for him, for virtue is a source
        of love not just for a true friend or peer,
        but for a stranger or a foe we fear.

At last he in his generous heart decides 72
    that aid to such a brave knight is most fit.
He digs his spurs into good Bayard's sides
    and for a sudden charge leaves loose the bit,
who, like a dart that curved steel drives, with strides
    as swift as lightning galloped and alit
        with as much force and fury among the foes
        as a rapacious goshawk among crows.

Rinaldo lifts his lance-guard to his chin 73
    and keeps the steel point level with his eyes.
It pierces one man, then one more, thrust in
    their entrails where the nurturing stomach lies.
Both slump like grass beneath the scythe and spin
    out of their saddles, nevermore to rise.
        Rinaldo does not check his furious way
        but, with no look at them, rejoins the fray.

Among the rest, behold a youth advance 74
    with rosy cheeks not yet adorned with hair
who, seeing the havoc that the knight of France
    was wreaking on his comrades gathered there,
took heart to face his wrath. Placing his lance
    in rest, he charged. His challenge rent the air.
        His daring was immense, and the sharp point
        hit his foe's gorget[147] at its topmost joint.

Rompe la lancia, e non trapassa il duro 75
    ferro ch'asconde l'onorata testa;
pur sotto l'elmo il paladin securo
    sente il furor de la percossa infesta,
onde con fero cor, con volto oscuro,
    con mano a la vendetta ardita e presta,
        spinge una punta e poi segue la spada
        col corpo, onde più forte a ferir vada.

Giunge a lo scudo e 'l rompe, e pur coperto 76
    è sette volte da villoso tergo;
rompe non men, bench'egli sia conserto
    di spesse ferree lame, il forte usbergo.
È dal ferro crudele il petto aperto,
    e quel si mostra sanguinoso a tergo:
        cade il garzon su la ferita, e afferra
        co' denti e morde l'inimica terra.

Forma fra tanto pur queste parole 77
    confuse, in suon di rabbia e di dolore:
— Soccorri, o padre, a l'unica tua prole,
    ch'io moro, oimè! degli anni miei nel fiore. —
Così detto finì, qual lume suole
    cui manchi in tutto il notritivo umore;
        ma si rivolse al suon di quella voce
        un cavaliero in vista aspro e feroce.

Questi, vedendo il figlio al pian sospinto 78
    morir, rabbioso a vendicarlo mosse,
ch'ancorché gli anni abbian domato e vinto
    sua robbustezza e le corporee posse,
l'ardir però del cor feroce estinto
    non era in lui, ch'altier più che mai fosse.
        Adopra l'armi, e fera ardente voglia
        di sanguinoso Marte ognor l'invoglia.

Ma qual gran foco e senza forze acceso 79
    in secca paglia in van s'infuria al vento,
perché nel colmo al suo furor conteso
    è 'l gir più inanzi, e manca il nutrimento,
tale ei s'infuria in van, di rabbia acceso,
    non send'egual la forza a l'ardimento;
        e nel collo aspramente al fin trafitto,
        al termin giunse a lui dal ciel prescritto.

The lance splinters and does not pierce the hard   75
    steel that conceals the hero's head, but — oh! —
Rinaldo, though the lethal tip is barred
    from entry, shakes to feel the luckless blow,
wherefore, seeking revenge, he stands on guard,
    rage in his heart, his furious face aglow,
        then lunges forward with sword held out straight
        and follows its thrust with his whole body's weight.

Its point pierces the shield, though covered by   76
    a seven-fold layer of tough, hairy hide,
pierces the chain-mail's rings that vainly try
    linked each to each to guard the stripling's side,
until the blade, intent to make him die,
    has made his breast discharge a bloody tide.
        Wounded, the brave lad falls and with his teeth
        wounds, as he bites the dust, the ground beneath.

He lived to speak these words, confused and wild,   77
    in tones of mingled anger and lament:
"Ah! help me, father, help your only child,
    too young to die! Ah, horrible event!"
So saying he died, and as he died, he smiled
    like a lamp that flickers when its oil is spent.
        But hearing him, there rose up in his place
        a knight of desperate and ferocious face.

He, seeing his son stretched dead upon the ground,   78
    ran to avenge him, spurred by sudden rage,
for though he in the course of years had found
    his strength diminished by advancing age,
yet was the ardor in his heart still sound,
    and his pride all the readier to engage
        a foe when his fierce mind, as on this day,
        felt honor-bound by bloody Mars to slay.

But as an ill-lit fire will swiftly wind   79
    its racing flames through dry straw, brightly flaring
in puffs of wind, but just as swiftly find
    its progress stopped by greedy heat outwearing
its fuel, so his fury's power declined,
    his strength not being equal to his daring,
        until, stabbed through the neck and dying, he
        fulfills the doom assigned by heaven's decree.

Rinaldo

Il paladin fra gli altri il destrier caccia,   *80*
   e rota in giro il suo fulmineo brando:
a chi parte la spalla, a chi la faccia,
   altri manda disteso a terra urtando.
Man, teste, busti e sanguinose braccia
   veggionsi andar per l'aria intorno errando;
      né men si mostra il suo compagno forte,
      ch'altrui piaga, stordisce e pone a morte.

Già l'inimico stuol tutto si dona   *81*
   in preda, e n'ha cagione, al vil timore;
e con l'ardir la speme anco abbandona,
   e cede a forza al fero ostil furore.
Ciascun di quei guerrier veloce sprona
   con timorosa fuga il corridore;
      ma i franchi vincitor, fermati insieme,
      non degnan di seguir chi fugge e teme.

Allor nel paladin le luci intende   *82*
   l'estran, colmo di nobil meraviglia,
e fissamente a ricercar lo prende
   dal capo al piè con inarcate ciglia,
tal ch'al fine il conosce, e lieto stende
   l'amiche braccia, e lui nel collo piglia,
      dicendo:— Or chi potea salvarmi in vita,
      se non chi sempre il giusto e 'l dritto aita?

O fratello, o signore, o fido, o caro   *83*
   amico, o prim'onor del secol nostro,
vedete qui chi di se stesso a paro
   v'ama: vedete qui Florindo vostro!
Or nulla più mi fia grave ed amaro,
   poiché benigno cielo a me v'ha mostro,
      ché per voi giusta cura, alto sospetto
      continuamente mi premeva il petto. —

Rimane a quel parlar l'altro guerriero   *84*
   qual chi per tema e per stupor s'adombra,
né certo è ben se quel sia vivo e vero
   corpo, o pur de le membra ignuda l'ombra.
Ma pur a mille segni il van pensiero
   e 'l folle dubbio al fin dal petto sgombra,
      e 'n lui manca il sospetto e 'l gaudio poggia,
      e cresce ognor qual rio per larga pioggia.

The paladin now frets the remnant bands   80
    with lightning sword, striking now here, now there,
cleaves this man's breast, cuts that man's face or stands
    to give a third good reason to despair,
till blood-stained entrails, severed arms, heads, hands
    are everywhere seen tumbling through the air.
       Nor does his comrade show less force and skill
       who wounds or stuns or slays wherever he will.

The pack of ruffian foes perforce take heed   81
    and yield with ample cause to caitiff fear.
Their ardor is much lessened when they bleed
    and see their hopes of triumph disappear.
At last each of these warriors spurs his steed
    to flight and speeds away in full career,
       but the brave victors stop together and
       scorn to pursue so cowardly a band.

At last the stranger fixes his firm gaze   82
    in noble wonder on the paladin,
and with raised eyebrows steadily surveys
    his form from head to toe, from brow to chin,
then, while his eyes fill with a joyful blaze,
    extends both arms and warmly draws him in,
       crying:"Who else could save my life but he
       who ever aids justice and probity?

O faithful friend, O brother, O my lord,   83
    O first inheritor of honor's throne,
behold Florindo here, the man whose sword
    and very self are yours more than his own!
Now that I have you back, by heaven restored,
    no grief shall ever come to make me groan,
       since for you only heartache and unrest
       have for so long weighed down my anxious breast."

It is now the other warrior's turn to speak,   84
    who stands there stunned, in fear and wonder lost,
unsure if this be truth or fancy's freak,
    his dear friend's living body or a ghost,
but memories crowding back at last make weak
    the foolish doubt by which his mind is tossed.
       Suspicion ebbs, joy grows and grows again,
       overflowing like a stream in heavy rain.

Rinaldo con quel volto e con que' detti,   *85*
   con cui s'accoglion le più care cose,
lieto l'accolse, e de' suo' interni affetti
   e nel volto e nel dir nulla gli ascose.
Poi che con mille esteriori effetti
   ciascun di loro il suo piacer espose,
      chiede a l'altro Rinaldo in qual maniera
      dal tempestoso mar salvato s'era.

Cominciò quelli: — Io mi credei sovente   *86*
   d'esser da l'onde rapide inghiottito,
poi ch'al furor del flutto violente
   e dal legno e da voi fui dipartito;
pur, come volse il Fato ultimamente,
   a gran pena arrivai notando al lito;
      ma tanto avea bevuto, e così lasso
      mi ritrovai, che non potei far passo.

Io giacea fuor de' sensi, e la mia vita   *87*
   già correva al suo fin senza ritegno,
s'in sorte così ria benigna aita
   porta non m'era dal celeste regno.
Ma quel che, mosso da pietà infinita,
   discese in terra a trionfar sul Legno,
      fece ch'un cavalier quindi passasse
      ch'a la morte vicina mi sottrasse.

Era costui del chiaro sangue altero   *88*
   degli antichi Corneli in Roma nato,
famoso in arme errante cavaliero
   che Scipion l'ardito era nomato,
e di sette città libero impero
   nel Lazio avea con titol di ducato.
      Questi m'accolse e mi condusse via
      in una sua città chiamata Ostia.

A medici d'illustre esperienza   *89*
   de la salute mia diede il governo,
né lasciò officio alcun di diligenza,
   come il moveva ascoso affetto interno;
ma mentre me, che giaceva egro e senza
   vigor, conforta con amor paterno,
      da quella parte ov'ha 'l suo albergo il core,
      mi vide un segno che rassembra un fiore.

Rinaldo with such looks and words as best   85
    greet dearest objects that seemed lost to night,
welcomed his friend and beamed with joy and blessed
    the day that brought him back in Fortune's spite.
Then, when each had by countless signs expressed
    love for the other and infinite delight,
        Rinaldo asked his friend to tell how he
        had come to safety from the stormy sea.

"When severed from our ship and you," he said,   86
    "and by the furious current swept away,
I kept on thinking I would soon be dead,
    too feeble to resist the surge's sway,
yet somehow I found strength to swim ahead
    and with great effort reached the strand that day
        yet, having swallowed so much water, found
        myself too weak to rise up from the ground.

I lay there senseless. My life seemed to race   87
    irrevocably towards its fated end,
unless in pity of my desperate case
    heavenly mercy would some succor send.
Yet he who once, moved by his infinite grace,
    to bear the Cross did to our Earth descend,
        inspired a knight near where I lay to roam
        who snatched me from near death and took me home.

That great knight proudly claimed direct descent   88
    from Rome's renowned Cornelii of old,
and had earned fame in war wherever he went.
    Known by the name of Scipio the Bold,
he ruled as duke and the free government
    of seven towns in Latium controlled.
        It was he who brought me, feeble and in pain,
        to Ostia, a town in his domain.

To soothe my pain and keep disease at bay,   89
    he hired physicians famous everywhere,
while he himself tended me night and day
    and my well-being seemed his only prayer.
It chanced that, coming to cheer me, as I lay
    feverish and faint, with fatherly love and care,
        he, looking at my breast, my poor heart's bower,
        saw there a rosy mark shaped like a flower.

Da la pelle il segnal rosso traspare   90
   come da vetro un fior d'orto vermiglio,
il che forse al signor fe' rimembrare
   d'un, ch'avea già perduto, unico figlio;
onde dal sommo a l'imo a risguardare
   mi cominciò con fisso immobil ciglio,
      pensando ch'esser forse io quel potea
      cui già bambino egli perduto avea.

Ed era tal credenza in lui più forte   91
   per quel che già gli disse un indovino,
che trovarebbe il figlio in dura sorte,
   ed a l'estremo d'ogni mal vicino,
e che tolto da lui fora a la morte,
   e sottratto al furor di reo destino.
      Tra sé volgendo ciò, rivolte e fisse
      in me le luci, al fin così mi disse:

"Signor, vorrei saper, se pur scortese   92
   mia richiesta od ingrata a voi non fia,
il nome e 'l sangue vostro, e qual paese
   è la vera di voi patria natia."
Io tosto a quel parlar gli fei palese
   che Numanzia tenea per patria mia,
      e che, forse dal fior ch'avea nel petto,
      venni nel mio natal Florindo detto.

Gli dissi ancor ch'a pien non era instrutto   93
   qual genitor m'avesse al mondo dato,
e seguendo oltra poi, gli narrai tutto
   ciò ch'a me l'idol prima avea narrato.
Allor quel non ritenne il volto asciutto,
   né ritenne il color del volto usato,
      e non frenò le voci; e con le braccia
      mi cinse e strinse, e giunse faccia a faccia.

Mi disse poi com'era io suo figliuolo,   94
   ch'essendo già bambin gli fui rapito
da un grosso di corsari armato stuolo,
   ch'a l'improviso dismontar sul lito:
onde mia madre se 'n morì di duolo,
   ed egli ne rimase egro e smarrito;
      nel tempo istesso ancora io seppi come
      Florindo no, ma Lelio era 'l mio nome.

Beneath the limpid skin this red mark glows　　　　90
　　　like a red garden flower under glass,
and in the duke's mind a vague memory rose
　　　of his only son, lost long ago — alas!
He stares at it and thinks or hopes he knows,
　　　then lets his fixed gaze to my visage pass
　　　　　at the sudden thought that I perchance might be
　　　　　that child lost long ago in infancy.

The thought grew stronger when he called to mind　　91
　　　a long-ago soothsayer's prophecy
that he would find his son one day, but find
　　　him only in extreme adversity,
at point of death, and find himself assigned
　　　the task of thwarting cruel Destiny.
　　　　　Rapt in a wild surmise, he once more cast
　　　　　a fixed look at my face and spoke at last:

'Friend, I would be obliged to know — unless　　　92
　　　this seems impertinent or impolite —
your name, your blood, your title of address
　　　and in what region you first saw the light.'
I answered, sensing his great eagerness:
　　　"Numantia nursed me, and I am a knight.
　　　　　I was named Florindo — perhaps to suggest
　　　　　the flower-shaped birthmark on my infant breast.'

I also said that I was never told　　　　　　　　93
　　　what father gave me to the world and so
proceeded all those matters to unfold
　　　that earlier the Idol made me know.[148]
No longer then could he his tears withhold,
　　　but pale with joy moved towards me to throw
　　　　　his arms about me in a fast embrace
　　　　　and, pressing his moist face against my face,

cried out, 'My son!' and then went on to say　　　94
　　　that while I was in my first infancy
a band of pirates suddenly one day
　　　overran his seashore and abducted me.
My mother died of grief, and he grew gray,
　　　a widower in childless misery.
　　　　　I also learned, in hearing him exclaim,
　　　　　that Laelius, not Florindo, was my name.

Disposi allor, dal dir paterno e saggio,   95
    anzi pur dal voler di Dio sospinto,
ed illustrato dal divin suo raggio,
    ch'aprì le nubi ond'era involto e cinto,
adorar lui che 'l nostro uman legnaggio
    salvò morendo, onde Pluton fu vinto;
      così asperso di sacra e lucid'onda
      fui, che lava le membra e l'alma monda. —

Qui si tacque il Romano; indi seguio   96
    ch'egli congiedo avea dal padre tolto,
spronato, lasso! dal crudel desio
    di riveder il vago amato volto,
e per tentar se mai potesse il rio
    sdegno ch'avea contr'esso Olinda accolto,
      sgombrar dal duro ed aggiacciato core
      con servitù, con fede e con amore.

Gli disse ancor ch'a l'apparir del giorno   97
    senza cagione, il che gli parve strano,
tutti gli fur que' cavalieri intorno,
    e l'assaltar con impeto villano,
per farli a lor potere oltraggio e scorno;
    onde Rinaldo ad un, che steso al piano
      giacea, ne chiese la cagione, e poi
      chi si fosse egli, chi quell'altri suoi.

Canto Eleven

I next, at my new father's wise request,   95
　　and urged indeed by heaven's gracious will
and by that Guiding Spirit, pure and blest,
　　who makes Faith's light our human darkness fill,
prepared to worship him who died to wrest
　　from Pluto by his death the power to kill,
　　　　and let those sacred droplets touch my skin
　　　　that bathe the limbs and cleanse the soul of sin."

The Roman here fell silent, but anon   96
　　said that he left his father, spurred by pain
of unfulfilled desire, which drove him on
　　to see the fair beloved face again,
and try, if ever to her presence drawn,
　　to melt Olinda's merciless disdain
　　　　and from her heart her icy scorn remove
　　　　by humble service, faithfulness and love.

He also told him that on the next morn   97
　　this pack of knights, as he rode northward-bound,
without all cause, like foul assassins sworn
　　to kill, attacked *en masse* and girt him round
to wreak on him their outrage and their scorn,
　　wherefore of one stretched wounded on the ground
　　　　Rinaldo asked what led to the affray,
　　　　and who they were, and what brought them that way.

CANTO DUODECIMO

Quegli, il parlar del paladino inteso,   1
   non dimostrossi a l'ubbedir ritroso,
ma da terra levando il capo offeso,
   ch'era di sangue caldo e rugiadoso,
su la destra appoggiò l'infermo peso,
   e con l'altra il sanguigno e polveroso
      volto fe' mondo; indi la voce e 'l guardo
      debil rivolse al cavalier gagliardo:

— Signor, convien che d'alto al mio sermoner   2
   principio dia, per sodisfarvi in tutto.
Il gran Mambrin ch'a l'Asia legge impone,
   or sospinto d'Amor s'è qui condutto,
e seco ha mille legni e di persone
   stuol grosso e forte ad ogni pugna instrutto,
      per far poi di Clarice intero acquisto,
      ch'acceso n'è, né 'l volto ancor n'ha visto.

Oltra di ciò, di vendicarsi brama   3
   contra un guerriero, il qual Rinaldo è detto,
perché gli tolse in mare una sua dama,
   lo stuol forzando a la sua guarda eletto;
e poi tre suoi fratei d'illustre fama
   gli uccise ancor con inimico affetto.
      Già son più dì che 'l re da' legni scese,
      e 'l più vicino porto a forza prese.

E con molti de' suoi scorse nascoso   4
   sin a Parigi, e tal fu sua ventura,
che Clarice trovò ch'in dilettoso
   prato godeasi l'ombra e la verdura;
quivi ardì di rapirla, a chi foss'oso
   di contradir dando morte aspra e dura;
      ed or al maggior passo egli camina
      ver' l'armata ch'è quinci assai vicina.

CANTO TWELVE

He heard the paladin, nor was he found   1
    slow to respond, but started in alarm,
lifted his wounded head and turned it round,
    with blood still trickling from it red and warm,
on his left arm from off the trampled ground,
    wiping the blood and dust with his right arm,
        then fixed with faltering voice and feeble eyes
        the brave knight and made answer in this wise:

"Sir, it is fitting that I should begin   2
    with the highest cause in answering your request:
Know then that Asia's sovereign lord, Mambrin,
    has come by Love's incitement to the West.
A thousand ships bear legions expert in
    all forms of war to fight at his behest.
        He comes for Clarice. It is her embrace
        he burns for though he never saw her face

and also to avenge an injury   3
    wrought by a knight — Rinaldo is his name —
who robbed him of a favored slave at sea
    and slew the warders of that peerless dame
and later in ferocious fight slew three
    of Mambrin's brothers,[149] warriors of great fame.
        He with his ships not long since steered his course
        hither and seized the nearest port by force,

and with a huge troop made his secret way   4
    as far as Paris, where by luck he found
Clarice who in a pleasant field that day
    took solace in a shaded plot of ground.
He seized her there and carried her away,
    killing her escort, and then turned around
        and soon will — doubt it not — himself appear
        to join his fleet anchored not far from here.

Rinaldo

Ma passando di qua questo guerriero 5
    vide, che fêa di sé superba mostra,
e impose a noi che tosto ei prigioniero
    fosse condutto infra la gente nostra:
ma troppo forte fu, troppo fu fiero,
    e troppo a tempo l'alta aita vostra. —
        Così disse il ferito e poi si tacque,
        e qual prima disteso in terra giacque.

Si sente il petto a quel parlar trafitto 6
    Rinaldo, e per dolor fremendo geme;
s'accoglie il sangue intorno il core afflitto,
    e fredde lascia l'altre parti estreme.
Par quasi omai ch'ei non si regga dritto,
    e così avien ch'ogni suo membro treme,
        come suol tremolar l'onda talora
        cui lieve increspi molle e placid'ora.

Poi, rosso il volto e torbido il sembiante, 7
    con fero, irato e minaccievol guardo,
e spesso nel girar sì fiammeggiante
    che di Giove parea l'acceso dardo,
chiede aita a Florindo; e ne l'istante
    medesmo verso 'l mar sprona Baiardo,
        e l'indirizza al più vicino porto
        per lo sentier ch'è più spedito e corto.

Non così in terra, in mar o 'n ciel giamai 8
    cervo, delfino o partica saetta
corse, notò, volò ratto, ch'assai
    non sia maggior de' cavalier la fretta:
già per gran spazio è dilungata omai
    dal luogo onde partì la coppia eletta,
        ma pare al lor desir pur troppo lento
        ogni destrier, benché rassembri un vento.

Tu sospesi per l'aria ir gli diresti, 8
    or chini e bassi, or alti e 'n su drizzati;
né dimora né requie in lor vedresti,
    né pur i calli dai lor piè segnati.
Fuman le membra sotto i colpi infesti
    che dagli sproni ognor son raddoppiati;
        i petti di sudor, di spuma i freni,
        d'arena i piedi son aspersi e pieni.

But earlier, seeing this warrior here pass by   5
   who seemed so bold, so stout, so unafraid,
he gave command that some of us should try
   to make him prisoner in an ambuscade.
But he, too fierce to yield, too strong to die,
   defied us and then found your timely aid."
      So spoke the wounded man and said no more
      but stretched out on the cold ground as before.

Appalled, Rinaldo hears him speak and grieves   6
   and vents his sore dread in half-stifled cries.
Blood rushes to his anxious heart and leaves
   his outward members cold as ice. His eyes
grow glazed in bitter woe, his bosom heaves,
   and over all his skin a shudder flies
      as when a soft, seemingly placid breeze
      rises to agitate and crisp the seas.

But then a look of furious menace came   7
   upon his face. He flushed and suddenly
wheeled round, his gazes shooting flame
   like Jupiter's dread bolts. One instant he
asked for Florindo's help and in the same,
   gave spur to Bayard and along the sea,
      taking the shortest path, without delay
      toward to the nearest harbor sped away.

With less speed through the woods or sea or sky   8
   a stag, a dolphin or an arrow sent
from a Parthian bow will run or swim or fly
   than that with which that pair of horsemen went.
Already mile on mile had passed them by
   since they set out, yet their incontinent
      desire made their galloping coursers, though
      they moved swift as the whirlwind, seem too slow.

To see them is to say they soar in air,   9
   now up, now down, upon their horses' backs,
or that their horses race suspended there
   with steps so swift they seem to leave no tracks,
attaining while their riders do not spare
   the lash or spur a speed that never slacks.
      Sweat bathes their chests, their muzzles froth with foam,
      and their great hooves are flecked with sandy loam.

Non sasso o sterpo o discosceso dorso   *10*
    d'orrido monte, o larga e cupa fossa
trovan, che porre a tanta furia il morso
    ed arrestarli in lor viaggio possa.
Lor tronca al fin l'impetuoso corso
    un gran torrente, che con grave scossa
        l'antico ponte avea pur dianzi rotto,
        togliendo ogni sostegno a lui di sotto.

Non sa che farsi allor l'amante ardito,   *11*
    ch'esporsi a rischio tal non fora ardire,
ma privo di ragion folle appetito,
    e di morte certissima desire.
Pur quando al fin gli manchi ogni partito,
    vol che lasciar l'impresa, anzi morire:
        tutto si scuote, e gli occhi intorno volve,
        né men del dubbio caso ei si risolve.

Venire in questa, onde deriva l'onda,   *12*
    un guerrier vede sovr'un gran battello,
che sì veloce gia per la seconda
    acqua, come per l'aria alato augello.
Rinaldo che 'l tragitti a l'altra sponda
    con dolce modo umil supplica quello,
        ché 'l cavalier gli sembra a l'armatura
        che già lo trasse da la valle oscura.

Colui non udir finge, e tuttavia   *13*
    de l'ondoso sentier gran spazio avanza,
tal ch'al baron di quel che più desia
    quasi manca del tutto ogni speranza.
Pur i preghi rinforza or più che pria,
    e cerca di piegarlo a sua possanza
        con offerte e promesse: ond'in lui fisse
        gli occhi al fin lo straniero, e così disse:

— Signor, se pur è ver che sì bramiate   *14*
    varcar sovra 'l mio legno esto torrente,
convien ch'un dono or voi mi promettiate,
    con fé di poi servarlo interamente. —
— Ogni cosa farò, se mi varcate
    di là — rispose l'altro impaziente.
        Quelli a la riva appressa allor la barca,
        e di peso novel la rende carca.

Nor crag nor mountain height nor steep ravine   10
    nor any other obstacle they met
could check their furious pace or come between
    them and the goal they hastened toward. And yet
at last a swollen river, unforeseen,
    stopped them, whose waves had earlier upset
        an ancient bridge athwart its raging path
        and swept it to the bottom in its wrath.

The impetuous lover knew not what to do.   11
    Not that he dared not risk his life and try
to swim, but also an uncanny yearning to
    plunge in lured him to end it all and die.
For certainly — if all else failed — he knew
    that he would rather perish here than fly.
        He shudders as he gazes all about
        assailed by indecisiveness and doubt.

At last he saw upstream an armed knight guide   12
    a sturdy boat with strong and steady oar,
making it over the waves as swiftly glide
    as through the clouds a bird will scud or soar.
To him Rinaldo in entreaty cried
    to come and take him to the other shore.
        Indeed, that knight seemed, by his armor's glow,
        much like his savior from the black vale's woe.

But he, pretending not to hear, moved on   13
    over the waves and kept on moving still,
until Rinaldo feared all hope was gone
    and felt his heart seized by a mortal chill.
More loudly yet, frantic and woebegone,
    he cried and sought to bend the boatman's will
        by promises, whereat the stranger eyed
        him with steadfast gaze and thus replied:

"My lord, if you are truly so intent   14
    to cross this torrent on my boat today,
then promise me a boon for my consent
    and swear to keep your promise, come what may."
"Ask what you will," the youth cried. "I'm content,
    but bring me to the other shore straightway."
        The bark draws toward the river's verge and straight
        sways as it feels a second rider's weight.

Rinaldo

Come furon di là, l'estran guerriero,   15
    volto a Rinaldo, a lui così ragiona:
— Signor, con voi di venir chieggio al fiero
    certame, ov'ora il gran desio vi sprona;
e perché il dono io ne riporti intiero,
    convien ch'altra armatura e via più buona,
        ch'io vi serbo, ha più dì, su quell'abete,
        vestiate; e questa qui lasciar potrete. —

Stupito il paladin drizza la vista   16
    u' la verde armatura era sospesa,
e vede lei con doppia aurata lista
    lucida lampeggiar qual fiamma accesa;
né men forte gli par che bella in vista,
    e qual conviensi a così dubbia impresa:
        onde lieto se n'arma e la dispende,
        e grazie a lo straniero alte ne rende.

Quelli a Florindo un destrier dona intanto   17
    c'ha vergate le gambe, a carbon spento
simil la coda e i crini estremi, e 'l manto
    mischio con poco nero a molto argento;
che sbuffa, ed or a questo, or a quel canto
    si volge, e par ch'al corso inviti il vento.
        Gli sprona il fianco allor, gli batte il dorso
        il buon Florindo, e gli rallenta il morso.

L'istesso ancora i suoi compagni fêro,   18
    e così insieme al maggior corso andaro.
Poi che 'l mondo vestì l'orrido e nero
    manto, e l'altro spogliò candido e chiaro,
posa a l'alma od al corpo essi non diero,
    anzi il viaggio lor pur seguitaro
        al raggio algente de la bianca luna,
        ch'intorno si scotea la notte bruna.

A lo scoprir del sol scopriro anch'essi   19
    l'avversa schiera a lor non molto lunge.
Rinaldo allor con radoppiati e spessi
    colpi così ne' fianchi il destrier punge,
che passa gli altri, e pria ch'alcun s'appressi
    ei tra' nemici impetuoso giunge;
        e scorge in mezo a lor Clarice bella,
        ch'egra e smarrita non si regge in sella.

When they had crossed, the stranger turned around   15
    to face Rinaldo, saying : "Sir, now hear
the boon I ask. First, that I shall be found
    fighting alongside you when foes draw near.
And second, that you fight in arms more sound
    than those you ride in. Here is better gear.
        I've hung it on yon spruce for you to find.
        Go put it on, and leave your own behind."

The paladin turns, and his astonished gaze   16
    finds a green armor hanging from a tree,
marked with two stripes of shining gold that blaze
    like fires. Nor does its splendor seem to be
less than the strength its tempered steel displays
    to ward off blows in doubtful fight. So he
        grasps it and with it girds his breast and flanks
        while rendering to the stranger joyful thanks,

The stranger on Florindo then bestows   17
    a stallion, dapple-haunched, on whose thick mane
and dusky tail and ashen hide there glows
    through varied black and gray a silvery stain.
Proudly he canters and with eager nose
    breathes in the wind and tugs against the rein.
        Florindo spurs his flank, lashes his back
        and lets the bridle at his bit go slack.

So did the other two and off they went,   18
    all three together, speeding on their way.
The world put on the black habiliment
    of night and threw off the bright garb of day,
yet they without repose or nourishment
    kept galloping onward by the moon's cold ray
        that with scant gleams of pale and ghostly light
        guided them through the darkness of the night.

When they see the sun, they also see nearby   19
    the gathered army of their enemies.
At once Rinaldo makes good Bayard fly,
    plying his sweating flank with spurs and knees,
and before his friends with a fierce battle-cry
    reaches the host and, as he does so, sees
        Clarice among them, riding pale and bowed,
        distraught, bewildered and sobbing aloud.

Fu da pietate ed ira insieme ei vinto;   20
    pur la pietate a l'ira allor diè loco,
onde il sembiante, di furor dipinto,
    vibrò dagli occhi strai di tosco e foco;
e tra' nemici il corridor sospinto
    diè principio di Marte al crudo gioco.
        Bene infelice è chi primier s'oppone
        al gran furor del gran figliuol d'Amone.

Musa, or narrami i duci onde Mambrino   21
    cinto n'andava largamente intorno,
de' quai fur molti allor dal paladino
    mandati con Plutone a far soggiorno.
Dimmi l'imprese ancor, ch'al saracino
    scielto drappel rendean l'abito adorno;
        perché la lunga età n'involve e copre
        non pur l'insegne omai, ma i nomi e l'opre.

In vermiglio color portava tinta   22
    l'incantata armatura il re famoso,
e la superba testa intorno cinta
    tenea di fregio imperial pomposo;
ne lo scudo l'impresa avea dipinta,
    un gran leon ferito e sanguinoso
        che la piaga mirava, e v'era scritto,
        "Io non perdono, e so chi m'ha trafitto".

Qual sanguigna cometa ai crini ardenti,   23
    o Sirio appar di sdegno acceso in vista,
che con orrida luce e con nocenti
    raggi nascendo, il mondo ange e contrista,
e sin dal ciel minaccia a l'egre genti
    morbi, ed a grave ardor ria sete mista:
        tal d'aspri mali annunzio egli risplende
        con squalido splendor ne l'armi orrende.

Gli va da la man destra il destro Olante,   24
    che di Francardo fu german secondo,
ed avea forma o forza di gigante,
    ma vago aspetto e crin aurato e biondo:
colui che porse aita al magno Atlante,
    quando cangiò la spalla al grave pondo,
        e resse il ciel che lui regger dovea,
        per impresa ne l'arme impresso avea.

Anger and ruth at once rush to his head,   20
    but pity at once gives way to burning ire,
so that his face, by fury stained all red,
    blazes forth venomous scorn and fateful fire.
He drives his steed amid the foe ahead
    to launch the game of Mars, cruel and dire.
      Woe to the man who happens first upon
      the matchless rage of Aymon's matchless son!

Say now, O Muse, what mighty warlords went   21
    leading that great host at Mambrino's call,
who by the paladin were later sent
    on their last journey, down to Pluto's hall.
Say also what heraldic ornament
    blazoned the shield or crest of each and all,
      so that the mist of times to come shall never
      hide their insignia, names and vain endeavor.

Enchanted armor did the king encase,   22
    dyed scarlet like a clinging, blood-red gown.
Circling his brow above his haughty face,
    he wore a sumptuous imperial crown.
His mighty shield showed, limned upon its face,
    a bleeding lion gazing with fierce frown
      upon his wound, with a legend round the rim:
      "I know who pierced me, nor will pardon him."

Like a blood-red comet trailing fiery hair,   23
    or angry Sirius[150] flaming in the sky,
at whose birth horrid rays spread everywhere
    their dismal glow and make the whole world sigh,
plunging weak men and sick in deep despair,
    as heat and parching thirst their entrails try,
      even so his armor augurs bitter ills
      and all the air with ghastly splendor fills.

See at his right hand dexterous Olas ride,   24
    King Francard's kinsman, strong beyond compare,
of giant girth, yet therewithal supplied
    with a handsome face and locks of golden hair.
Upon the shield that hangs at his left side
    see pictured him who helped great Atlas bear
      the world, taking that burden all alone
      from off the Titan's shoulders on his own.

Da l'altro lato va 'l superbo Alcastro,   25
    nato ov'il Nilo impingua il verde Egitto,
nel cui natale in ciel regnava ogn'astro
    che torce l'uom dal camin buono e dritto.
Porta un villan che con la zappa e 'l rastro
    frange le glebbe e si procaccia il vitto.
        L'impresa è poi del suo compagno Olpestro,
        congiunto ad una ninfa un dio silvestro.

V'è 'l signor degli Assiri, il cauto Altorre,   26
    accerbo d'anni e di pensier maturo:
una destrutta e fulminata torre
    ha ne lo scudo in campo verde oscuro.
Porta un fanciul che fra le mani accôrre
    gli attomi tenta, il re dei Siri Arturo;
        quel di Cilicia, da fier disco estinto
        sovr'un letto di fiori il bel Giacinto.

Atteone il formoso, ond'un più bello   27
    non forse allor la terra in sen nudria,
se non che ferro, di pietà rubello,
    tagliolli un piè del qual or zoppo ei gia,
pinto avea di Giunon l'adorno augello
    che nel guardarsi i piè mesto apparia;
        e v'era un motto che 'l suo grave duolo
        accennava, dicendo, "In questo solo".

Siegue il saggio Orimeno, a cui son noti   28
    de la madre natura i gran secreti:
antivedea costui gli effetti e i moti
    de le sfere celesti e de' pianeti,
le pioggie, i tuoni e lo spirar de' Noti,
    e quando il mar si turbi o pur s'acquieti;
        antivide sua morte, e de l'istessa
        la vera forma avea ne l'arme impressa.

Va seco il re di Lidia, e porta un lauro   29
    ch'al suol sparge di fronde un ricco nembo;
lo scudo orna al fratel la pioggia d'auro
    ch'accolse Danae simplicetta in grembo.
Rosso ha lo scudo il fier gigante Oldauro
    senza pittura, e sol d'argento ha il lembo;
        e le tre dive ignude il forte Almeno,
        che regge altier de' Cappadoci il freno.

On the king's left see proud Alcaster go,   25
    born where the Nile paints Egypt green, at whose
birth all the sky's malignant stars did glow
    that tempt men to spurn good and foully choose;
his sign: a peasant who with rake and hoe
    opens the glebe to harvest food for use.
      His friend Olpester shows, painted upon
      his shield, a wood-nymph bedded by a faun.

There rides Assyria's lord, Altorres, green   26
    in years but early ripe in thoughts profound.
A tower struck by lightning bolts is seen
    depicted on his targe's dark-green ground.
A boy, hands gathering grain as though to glean,
    on Syrian Arcturus's shield is found.
      Cilicia's shows pale Hyacinth, struck dead
      by the discus, prostrate on a flowery bed.

The handsome Actaeon — few men had heard   27
    of a man of greater beauty far and wide,
save that a sword slash, by ill luck conferred
    on his foot one day, gave him limping stride —
bore for device great Juno's gaudy bird,
    which seemed abashed to have its foot descried,
      marked with a cryptic motto hinting at
      his grief in these words: "Through
        no more than that…"

There follows Orimen, sagest of seers,   28
    adept in Mother Nature's mysteries.
He could predict the motions of the spheres
    and planets, foretell calm or troubled seas,
storms, thunder, rains, barren or prosperous years —
    nothing was hidden from his prophesies.
      He now foresees his death and shows Death's true
      semblance on his escutcheon in plain view.

On Lydia's monarch's shield, a laurel tree   29
    makes leafy branches toward the sunlight spread,
and on his brother's, guileless Danaë
    receives the golden shower in her bed.
Giant Oldauros shows no heraldry,
    his shield a great silver-rimmed disk of red.
      Three naked goddesses[131] dancing in a ring
      Almenos carries, Cappadocia's king.

Se 'n va presso costor l'empio Odrimarte,   *30*
    cui sol legge era il suo volere istesso,
che 'l vero e i falsi divi a parte a parte
    in odio aveva ed in dispregio espresso;
porta egli sé dipinto, e 'l fiero Marte
    incatenato e da' suoi piedi oppresso;
        l'accompagnan Corin, Pirro ed Aiace,
        ai quali orna lo scudo un'aurea face.

Né tu da questi vai molto lontano,   *31*
    o Floridor, cui la novella sposa
col pianto indarno e col pregar umano
    tentò ritener seco in dolce posa:
ché lei lassata, ch'aspettando in vano
    mena fredda le notti e i dì pensosa,
        armato spieghi in verde campo il fiore
        che col pianto formò la dea d'amore.

Vengon teco anco Almeto ed Odrismonte,   *32*
    che portan Cinzia ed Atteon scolpiti:
ambo germani, ambo di forze conte,
    ambo d'aurato acciar cinti e guerniti.
Vi viene il re de' Parti, il fier Corsonte,
    e scopre tre spinosi arbor fioriti;
        e riman lo sdegnoso Altin lo scempio:
        mostra di Vesta impresso il sacro tempio.

Sovra un destrier via più che neve bianco   *33*
    di candid'arme altier ne va Filarco,
non impugn'asta e non ha spada al fianco
    questi, ma porta ben la mazza e l'arco:
è la su' impresa un uom dagli anni stanco,
    di crespe rughe il volto ingombro e carco.
        Niso, Alcastus, Orion, Breusso e Taumante,
        cinque germani, han per impresa Atlante.

Al gigante Lurcon lo scudo indora   *34*
    in campo azuro uno stellato cielo;
al re di Caria, Aridaman, l'infiora
    una rosa che s'apre in verde stelo;
ne lo scudo d'Aldriso appar l'Aurora
    che sparge i fiori e 'n perle accolto il gielo;
        di Damasco il signor mostra dipinto
        il vago Adon, da l'empia fera estinto.

Next comes vile Odrimart, supreme in vice,   30
    whose one law is his will, a man who'll greet
with cold contempt all faith or sacrifice,
    considering trust in any god a cheat.
An image of himself is his device
    with fearsome Mars in chains beneath his feet.
        Pyrrhus, Corin and Ajax, all three, hold
        shields with the same device: a torch of gold.

Nor are you far behind, O Floridor,   31
    whom your new-wedded bride not long ago
with hot tears and soft prayers did implore,
    as you lay in her sweet bed, not to go.
In vain she waits for your return from war,
    doomed to cold nights and weary days of woe.
        Upon your shield on a green ground appears
        the flower Love's goddess watered with her tears.[152]

Almethos and Odrismont come bearing   32
    arms that show Actaeon's flight and Cynthia's bower.
They are brothers, both arrayed in glistening
    armor of gilded steel, both men of power.
Then there's fierce Corsont, Parthia's potent king,
    whose targe displays three thorny trees in flower.
        Altin the Proud is next to take the field
        with Vesta's temple graven on his shield.

In glittering armor see Philarcos ride   33
    upon a stallion whiter than new snow.
Bearing no lance, with no sword at his side,
    his only weapons are his mace and bow,
and his device a graybeard, rheumy-eyed,
    wrinkled of face, white-haired and stooping low.
        Nisus, Orion, Breussos, Alkast, Thaumas,
        five brothers, next. Their joint device: Atlas.

Gigantic Lurcon on his shield displays   34
    gold stars bespangling a dark ground of blue.
Carian Aridaman's royal targe lets blaze
    on a green stem a rose of crimson hue,
and on Aldriso's, bright Aurora sprays
    a flowering field with drops of pearly dew.
        Royal Damascus on his splendid crest
        bears fair Adonis by the boar oppressed.

Olindo e Floridan nati ad un parto,   35
    d'un valor, d'un parlar, d'un volto stesso,
hanno un prato di fior varii consparto,
    in cui giace dal vin Sileno oppresso.
Il signor d'Antiochia, il mesto Alarto,
    porta tronco nel mezzo un gran cipresso,
        cui con più nodi un motto tal s'attiene:
        "Seccò per mai non rinverdir mia spene".

Tra questi e tra molt'altri, onde corona   36
    larga fatta era intorno al re gagliardo,
arrestando il troncon Rinaldo sprona
    con furioso assalto il suo Baiardo.
Fuggi, Odrimarte, ché 'l tuo giorno a nona
    si chiuderà, sì nel fuggir sei tardo:
        ecco che te, cui d'ogni dio più forte
        credevi, ora un solo uom conduce a morte!

Sanguigna trae da la sanguigna fronte   37
    il forte vincitor l'intera lancia,
e Lurcon percotendo, un largo fonte
    uscir gli fa da la piagata guancia.
Là dove corron Stige e Flegetonte,
    e 'l severo Minòs l'alme bilancia,
        fuggì l'altero spirto, e fe' fuggire
        a molti allora il lor soverchio ardire.

Passa sdegnoso il cavaliero, e senza   38
    vita abbandona questi e senza onore;
poi trova i duo fratei ch'in apparenza
    indifferenti, ahi! con che dolce errore,
spesso i padri ingannar: ma differenza
    dura troppo or vi fa l'ostil furore,
        che scema Floridan d'ambe le braccia,
        e per mezzo ad Olindo apre la faccia.

Contra Rinaldo allor si move Aldriso,   39
    non men ch'irato il cor, sdegnoso il ciglio.
Morta la madre, uscio dal ventre inciso
    questi, e picciol schivar l'aspro periglio
poteo del ferro, onde già grande ucciso
    poi fu, né gli giovò forza o consiglio.
        Né tu men gli giovasti, o biondo Apollo,
        cui da bambino il genitor sacrollo.

Olindo and Floraman, born on the same day,   35
 alike in looks, in speech, in bravery,
show a green meadow strewn with flowers of May
 where, drunk with wine, Silenus[153] seems to lie.
Sad Alart, lord of Antioch, makes display
 of a cypress whose great branches seek the sky.
  Tied unto its trunk, this motto can be seen:
  "My hope, once dry, shall nevermore grow green."

Amidst these men, massed round their gallant king 36
 with a host of others, Rinaldo makes his way
on Bayard, lance in rest now, galloping
 bent forward in his saddle toward the fray.
Flee, Odrimart, for the ninth hour will bring
 ruin upon you if you make delay.
  You thought no god could match your
   strength — but lo! —
  now a mere man shall wreak your overthrow!

With lance still bloody from your bloodied head 37
 and still unbroken, the bold victor hits
Lurcon and makes a crimson fountain spread
 his gore over his cheek. His spirit flits
to Styx and Phlegethon below, where dread
 Minos upon the throne of judgment sits.
  Next countless other champions who advance
  to face it fall, pierced by that fatal lance.

The raging hero leaves them all behind,   38
 bereft of life and honor, then attacks
two brothers so alike no man could find
 which one was which — yea, their fond father lacks
all skill to tell — but now — ah fate unkind! —
 war marks the difference, for Rinaldo hacks
  both arms off Floraman[154] and through Olindo's face
  thrusts his sharp lance's point from tip to base.

Aldriso next he rides at to destroy,   39
 whose face and heart fill with both rage and gloom.
His mother dead, he as a newborn boy
 was freed from the harsh peril of her womb
by steel, which, once his means to life and joy,
 is now the instrument that wreaks his doom.
  Nor could you, blond Apollo, help him now,
  who at his birth once heard his father's vow.

Rinaldo

Rinaldo poi con cinque aspre ferite   40
    que' cinque frati un dopo l'altro uccise,
le cui speranze al fin lasciò schernite
    Fortuna, che lor destra un tempo arrise.
L'alme nel corpo già tra lor sì unite,
    né disciolte da quel, restar divise,
        perché Pluton tutte albergolle insieme
        nel cerchio ov'i superbi aggrava e preme.

Mentre, come villan che 'n verde prato   41
    stenda l'adunca falce in largo giro,
ruota Rinaldo intorno il brando irato,
    dando sempre ai pagani aspro martiro,
i due compagni suoi da l'altro lato
    il nemico drappel feri assaliro,
        come due tigri cui digiuno e rabbia
        spingan fra' tori a insanguinar le labbia.

E ben lo san color che d'aurea face   42
    portano il campo de lo scudo adorno,
de' quali un già vil busto in terra giace,
    privo del lume del sereno giorno.
L'altro, trafitto il cor, si more e tace,
    pensando al suo natio dolce soggiorno,
        ed a l'amata moglie, omai vicina
        a le prime fatiche di Lucina.

Restava il terzo ancor, quand'il romano   43
    eroe ne' danni suoi la spada strinse.
Miser! la forza e lo schermirsi è vano
    contra colui ch'in ogni impresa vinse.
Già la rapace Morte alza la mano,
    e 'l manto squarcia onde Natura il cinse;
        l'alma, qual lieve fumo o poca polve,
        nel puro aer si mischia e si dissolve.

Atteon, che quel colpo orribil scorse,   44
    aggiacciò di stupor, d'ira s'accese,
e verso 'l buon Florindo il destrier torse
    con fere voglie a darli morte intese;
ma pria parole a lui che colpi porse,
    e 'n questa guisa ad oltraggiar lo prese:
        — Credi forse irne impune? Ahi! che s'aspetta
        a te gran pena, al morto aspra vendetta!

Rinaldo next with five stupendous blows   40
    cast down the five bold brothers[155] one by one.
The time had come for Fortune to oppose
    the hopes of those she long had smiled upon.
Their souls, disjoined from bodies by death's throes,
    joined each to each, fled down to Acheron,
        where Pluto welcomed them and side by side
        assigned them to the ring of punished pride.

While, like a mower in a grassy sward   41
    swinging his sickle in still widening rings,
Rinaldo swung his never-failing sword,
    which with each stroke a bitter torment brings,
both of his comrades with like fierceness gored
    and gashed and stabbed and harrowed knights and kings
        and, like two tigers mad for blood who maul
        a herd of bulls, wrought havoc on them all.

And this is all too evident for the three[156]   42
    with golden torches for escutcheons: one,
already a cadaver, will not see,
    another fight nor gaze upon the sun;
the second lies with heart pierced, silently
    struggling to fix his dying thoughts upon
        his dear home and his sweet, young wife, in whom
        even now Lucina first quickens her womb.

The third still fights on, but the Roman[157] knight   43
    now tries his falchion's edge upon his skin.
Poor wretch! Your strength and utmost skill are quite
    vain in opposing power destined to win.
Lo! Grinning Death appears before his sight
    and rips the coat that Nature clothed him in.
        His soul, torn from him by that fateful stroke,
        mingles with air like a light puff of smoke.

Lovely Actaeon[158] at that blow's huge force,   44
    froze with astonishment and seethed with wrath
and toward brave Florindo spurred his horse,
    seized by fierce longing for his instant death,
but before charging him, in this discourse
    proudly addressed him as he barred his path:
        "Do you think that you shall scot-free quit this place?
        Ah no! For vengeance, death and foul disgrace

Tu qui morrai su questi incolti piani,   45
 né rendrai gli occhi anzi il morir contenti;
né chiuderanti con pietose mani
 quei già cassi di luce, i tuoi parenti:
ma preda rimarrai di lupi e cani,
 esposto a l'onde, a le tempeste, ai venti. —
  Così detto, il destrier spronando punse,
  e d'un gran colpo a mezzo scudo il giunse.

L'empio ferro crudel rompe il ferrigno   46
 scudo, e col duro usbergo il molle petto.
Lelio, che quindi uscir vede il sanguigno
 umor macchiando il ferro terso e netto,
d'ira infiammato e di furor maligno
 percosse e franse l'inimico elmetto,
  e 'n sino al naso penetrò la spada,
  onde convien che quel morendo cada.

Il leggiadro garzone in terra langue,   47
 pallido il volto e nubiloso il ciglio,
e da la fronte un ruscellin di sangue
 versa qual ostro lucido e vermiglio;
ma bench'egli sia già freddo ed esangue,
 e provi omai di morte il crudo artiglio,
  è però tal che puote a un solo sguardo
  ferire ogn'alma d'amoroso dardo.

Molti piagati e molti estinti avea   48
 in questo mezzo il paladin feroce,
ed egli illeso ancor se 'n rimanea,
 ch'a l'arme sue non taglio o punta noce,
ma pesto il corpo omai pur si dolea.
 Non perciò appar men destro e men feroce,
  anzi gagliardo i suoi nemici offende,
  e da lor si schermisce e si difende.

Mambrino allor, che, quasi a sdegno avendo   49
 di trar la spada per sì vil impresa,
l'empie brame di sangue entro premendo,
 fermo stava a mirar l'aspra contesa,
si trasse avanti in fier sembiante orrendo,
 che minacciava altrui mortale offesa,
  e 'l folgorante sguardo ai suoi rivolse;
  indi in grave parlar la lingua sciolse:

are here. You'll die here in this barren land,   45
    nor shall you merely die like this, with not
one kinsman by to close with pitying hand
    your failing eyes; your corpse in some dank spot,
wind-tossed or rain-soaked on a foreign strand,
    food for stray dogs and wolves shall lie and rot."
      This said, he urged his steed against his foe
      and struck him mid-shield with a mighty blow.

The cruel iron breaks the iron guard   46
    of shield and hauberk, reaching the soft breast.
Laelius, astonished, sees his armor marred
    and moisture stain the steel that clads his chest.
In mad rage he strikes back and strikes back hard.
    His keen blade smashes through his foeman's crest
      and splits his brow and nose down to his chops.
      He totters on his courser's back and drops.

The gallant youth is prostrate, ashen pale,   47
    eyes clouding in his final agony,
while trickling rills of lucid crimson trail
    down from his ivory brow. And although he
lies drained of blood and all his forces fail
    and death claws at his life, he seems to be
      a man whose lightest glance could wound the hearts
      of all it greets with Cupid's amorous darts.

Meanwhile the furious paladin had slain   48
    many a man and wounded many more,
himself unwounded, since all blows were vain
    against the enchanted armor that he wore.
Proof against wounds but not against the pain,
    he no less nimbly or fiercely fought therefore,
      now lunging at the foe with lance or sword,
      now parrying blows or leaping to his ward.

Mambrin, as though in scorn to draw his blade   49
    in such a petty quarrel, had long been
standing aloof to watch the fight and made
    his wonted thirst for blood tarry within,
but now his fiendish countenance displayed
    death-threatening wrath and desperate chagrin.
      He looked about with flaming gaze and then,
      loosing his tongue, thus spoke unto his men:

Rinaldo

— *Traggasi ognuno indietro: a me s'aspetta*   50
   l'impresa, a me voi vendicar conviene,
a me domar costui ch'in sì gran fretta
   ad incontrar la morte audace viene.
Voi, gente infame, vil turba negletta,
   la qual io... ma tempo è che l'ira affrene,
      anzi pur che la volga e sfoghi altrove:
      state in disparte a rimirar mie prove! —

Al superbo parlar del fier Mambrino   51
   alcun non è ch'ad ubbedir ritardi;
fassi gran piazza intorno, e 'l Saracino
   volge a Rinaldo i detti alteri e i guardi:
— *Deh! perché teco non son or, meschino,*
   Carlo e di Carlo i paladin gagliardi,
      e quanta gente nutre Italia e Francia,
      a provare il furor de la mia lancia?

I tuoi compagni almen de la tua sorte   52
   fian testimonii, e non potranno aitarti.
Tu giacendo vedrai vicino a morte
   da la vittrice man l'arme spogliarti. —
Rinaldo a quello: — *Io qui morrò qual forte,*
   s'è fisso in ciel, né tu pria déi vantarti;
      o pur, ucciso te, che Giove il voglia,
      altier n'andrò de l'acquistata spoglia. —

Mentre egli ancor così gli parla, arresta   53
   il re superbo la massiccia antenna;
e spronando il corsier sovra la testa
   di voler côrre il paladino accenna:
ma si sottragge a la percossa infesta
   Baiardo, lieve più ch'al vento penna.
      Rinaldo, nel passar presso la mano,
      tronca l'asta d'un colpo al fier pagano.

Indi, ogni suo vigore in un raccolto,   54
   dechina il braccio e maggior colpo tira,
e lo percuote a punto a mezzo il volto,
   là 've per stretta via si vede e spira.
L'elmo che, dove 'l gran Tifeo è sepolto,
   temprò Vulcan, resse del brando a l'ira,
      ma china a forza il capo il re feroce,
      per ira e duol stridendo in aspra voce.

"Withdraw now, all of you. This fight is mine,   50
    mine here is vengeance, mine the task to wage
combat with anyone in such haste to shine
    and play the hero's role upon death's stage.
You, worthless rabble, who fight like dogs and swine,
    cowards whom I... —but I shall check my rage
        that it may elsewhere turn to wreak my spite.
        Stand back and watch, for now your king will fight!"

This proud command of insolent Mambrin   51
    no man is tardy to comply withal.
They fall back round him, and the Saracen
    says to Rinaldo with a jeering drawl:
"Villain, why not ask all your comrades in:
    Great Charles and Charles' paladins, yea all
        the chivalrous fools whom Italy and France
        have spawned to feel the fury of my lance?

Two of your ilk at least are here to be   52
    witnesses, helpless at your downfall, and
when you lie dying at my feet, they'll see
    your arms despoiled by my victorious hand."
To him, Rinaldo: "If heaven should decree
    that I must die, I shall not die unmanned.
        Don't boast till then, for you may die. All toil
        may fail and hands unlooked-for seize the spoil."

He was still speaking when the insolent king   53
    put his enormous shaft in rest and sped
on his huge courser toward him galloping,
    intent to wound the paladin in the head,
but Bayard dodged the dreadful charge, veering
    light as a feather sideways, while instead
        Rinaldo, leaning to the right drew near,
        hitting the pagan's shield, but broke his spear.

He now, as both recover, comes to make   54
    his sword descend with a still mightier blow
on the spot mid-face, which air and vision take
    for a path of entry, and it strikes his foe,
whose Vulcan-tempered helmet does not break,
    wrought where Enceladus[59] lies, although
        the savage king perforce, touched to the brain,
        slumps in his seat and howls in rage and pain.

Né sì di rabbia il tauro ardendo mugge,   55
   né sì percosso il mar da' venti geme,
né sì ferito a morte il leon rugge,
   né sì sdegnato il ciel tonando freme:
a l'orribil gridar s'asconde e fugge
   ogni animal, non pur ne dubbia e teme;
      si rinselvan le fere a stuolo a stuolo,
      e rivolgon gli augelli indietro il volo.

L'irato re, ch'a vendicarsi intende,   56
   raggira il ferro in fiammeggiante ruota:
l'aria si rompe ed alto suon ne rende,
   quasi di Giove il folgor la percuota;
quando dal braccio il colpo orribil scende,
   par ch'intorno il terren tutto si scuota,
      com'avien se i vapor, secchi e rivolti
      in venti, stanno a forza entro sepolti.

Ma 'l cauto paladin, che scorge aperto   57
   lo sdegno ostile e 'l fier rabbioso affetto,
qual cavaliero in tai battaglie esperto,
   indi per sé n'attende utile effetto;
e ne l'armi si tien chiuso e coperto,
   ed in se stesso sta raccolto e stretto,
      facendo or con lo scudo or con la spada
      che la percossa avversa indarno vada.

Tal volta ancor con lieve e destro salto   58
   il veloce destrier tragge in disparte,
e così van l'impetuoso assalto
   rende non men de l'inimico Marte;
poi, vibrando la spada or basso or alto,
   sì lo schermirsi col ferir comparte,
      che n'è 'l gigante in molte parti offeso,
      ed egli ancor se 'n va salvo ed illeso.

Chi visto ha mai ne l'africane arene,   59
   quando il leon l'alto elefante assale,
com'egli destro ad affrontar lo viene,
   come de l'arte e del saltar si vale,
che non fermo in un luogo il passo tiene,
   ma gira sempre, e par ch'al fianco aggia ale,
      Mambrino a questo e 'l gran Rinaldo a quello
      potria rassomigliar nel fier duello.

Canto Twelve

No bull in heat more fiercely bellows, nor   55
    with ghastlier noise resounds a storm-tossed sea,
nor does a wounded lion's dying roar,
    nor rolling thunder shattering rock or tree.
All nearby creatures, shaken to the core,
    hearing that horrid outcry, hide or flee.
        Beasts haste in throngs toward the woods nearby,
        and flocks of birds reel backward in the sky.

The furious king, intent on vengeance, swings   56
    his falchion in a flaming arc. The air
is broken by its sweeping course and rings
    as if Jove's piercing bolt were whizzing there,
and the blow that from that strong arm falls then brings
    a devastating shock of force to bear,
        as when hot vapors forced from underground
        erupt and make earth tremble all around.[160]

But the paladin is wary, for he sees   57
    clearly what his foe's potent wrath intends,
having long learned the knightly expertise
    of turning an assault to his own ends.
Sheathed in his armor, self-possessed, at ease,
    he watches for his vantage and defends
        himself now with his shield, now with his blade,
        standing his ground or parrying undismayed.

Sometimes he makes his swift steed sideways go   58
    with nimble curvetings or leaps, whereby
he renders vain each devastating blow
    that hostile Mars brings crashing from on high,
and then, with sword now held aloft, now low,
    fends every stroke even as his own strokes fly,
        causing his giant foe grief and travail,
        while he himself remains unscathed and hale.

He who has seen a maddened lion fight   59
    a monstrous elephant on Afric sands —
he leaps at him to claw his hide and bite,
    and using every artifice he commands,
now seems to stay in place, but never quite,
    now flies at him as if on wings, now stands —
        would see Rinaldo truly imaged in
        the one, and in the other, fierce Mambrin.

Tra mille colpi al fin colse il gigante 60
    pur una volta il paladino in fronte,
mentre spingendo il corridore avante
    quel ne venia per farli oltraggio ed onte.
Quasi allor giacque da l'acciar pesante
    oppresso, qual Tifeo dal vasto monte;
        e, com'il mondo oscura notte adombre,
        agli occhi gli apparir tenebre ed ombre.

Ma le membra il vigor, gli occhi la vista 61
    racquistar tosto, e 'l cor l'usato ardire.
Di sì rio caso il cavalier s'attrista,
    ed apre il petto a novi sdegni ed ire;
e tanto più che n'ha Clarice vista
    gli occhi oscurar, le guancie impallidire:
        onde fiere il pagan con tanta possa
        che se no 'l ferro, il duol ben giunge a l'ossa.

Temendo a sé rio scorno, a lui ria morte, 62
    mira Clarice il suo gradito amore,
e come varia del pugnar la sorte,
    varia ella il viso e varia stato al core:
or con le guancie appar pallide e smorte,
    or di roseo le sparge e bel colore;
        tal, quando il giel dà loco a primavera,
        l'aria fassi nel marzo or chiara or nera.

Intanto di lor forze orrendo saggio 63
    fanno i due cavalier ch'a fronte sono.
Le spade nel girar sembrano un raggio
    che scorra il ciel con strepitoso tuono.
Non è sempre l'istesso il lor viaggio,
    né sempre fanno ancor l'istesso suono,
        perché, sì come or punta or taglio n'esce,
        diverso il suono e 'l lor camin riesce.

Caggion su l'ampie fronti e su le cave 64
    tempie l'aspre percosse a mille a mille:
non quando l'aria più di pioggia è grave
    versa Giunon sì spesse aquose stille.
L'armi, s'avien che lor gran colpo aggrave,
    spargon di fuoco al ciel vive faville,
        ed a' brandi la via darebbon sempre,
        s'elle non fosser d'incantate tempre.

At last one of the paladin's countless blows —   60
    one and one only — found the giant's head
just as he, giving spur, turned to oppose
    Rinaldo's charge and madly toward him sped.
He sprawls, stunned by the steel as his eyes close,
    like Typhoeus under Etna, arms outspread,
        and even as day turns black with sudden night,
        so thickening gloom obliterates his sight.

But look! His limbs regain their strength, his eyes   61
    their sight, his heart its savage ruthlessness.
The knight feels heightened scorn and anger rise
    at this cursed obstacle to his success,
and all the more when he nearby descries
    Clarice, all pale and weeping in distress.
        Doubling his blows, he makes sharp pain invade
        the pagan's bones, though proof against to his blade.

In dread of his disgrace and death, yea her   62
    disgrace and shame, Clarice looks on. Her face
grows pale or glows, her eyes brighten or blur
    as bane to weal or weal to bane yields place.
Now languid teardrops down her white cheeks err,
    now blushes sprinkle them with rosy grace.
        Even thus, when snow gives way to spring, the air
        of March bodes sometimes ill and sometimes fair.

Now the two knights are locked in furious fight,   63
    each offering horrid proof of martial skill.
Their swords whirl wildly, glinting as they smite
    like lightning flashes that the welkin fill,
but rarely twice in the same place alight
    or by the same sound show that they can kill,
        for here a point and there an edge proclaims
        in diverse sounds that both have found their aims.

Thousands on thousands of their ponderous blows   64
    on their broad brows and concave temples fall,
countless as drops when Juno's wrath o'erflows
    the skies in an annihilating squall.
Being struck, each of their armors' surface throws
    off sparks but shows no dent or gash at all,
        yet both, had sorcery not charmed their stuff,
        would have been smashed or punctured soon enough.

Ecco il fiero Mambrin, che folgorando   65
    tutto negli occhi, di furore ardente,
alto si leva e in alto leva il brando,
    ed in giù poi n'avalla un gran fendente;
ma non l'aspetta il paladin che, quando
    calar lo scorge e sibilar lo sente,
        tira tosto da canto il buon destriero,
        e van rende del reo l'empio pensiero.

Il grave colpo, ch'è commesso al vento,   66
    tira il guerrier col suo gran peso a basso;
sovra 'l ferrato arcion Mambrino il mento
    batte, e la spada sovr'un duro sasso.
Non è Rinaldo ad oltraggiarlo lento,
    ma con tal forza il fiede e tal fracasso,
        e sì raddoppia ognor l'aspre percosse,
        ch'al fin de' sensi e di vigor lo scosse.

Rassembra il paladin che, preso il ferro   67
    ad ambe man, raddoppia i colpi in fretta,
forte villan che 'l noderoso cerro
    brami tagliar con la pesante accetta;
pur tra sé disse alfin: — Vaneggio ed erro
    s'io credo penetrar la tempra eletta:
        tronchinsi i lacci a l'elmo, il capo al busto,
        mentre è stordito il Saracin robusto. —

E ben avrebbe, il suo desir a riva   68
    guidando, il fier gigante a morte posto,
ma vide il grosso stuol che ne veniva
    a vendicar il suo signor disposto;
onde l'ira temprò ch'in lui bolliva,
    ed a miglior pensier s'apprese tosto:
        ché ne l'immenso ardir che 'n lui regnava,
        luogo ognor la prudenza ancor trovava.

Vanne a Clarice, che nel dolce guardo   69
    gli dimostrava quel che 'l cor chiudea,
perch'a la voce ed al destrier gagliardo
    già prima lui riconosciuto avea;
e la si recca in groppa al suo Baiardo,
    dicendo: — Non vi spiaccia, alma mia dea,
        accettar di colui la pronta aita,
        ch'ama più il vostro onor che la sua vita. —

Canto Twelve

Behold! Now fierce Mambrin, his eyes afire   65
     his brow in fury knotted, black and grim,
lifts himself high and lifts his sword still higher,
     then lets it fall to hew off head or limb,
but the nimble paladin escapes its ire
     and sensing it come whistling down on him,
         makes his steed leap aside and brings to naught
         his murderous enemy's malicious thought.

Spent on the wind, the blow by its own weight   66
     carries Mambrino forward on his horse
and makes the iron saddle-bow meet his pate
     while stone ground stops his blade's descending course.
Rinaldo sees and does not hesitate
     but strikes with so much energy and force,
         redoubling every blow, that he at length,
         addles the pagan's sense and saps his strength.

The paladin pelts him with unnumbered cruel,   67
     two-handed blows, like a stout peasant who
is hacking with his heavy, sharp-edged tool
     at the thick trunk of a huge oak or yew,
but then he tells himself, "I am a fool
     to seek, as he lies stunned here, to pierce through
         his spell-charmed armor, when I might instead
         unlace his helmet and cut off his head."

He would indeed have followed up this thought   68
     and slain the unconscious giant then and there
but that he saw, converging on the spot
     just then, huge throngs of vengeful foes appear,
wherefore he tempered boiling rage and taught
     his ardor to proceed with prudent care,
         for, though the utmost daring ruled his soul,
         he never lacked discretion or control.

He turns to Clarice — who, angry no more,   69
     now shows her heart's love clearly in her face,
for she had recognized him long before
     by his voice and steed — and lifts her to a place
on Bayard's croup. "Goddess whom I adore,"
     he cries, "vouchsafe your servant by your grace
         to take you from this scene of death and strife
         who holds your honor dearer than his life."

Così disse ei, che fisso ha nel pensiero 70
   di ritrarsi al sicur con la donzella;
ma 'l sovragiunse con assalto fiero,
   come suol nave rapida procella,
l'aversa turba: allor l'estran guerriero
   spargendo gio certo liquor tra quella,
      e con sommesso mormorar fra' denti,
      formava intanto non intesi accenti.

Deggio 'l dire o tacer? Di quei che prima 71
   moveano al paladin spietata guerra,
tenta or ciascun com'il compagno opprima,
   e contra lui l'arme sdegnoso afferra:
così tra lor conversi oltr'ogni stima
   rendon del sangue lor rossa la terra.
      Ne stupisce Rinaldo, e ciò che vede
      agli occhi suoi medesmi a pien non crede.

E pensa ben tra sé che tale incanto 72
   solo opra sia del mago a lui germano;
fissamente colui rimira intanto,
   né l'imaginar suo gli sembra vano;
pur non parla di ciò, ma 'l prega alquanto
   che disfar voglia quell'incanto strano,
      ché fora biasmo lor se sì vilmente
      uccidesser sì forte e nobil gente.

— Il farò ben — rispose quelli allora, 73
   e dal più oltre caminar si tolse.
Tre volte ai regni de la bianca Aurora,
   tre volte gli occhi a l'occidente volse,
ed altre tante in sacri detti ancora
   la sacra lingua mormorando sciolse;
      alcune erbe non men sparse tre volte,
      che nel sen de la terra avea raccolte.

Lassa il pagano stuol l'aspra battaglia, 74
   in cui ciascun di lor fora al fin morto,
e contra 'l paladin allor si scaglia,
   stupido tutto, e del su' errore accorto;
ma, strano a dir, la via gli vieta e taglia
   fuoco d'incanto a l'improviso sorto,
      simile a quel che già Scamandro scerse,
      ch'in cener poi l'alto Ilion converse.

This said, he speeds off with her, being intent   70
    to bring her somewhere safe, but finds their flight
overtaken by the pagan rabblement.
    So might a boat on the wide sea catch sight
of a swift corsair on rape and pillage bent.
    Just then between them steps the stranger knight,
        sprinkling some liquid toward the infidels
        and muttering through clenched teeth some
            nameless spells.

Should I speak or bid my tongue be still? For lo!   71
    Half the pursuing host turns in its tracks,
and each foe turns upon a fellow foe,
    and not the paladin, but him attacks.
Rivers of blood beyond all measure flow
    to redden earth from mangled chests and backs.
        Rinaldo, thunderstruck, can scarce believe
        the evidence that his own eyes receive.

Indeed he deems that magic such as this   72
    none but his sorcerer cousin could command,
and finding his conjecture not amiss
    when he his face somewhat more closely scanned,
but keeping mum, he begs him to dismiss
    the dark spell, begging him to understand
        that death by sorcery brought naught but shame
        on all these many knights of worth and fame.

"Agreed," said he, "you shall not ask in vain,"   73
    and moved some steps apart from all the rest.
Three times he bowed toward white Aurora's reign,
    and three time turned his eyes toward the west,
and then in hallowed words three times again
    the vacant air with reverent tongue addressed,
        thrice scattering some herbs of sovereign worth
        plucked by him from the bosom of the earth.

The pagans ceased their fratricidal war,   74
    in which they to a man would soon have died,
and turned against the paladin once more,
    aware of their mistake and stupefied,
but, strange to say, enchanted flames now roar
    to block the path they would assail him by
        like those that from Scamander did ascend
        and made great Ilium in cinders end.[61]

Né stella che risplenda a mezzo giorno,   75
    o ch'aggia a notte i crin di sangue aspersi,
né ciel ch'appaia di tre soli adorno,
    né ruggiada che rossa indi si versi,
né l'eclipsar di quel che suolsi intorno
    scuoter l'ombre e mostrar color diversi,
        recaro altrui giamai tal maraviglia,
        qualor ciascun del novo incanto piglia.

Di là stanno i pagani alto fremendo   76
    e minacciando il nobil paladino,
ch'entrar a piè volea nel foco orrendo
    per l'orgoglio domar del Saracino;
ma lo strano guerrier, la man tendendo,
    il prese e 'l distornò da quel camino,
        ché gli disse che 'l fuoco in un sol punto
        lui con l'armi e le veste avria consunto;

e che ben tosto in sanguinoso Marte   77
    potrebbe essercitar gli sdegni e l'ire,
quando non fia chi con astuzia ed arte
    la battaglia tra lor cerchi impedire;
e 'l prega poi che seco in altra parte
    con la sua compagnia degni venire,
        ad onorare il suo più caro albergo,
        che d'un bel colle preme il verde tergo.

Rinaldo, ch'oltramodo a lui desia   78
    di compiacere, a pien ciò gli concede.
Così partirsi, e l'altra compagnia
    di ragionar modo agli amanti diede:
ond'il barone a la sua donna gia,
    dimostrando il su' amore e la sua fede,
        e purgandosi in quel ch'era sospetto
        con destro modo e con acceso affetto.

Il sentier, ch'è ben lungo e discosceso,   79
    pian sembra e curto ai duo fidi amadori;
veggion splendere al fin, qual raggio acceso
    che sorgendo dal Gange il mondo indori,
il bel palagio, e così bene inteso,
    ch'opra par di celesti architettori:
        quadra la forma, e la materia è d'aspro
        per molti intagli oriental diaspro.

No prodigy — not some star at mid-day bright,   75
    nor one that trailing red hair blazes through
nocturnal darkness nor the threefold light
    of three suns in the sky nor bloody dew
nor the eclipse of what restores to sight
    the hues and shades that black night blots from view —
        ever made any man so gape and stare
        as did this new enchantment's scorching glare.

On one side of the blaze the pagans stand   76
    uttering loud threats against the paladin,
who himself looks keen to meet the fierce flames and
    to tame the vain pride of the Saracen,
but the strange warrior takes him by the hand,
    turns him aside and says that leaping in
        would have meant instant death: the fiery wall
        would have consumed him, arms and clothes and all.

He adds that he would soon enough be free   77
    to give full scope to Mars in bloody wrath,
when no man should by art or sorcery
    beguile him of his foe or bar his path.
Meanwhile he asks him and his company
    to follow him and spend the aftermath
        of combat at his best-loved place of rest
        nearby, resplendent on a green hill's crest.

Rinaldo, well disposed in any case   78
    to yield to his desire, does not say no.
He follows with the others toward that place,
    the pair of lovers talking as they go.
The baron, once more in his lady's grace,
    assures her of his love and faith and so
        silences the last remnants of suspicion
        with words of ardent love and meek submission.

The path is steep and arduous but seems   79
    easy and level to the lovers' eyes.
At last they see, bright as the blazing beams
    that gilding all the world from Ganges rise,
the palace, fronting like a house of dreams
    built by celestial architects the skies,
        splendid, four-square, its splendor much increased
        by carvings wrought in jasper from the East.

Con benigne accoglienze e con reale   80
   pompa accolti ambo fur nel tetto altero,
e sùbito curato, e del suo male
   quasi guarito fu 'l roman guerriero.
Fu la cena abbondante, e forse quale
   Cleopatra e Locullo un tempo fêro;
      e qui lor poi l'albergator cortese
      fe' d'esser Malagigi al fin palese.

Oh con che lieto affetto, oh con qual caro   81
   modo Rinaldo il suo cugino abbraccia!
Quasi il dolce piacer in pianto amaro
   accolto sparge su l'allegra faccia,
perciò che lor d'amor perfetto e raro
   indissolubil nodo i cuori allaccia.
      Fa quell'altro il medesmo; indi da canto
      Clarice e 'l su' amador ritira alquanto.

Quivi, poi che disgombro ebbe da quella,   82
   con mille rai di ragion vive e vere,
del rio sospetto l'ombra iniqua e fella
   che rendea le lor menti oscure e nere,
così aperse le labra a la favella,
   principio ad ambeduo d'alto piacere:
      — Dire a ragion colui si dee prudente
      che scorge più di quel ch'egli ha presente.

Colui che col presente e col passato   83
   così bene il futur misura e scorge,
che, se gli è da Fortuna appresentato,
   al suo crine la man veloce porge,
né da nessuno error folle adombrato,
   lassando il peggio, del miglior s'accorge:
      ciò vi dico io, perché possiate voi
      prudenti e saggi dimostrarvi poi.

Ed or che vi si porge e tempo e loco   84
   commodo a terminar vostri martiri,
ché so ben ch'ambo in amoroso foco
   per l'altro ardete e 'n casti e bei desiri,
a quel ch'avvenir può pensate un poco,
   ai varii di Fortuna instabil giri,
      a le guerre, agli incendi onde la Francia
      n'andrà più giorni in lacrimosa guancia.

Received with great pomp at the palace door,   80
    they enter the high hall. At once appear
healers to soothe the fresh wounds and restore
    the Roman warrior to health and cheer.
A banquet follows, sumptuous as of yore
    Cleopatra's or Lucullus's.[162] And here
        their host at last discloses who he is:
        the sorcerer-knight of Clairmont, Malagis.

Oh, with what gladness now, what tender pride,   81
    Rinaldo meets his cousin's fond embrace!
What joy, overflowing as it were, now spills
    in streams of salt tears on his beaming face
knowing the rare and perfect love that tied
    their hearts by laws no power could erase!
        The other equally shows his delight,
        then draws apart with Clarice and her knight.

To Clarice first he speaks to make her free,   82
    by lucid arguments of every kind,
of the last shadows of foul jealousy
    that long in both had darkened heart and mind,
then utters words in which both he and she
    plenteous cause for unmixed pleasure find:
        "Whatever one's present fortune be, one should
        not be kept ignorant of future good.

A man who knows both past and present weal   83
    by prudent thought may know the future's, too.
At the approach of fickle Fortune, he'll
    grasp at her forelock when she sails in view.
That man will, undeceived by things unreal,
    forget the worse and find the better true.[163]
        I say this, so that you yourselves may find,
        while time is ripe, such prudence of the mind.

Now that the place and time seem apt and near   84
    to end the torment of your hearts that yearn —
I well know how you for each other here
    in amorous fire and chaste longing burn —
think of the time to come, the time of fear,
    of havoc when great Fortune's wheel shall turn,
        of war that in a few short days or weeks
        shall stain with bitter tears poor France's cheeks.

Fia ben vittrice al fin, ma non d'amore 85
    fiano i nostri pensier per molti mesi,
ma sol d'odio, di rabbia e di furore,
    e di desio d'aspre vendette accesi;
a sangue, a morti, a stragi, a tutte l'ore
    gli animi incrudeliti avremo intesi.
        Dunque or che 'l tempo par ch'a ciò v'invite,
        con laccio maritale in un v'unite.

Né rimagniate già, perché lontani 86
    ed ignari ne sian vostri parenti,
ché questi abusi sono, e folli e vani
    respetti sol de le vulgari genti.
E quel sommo Signor, de le cui mani
    opra son gli alti cieli e gli elementi,
        n'impose sol che di concordi voglie
        concorrà col marito in un la moglie. —

Spinti i fidi amador da questi detti, 87
    e dal desir ch'in lor ne gia di paro,
venner concordi a' maritali effetti,
    ch'in presenza d'ognun si celebraro.
Fur i lor cuor da gentil laccio stretti,
    ch'Amore e Castità dolce annodaro;
        sorrise Giove, e con secondo tuono
        veder gran luce, udir fe' lieto suono.

Già ne venia con chiari almi splendori 88
    Cinzia versando in perle accolto il gielo,
e senza ombre noiose e senza orrori
    candido distendea la Notte il velo.
Già spargeva Imeneo coi vaghi amori
    fiori e frondi nel suol, canti nel cielo,
        quando di propria man Venere bella
        congiunse in un Rinaldo e la donzella.

Or che sì destro il cielo a voi si gira, 89
    godete, o coppia di felici amanti,
godete il ben che casto Amor v'inspira,
    e l'oneste dolcezze e i gaudi santi.
Ecco che tace omai la roca lira
    che cantò i vostri affanni e i vostri pianti;
        e che voi insieme il desir vostro, ed io
        ho qui condutto a fin il canto mio.

Though she will triumph in the end, meanwhile   85
    for months our minds will be preoccupied
with hostile slaughter, treachery and guile,
    with thoughts of vengeance still unsatisfied
making us cruel, with no time to smile
    for love till we have crushed the pagan's pride.
        Therefore propitious time invites you now
        to be united by the nuptial vow.

Think not your parents, being far away   86
    and unaware of this, are thus abused:
that is what vain and vulgar folk would say
    whose acts are foolish and whose minds, confused.
The highest Lord, whom earth and heaven obey
    ordains no marriage vow can be refused
        so long as, by concordant judgment led,
        a woman and a man agree to wed."[164]

Urged by these words, urged no less strongly by   87
    their keen desire, the loving pair made haste
whither the nuptial altar rose on high
    and, plighting troth in sight of all, embraced,
letting those chains their hearts together tie
    that Love and Chastity around them placed.
        Jove smiled and his auspicious thunder rent
        the air with sound, with light the firmament.

Now rises, scattering dew like clustered pearls   88
    in all her splendor Cynthia, kind and clear.
Now starry Night her lambent veil unfurls,
    and no dark sprites or baleful shades draw near.
Now Hymen, with his crew of cupids, whirls
    his flowering staff and greets with song the ear,
        while Venus by her own hand joins in one
        Rinaldo and the love that he has won.

Now that kind heaven rights your former wrong,   89
    enjoy your new-found life, O happy pair,
enjoy the sweets that to chaste Love belong.
    Let their delight repay your former care.
Lo! The hoarse lyre falls silent that so long
    made your laments re-echo through the air.
        You have reached the end of your desires, and I
        must end this song of mine and say good-bye.

Rinaldo

Così scherzando io risonar già fèa 90
    di Rinaldo gli ardori e i dolci affanni,
allor ch'ad altri studi il dì togliea
    nel quarto lustro ancor de' miei verd'anni:
ad altri studi, onde poi speme avea
    di ristorar d'avversa sorte i danni;
        ingrati studi, dal cui pondo oppresso
        giaccio ignoto ad altrui, grave a me stesso.

Ma se mai fia ch'a me longo ozio un giorno 91
    conceda, ed a me stesso il ciel mi renda,
sì ch'a l'ombra cantando in bel soggiorno
    con Febo l'ore e i dì felici spenda,
portarò forse, o gran Luigi, intorno
    i vostri onori ovunque il sol risplenda,
        con quella grazia che m'avrete infusa,
        destando a dir di voi più degna musa.

Tu de l'ingegno mio, de le fatiche 92
    parto primiero e caro frutto amato,
picciol volume ne le piagge apriche
    che Brenta inonda, in sì brev'ozio nato:
così ti dian benigne stelle amiche
    viver, quando io sarò di vita orbato;
        così t'accoglia chiara fama in seno
        tra quei de le cui lodi il mondo è pieno.

Pria che di quel signor giunghi al cospetto, 93
    c'ho nel core io, tu ne la fronte impresso,
al cui nome gentil vile e negletto
    albergo sei, non qual conviensi ad esso,
vanne a colui che fu dal cielo eletto
    a darmi vita col suo sangue istesso:
        io per lui parlo e spiro e per lui sono,
        e se nulla ho di bel, tutto è suo dono.

Ei con l'acuto sguardo, onde le cose 94
    mirando oltra la scorza al centro giunge,
vedrà i difetti tuoi, ch'a me nascose
    occhio mal san che scorge poco lunge;
e con la man ch'ora veraci prose
    a finte poesie di novo aggiunge,
        ti purgarà quanto patir tu puoi,
        aggiungendo vaghezza ai versi tuoi.

IL FINE

Thus I once made, as though in sport, resound   90
     Rinaldo's hurtful loves and pleasing tears,
truant from other studies' dismal round
     in the fourth lustrum[165] of my unripe years,
from other studies to which I seemed bound
     to fill my hopes and to allay my fears,
         unpleasant studies, by whose weight oppressed
         I found, still nameless, neither joy nor rest.

But one day, granted leisure and strength to bring   91
     myself to claim my own God-given right,
I may, seated at ease in pleasant shade to sing
     with Phoebus and his deathless crew, take flight
to make your fame, august Luigi,[166] ring
     in every clime to which the sun gives light,
         and by the grace that you in me infuse
         arouse, to speak of you, a worthier Muse.

Go then, first birth and dear-beloved fruit   92
     that heavy toil unto my genius bore.
Go little book that in short time took root
     from leisure snatched on Brenta's sunlit shore.[167]
May friendly stars lend aid in your pursuit
     of deathless fame when I shall be no more,
         and may your words inspire in future days
         all those who best deserve the whole world's praise.

Yet, before seeking him whose name is found   93
     engraved on your first page and in my heart —
lodgings too humble for a name renowned
     and worthy to be served by loftier art —
first seek out him whom generous heaven bound
     by ties of blood to me even from the start.
         He gave me breath and speech, yea life and limb,
         and all my best gifts are but gifts from him.

He surely, with that keen gaze by which he   94
     pierces the superficial husk and knows
the core, will spy out flaws I could not see
     when Truth's light made my poor eyes blink or close.
Let his firm hand that to feigned poetry
     joins once again now plain and honest prose,[168]
         cleanse or emend as much as you'll endure
         to make your verse ring effortlessly pure.[169]

THE END

NOTES

*Asterisks precede names and terms defined in the Glossary

1. An echo of Virgil's fourth *Eclogue* and of the opening lines of his *Aeneid* (eventually cancelled). Tasso's use of this topos is primarily conventional, since the bulk of his lyric poetry in fact postdates the composition of *Rinaldo*; however, by the time of publication he had indeed written a number of lyrics for Lucrezia Bendidio (whose "beloved name" is likely intended by line 4). The topos reappears in the opening sonnet of Tasso's *Rime d'occasione e d'encomio* (S.500).

2. The dedicatee of the poem was Luigi d'Este (1538–86), second child of Ercole II d'Este and Renée, daughter of Louis XII of France. An avid supporter of art and music, he was Bernardo Tasso's patron, and Tasso himself eventually entered his service in 1565. The "device" is probably the Este family coat-of-arms: a silver eagle on a blue ground (flying heavenward?). Luigi's personal emblem, however, was "Prometheus bearing fire in a stalk of fennel."

3. Wearing the cardinal's hat.

4. Luigi d'Este, then just twenty-three years old, was elevated to the cardinalship a year prior to the publication of *Rinaldo*. He was eventually named cardinal-protector of France, a position that gave him enormous influence in the Roman Curia; hence Tasso's not unreasonable reference to the papal tiara in the next stanza, inferring that Luigi would eventually become pope. He did not.

5. The Holy Land.

6. The lyre is a symbol of the lower (lyric and romantic) reaches of poetry; the trumpet, of the higher (epic and tragic). Tasso adds this dichotomy to the one already introduced earlier (n.1 above).

7. In the earliest source for Tasso's epic, the Old French *Quatre Fils d'Aymon*, Renaud (Rinaldo) has three brothers. Tasso, perhaps from an unknown later source, gives him only two (see 1.27). They are occasionally mentioned in the narrative but never named. (See also 9.47–51.)

8. According to Carolingian legend, Bernard of *Clairmont fathered two sons, Milo and *Aymon, who respectively fathered Orlando and Rinaldo. Tasso makes Rinaldo eventually discard this leopard shield (see 8.72).

9. In Greek mythology, the *Fates.

10. Lance and spear are not, strictly speaking, synonyms — a lance is for thrusting; a spear for throwing. However, where a rhyme is involved I have sometimes used these interchangeably.

Rinaldo

11. The first Christian emperor of Rome. In medieval legend, many
    rulers and heroes (including *Charlemagne and *Orlando) claim
    descent from him; conversely, villains (such as Ganelon) are often
    said to be descendants of Constantine's rebel son, Licinius. These
    villains, in turn, sometimes legitimize offspring by naming them
    Constantine — no doubt Tasso's reason for also giving the name to
    an evil pagan. See Index and 8.75.

12. Region in northeast-central Greece, associated in classical literature
    with magicians, centaurs, and the Argonauts.

13. The stanza presents one of the few instances of authorial moralizing
    in the narrative, expressly deemed undesirable in *Torquato Tasso to
    His Readers* (see Appendix, pp. 438–46). For the handful of other
    infractions of this rule see 6.12.1–6; 6.62.1–63.12, 10.6.11–12 and
    11.5.1–12.

14. *English baron:* This knight is never named. Tasso perhaps intended
    him for Astolfo, the British prince in Ariosto's *Orlando Furioso,* who
    rides not only the fierce stallion, Rabican, but also the Hippogriff.
    He, at any rate, disappears from Tasso's poem after a dozen stanzas.

15. This passage is obviously indebted to Virgil (*Aeneid* 12.896–98) and
    Homer (*Iliad* 21.403–5).

16. The region around Pozzuoli, a city north-west of Naples, is noted
    for volcanic activity.

17. Mythological steed tamed by *Pollux.

18. *Cupid.

19. Rinaldo, it will be remembered, has no sword to draw, since he
    vowed to employ none unless he first wrests it in battle from a
    worthy foe (1.26–27). His present opponent is evidently unworthy;
    thus it is Ysolier who must now take up the quarrel.

20. Rinaldo's future fight with the giant Atlas, from whom he will take
    the sword Fusberta (6.25–36).

21. Though not named, this can be none other than Clarice. Tasso's
    account of her movements is somewhat vague. It seems she has run
    into the Knight of the Siren after his mission to her brother Ives
    (3.48) and run off alone when their horses are killed by Ransald
    (3.20). We next find her among Queen Galerana's attendants (4.11).

22. Gharb-al-Andalus, historically the Umayyad region of southern
    Spain and northern Morocco.

23. Tyre was a city in ancient Phoenicia, now in Lebanon; in Tasso's
    day considered part of Syria.

24. For *Babylon, see Glossary. Kurdistan does not appear in Tasso's
    original. It has been added for the sake of rhyme.

Notes

25. Atlante is the sorcerer who acts as Ruggiero's protector in Ariosto's *Orlando Furioso*; Zoroaster or Zarathustra is the great magus of ancient Persia.

26. In Arthurian romance, Tristan of Lyoness and Lancelot of the Lake are both great champions and great lovers (of their liege-lords' wives). In some late-medieval accounts, notably *Tristan et Lancelot* by Pierre Sala (1457-1529), they fight a great duel.

27. The builder of the Parthenon, the most illustrious sculptor of ancient Greece.

28. See n. 8 above.

29. The passengers of this vessel and the reasons for its rendezvous with the land-carrack are never specified. One conjectures that the battle that soon follows prevents an intended ritual betrothal of Clarice and Mambrin.

30. Barbarous region in present-day southern Russia.

31. Venus' husband, the god *Vulcan.

32. The word usually carries the broader sense of *Africa*.

33. Varying…varying: the repetitiveness of the diction in my translation does not exceed that of the original.

34. Ursa Major is a constellation in the northern hemisphere.

35. The god of *Love.

36. In Ariosto's *Orlando Furioso*, Ysolier is brother to one of the poem's main figures, Ferraù. In Tasso's work he now disappears without explanation from the poem. His narrative function as Rinaldo's *fidus Achates* is taken over (5.31ff) by Florindo, seemingly also a Spaniard, though eventually recognized as a Roman foundling.

37. *Lustra* (pl. of Latin *lustrum*), a five-year period, originally the interval at which censors in ancient Rome offered a purification sacrifice ("lustration"). Tasso was pedantically fond of this term as a synonym for the passing of the years. He employed it twice again in *Rinaldo* (9.33.8 and 12.90.4) and — no less than four times! — in *Gerusalemme liberata* (1.60, 4.44, 8.10, 10.22).

38. *Venus.

39. In the original Italian the boy's skin is both "silver" (*argento*) and "ivory" (*avorio*). No ringdoves fill the air in the Italian; they're needed for the rhyme.

40. *Phosphorus, the morning star, is the son of *Aurora, the dawn. His brother is Hesperus (the evening star). Both are in actual fact the planet Venus. Their identity is hinted at in the stanza that follows.

41. The discovery of a lover lamenting in solitude is a commonplace of both chivalric and pastoral literature. Compare Boiardo, *Orlando Innamorato* 1.16.60, Ariosto, *Orlando Furioso* 1.40ff, Alamanni, *Girone* 4.32 and Sannazaro, *Arcadia* I.

42. A famous madrigal setting of this octave is contained in Luca Marenzio's *Madrigali a quattro voci*, Book One (1585).

43. Another octave set as a famous madrigal, in Stefano Felis' *Madrigali a cinque voci*, Book Six (1591). Note the late date: almost thirty years after *Rinaldo*'s first publication.

44. A literal translation gives an idea of the artificiality of Tasso's rhetoric here. "Always there is hope where there is the fire of love; / in me the first [i.e., hope] is not, the other [i.e., the fire of love] indeed."

45. Florindo's speech, which follows here, is the longest (259 lines) of the half dozen or so inserted secondary narrations in the poem, longer by far than its nearest competitors: the lament of Clytie's widower in Canto Seven (180 lines) and Rinaldo's account of his quarrel with Ginam in Canto Nine (168 lines).

46. A city in Spain, famous for its resistance to Rome. After a cruelly protracted siege, it was taken and razed by Scipio Aemilianus in 133 BCE. The city's heroic resistance is noted by many ancient historians, notably Appian (*Iberian Wars* 6.90–98). Appian's work had been known in Latin translation since the beginning of the 16th century. There were numerous Venetian editions before 1562, including those by Ludovico Dolce (1559), who may have known the *editio princeps* (Paris, 1551) of the Greek original. Another edition, by Girolamo Ruscelli, appeared in Venice one year after *Rinaldo*.

47. Mahoun (or Mahound) is Muhammad, imagined by most medieval and Renaissance authors as a demon or pagan divinity, rather than as the founder of a religion.

48. A kissing contest (albeit among boys — but see 5.29) occurs in Theocritus' *Idylls* (12.30–34). More interestingly, some thirty years after *Rinaldo*, Battista Guarini introduces a far more similar contest in his vastly popular *Pastor Fido* (2.1.59–336). Guarini, Tasso's rival and eventual successor as court-poet in Ferrara, may have taken his cue from *Rinaldo*, but Navone's suggestion ("Intersezione," p. 10) that both poets drew on an unknown common source cannot be ruled out.

49. Such a disguise, with a similar end in view, is found in Boccaccio's *Nymphs of Fiesole* (200 ff.). Boccaccio's account, it must be said, is rather more lascivious, and his lovers end unhappily.

50. Tasso's eighteenth-century English translator, John Hoole, first suggested that the fire blocking access to the Cave of Love may

have inspired Edmund Spenser's similar wall of flame in *Fairie Queene* (6.12), through which Britomart passes to view the Masque of Cupid. If so, Spenser expanded Tasso's mention of Cupid's conquests, supposedly depicted on the slab outside the cave (6.59.6–8), into an elaborate ekphrasis of Cupid's triumphs on the tapestries inside the vestibule (*FQ* 3.11.28–46).

51. *Victories…gods above:* Tasso is probably thinking of Arachne's depiction of the loves of the gods in Ovid's *Metamorphoses* (6.103–128). This is exactly what Spenser later supplies (see n. 50 above). Readers who feel cued to expect a similarly elaborate ekphrasis will, however, be disappointed. Tasso's failure here and elsewhere to fill in such specifics is perhaps a sign of the haste in which the poem was composed. (For a satisfactory ekphrasis, see 8.19-23.)

52. The quintessence or ether, a supposed incorruptible and non-corporeal element that filled the space above the corporeal other four: earth, water, air and fire.

53. He has, of course, joined in it already. The piously orthodox feeling of this stanza seems false in *Rinaldo,* but anticipates a tone characteristic of the *Gerusalemme.*

54. *Venus.

55. Julius Caesar, who conquered Transalpine Gaul. i.e., France and much of Spain and the Netherlands in 58–51 BCE.

56. Hannibal, the Carthaginian general who led his army across the Alps to invade Rome during the Second Punic War in 218 BCE.

57. This encomium of Italy seems to be a free imitation of Virgil's *Georgics* 2.167-74.

58. The region of the Hesperides or Blessed Isles, traditionally located far west of Europe's Atlantic coast.

59. The borderland between Arabia and Syria from the Euphrates to the Red Sea.

60. Lust or drunkenness.

61. Anachronistic reference to the Roman equivalent of the boxing glove, made of lead-weighted strips of leather tied around the fist.

62. The two stanzas that follow here are the longest incursion of the authorial voice in the body of the narrative. (See also notes to 1.91.1-12, 10.6.11-12 and 11.5.1-12).

63. The dragon stands for the Turks, who, after seizing Constantinople in 1492, had overrun most of the Balkans. All through his life Tasso supported the call for a crusade to retake the formerly Christian East.

64. Rinaldo, true to his vow, still wears no sword.

65. In Tasso's massing of names in single stanzas some names have been altered for the sake of rhyme — a perhaps pardonable liberty when hundreds of combatants appear and are named only once in the poem.

66. Otho is a Christian, drawn into battle by envy of Rinaldo's achievement. The first blood drawn by the pagan sword conquered by Rinaldo is Christian, an irony that Tasso probably intended.

67. The translation is exact, but Tasso's need for a rhyme (*lancia* rhyming with *Francia*) has made him forget that Hugh fell to a sword, not to a lance. Hugh's death results from a breach of the chivalric code. A jouster was forbidden to use his sword while lances were still in play. Rinaldo's anger at being almost thrown makes him break this rule. Compare the earlier combat with Atlas, in which the Saracen, wielding the same sword, takes similarly unfair advantage.

68. The combatants are close relatives. See 1.19.

69. In post-Homeric tradition, *Achilles was invulnerable, except for his heel. He fought with Neptune's son Cycnus, and, finding him impervious to wounds, strangled him with the laces of his helmet. Neptune transformed him into a swan (Ovid, *Metamorphoses* 12.72).

70. A foreshadowing. All three of these are fated to be killed by Rinaldo in Canto Eight.

71. The pile-up of casualties here (mentioned here for the first and only time in the poem) has once again led me into renaming for rhyme (see 6.23), but in this case Tasso's Italian is equally lame.

72. *Charlemagne's camp on its hillside, the Saracens' in the plain below, with Namo's and Aymon's on either side. See 6.7.

73. This lamentation by Hugh's father is clearly indebted to Evander's lament for Pallas in Virgil's *Aeneid* (11.148–81), but the grisly episode of the severed head that follows is Tasso's own invention.

74. The story that follows clearly imitates Ovid's accounts of Cephalus and Procris (*Ars Amatoria* 3.683–746 and *Metamorphoses* 7.694–862). Tasso had apparently written an early poem (now lost) on this subject. He specifically refers to it in one of his lyrics (*Rime* S.500). The present passage is perhaps a rewriting of that work.

75. Tasso is planting, I think, a deliberately misleading suggestion. By the conventions of courtly-love rhetoric, the line suggests that the speaker was "dying with love" for Hermilla. Its true meaning turns out to be that Hermilla's beauty is fatal for the speaker by causing his wife's jealousy and death.

76. The stanza alludes to three famous just-so stories from Ovid's *Metamorphoses*. Hyacinthus was accidentally killed in a discus contest with his lover *Apollo, who transformed him into a hyacinth (10.162ff.). Narcissus was turned into the flower that bears

his name after he drowns in a pool while trying to embrace his reflection (3.407ff.). Adonis, beloved of *Venus, after being killed by a boar, was transformed by her into an anemone (10.524ff. and 708–35). The "third sphere" in Ptolemaic astronomy is the sphere of Venus.

77. Here used in the general sense of "the sea," but compare with the Glossary entry.

78. A seaside village north-west of Naples, now part of the city, long famed for its natural beauty and its association with Virgil whose reputed tomb is nearby. Tasso, no doubt, had fond memories of it from his boyhood. In the 1540s, his father praised its beauty in a well-known letter to G.B. Peres reprinted in *Napoli Nobilissima* 13 (1904): 172–74.

79. Chloris is the Greek name of Flora, goddess of flowers and the springtime. Pomona is the goddess of fruits and autumn. The Three Graces (Greek *Charites*), symbols of natural beauty and human comeliness, are usually imagined as three naked goddesses joining hands in a dance.

80. Mediterranean island closely associated with *Venus. See also n. 132 below.

81. The hall here described seems to be modeled on the central salon of the Villa Imperiale near Pesaro, summer residence of the dukes of Urbino, visited by Bernardo Tasso in 1557 and 1559 and described by him in a letter dated February 10, 1557 (Bernardo Tasso, *Lettere*, ed. Comino, v. 2, p. 243).

82. Apelles of Kos (4th century BCE) singled out by Pliny the Elder (*Natural History* 35–36) as the best painter in antiquity.

83. Francesco de' Rossi (1510–63), called 'Il Salviati,' Florentine painter and student of Andrea del Sarto. Tasso, however, is probably referring to his student, Giuseppe Porta (1520–75), who adopted his master's name and had recently been active in Padua, completing a notable fresco cycle in the Selvatico Palace in 1552. This is no longer extant; his best-known surviving works are a series of tondos in the Biblioteca Marciana, Venice.

84. Cancer and Taurus: the sun rises and sets in these two signs of the Zodiac once every year.

85. David Quint in "The Boat of Romance and the Renaissance Epic," in *Romance: Generic Transformation from Chrétien de Troyes to Cervantes*, edited by Kevin Brownlee and Marina Scordilis Brownlee, 178–202 (Hanover, NH: University Press of New England, 1985) has shown that the Ship of Adventure is a commonplace of European romance.

86. An echo of Homer's "rosy-fingered dawn."

87. Tasso's catalogue of imaginary portraits seems to imitate (if less elaborately and somewhat feebly) two passages in Ariosto's *Orlando Furioso:* *Merlin's paintings in Tristan's castle of future invaders of Italy (33.13–57) and the statues on the Fountain of Chaste Women (42.78–95). In the latter, Ariosto, like Tasso, features Rinaldo as the auditor and several personages connected with the House of Este as subjects.

88. Ippolito d'Este (1509–72), son of Alfonso I, noted patron of letters, created cardinal (i.e., vested in the "sacred purple") in 1538.

89. Ercole Gonzaga (1505–63), son of Francesco II, duke of Mantua, and Isabella d'Este; created cardinal at age twenty; papal legate to the Council of Trent and elected its president in 1561.

90. Luigi d'Este. See nn. 2 and 4 above and 12.91–93.

91. This stanza, with 8.10 and 10.80, is one of three dropped in the second Venetian edition (1570). No satisfactory reason for their deletion has been discovered.

92. Alfonso II d'Este (1533–97), fifth and last duke of Ferrara, who became Tasso's patron in 1572. A youthful portrait of him by Girolamo da Carpi can be seen in the Prado, Madrid.

93. *Maria Francesco's son:* Maria Francesco della Rovere (1490–1538) was succeeded as duke of Urbino by his son, Guidobaldo II (1514–74), to whom Tasso dedicated the fragmentary first draft of his *Gierusalemme.*

94. Francesco Maria della Rovere (1548–1641), Guidobaldo's heir; a fellow student of Tasso's at Urbino and a life-long friend.

95. See note to 8.6 above.

96. Neapolitan priest and writer, later bishop of Naples (d. 1595), a friend and classmate of Tasso's at Padua.

97. A Polish nobleman who also studied with Tasso at Padua.

98. Scipione Gonzaga of Gazzuolo (1542–93), collateral relative of the dukes of Mantua, man of letters and fellow student with Tasso in Padua, a founding member of the Accademia degli Eterei. He later (1575) convened and became a member of the committee to whose judgment Tasso entrusted the first version of his *Gerusalemme liberata.* He was eventually (1587) created cardinal.

99. *Fulvio Rangon:* Marquess of Livisano and Castelvetro (1536–1588), brother of Claudio Rangoni (1559-1621, later bishop of Reggio) and a diplomat and amateur author, who patronized both Bernardo Tasso and his son. In 1564, he gave shelter at his castle to Tasso, driven from Bologna for supposedly writing a seditious pamphlet (see Chronology).

100. Ercole Fregoso may be a son of Giani Fregoso, doge of Genoa and later Venetian condottiere. The Fregoso funeral monument in S. Anastasia,Verona, is by Danese Cataneo (see p. xvi, n.8). Santinello has not been satisfactorily identified.

101. Vittoria Farnese (1519–1602), wife of Guidobaldo II della Rovere, duke of Urbino. A portrait of her is also found along with that of Claudia Rangoni (n. 104 below), in the Temple of Chastity of Bernardo Tasso's *Amadigi* (Canto 44).

102. Lucrezia d'Este (1535–98), sister of Alfonso II, who married Francesco Maria II of Urbino in 1570 and later became, along with her sister Eleonora, a patron frequently celebrated in Tasso's poetry.

103. Anna (1531–1607) and Eleonora (1537–81) d'Este, sisters of Lucrezia and Alfonso II. Tasso never met Anna. She left Ferrara for France after her marriage to the duke of Guise in 1548 and never returned to Italy. Her husband was killed by a Huguenot assassin in 1563. Nine years later (the year of *Rinaldo*'s publication), she was widely thought to have instigated the assassination of the Huguenot leader Coligny, which precipitated the infamous St. Bartholomew's Day Massacre in Paris. Eleonora d'Este, along with Lucrezia (n. 102 above and Chronology, pp. xlii–xliii, for the years 1565, 1570 and 1575) became a lifelong patron of Tasso's.

104. Claudia Rangoni (d. 1593); sister of Claudio and Fulvio Rangoni (n. 99 above), married in 1550 to Gilberto VIII, count of Correggio and separated from him in 1562. Though Tasso implies that she was a writer, no works by her seem to have survived.

105. The youngest of the classical *Hours, goddess of Peace. Classical myth does not particularly connect her with needlework.

106. In a myth famously retold by Ovid (*Metamorphoses* 6.5–140), Arachne challenges *Minerva to a weaving contest and is punished by being transformed into a spider.

107. *Sister of the sun:* *Diana, *Apollo's sister, and daughter of *Latona. One of her best-known "exploits" is her role in the story of *Niobe, the subject of the ekphrasis in the five stanzas that follow.

108. In Ovid's *Metamorphoses* 6.165–312), the source closely followed by Tasso, the sons are slain first and Niobe discovers their bodies. (Tasso picks up the story at this point.) Then the daughters are dispatched one by one.

109. The seventh line of this stanza in the Italian original (*intanto fugge e si dilegna il lito*) was later cited by Tasso in his *Discorsi sull' arte poetica* (and attributed to Ariosto!). See Lawrence F. Rhu, *The Genesis of Tasso's Narrative Theory* (Detroit, MI: Wayne State University Press, 1993), p. 144, n. 75.

110. It is unclear to whom this refers. In the singular, *barone* is usually used for Rinaldo. It is technically a feudal title that Florindo, who at this point in the narrative doesn't even know who his father is, could not claim. On the other hand, Rinaldo and Florindo as a pair are thrice called *baroni* (7.72, 8.45, 9.6). The knight who rallies here may thus either be Rinaldo, who in order to save his friend breaks the chivalric code that he has earlier invoked, or Florindo, who has ignored the code in the first place. On balance, the first explanation seems to me more probable.

111. See 1.25.

112. *Diana. *Latona gave birth to her and her twin *Apollo on the island of Delos.

113. "He" is *Apollo, the sun, who successively rises at points on the horizon corresponding to signs of the Zodiac. The literal sense of this epic periphrasis is "Two months had gone by."

114. Ancient kingdom in north-eastern Iran.

115. The stanzas that follow give the first physical description of Rinaldo in the poem.

116. Floriana's bard, Musaeus, is Tasso's variation on Dido's bard, Iopas, in Virgil' *Aeneid* (1.740–46). His song (stanzas 27–29) is an abstract of most of Book One of Ovid's *Metamorphoses*: the origin of the world from Chaos (*Metamorphoses* 1.5–88), the Four Ages (89–150), Deucalion's flood (253–415), *Apollo and *Daphne (452–567), *Argus and Io (568–688, 713–46), Pan and *Syrinx (689–712).

117. Tasso echoes the doctrine of Empedocles, according to which all creation mirrors the harmony and discord of the four elements.

118. *Apollo

119. Domenico Veniero (see p. xxvii, n. 9 and p. xxviii, n. 13 above). Among his works was a translation from Ovid, which survives only in fragments.

120. See n. 37 above and n. 165 below. This makes Rinaldo fourteen years old at the time of this early exploit. When recalling it here, he is, one must suppose, of about the same age — sixteen or seventeen — as Tasso when composing the poem.

121. City in southwestern France, seat of the treacherous *Maganza clan.

122. For some reason, Tasso departs from all known sources in giving Aymon three rather than four sons. See 1.24 and n. 7 above. Interestingly, Ariosto (*Orlando Furioso* 94.2) errs in the opposite direction by increasing the number of sons to five.

123. The virago or woman-warrior was a standard feature of Italian chivalric romance. Tasso here seems to make Rinaldo replicate his

own past in his offspring. In Ariosto, Rinaldo himself (although Tasso does not mention the fact) has a virago twin-sister, Bradamante. She eventually marries Ruggiero, who also has a warlike female twin, Marfisa (the protagonist of Danese Cataneo's *Amor di Marfisa*, 1562).

124. The biblical Ekbatana (*Acatana* in Italian), Iranian mountain city south of the Caspian Sea and ancient capital of Media.

125. *Antica fiamma*, a commonplace dating back to Dante (*Purgatorio* 30.46–48) and ultimately to Virgil (*Aeneid* 4.23).

126. The first thirty-five stanzas of this canto employ, for the first and last time in the main narrative of the poem (not counting narrated flashbacks), a point of view other than Rinaldo's.

127. Authorial comment. Cf. 1.91.1–12, 6.12.1–6.13.12, 11.5.1–12 and corresponding notes.

128. According to legend, the eagle has eyes that can gaze directly into the sun.

129. Another name for *Hercules. Calpe is an ancient name for Gibraltar.

130. See n. 125 above.

131. Francard, killed by Florindo (8.62).

132. The island of Cyprus is sacred to the goddess *Venus, who also governs her planet (the third sphere of the Ptolemaic cosmos).

133. The island of Crete, where *Jupiter was born.

134. The peninsula of the Greek Peloponnese.

135. Sicily was called Trinacria (land of the three peaks) after the mountain tops at its three extremities: Pelorus (near Messina), Lilybaeum (near Marsala) and Passerus (near Syracuse).

136. An allusion to the story of *Diana and *Actaeon.

137. Juno is a weather goddess, so her "cry" here perhaps refers to storm noise in general, but Tasso may be alluding more specifically to the war-cry that launches the central conflict in Virgil's *Aeneid* (7.514–15) — though the crier is Alecto, albeit at Juno's urging.

138. A commonplace derived from Empedocles: the world grows perfect when Love joins the elements and returns to chaos when Strife disjoins them.

139. A hot and violent wind from the south-west.

140. See 10.66. Though rarely mentioned, squires can usually be assumed to accompany their knights.

141. One of the Cyclopes in *Vulcan's smithy supposedly located beneath Mount *Etna.

142. See n. 91 above.

143. A rare stanza of authorial comment (cf. 1.91.1–12, 6.12.1–6.13.12, 10.6.11–12 and notes).

144. See nn. 7 and 122 above.

145. Orlando.

146. This figure almost immediately disappears from the poem. He is Despair personified and inhabits an allegorical landscape, the Black Vale. Rinaldo is trapped there (stanzas 50–55) until the disguised Malagis lures him (56–59) to the Green Hill (60–67), where he is greeted by a personification of Hope, Despair's opposite. The allegory here is of a kind familiar to readers of Spenser.

147. Linked plate-armor just below the helmet, protecting the neck. The original Italian text translates as "the point where the helmet rises."

148. See 5.68.

149. The favorite is, presumably, Auristella, one of the damsels rescued earlier (8.27–42); Mambrin's brothers are Clarel, Brunamont and Constantine (2), all killed in the fight over Clarice's image (8.49–77).

150. The brightest star in the night sky. According to superstition, when its rising is unusually bright, this portends a summer of heat, drought, infertility and pestilence.

151. The Three *Graces.

152. The anemone, formed by *Venus of the dead *Adonis.

153. Companion and tutor of the god *Bacchus, usually portrayed as a naked, fat and drunken old man.

154. The text here has "Floridan," the name of Floriana's brother (see 9.10.1), clearly a slip of the pen. I have substituted the name of Olindo's twin from stanza 35.

155. See 12.33.

156. Pyrrhus, Corin and Ajax. See 12.50.

157. Florindo/Laelius, who was born in Rome (see 11.94). He is again referred to in this way at 12.80.

158. See 12.27.

159. *Enceladus* is changed to *Typhoeus* in the 1570 edition, perhaps for the sake of consistency with 12.60.

160. According to pre-modern meteorology, earthquakes are caused by a lighter element (air) unnaturally lodged in a heavier (earth) and exploding upward.

Notes

161. An allusion to the episode in Homer's *Iliad* (21.211ff.) when the river god *Xanthus (Scamander) rises to defend the Trojans against *Achilles. Achilles almost defeats the river until *Juno calls upon the god *Vulcan, who turns Xanthus' waves into flames. Juno herself vows to raise a fire storm to destroy Troy.

162. In the works of Plutarch, Cleopatra, queen of Egypt, and the Roman patrician and general, Lucullus, are both noted for elaborate and luxurious banquets and entertainments.

163. These six lines are self-consciously gnomic.

164. Malagis here perhaps reflects the position of the Council of Trent, which quietly excludes "parental consent" from the conditions for a valid marriage, though he neglects to mention two conditions the council *does* insist upon: an officiating priest and at least two witnesses. At any rate, theologians had long distinguished between "natural marriage" —requiring solely the consent of a man and a woman — and "Catholic marriage" requiring a sacramental rite.

165. See nn. 37 and 120 above.

166. Cardinal Luigi d'Este, the dedicatee of the poem, patron of Bernardo Tasso at the time, and later of Tasso himself. See Chronology, pp. xl–xlv for the years 1561, 1565, and 1570-71; also see 1.3 and 8.5, and the opening of stanza 93, as well as the Dedication on p. 438–39.

167. The river Brenta runs through Padua, though in earlier times its bed was occupied by the nearby Bacchiglione, with which it was sometimes confused. In Roman times, the Brenta and the Bacchiglione both counted as arms of the same river, the Medoacus. Tasso's reference here it may well be to the Bacchiglione. It passes near the Este summer palace at Bagni Abano (present-day Abano Terme), where Tasso was in attendance during the summer of 1561 and where he most likely finished his poem and fell in love with Lucrezia Bendidio. This would sharpen the contrast between tedious study (Padua) and hours of sunny leisure snatched for the composition of poetry.

168. Bernardo's *Epistolario*, for some time after considered a model of literary prose, was published in the same year as *Amadigi*, 1560. It was followed two years later by his *Ragionamento della poesia*.

169. The word *vaghezza*, has, like its cousin *sprezzatura*, no satisfactory English equivalent. It may mean "grace," "charm," "loveliness," "elegance," as well as "vagueness." "Effortless purity" seems a reasonable English equivalent. It is at any rate odd that young Tasso makes his father a judge of an aesthetic quality to which the author of *Amadigi* can arguably *least* lay claim.

—◆—

Glossary of Mythological and Topical Allusions

Cross references indicated by SMALL CAPS.

ACHERON: The black river; with LETHE, STYX, Cocytus and PHLEGETHON, one of the five rivers of the classical underworld..

ACHILLES: Foremost Greek hero in the Trojan War, son of THETIS and Peleus, slayer of HECTOR; in post-Homeric tradition, invulnerable except for his heel.

ACTAEON: In Greek myth, a hunter who, when he spied on the naked DIANA, was transformed by her into a stag and torn apart by his own hounds. (For the homonymous Saracen in *Rinaldo*, *see* Index of Proper Names.)

ADONIS: A hunter loved by VENUS; when he is killed by a boar, she transforms him into an anemone.

AEOLUS: In Greek myth, the god of the winds, who supposedly keeps them in caves on the island of Lipari.

ALMONT: In Carolingian romance, a Moorish champion, son of ANGLANT and brother of TROYAN; possessor of a magic helmet that passes to ORLANDO when he slays Almont in battle. *Also see* Index of Proper Names.

AMADIS (Amadigi): Legendary French king; hero of Garcí Rodriguez de Montalvo's celebrated Spanish chivalric romance, *Amadis de Gaula*, and of Bernardo Tasso's *Amadigi*. *Also see* Index of Proper Names.

AMYCLEA: Spartan city ruled by POLLUX.

AMOR: *See* CUPID.

ANGLANT (Agolante): in Carolingian romance, a Moorish king, supreme commander of the Saracen army in ASPROMONTE, father of TROYAN and ALMONT. *Also see* Index of Proper Names.

413

Glossary

APOLLO (also called Phoebus): God of the sun, of medicine and of Poetry; son of LATONA and born with his twin-sister DIANA on the island of DELOS.

AQUILO: *See* BOREAS.

ARDEN: The Ardennes, a forested region in present-day Belgium and northern France; in Carolingian romance, the setting of many magical adventures.

ARGUS: Giant with a hundred eyes, at least one of which never shuts. JUNO makes him guard IO whom she has transformed into a cow, but MERCURY plays a flute to put him to sleep and kills him. His eyes become the marks on Juno's sacred bird, the peacock.

ASPROMONTE: Mountainous region in Calabria in southern Italy, the traditional setting of many exploits in Carolingian romance.

ATHENA: *See* MINERVA.

ATLAS: *See* HERCULES.

AURORA (Greek *Eos*): Goddess of the dawn, mother of HESPERUS and PHOSPHORUS.

AUSTER (Notus): The South Wind.

AVERNUS: A volcanic crater east of Naples. Lake Avernus was thought to be the entrance to the Roman Hades.

BABYLON: (a) Famed Mesopotamian capital. (b) In medieval and Renaissance literature, a common designation of Islamic Cairo or (by extension) of Egypt.

BACCHUS: (Greek *Dionysus*), god of wine and drunkenness.

BOEOTES: The constellation of the Plow in the northern sky.

BOREAS (Aquilo): The North Wind (more accurately NNE).

CASTOR: *See* LEDA.

CARLO: *See* CHARLEMAGNE.

CHARLEMAGNE (Charles, Carlo): Son of PEPIN, king of France, and later the first Holy Roman Emperor; in Carolingian romance, the commander-in-chief of the Christian army against the infidels, followed by the twelve paladins including ORLANDO (the French Roland). *Also see* Index of Proper Names.

CHARLES: *See* CHARLEMAGNE.

CLAIRMONT: The noble house to which ORLANDO and Rinaldo belong; *see* MAGANZA.

CORUS: The North-West Wind (more precisely WNW).

CUPID (Greek *Eros*, also *Amor*): The god of love, son of VENUS; conventionally portrayed as a winged and naked boy armed with bow and arrow.

CYCNUS: A son of NEPTUNE who was, like ACHILLES, invulnerable. When the latter fought him and found him impervious to wounds, he strangled him with the laces of his helmet, whereupon Neptune transformed him into a swan.

CYNTHIA: *See* DIANA.

DANAË: In classical myth, a princess whose father, hearing a prophecy that her son will kill him, imprisons her in a tower. JUPITER visits her, disguised as a shower of gold; the child born of this union is the hero Perseus.

DAPHNE: A nymph loved by APOLLO. When he pursues her, she evades his embrace by turning into a laurel tree. Ever after laurel leaves are sacred to Apollo.

DELOS: Aegean island, birthplace of APOLLO and DIANA.

DIANA (Greek *Artemis*): Virgin goddess of chastity, of the hunt and of the moon; daughter of LATONA along with her twin-brother APOLLO; also called Cynthia, after her birth place, Mount Cynthus on the island of DELOS.

DIOSCURI: *See* LEDA.

ENCELADUS: *See* TYPHOEUS.

ENDYMION: A shepherd loved by DIANA.

ETNA: An active volcano, the tallest mountain in Sicily; *see also* VULCAN, TYPHOEUS.

EURUS (also *Vulturnus*): The East Wind (more accurately ESE).

FATE: *See* FORTUNE; also PARCAE.

FORTUNE (or *Fate*): The goddess of chance. Though sometimes introduced as a mere abstraction, traditionally personified as a blindfolded female figure, who controls a great wheel on which men and women ride up from bad fortune to good and back down. She is bald except for a lock of hair blown over her forehead. Proverbially, "to grasp Fortune by the forelock" means to seize an opportunity when it offers itself. (*See also* PARCAE.)

GANELON (Gano): In Carolingian romance, chief of the MAGANZA clan, treacherous enemies of ORLANDO and the CLAIRMONTS. *Also see* Index of Proper Names.

GANGES: River in India; in poetic diction, the origin of the rising sun.

GANO: *See* GANELON.

GEMINI: *See* LEDA.

GRACES (Greek *Charites*): Symbols of natural beauty and human comeliness, usually imagined as three naked goddesses joining hands in a dance.

HECTOR: Homeric hero, Trojan prince, eldest son of Priam and Hecuba, and chief champion of Troy. He is killed in combat by ACHILLES.

HELICON: Greek mountain sacred to the MUSES, symbolic of poetry.

HERCULES (also *Alcides*): Mythic hero, son of JUPITER and Alcmena; best known for his Twelve Labors. The eleventh labor ("Stealing the Apples of the Hesperides") is several times alluded to in *Rinaldo*: ATLAS, the Titan who carries the world on his shoulders, has access to the Hesperides, and Hercules temporarily relieves him of his burden; at his return Hercules designates the nearby Straits of Gibraltar ("the Pillars of Hercules," referred to as "Alcides' signposts") as the limit of all navigation.

HESPERUS (Latin *Vesper*): Divinity of the evening star, brother of Phosphorus, the morning star. In myth, both are the sons of AURORA, the goddess of the dawn. They are sometimes identified with each other, since to astronomers they are the same "star," the planet VENUS.

Hours (Greek *Horae*): Goddesses of the seasons and other temporal processes.

HYACINTH (Hyacinthus): In classical myth, a youth loved by APOLLO. He is accidentally killed in a friendly discus contest with the god and transformed by him into a hyacinth.

HYMEN: The Greco-Roman god of marriage.

IDA: Mountain near TROY. During the Trojan War, JUPITER observes the combat of HECTOR and ACHILLES from its summit.

ILIUM: *See* TROY.

IO: Argive princess abducted by JUPITER, who transforms her into a cow to hide her from the jealous JUNO. Juno is suspicious and asks Jupiter to give her the cow. He cannot refuse, and she sets the hundred-eyed ARGUS to guard Io. After MERCURY kills Argus, Io wanders the earth, harried by gadflies sent by Juno, until she arrives in Egypt, where she is worshiped as a goddess. She is later restored to human form and mothers a long line of heroes.

JOVE: *See* JUPITER.

JUNO (Greek *Hera*): Wife and sister of JUPITER; goddess of marriage, domestic order and the weather; often also identified with Lucina, the goddess of childbirth. Her sacred bird is the peacock. In Virgil's *Aeneid* and elsewhere, she is a great causer of storms.

JUPITER (Greek *Zeus*): Also known as Jove, god of the sky and ruler of the Olympian deities. His sacred bird is the eagle, and his weapon is the thunderbolt. He is married to his sister JUNO and the father of most of the other Olympian gods.

LATONA (Greek *Leto*): Mother of APOLLO and DIANA, to whom she gave birth on the island of DELOS.

LEDA: Spartan queen who, is loved by JUPITER in the shape of a swan. She bears him two sets of twins, Helen and Clytemnestra and Castor and Pollux (the Dioscuri). Castor was mortal, Pollux immortal, but when Castor died, Pollux decided to spend half his immortality with his brother in the underworld. The two later became the constellation Gemini, protectors of vessels at sea.

LETHE: The river of forgetfulness in the classical underworld.

LETO: *See* LATONA.

LOVE: Even where the modern reader sees this term as a mere abstraction, Tasso often intends a personification. *See* CUPID.

LUCINA: see JUNO.

MAGANZA: In Carolingian romance, a clan in deadly enmity with the CLAIRMONT clan; the death of ORLANDO, chief hero of

Glossary

the Clairmonts, is the result of treachery by the Maganzan GANELON.

MARS (Greek *Ares*): The god of war.

MERCURY (Greek *Hermes*): Classical messenger of the gods and god of physicians and tradesmen; conductor of souls to the underworld; in Renaissance lore often associated with higher learning.

MERLIN: Legendary magician of Arthurian romance, reputed builder of the four magic fountains in the Forest of ARDEN. *Also see* Index of Proper Names.

MINERVA (Greek *Athena*): Goddess of prudence, weaving and warfare.

MINOS: Mythical king of Crete who after his death becomes (along with Rhadamanthus) one of the judges of the underworld.

MUSE (Muses): In ancient myth, the daughters of JUPITER and Mnemosyne (Memory), votaries of APOLLO and guardians of the two sacred springs on Mount HELICON; goddesses of inspiration. Invoked by poets both in the singular and in the plural. There are traditionally nine of them: Calliope (epic), Clio (history), Euterpe (lyric), Erato (love poetry), Melpomene (tragedy), Polyhymnia (sacred poetry), Terpsichore (dance), Thalia (comedy) and Urania (astronomy). Muse in the singular sometimes merely personifies the poet's genius.

NEPTUNE (Greek *Poseidon*): God of the sea, brother of JUPITER and PLUTO.

NIOBE: Legendary Theban queen, mother of seven sons and seven daughters. When she arrogantly boasts of being superior to LATONA, who has only two children, Latona's offspring, APOLLO and DIANA, kill all Niobe's children in front of her eyes. Her grief petrifies her into a rocky column.

NOTUS: *See* AUSTER.

ORLANDO: In Carolingian romance, count of Brittany, CHARLEMAGNE'S nephew and chief paladin in his court, hero of numerous exploits until killed through the treachery of his step-father GANELON in a mountain ambush at Roncesvalles; in Italian literature, a hero in epics by Pulci, Boiardo, Ariosto, Tasso and many others. *Also see* Index of Proper Names.

PAN: Greek woodland deity, usually imagined as goat-footed and lecherous. When the nymph SYRINX frustrates his advances by turning into a reed, he cuts the reed and fashions it into a pipe.

PALADIN: Title given to any of the Twelve Peers of CHARLEMAGNE, traditionally consisting of ORLANDO, his friends OLIVER and Florismart, his cousin Astolfo, Ogier the Dane, GANELON, Rinaldo, Malagis, Guy de Bourgogne, Namo and two converted Saracen knights, Ferumbras and Otuel. Some sources substitute or add names to the list.

PARCAE: In Greek mythology, the three Fates who weave, measure and cut the threat of human life. They are called Clotho (the Spinner), Lachesis (the Disposer of Lots) and Atropos (the Inevitable).

PEPIN: King of France, father of CHARLEMAGNE.

PHIDIAS: Athenian sculptor and architect (5th century BC), largely responsible for the Parthenon of Athens; traditionally considered the greatest sculptor of antiquity.

PHLEGETHON: A stream of fire, one of the rivers of the classical underworld, along with STYX, LETHE, Cocytus and ACHERON.

PHOEBUS: *See* APOLLO.

PHOSPHORUS: *See* HESPERUS.

PLUTO: The god of the Underworld, also referred to by his Greek names, Dis or Hades; brother of JUPITER and NEPTUNE; husband of Proserpina. In Renaissance literature often identified with the Christian devil.

POLLUX: *See* LEDA.

PROMETHEUS: A Titan, who created human beings by breathing life into images of clay and who, finding them naked and cold, gave them fire stolen from heaven. JUPITER punished him by chaining him to a rock in the Caucasus, where every night a eagle came to eat his liver. The story is treated by Aeschylus *(Prometheus Bound)* and Ovid *(Metamorphoses* 1.90ff.). The *editio princeps* of Aeschylus's plays (Venice, 1552) was issued by Francesco Robortello (d. 1567), who was still teaching at Padua while Tasso was a student there, and whose work on ARISTOTLE is specifically mentioned by the poet.

Glossary

PYRRHA: In classical myth, she and her husband, Deucalion, are the only survivors of the flood sent by JUPITER to destroy mankind. Hoping to repopulate the earth, they consult an oracle which instructs them to cast the bones of their mother behind them. Deucalion and Pyrrha, rightly interpreting "mother" as the Earth and her "bones" as rocks, throw stones behind their backs, which rise back up as humans. The story is retold at length in Book One of Ovid's *Metamorphoses*.

SCAMANDER: *See* XANTHUS.

SEPTENTRIO: The North Wind.

SILENUS: Companion and tutor of the god BACCHUS, usually portrayed as a naked, fat and drunken old man.

SIREN: A mythical island creature, half woman, half bird, who lures sailors to shipwreck by her irresistible song.

SORIA: Ancient name for Syria.

STYX: Along with PHLEGETHON, LETHE, Cocytus and ACHERON, one of five the rivers of the classical Underworld; in some accounts these rivers converge in a marsh also called Styx.

SYRINX: See PAN.

TARTARUS: The place of punishment in the classical underworld; hell.

THETIS: A sea-nymph who marries a mortal, Peleus. At their wedding feast, the goddess of Strife drops the Golden Apple contested by JUNO, MINERVA and VENUS, which becomes the cause of the Trojan War. Thetis' son by Peleus is ACHILLES.

TIGRIS: With the Euphrates, one of the chief rivers of Mesopotamia.

TROY (Ilium): City in Asia Minor destroyed by the Greeks in the Trojan War. *See also* ACHILLES, HECTOR, IDA, XANTHUS.

TROYAN (Troiano): In Carolingian romance, a Moorish king of Africa, son of ANGLANT, brother of ALMONT, champion of the pagan army in ASPROMONTE; killed by ORLANDO. *Also see* "Index of Proper Names".

TYPHOEUS: With his brother Enceladus, one of the monstrous giants who warred against the Olympian gods until struck them down by JUPITER's lightning. Since they were immortal,

Jupiter confined them under Mount ETNA, where they still shake the ground from time to time.

VENUS (Greek *Aphrodite*): Goddess of beauty and love, wife of VULCAN, mistress of MARS and lover of ADONIS.

VESPER: *See* HESPERUS.

VULCAN (Greek *Hephaistos*, also Mulciber): God of fire and smiths; son of JUPITER and JUNO, husband of VENUS. His forge is supposedly located beneath Mount ETNA. In the *Iliad*, he fashions the shield of ACHILLES, and in the *Aeneid*, the arms of Aeneas.

VULTURNUS: *See* EURUS.

XANTHUS: (a) A river near TROY, sometimes identified with the Scamander. (b) One of the horses of HECTOR.

ZEPHYR: The West Wind, but sometimes simply a term for any mild breeze.

Index of Proper Names in *Rinaldo*

This index is limited to the named characters, animals and objects in Tasso's poem. Other names and terms are explained in the notes. References are by canto and stanza number. Italian names, where they differ from their English equivalents, appear in parentheses and are cross-listed. Internal cross-references are indicated by SMALL CAPS, cross-references to the Glossary and Notes are indicated by *asterisks.

ACTAEON (Atteone):   Saracen champion; in Mambrin's muster (12.27); killed by Florindo (12.44–47). For the homonymous character in Greek myth, *see* Glossary.

AGOLANTE: *See* *ANGLANT.

AJAX (Aiace): Saracen champion; in Mambrin's muster (12.30).

ALARD (Alardo):   One of Rinaldo's brothers; knighted by *CHARLEMAGNE (1.26).

ALARTOS (Alarto):   Saracen king of Antioch; in Mambrin's muster (12.35).

ALBERNIOS (Albernio):   Median champion; overthrown by Rinaldo and Florindo (9.7).

ALBERT (Alberto):   English champion; overthrown by Florindo (6.74).

ALCASTER (Alcastro):   Egyptian warrior, companion of Olpester; in Mambrin's muster (12.25).

ALCHISO: Magician at the court of*AMADIS de Gaul; enchants Bayard (1.42–43).

ALDA: Sister of Oliver, Orlando's betrothed, friend of Rinaldo (4.19); unsuccessfully wooed by Gryphon (10.84, 11.1); simultaneously asked to dance by Rinaldo and Anselm (11.24–26).

ALDRIMANTE: *See* DRIMANT.

ALDRISUS (Aldriso): Saracen champion; in Mambrin's muster (12.34); killed by Rinaldo (12.39).

ALFERNO: Saracen pirate; defeated by Rinaldo, saved by Foleric and Lanfranco (8.33).

ALGA: Lady-in-waiting to Galerana, beloved of Oren (4.19).

ALGARD (Algardo): Saracen champion; defeated by Francard (3.31).

ALKAST (Alcasto): (a) Prince of Thessaly, exiled enemy of *CHARLEMAGNE in Clarice's retinue; killed by Rinaldo (1.72–78). (b) Brother of Nisus, Orion, Breussos and Thaumas; in Mambrin's muster (12.33); killed by Rinaldo (12.40). (c) Moorish knight overthrown by Rinaldo (6.23).

ALMA: Sorceress and queen of Naples who established the Inn of Courtesy (7.75ff.); fashioned the Ship Adventurous (7.83–84, 8.2).

ALMENOS (Almeno): King of Cappadocia; in Mambrin's muster (12.29).

ALMETHOS (Almeto): Saracen champion; in Mambrin's muster (12.32).

ALMONT (Almonte): See Glossary; killed by Orlando (1.6, 6.42); his helmet (6.44, 11.31).

ALTIN (Altino): Saracen champion; in Mambrin's muster (12.32).

ALTORRES (Altorre): King of Assyria; in Mambrin's muster (12.26).

AMADIS (Amadigi): See Glossary; original owner of Bayard (1.41f.).

AMONE: See *AYMON.

ANACHRONE (Anacro): Pagan necromancer; builder of the Temple of Beauty (3.40).

ANDROLIUS (Androglio): Pagan champion, companion to Argos; defeated by Rinaldo and Florindo (9.8–9).

ANGIOLIN: One of *CHARLEMAGNE's paladins (in Boiardo, Angelino of Bordeaux); overthrown by Rinaldo (6.20).

ANGLANT (Agolante): (1.1). See Glossary.

ANSELM (Anselmo): Lord of Altaripa, member of the *MAGANZA clan; overthrown by Florindo (6.73); killed by Rinaldo (11.26–41).

ANSUIGI: Overthrown by Florindo (6.73).

ARBAN (Arbano): Pagan knight, the second of three brothers (with Orin and Drimant) felled by Rinaldo (6.24).

ARCTURUS (Arturo): King of Syria; in Mambrin's muster (12.26).

Index of Proper Names

ARGOS: Median champion, companion of Androlius; overthrown by Rinaldo and Florindo (9.8–9).

ARIDAMAN (Aridamano): King of Caria; in Mambrin's muster (12.34).

ARIDAN (Aridano): Knight in Galerana's escort; killed by Rinaldo (4.22).

ARNANQUE (Arnanco): Knight from Vercelli, in Galerana's escort; killed by Ysolier (4.27).

ARTURO: *See* ARCTURUS.

ASTOLFO: *See* ENGLISH KNIGHT.

ATLAS (Atlante): A Saracen giant, lord of Algiers (3.25); killed by Rinaldo and forfeits Fusberta (6.25–35). (For the homonymous character in Greek myth, *see* Glossary.)

ATTEONE: *See* ACTAEON.

AURISTELLA: Arabian princess, daughter of Pandion; freed from Mambrin's pirates by Rinaldo (8.42).

AVIN (Avino): Overthrown by Florindo (6.73).

AVOR (Avorio): Overthrown by Florindo (6.73).

AYMON (Amone): Duke of Dordogne, chief of the *CLAIRMONT family, paladin of France, uncle of Orlando, father of Rinaldo and several other famous sons (1.12, 64, 71); commands third wing of *CHARLEMAGNE's army (6.7); wins Beatrice over rival Ginam (9.34); Ginam slanders his wife's honor (9.40–46); intends to kill his wife (9.47); finds her vindicated by Rinaldo (9.54).

BAYARD (Baiardo): Rinaldo's horse, previously owned by *AMADIS and enchanted by Alchiso; Rinaldo told about him by Malagis (1.32–45); found by Rinaldo and Ysolier (2.30-45); helps Rinaldo defeat the Knight of the Siren (3.4–5); falls atop Rinaldo (4.55–56, 5.4); in Rinaldo's fight with Atlas (6.28); in fight with Orlando (6.47); wounded by Clarel's lion (6.67–69, 8.64, 8.67); stolen from Rinaldo (10.52–53); reconquered by Rinaldo (10.66–74); abducted by Malagis (11.55); restored to Rinaldo (11.59, 72; 12.36, 53–69).

BEATRICE: Wife to Aymon, Rinaldo's mother; in Paris with Rinaldo (1.15); won by Aymon (9.39); her honor called into question by Ginam (9.40–46); flees to her father with her sons (9.49);

DRIMANT (Aldrimante): Pagan knight; the third of three brothers, with Orin and Arban felled by Rinaldo (6.24).

DRUSE (Druso): Overthrown by Rinaldo (6.20).

DULICON (Dulicone): Saracen champion; defeated by Francard (3.31).

ELIDONIA: *See* HELIDONIA.

ENGLISH KNIGHT: Perhaps identified with Ariosto's *ASTOLFO; in Ysolier's company, encountered by Rinaldo (2.12); fails to tame Bayard (2.16); fails to avert combat between Rinaldo and Ysolier (2.17–18); makes peace between them, leads them to Bayard's cave and departs (2.25–29).

ERMILLA: *See* HERMILLA.

ERNANDO: Knight in Galerana's escort; Ysolier strikes off his left arm (4.28).

EURYBAS (Euribante): Saracen pirate; killed by Rinaldo (8.33).

EURYDICE (Euridice): Princess of Capua, daughter of Guilant; welcomes and describes Inn of Courtesy to Rinaldo and Florindo (7.65–85); shows Rinaldo and Florindo pictures of Italian worthies (8.2–13).

FAUSTUS (Fausto): Knight in Galerana's train; fight with Ysolier, loses his left hand while sustaining a friend, but wounds Ysolier and Rinaldo (4.34–35).

FERNAND (Fernando): Knight in Galerana's escort; wounded by Rinaldo (4.37).

FILARCO: *See* PHILARCOS.

FLORAMAN: Saracen champion, twin brother of Olindo; in Mambrin's muster (12.35); killed by Rinaldo (12.38).

FLORIANA: Queen of Media; invites Rinaldo and Florindo to joust (9.5–10); falls in love with Rinaldo (9.11–20, 56–57); entertains him (9.21–32); ; recalls prophecy that he will father her twins (9.58–59); conducts him on tour of Hamadan (9.63); confides her love to Helidonia (9.66–73); seduces Rinaldo (9.74–81); her grief at being abandoned by him (10.1–6); unsuccessfully sends knights in pursuit (10.7–14); prepares for suicide (10.15–26); prevented by Medea and abducted to the Joyous Isle (10.27–35).

Index of Proper Names

FLORIDAN: Brother to Floriana; partnered with Lucindo in joust, overthrown by Rinaldo and Florindo (9.10–14).

FLORINDO: Spanish shepherd, a foundling eventually recognized as Laelius, son of Scipio; encountered by Rinaldo (5.31–40; his complaint to Love 5.17-19; [tells his story to Rinaldo: his shepherd upbringing (5.20–25); at May festival falls in love with Olinda (5.31); attends her while hunting (5.43–46); at next May festival, tries to kiss her in woman's disguise and is exiled by her 5.47-54;] with Rinaldo continues to the Cave of Cupid (5.55–67); his noble birth and prophesy of his marriage to Olinda (5.68).

He travels to Italy with Rinaldo (6.1–8); knighted by *CHARLEMAGNE (6.9); issues challenge on behalf of Rinaldo (6.17); defeats a number of champions (6.73–74); leaves *CHARLEMAGNE's camp with Rinaldo and arrives with him at Clytie's tomb (7.2–50); with Rinaldo to Posillipo (7.51–57); at Inn of Courtesy (7.58–85); given a surcoat embroidered with story of NIOBE (8.16–21); embarks with Rinaldo on Ship Adventurous and fights with pirates (8.22–25); with Rinaldo on ship to Asia (8.44–45); kills Francard (8.57–60); with Rinaldo kills Clarel and lion (8.62–67); routs Francard's followers (8.71); exploits in Asia (8.74–75).

He jousts at Floriana's court (9.1–30); leaves Media with Rinaldo (9.90–92); with Rinaldo, traverses Asia and boards ship (10.36–37); with Rinaldo in storm at sea (10.38–53); separated from Rinaldo in shipwreck (10.54–61); waylaid by Mambrin's knights, rescued and recognized by Rinaldo (11.68–85); [his account to Rinaldo: recovers from shipwreck in Scipio's care, is recognized as Scipio's long-lost son Laelius and baptized (11.87–96)]; sets out with Rinaldo to rescue Clarice (12.7–17); given magic steed by Malagis (12.18); in battle alongside Malagis (12.41); kills various Saracen champions (12.42–47); with Rinaldo and Clarice to Malagis's castle (12.79ff.).

FOLERIC (Folerico): Saracen pirate; killed by Rinaldo (8.33).

FRANCARD (Francardo): King of Armenia, cousin of Mambrin and Olas; his emissary met by Rinaldo (3.1–8); sets out to champion Clarinea's name (3.28–31); finds Clarice's picture in the Temple of Beauty, deserts Clarinea (3.35–40); offers his services to *CHARLEMAGNE in exchange for Clarice's hand

(3.43); *CHARLEMAGNE reminded of him by Rinaldo's valor 6.56; discovered worshipping Clarice's statue, challenges and attacks Rinaldo, who refuses to fight him because he wears no armor (8.50–58); killed by Florindo (8.59–62, 10.37, 12.24).

FUSBERTA: Rinaldo's sword; originally owned by Atlas (6.29, 6.31); taken from Atlas by Rinaldo (6.36); lost by Rinaldo in shipwreck (10.52–53); regained by Rinaldo (10.66–74).

GALASSO: Median champion; overthrown by Rinaldo and Florindo (9.7).

GALERANA: Queen of France, wife of *CHARLEMAGNE; appears in chariot attended by Clarice (4.11); unable to keep Rinaldo from abducting Clarice (4. 41–44).

GALVEN (Galveno): Knight in Galerana's retinue; killed by Rinaldo (4.23–24).

GANELON (Gano): Treacherous paladin at *CHARLEMAGNE's court, head of the *MAGANZA clan, see Glossary; leads attack against Rinaldo (11.31); counsels *CHARLEMAGNE to banish Rinaldo (11.36).

GINAM (Ginamo): *MAGANZA noble, lord of Bayonne, cousin of Ganelon; rejected suitor to Beatrice (9.34); slanders Beatrice (9.41–46); falls in duel with Rinaldo and confesses treason (9.52–54).

GISMOND (Gismonodo): Pagan knight, brother of Orin and Aldrimas; overthrown by Rinaldo (6.24).

GRIFONE: See GRYPHON.

GRYPHON (Grifone): *MAGANZAN lord of Ponthieu, in some accounts Ganelon's father; overthrown by Florindo (6.71–73); challenges Rinaldo (10.83); poses as Clarice's champion (10.84); overthrown by Rinaldo (10.85–92, 11.1).

GUALTIER DI MONLEONE: See WALTER OF MOLLIONE.

GUILANT (Guilante): Lord of Capua, father of Eurydice (7.86).

GUISCARD (Guiscardo): One of Rinaldo's brothers; knighted by *CHARLEMAGNE (1.26).

HELIDONIA (Elidonia): Nurse to Floriana; hears Floriana confess her love for Rinaldo and counsels her (9.66–73).

HERMILLA (Ermilla): A wood nymph; Clytie's husband wrongly suspected of sleeping with her (7.30–31, 39).

ferries Rinaldo and Florindo across river, bestows magic armor (12.12–17); rides with them to confront Mambrin (12.18–20); fights alongside Florindo (12.41); stops attackers with magic spell (12.70–71); lifts spell at Rinaldo's request (12.73–74); stops renewed attack with magic fire (12.75); prevents Rinaldo from entering fire, brings him and his company to his castle (12.76–77); his palace (12.79); reveals himself to Rinaldo (12.80); prophesies war, advises Rinaldo and Clarice to marry (12.82–86).

MAMBRIN (Mambrino): Asian king, brother of Constantine (B), Brunamont and Clarel; cousin of Francard (3.27); remembered by *CHARLEMAGNE seeing Rinaldo fight (6.56); overlord of the pirates routed by Rinaldo (8.36–38, 8.62); invades France, captures Clarice (12.1–6); heads muster of Saracen champions (12.21–23); in combat with Rinaldo (12.49–67).

MEDEA: A Saracen sorceress, Floriana's paternal aunt; prevents Floriana's suicide and transports her to the Hesperides (10.27–36).

MERLIN (Merlino): *See* Glossary; his magic fountains in the Forest of *ARDEN (1.50); artificer of the lances and magic statues of *TRISTAN and *LANCELOT (3.61, 63); creator of the Cave of Cupid (5.64).

MUSAEUS (Museo): Bard at Floriana's court; entertains Rinaldo and Florindo (9.26–30).

NAMO: Duke of Bavaria, one of *CHARLEMAGNE's paladins; commands second wing of Charles's army (6.7).

NIOBE: *Also see* Glossary; her story in embroidery (8.19–24).

NISUS (Niso): (a) A knight in Galerana's escort; killed by Rinaldo (4.37). (b) Saracen champion, brother of Alkast (b), Orion, Breussos and Thaumas; in Mambrin's muster (12.33); killed by Rinaldo (12.40).

ODRIMAS (Odrimante): Median champion; overthrown by Rinaldo and Florindo (9.7).

ODRIMART (Odrimarte): Perhaps the same as ODRIMAS, Saracen champion in Mambrin's muster (12.30).

ODRISMONT (Odrismonte): Saracen champion; in Mambrin's muster (12.32).

Index of Proper Names

OLAS (Olante): Saracen lord, second cousin of Francard; in Mambrin's muster (12.24).

OLBRAND (Olbrando): King of Tyre; defeated by Francard (3.31).

OLDAUROS (Oldauro): Saracen champion; in Mambrin's muster (12.29).

OLINDA: Spanish princess; Florindo falls in love with her (5.31–40); attended by Florindo while hunting (5.43–46); when kissed by Florindo in woman's disguise, exiles him (5.47-54); her marriage to Florindo foretold (5.68).

OLINDO: Saracen champion, twin brother of Floraman; in Mambrin's muster (12.35); killed by Rinaldo (12.38).

OLIVER (Oliviero): Paladin of *CHARLEMAGNE, Orlando's best friend, brother of Alda; his sister courted by Gryphon (10.84).

OLIVIERO: See OLIVER.

OLPESTER (Olpestro): Companion of Alcaster; in Mambrin's muster (12.25).

OREN: Bayonne-born son of Aridan, in love with Alga; killed by Rinaldo (4.19–21).

ORGOLT (Orgolte): Saracen pirate; killed by Rinaldo (8.33).

ORIANA: Daughter of Lisuart, king of Brittany, wife of *AMADIS (1.40).

ORIMEN (Orimeno): Saracen warrior and soothsayer; in Mambrin's muster (12.28).

ORIN: Pagan knight, the eldest of three brothers (with Arban and Drinant); felled by Rinaldo (6.24).

ORION: (a) Moorish knight; killed by Rinaldo (6.23). (b) Saracen champion, brother of Alkast 2, Nisus, Breussos and Thaumas; in Mambrin's muster (12.33); killed by Rinaldo (12.40).

ORLANDO: Count of Brittany, *CHARLEMAGNE's nephew and chief paladin in his court, cousin of Rinaldo; slayer of *ALMONT and *TROYAN (1.6); his exploits and rising fame (1.9–10); Rinaldo vows to equal him (1.65–67, 70; 3.25); assists at Florindo's knighting (6.16); urged to fight Rinaldo to avenge Hugh's death (6.39–43); combat with Rinaldo (6.44–60); makes peace with Rinaldo (6.61–67); assists Rinaldo in fight against the *MAGANZANS (11.31).

OTHO (Ottone): Son of Namo of Bavaria and brother of Berlingher; overthrown by Rinaldo (6.37).

PANDION: King of Arabia, father of Auristella; Rinaldo rescues his daughter (8.42).

PEPIN (Pipino): *See* Glossary; 6.1, 56; 7.12; 10.12.

PHILARCOS (Filarco): Saracen champion; in Mambrin's muster (12.33).

PIRRO: *See* PYRRHUS.

PULION: Moorish knight; killed by Rinaldo (6.23).

PYRRHUS (Pirro): Saracen champion; in Mambrin's muster (12.30).

RANSALD (Ransaldo): Ransald the Fierce, Saracen knight; unhorsed by Rinaldo and overcome by Ysolier (2.47–55); Rinaldo assaulted after being mistaken for him (3.1–8); slew the steeds of the Knight of the Siren and Clarice (3.13–22).

RICCARDO: *See* RICHARD.

RICHARD (Riccardo): (a) one of Rinaldo's brothers; knighted by *CHARLEMAGNE (1.26). (b) Carolingian champion (perhaps Richard of Normandy); overthrown by Rinaldo (6.23).

RINALDO: Rinaldo of Montalban, champion of the *CLAIRMONT clan, future paladin at *CHARLEMAGNE's court; youngest of the three sons (four in Tasso's sources) of Aymon and Beatrice, cousin to Orlando; first named (1.1); leaves Paris (1.11–15); after lamenting his lack of fame, finds mysterious horse, armor and weapons, takes all except sword (1.16–26); has vowed never to use a sword until he wins one in battle (1.27); wanders in Forest of Arden, encounters Malagis, who tells him of Bayard (1.41–48); rides in quest of Bayard, rests at *MERLIN's Well (1.49–51); meets Clarice and routs her knights (1.52–85); accompanies Clarice to her castle but declines her offer to sleep with him (1.86–93).

His amatory soliloquy (2.1–8); encounters Ysolier and the English knight (2.11–13); unhorses Ysolier who joins him in quest for Bayard (2.14–30); finds and tames Bayard (2.31–45); challenges and unhorses Ransaldo, seizes Ransald's Cupid shield (2.46–55).

He is mistaken for Ransaldo, challenged by and defeats the Knight of the Siren (3.1–12); hears the Siren Knight's story and leaves with Ysolier (3.24–54); discovers *MERLIN's statues of *LANCELOT and *TRISTAN (3.55–63); gains *TRISTAN's lance (3.64–65).

At the mouth of the Seine, he sees bark arriving and met by Galerana's chariot, with Clarice among her followers (4.1–11); thinks Clarice is intended for another man (4.12–18); kills the knights guarding the chariot (4.19–37ff.); offers excuses to Galerana (4.41–43); abducts Clarice (4.44–48); contemplates raping her (4.49–51); confronted by Malagis disguised as Dragon knight, sees Clarice abducted by him on a magic chariot (4.57–60).

He goes in quest of Clarice (5.1–10); meets Florindo and hears his story (5.11–54); proceeds with him to the Cave of Cupid (5.55–66); Cupid's oracle prophesies his marriage to Clarice (5.67).

He and Florindo travel to Italy (6.1–6); arrives near *CHARLEMAGNE's camp (6.7–8); overthrows many knights (6.25-36); kills Hugh (6.37–38); combats and kills Atlas, gaining the sword Fusberta 6.25-36; overthrows Otho and kills Hugh 6.37–38; engages in battle with Orlando (6.44–60); makes peace, but refuses to reveal his name (6.67–71); rejoices at Florindo's victories (6.74); with Florindo, leaves *CHARLEMAGNE (6.75).

He witnesses the lament of Hugh's father (7.2–11); arrives at Clytie's tomb and overthrows her widower (7.12–24); hears his story (7.25–46); frees Clytie's funeral cortege from enchantment (7.49–51); proceeds to Posillipo (7.51–57); invited to Inn of Courtesy (7.58–64); welcomed by Eurydice (7.65–85).

He is shown pictures of Italian worthies (8.2–13); embarks on Ship Adventurous (8.22–24); overcomes Mambrin's pirates (8.25–43); sails with Florindo on Ship Adventurous to Asia (8.44–45); finds statue of Clarice (8.46–49); fights with Francard (8.50–56); assisted by Florindo, kills Clarel and lion (8.62–69); adopts lion as heraldic device (8.70); takes possession of Clarice's statue and wanders in Asia with Florindo (8.74); kills Constantine (b) and Brunamont (8.75).

He arrives in Media with Florindo, welcomed by Floriana (9.1–6); with Florindo, defeats her champions in joust (9.7–10); entertained by her (9.21–32); [in flashback, tells Floriana how he vindicated his mother from Ginam's slander (9.33–54)]; seduced by Floriana (9.58–81); sees Clarice in a dream (9.82–86); realizes his error and leaves Media (9.87–92).

He repulses knights sent in pursuit (10.11–14); with Florindo, traverses Armenia and Syria, and boards ship (10.36–37); storm at sea (10.38–51); his horse and sword stolen (10.53–54); separated from Florindo in shipwreck (10.55–61); swims to shore (10.62–65); regains Bayard and Fusberta in combat (10.66–74); acquires unlucky shield (10.75–77); returns to France (10.78–82); defeats Gryphon (10.83–92).

His unlucky shield provokes Clarice's jealousy (11.6–7); he is repulsed by Clarice (11.9–20); hoping for intercession, he asks Alda to dance and kills Anselm (11.26–30); attacked by Ganelon and the *MAGANZANS (11.31–35); banished by *CHARLEMAGNE (11.36); his letter to Clarice refused (11.38–43); leaves Paris (11.44–45); discards the shield and despairs (11.46–54); lured by disguised Malagis to the hill of hope, his hope restored (11.60–67); rescues stranger (11.68–76); kills young son and father (11.77–79); recognizes the stranger as Florindo and hears his story (11.80–96).

He is told of Mambrin's invasion and Clarice's capture (12.1–6); with Florindo, rides to the rescue (12.7–17); sees Clarice captive (12.18–20); kills Mambrin's champions (12.36–40); single combat with Mambrin (12.49–67); attacked by remainder of Mambrin's army (12.68); with Clarice is rescued through magic spells of Malagis (12.69–75); brought to Malagis's castle (12.76–79); recognizes Malagis (12.80–81); marries Clarice (12.87–89).

SCIPIO: Roman patrician of the Cornelii family, lord of Ostia and other Latin cities, Florindo's long-lost father; finds Florindo and nurses him to health (11.88–89); recognizes him as his lost son Laelius (11.90–94).

SIREN, KNIGHT OF THE: Armenian knight, emissary of King Francard; mistakes Rinaldo for Ransald and assaults him (3.1–12); tells his story (3.13–22); identifies himself as ambassador to

—ᙡ—

APPENDIX:
PREFATORY MATTER FROM THE ORIGINAL EDITION

DEL RINALDO DI TORQUATO TASSO ALL'ILLUSTRISSIMO E REVERENDISSIMO SIGNOR DON LUIGI D'ESTE CARDINALE

—◊◊◊—

TORQUATO TASSO AI LETTORI

Non m'era nuovo, benignissimi lettori, che sì come nessuna azione umana mai fu in ogni parte perfetta, così ancora a nessuna mai mancaro i suoi reprensori. Là onde, quando diedi principio a quest'opera, la qual ora è per venir a le vostre mani, e quando di stamparla mi disposi, chiaramente previdi che alcuno, anzi molti sarebbono stati, quali l'una e l'altra mia deliberazione avriano biasimata, giudicando poco convenevole a persona che per attender agli studii de le leggi in Padova dimori, spendere il tempo in cose tali; e disconvenevolissimo ad un giovane de la mia età, la quale non ancora a XIX anni arriva, presumere tant'oltre di se stesso ch'ardisca mandare le primizie sue al cospetto degli uomini ad esser giudicate da tanta varietà di pareri.

Nulla di meno, spinto dal mio genio, il quale alla poesia sovra ad ogn'altra cosa m'inchina, e dall'esortazioni de l'onoratissimo M. Danese Cattaneo, non meno ne lo scrivere che ne lo scolpire eccellente; essendo poi in questa opinione confermato da M. Cesare Pavesi, gentiluomo e ne la poesia e ne le più gravi lettere di filosofia degno di molta lode, osai di pormi a quest'impresa, ancor che sapessi che ciò non sarebbe per piacere a mio padre, il quale e per la lunga età, e per li molti e varii negozii che per le mani passati gli sono, conoscendo l'instabilità de la fortuna e la varietà de' tempi presenti, averebbe desiderato ch'a più saldi studi mi fossi attenuto, co' quali quello m'avesse io potuto acquistare ch'egli con la poesia, e molto più col correr de le poste in servigio de' principi, avendo già acquistato, per la malignità della sua sorte perdè, né ancora ha potuto ricuperare; sì che, avendo io un sì fermo appoggio com'è la scienza delle leggi, non dovessi poi incorrere in quegli incomodi ne' quali egl'è alcuna volta incorso.

To The Most Illustrious And Most Reverent Lord Luigi d'Este, Cardinal

—⧓—

Torquato Tasso to His Readers

It was no secret to me — my most esteemed readers — that since no human action has ever been perfect in every detail, none has ever been in want of detractors. Wherefore I, both in beginning the work that now comes into your hands and in deciding to have it printed, clearly foresaw that there would be some people, however many, who would condemn one or the other of these decisions, deeming it unsuitable for a man residing in Padua as a student of law to waste his time on such matters; and especially improper for a youth of my age, who has not yet completed his nineteenth year, to presume so far as to submit his first efforts to the public and to the judgment of such a diversity of peers.

All the same, prompted by my genius — which impels me toward poetry above all other goals — and by encouragement from the most honorable Master Danese Cattaneo[1] — who excels no less as a writer than as a sculptor — and finding his opinion confirmed by Master Cesare Pavese[2] — a gentleman deserving of high praise for both poetry and profoundest philosophy — I ventured to launch this enterprise, though I knew that doing so would displease my father, who, taught by his advanced age and the manifold duties that had passed through his hands, and knowing the fickleness of Fortune and the instability of modern times, would have preferred me to pursue more useful studies, by which I might fare better than he did by poetry, and enjoy a success even greater than his — though since lost by the malignity of his fate and never recovered[3] — in the service of princes, so that I, by a solid grounding in the science of law, should be spared those vexations that he had sometimes encountered.

Appendix

Ma sendo stata di maggior forza in me la mia naturale inchinazione, il desiderio di farmi conoscere, il che forse più facilmente succede per lo mezo de la poesia che per quello de le leggi, e l'esortazioni de' molti amici miei, cominciai a dare effetto al mio pensiero, cercando di tener quello ascoso a mio padre. Ma non era giunto ancora di grande spazio a quel termine che ne la mente proposto m'avea, ch'egli ne fu chiarissimo; ed ancor che molto gli pesasse, pure si risolvè a la fine di lasciarmi correre dove il giovenil ardor mi trasportava.

Sì ch'avendo ne lo spazio di dieci mesi condutto a fine questo poema, come il S. Tommaso Lomellino, gentiluomo onoratissimo e di pulitissimi costumi, ed altri molti render ne possono testimonio, e mostrandolo ai clarissimi signor Molino e Veniero, il valor de' quali supera di gran lunga la grandissima fama, fui da loro esortato caldamente a darlo fuori; e si può veder una lettera del predetto S. Veniero scritta in questa materia a mio padre, il quale senza l'auttorità ed il parere di questi dottissimi e giudiziosissimi gentiluomini non m'avrebbe giamai ciò permesso, ancor che dal Danese e dal Pavese, il giudizio de' quali è però da lui molto stimato, ne gli fosse prima stato scritto, non avendo egli veduto se non parte de l'opera mia.

Viene dunque il mio Rinaldo a dimostrarsi al vostro cospetto, sicuro sotto lo scudo di tali auttorità da l'arme de le maledicenze altrui. Pregherò ben voi, gentilissimi lettori, che lo vogliate considerare come parto d'un giovinetto, il qual se vedrà che questa sua prima fatica grata vi sia, s'affaticherà di darvi un giorno cosa più degna di venire ne le vostre mani, e ch'a lui loda maggior possa recare.

Né credo che vi sarà grave ch'io, discostatomi alquanto da la via de' moderni, a que' miglior antichi più tosto mi sia voluto accostare: che non però mi vedrete astretto a le più severe leggi d'Aristotile, le quali spesso hanno reso a voi poco grati que' poemi che per altro gratissimi vi sarebbono stati; ma solamente que' precetti di lui ho seguito i quali a voi non tolgono il diletto: com'è l'usare spesso gli episodi, ed introducendo a parlar altri, spogliarsi de la persona di poeta, e far che vi nascano l'agnizioni e le peripezie o necessariamente o verisimilmente, e che vi siano i costumi e 'l discorso espressi.

But since my natural inclination had greater power over me, the desire to become known — which perhaps succeeds more readily by poetry than by jurisprudence — together with the encouragement of many of my friends, caused me to act on this idea of mine, while trying to keep it hidden from my father. Yet had I not progressed far toward the goal on which my mind was fixed, when it became very clear to him; and indeed he, after much meditation, resolved at last to let me run whither my youthful ardor carried me.

So, having brought this poem to its conclusion in the space of ten months — as Lord Tommaso Lomellino,[4] a highly honored gentleman and of the most polished manners, and many others can testify — and having shown it to the most renowned Masters Molino and Veniero[5] — whose worth has long ago achieved exalted fame — I was warmly exhorted by them to publish it. A letter is extant, written on this subject by the aforesaid Master Veniero to my father, who would never have given me permission without the authority and example of these most learned and judicious gentlemen — not to mention Danese or Pavese earlier — whose judgment he holds in the highest esteem. Nor would my work have been written in the first place, had he not himself seen at least a part of it.

My *Rinaldo* therefore here comes into your view, shielded by authorities like these against the weapons and disparagements of others. I beg you very urgently, most gentle readers, to consider that it issues from a young man, who, if he finds that this first labor of his pleases you, will make every effort to give you some day a work worthier of your hands and with a better claim to your praise.

It will not, I imagine, displease you if I, departing somewhat from the practice of modern writers, have rather emulated the best ancient ones: for though you will not see me constrained by Aristotle's severest laws, which now and then decrease your delight in poems that you otherwise like best, yet have I at least followed those of his precepts that will not spoil your pleasure — such as the frequent use of episodes, the introduction of a variety of speakers, the avoidance of speeches in the poet's own person, the inclusion of recognition and peripety[6] resulting from either necessity or verisimilitude, and the faithful depiction of human manners and discourse.

Appendix

È ben vero che ne l'ordir il mio poema mi sono affaticato ancora un poco in far sì che la favola fosse una, se non strettamente, almeno largamente considerata; e ancora ch'alcune parti di essa possano parere oziose, e non tali che sendo tolto via il tutto si distruggesse, sì come tagliando un membro al corpo umano quel manco ed imperfetto diviene, sono però queste parti tali, che se non ciascuna per sé, almeno tutte insieme fanno non picciolo effetto, e simile a quello che fanno i capelli, la barba, e gli altri peli in esso corpo, de' quali se uno n'è levato via, non ne riceve apparente nocumento, ma se molti, bruttissimo e difforme ne rimane. Ma io desiderarei che le mie cose né da' severi filosofi seguaci d'Aristotile, c'hanno innanzi gli occhi il perfetto essempio di Virgilio e d'Omero, né riguardano mai al diletto ed a quel che richieggono i costumi d'oggidì, né dai troppo affezionati de l'Ariosto, fossero giudicate; però che conceder non mi vorranno che alcun poema sia degno di loda, nel qual sia qualche parte che non faccia apparente effetto, la qual tolta via non però ruini il tutto; ancor che molti de' tai membri siano nel Furioso, e ne l'Amadigi, ed alcuno negli antichi greci e latini. Quest'altri gravemente mi riprenderanno che non usi ne' principii de' canti quelle moralità e quei proemi ch'usa sempre l'Ariosto; e tanto più che mio padre, uomo di quell'auttorità e di quel valore ch'il mondo sa, anche egli tal volta da quest'usanza s'è lasciato trasportare. Benché da l'altra parte, né il principe de' poeti, Virgilio, né Omero, né gli altri antichi gli abbiano usati, ed Aristotile chiaramente dica ne la sua Poetica, la qual ora con gloria di sé e stupore ed invidia altrui espone in Padoa l'eloquentissimo Sigonio, che tanto il poeta è migliore quanto imita più, e tanto imita più quanto men egli come poeta parla e più introduce altri a parlare. Il qual precetto ha benissimo osservato il Danese in un suo poema composto ad imitazione degli antichi e secondo la strada ch'insegna Aristotile; per la quale ancora me egli esortò a caminare. Ma non l'han già servato coloro che tutte le moralità e le sentenze dicono in persona del poeta, né solo in persona del poeta, ma sempre nel principio de' canti, ch'oltre che ciò facendo non imitino, pare che siano talmente privi d'invenzione e che non sappiano tai cose in altra parte locare che nel principio del canto.

I certainly have taken pains to make the plot unified — if not strictly so, yet at least in a general way — as well as to prevent apparently superfluous parts from destroying the whole if removed. For granted that cutting off a member of the human body cripples it and destroys its perfection, there are nevertheless parts that by their nature create a not negligible effect, if not each by itself, yet all of them together, like tresses, beard and other hair on a man's body, which receives no apparent harm by the removal of one or the other, but is left in a very brutish and deformed condition by the removal of all. But I want my work to be judged neither by the severest philosophical followers of Aristotle, who have the perfect example of Virgil and of Homer before their eyes, with never a regard for delight and contemporary taste; nor by those who are infatuated by Ariosto. For the former would consider any poem unworthy of praise which contained a single part that, while producing no definite effect, would ruin the whole if removed — although there are in fact many such parts in the *Furioso,* and in the *Amadigi,* and some in ancient Greek and Latin classics. The others will severely scold me for not beginning each canto with one of those moral sayings and little proems that Ariosto always employs[7] — all the more so since even my father, a man whose authority and worth are known throughout the world, here and there let himself be caught up in that practice. On the other hand, neither Virgil, the Prince of Poets, nor Homer, nor the other ancients ever used it, and Aristotle clearly declares in his *Poetics* — which even now the most eloquent Sigonio is expounding at Padua to the glory of himself and to the astonishment and envy of others — that the better a poet is, the more he imitates, and the more he imitates, the less he speaks in his own person but rather through his characters. Danese has scrupulously observed this rule in his poem imitating the ancients,[8] proceeding along the path shown by Aristotle — a path along which he exhorted me to walk as well. But its advantages were lost on those who declare that all morality and maxims must be voiced by the poet in person, and not only in the poet in person, but invariably at the beginning of a canto. These authors, aside from the fact that they thereby fail to imitate, seem bankrupt of invention in their inability to express such sentiments anywhere but the outset of a canto. For

Appendix

E come questo ad alcuni potrebbe parere soverchia ambizione di volere mostrarsi dotto, o pur d'esser, scherzando, piacevole e faceto tenuto dal vulgo, così forse non è senza affettazione. Ed io credo che vero sia ciò che il dottiss. S. Pigna dice in questa materia, che l'Ariosto tai proemi non avrebbe fatto, se non avesse stimato che trattando di vari cavalieri e di varie azioni, e tralasciando spesso una cosa e ripigliandon'un'altra, gli era necessario render tal volta docili gli auditori, il che quasi sempr'in tai proemi si fa, preponendo quel che nel canto si dee trattare, e congiungendo le cose che s'hanno a dire con quelle che già dette si sono; e la medesima cagione, oltre l'usanza, ha mosso mio padre ad imitarlo. Ma io, che tratto d'un sol cavaliero, ristringendo, per quanto i presenti tempi comportano, tutti i suoi fatti in un'azione, e con perpetuo e non interrotto filo tesso il mio poema, non so per qual cagione ciò mi dovessi fare: e tanto più che vedeva la mia opinione dal Veniero, dal Molino, e dal Tasso essere approbata, l'auttorità de' quali può molto appo ciascuna persona. Sapeva oltra ciò questo essere prima stata opinione de lo Sperone, il qual tutte l'arti e le scienze interamente possiede. Non vi spiaccia dunque di vedere il mio Rinaldo parte ad imitazion degli antichi e parte a quella de' moderni composto.

—◊—

some this may spring from a sovereign desire to appear learned, for others from a wish, by speaking playfully, to be considered pleasant and amusing by the vulgar, an end that — I suggest — cannot be achieved without affectation.

Moreover, I am convinced by the most learned Master Pigna's opinion on this subject: that Ariosto would not have composed such proems, if he had not believed that, in his treatment of diverse knights and diverse stories, frequently putting one aside to take up another, it was sometimes necessary to prompt his audience, an end which is almost always achieved in these proems by anticipating what is about to happen in a particular canto and connecting what is about to be said with what has been said earlier. That same consideration, apart from common practice, moved my father to imitate him.

But I, who treat of no more than a single knight, encompassing all his exploits, so far as present usage permits, in a single action, and weaving my poem along a perpetual and uninterrupted thread, see no reason to do this: all the more because I find my opinion seconded by Veniero, by Molino,[9] as well as by Tasso,[10] whose authority enjoys universal force among men. It is known besides that, even before them, this was the opinion of Sperone, that consummate master of all arts and sciences. Do not therefore let it displease you to see my *Rinaldo* composed in imitation partly of the ancients, and partly of the moderns.

NOTES

1. For Danese Cataneo, Domenico Venièr, Carlo Sigonio and Giovan Battista Pigna, see pp. xxvi–xxvii, nn. 8–12.

2. Also Pavesi (d. 1594); Venetian author and intellectual who befriended Tasso shortly after 1559. He published a collection of fables under the pseudonym of Pietro Targa in 1569. A letter by Bernardo Tasso dated April 15, 1562 thanks him for supervising the printing of *Rinaldo*. One of Tasso's sonnets (Rime S.388) is dedicated to him.

3. The blow from which Bernardo never recovered was the loss of his patron, Ferdinando Sanseverino, prince of Salerno, with whom he was exiled from Naples in 1552. (See Chronology.) Sanseverino left for France, his fiefdoms in Italy passed into other hands, and Bernardo was cast adrift.

Appendix

4. Unidentified, but Lomellino (or Lomellini) is the name of a prominent family in Genoa.

5. Girolamo Molino (1500–1569), Venetian poet and intellectual instrumental in inviting Tasso's father to join the Venetian academy. As a young man, he had enjoyed the friendship of Gian Giorgio Trissino and Pietro Bembo. His *Rime* were published posthumously in 1573.

6. In Aristotle's *Poetics, anagnorisis* (recognition) and *peripeteia* (reversal) are plot criteria for tragedy. Tasso, however, like many of his contemporaries, extends their applicability to epic. He also weakens Aristotelian *peripeteia* by allowing it to spring from "verisimilitude" (including the *ex machina* marvelous) as well as from necessity.

7. Tasso objects to Ariosto's frequent, and often ironic, insertion of authorial moralizing in the body of the narrative, usually near the beginning of a canto. This, with a very few, perhaps inadvertent, exceptions (see 1.91 and note) is avoided in *Rinaldo.*

8. The reference seems to be to Danese's unpublished *Teseide,* rather than to his *Amor di Marfisa,* printed in the same year as *Rinaldo.*

9. See note 5 above.

10. Probably not Bernardo Tasso, the poet's father, whom the preface elsewhere always calls "mio padre" and never names. The person intended is probably the poet's cousin, Ercole Tasso or Tassoni (1540–1613), a philosopher, writer and jurist, to whom Tasso addressed several of his letters and lyrics (*Rime* S.22, S.535, S.1148, S.1251). Years later, they defended opposing views of marriage in *Dello ammogliarsi* (1593) — Ercole, a married man, taking a misogynistic view of the institution and Torquato, a lifelong bachelor, praising it. An English version, *Of Marriage and Wiving,* by Robert Tofte, the translator of Boiardo, appeared in 1598.

—◆—

This Book Was Completed on 19 June 2017
at Italica Press, New York. It Is
Set in Bembo and Printed
on Acid-Free
Paper.

—◆— —◆—

—◆—

CPSIA information can be obtained
at www.ICGtesting.com
Printed in the USA
FFOW04n1455190717
37966FF